HUMOR C   N
Theory, Impact, and Outcomes

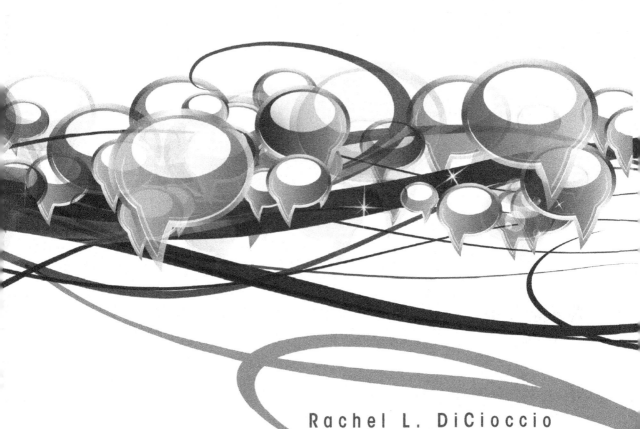

Rachel L. DiCioccio

Kendall Hunt
publishing company

Book Team

Chairman and Chief Executive Officer   Mark C. Falb
President and Chief Operating Officer   Chad M. Chandlee
Vice President, Higher Education   David L. Tart
Director of Publishing Partnerships   Paul B. Carty
Editorial Manager   Georgia Botsford
Senior Editor   Angela Willenbring
Vice President, Operations   Timothy J. Beitzel
Assistant Vice President, Production Services   Christine E. O'Brien
Senior Production Editor   Carrie Maro
Permissions Editor   Renae Horstman
Cover Designer   Jenifer Fensterman

Cover image © 2012 Shutterstock, Inc.

Kendall Hunt
publishing company

www.kendallhunt.com
Send all inquiries to:
4050 Westmark Drive
Dubuque, IA 52004-1840

Printed in the United States of America
10   9   8   7   6   5   4   3   2

DEDICATION

This book is dedicated to my family—the funniest people I know!

CONTENTS

PREFACE

The ubiquitous nature of humor in our society is undeniable. We experience humor in our everyday interactions with family, friends, and coworkers. We are exposed to and even bombarded by humor in the media. We are entertained, charmed, shocked, and sometimes offended by its uses. An integral part of our relationships, the complexity and subtle nuances of humor outstrip the stereotypical joke to reveal a powerful communication tool.

This edited volume encapsulates the fast growing area of humor research in the communication discipline. Collectively, the examination of humor communication represents a significant area of scholarship in the field of Communication Studies, which to date has been scattered across numerous venues and disciplines. The breadth and depth of research in this area reveals a rich literature, encompassing multiple theoretical and conceptual perspectives, numerous contexts, and a plethora of related issues. The purpose of this book is to systematically showcase emerging directions in the study of humor communication.

The nineteen chapters advanced in this text explore and demonstrate the multifunctional importance of humor. Contributing scholars examine the uses, outcomes, and impact of humor using forward-looking disciplinary contours of communication. The wide-ranging scholarship reflected in this book addresses the unique theoretical perspectives, as well as, contextual explorations of the communication of humor. By examining humor at both macro and micro levels, these diverse scholarly voices articulate how humor is being recognized and positioned in theory and research. The text is divided into two sections: foundational issues and contextual research.

Part 1 of the book introduces issues central to the conceptualization of humor communication. The seven chapters spanning this section elucidate theoretical and operational approaches that establish the foundation for examining humor and inform our understanding of what constitutes humorous messages. This section introduces four major contemporary theories that explain humor from a communication perspective, presents a functional model of humor, addresses humorous message production, and surveys the primary measures of humor in the fields of communication and psychology. In this introductory section authors also review the development and future directions of the Humor Assessment instrument, examine humor as aggressive expression, and illuminate how humor may act as a Verbal Trigger Event—a situational determinant of verbal aggression.

Part 2 of the book reflects the unique and pioneering programmatic lines of research that have emerged in the last two decades. Twelve chapters explore diverse contextual avenues by discussing extant research, reporting new research findings, and suggesting future research directions. In this section, authors report on the relationship between sexual humor use and sexual communication satisfaction in close relationships, utilize a lifespan approach to studying humorous communication development, apply emic sociolinguistic research to further understand humor use in the family, and operationalize work place humor through an in-depth case study of an organizational crisis and labor negotiation.

Melissa Bekelja Wanzer

Melissa Bekelja Wanzer (Ed.D., West Virginia University, 1995) is Professor in the Communication Studies Department at Canisius College, where she teaches graduate seminars in interpersonal communication and persuasion and undergraduate courses in health communication, family communication, interpersonal communication, gender and humor. Dr. Wanzer studies the benefits of humor in instructional, corporate, and health care contexts. Her research appears in *Communication Education, Communication Teacher, Communication Studies, Communication Quarterly, Health Communication, Journal of Health Communication,* and *Communication Research Reports.* In April 2009 Dr. Wanzer received the Donald Ecroyd and Carolyn Drummond-Ecroyd Teaching Award from the Eastern Communication Association and was recognized as a Teaching Fellow from the same association.

Charles J. Wigley III

Charles J. Wigley III (Ph.D., Kent State University; J.D, University of Akron; A.B., Youngstown State University) is Professor of Communication Studies at Canisius College. He is primarily interested in communication traits (especially verbal aggressiveness) and the powerful role of communication traits in the jury selection process. He has published articles in *Communication Monographs, Communication Quarterly, Communication Research Reports,* and *Communication Reports* as well as a number of book chapters.

Jason S. Wrench

Jason S. Wrench (Ed.D., West Virginia University) is Associate Professor in the Communication and Media Department at SUNY New Paltz. He is the author of over 30 research articles and 10 books, including *Casing Organizational Communication* with Kendall Hunt. He specializes in organizational communication, but the bulk of his early research examined humor as a communication trait.

PART ONE
FOUNDATIONS OF HUMOR COMMUNICATION

Theories of Humor – *Andrew S. Rancer & Elizabeth E. Graham, University of Akron*

Humor Functions in Communication – *John C. Meyer, University of Southern Mississippi*

Humor and Message Production – *Nathan Miczo, Western Illinois University*

Introduction to the Measurement of Humorous Communication – *Melissa Bekelja Wanzer, Canisius College, & Melanie Booth-Butterfield, West Virginia University*

Understanding the Development of the Humor Assessment Instrument – *Virginia Peck Richmond, University of Alabama at Birmingham, & Jason S. Wrench, State University of New York at New Paltz*

Humor as Aggressive Communication – *Rachel L. DiCioccio, University of Rhode Island*

Humor as a Verbal Trigger Event – *Charles J. Wigley III, Canisius College*

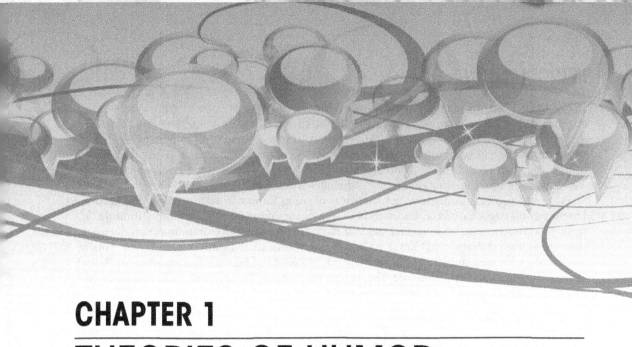

CHAPTER 1
THEORIES OF HUMOR

Andrew S. Rancer
University of Akron

Elizabeth E. Graham
University of Akron

INTRODUCTION

In this chapter, we provide the reader with a description of the most popular, contemporary, and accepted theoretical approaches to understanding what constitutes "humor." First, we define and describe what constitutes a "theory." Next, we briefly discuss the role and importance of theory in the explanation of communication phenomenon, with a specific focus on its applicability to humor. We then provide a few contemporary definitions of humor. In the following section, we introduce a conceptualization of the "individual differences" (trait) approach to humor and reveal some positive and negative consequences of using humor in relational communication. Humorous messages have been found to have significant effects in several communication contexts. As a consequence, we introduce some of the extant work in the Communication discipline that has explored the impact of humor in the contexts of education, health care, and work. Finally, we describe what are considered to be the four major theories of humor today: (a) Arousal/Relief/Release Theories, (b) Psychoanalytic Theory, (c) Incongruity Theory, and, (d) Superiority and Disparagement Theories.

For many of you, it may seem incongruous that we are using the terms "theory" and "humor" in the same chapter. The term "oxymoron" might come to mind when discussing theory and humor. An oxymoron is used here to mean a contradiction in terms,[1] such as when we use the phrase non-alcoholic beer. Thus, it may appear oxymoronic that individuals talk of theories when they discuss what makes something funny or comical (take note, as we have just foreshadowed one of the explanations of what makes something humorous, that being incongruity). However, once you understand what a theory is and the importance of theory, we believe you will have a greater understanding and appreciation of why theories have been created to explain humor.

What Is a Theory?

As students of human communication, you may already be familiar with the term theory from several of your classes, especially if you have taken a class in communication theory. Infante, Rancer, and Avtgis (2010) define theory as a "group of related propositions designed to explain why events take place in a certain way" (p. 501). Theories are employed to investigate phenomena and events that occur in nature, and humor is often identified as one of the most important phenomena we can employ across communication contexts (Lynch, 2002; Meyer, 2000). Communication theorist Charles Gruner states that theories direct researchers what to look for to see if the theory corresponds with reality (1997, p. 10).

The Importance of Theory

The goal of any theory is to *describe, explain,* and *predict* events, with the goal being to more effectively *control* our world, our environment, and especially the outcomes we seek for our communication behavior. The description goal of a theory focuses attention on particular parts of an event. In the arena of humor theories, the focus would be on *what* exactly constitutes humor? By ensuring everyone has the same concept of "humor," we can have a description of it that is understood by others (Infante et al., 2010, p. 42). The explanation goal of a theory concerns understanding *how* a phenomenon occurs (Infante et al., 2010, p. 42). In the arena of humor we need to be able to explain how humor works, that is, how does a verbal or nonverbal message (or behavior) stimulate or create a jovial, lighthearted, or funny response or reaction in someone? Putting it more succinctly, exactly how does humor work? The prediction goal of a theory concerns knowing what events or outcomes *will occur* in the future. For communication scholars, an important goal of a theory is the ability to predict communication behavior. In the arena of humor, we could utilize a theory that would allow us to predict *whether* a person will find some message or behavior humorous. Finally, the control goal of theory concerns how we can use a theory to enhance the chances of obtaining certain *outcomes* we seek or desire in a communication event or interaction. When we use the term control, "we are referring to the ability to alter elements in the present to achieve a specified outcome given certain situational factors" (Infante et al., 2010, p. 42). In the context of humor, we often ponder how we can utilize humor in its many forms to achieve a specific response and/or a desired outcome. These outcomes could include creating a more favorable impression during an employment interview, diffusing a tense or angry interpersonal encounter between colleagues, or enhancing the chances of success in a persuasive or compliance-gaining effort designed to get a friend to do something for you.

What Is Humor?

What constitutes humor? The *Oxford English Dictionary* defines humor as "that quality of action, speech, or writing which excites amusement; oddity, jocularity, facetiousness, comicality, fun" (as cited in Martin, 2007, p. 5). The *Merriam Webster On-line Dictionary* says humor is "the mental faculty of discovering, expressing, or appreciating the ludicrous or absurdly incongruous" (www.merriam-webster.com/dictionary).[2]

How do scholars define humor? Apte (1985) states that humor "is viewed as a cognitive experience involving an internal redefining of sociocultural reality and resulting in a 'mirthful' state of mind, of which laughter is a possible external display" (as cited in Meyer, 2000, p. 311). Martin (2007) suggests that humor is "a broad term that refers to anything that people say or do that is perceived as funny and tends to make others laugh, as well as the mental processes that go into both creating and perceiving such an amusing stimulus, and also the affective response involved in the enjoyment of it" (p. 5). Martin (2007) goes on to state that humor is a type of social interaction that can take many forms and occurs everywhere (p. 14).

The scope and significance of the study of humor is reflected in the interdisciplinary nature of scholarship on the subject spanning the fields of philosophy, psychology, sociology, mathematics, anthropology, communication, film, medicine, and literature. Consequently, attempts to define humor have been as elusive as reaching consensus on the most fruitful theory of humor. Speaking most broadly, definitions of humor fall into two categories: appreciation/interpretation of humor and creation/production of humor (Martin & Lefcourt, 1984). Parsing the two is critical to understanding how one can appreciate humor but may not be capable of creating and producing humor. However, if one can produce humor, more than likely one can appreciate humor. It makes sense that you might thoroughly enjoy *The Daily Show with Jon Stewart* but be incapable of producing the same humor he so masterfully creates.

The Social Implications of Humor

Why discuss humor or theories of humor in a communication text? As we have already stated, humor involves the encoding and decoding of verbal and nonverbal messages. Lynch (2002) argues, "All humor is fundamentally a communicative activity. At its most basic level humor is an intended or unintended message interpreted as funny" (p. 423). Meyer (2000) suggests that "communication is a key factor in nearly all theories of humor because of its resulting from a message or interaction perceived by someone" (p. 311).

The relational benefits of humor are well documented. Bippus (2000) claims that "people use humor to do important relationship work" (p. 380). Humor has been reported to increase bonding and reduce tension for couples. Sometimes humor can be used to avoid certain conversations that might provoke an argument or an uncomfortable situation (Priest & Thein, 2003). Humor has also been related to liking, closer information processing, and reduced counterargument (Nabi, Moyer-Guse, & Byrne, 2007).

The study of interpersonal communication in general, and humor in particular, privileges the more prosocial positive aspects of social interaction to the neglect of the full spectrum of relationship life (Graham & Titsworth, 2009). Meyer (2000) argued that humor serves two functions: unification and division. We know the positive uses of humor, but now let's turn our attention to the negative uses. Researchers have found that humor can be useful in delivering negative and hurtful remarks (Vangelisti, 1994; Young & Bippus, 2001) and putdowns (Butzer & Kuiper, 2008). Negative humor can serve a corrective function in a relationship, too (Ziv, 2010). However, this type of communication (i.e., aggressive humor) is negatively related to romantic relationship satisfaction (Cann, Zapata, & Davis, 2009). Humor used as weaponry, termed aggressive humor, is rooted in superiority theory (Ziv, 2010, p. 18). Wanzer and colleagues (Wanzer, Booth-Butterfield, & Booth-Butterfield, 1996) found that verbally aggressive individuals are more likely to target others in their humor rather than target themselves and view aggressive remarks as humorous. "Disparagement is an implicitly aggressive, negative act by one person of belittling another" (Opplinger & Sherblom, 1992, p. 106). Chapter 6, "Humor as Aggressive Communication," and chapter 7, "Humor as a Verbal Trigger Event (VTE)," in this text discuss aggressive humor in detail.

Humor as Communication

Like communication, humor is a relational activity made manifest in talk and rendered meaningful by the negotiated relationship between parties. True to its relational moorings, scholarship in communication has featured humor from both a production (i.e., sender) and an appreciation (receiver) standpoint. Not surprisingly, in the past 25 years, the study of humor has found a welcoming home in interpersonal communication (Cann et al., 2009). The next section of this chapter focuses on humor as a personal predisposition of which individual differences abound. We also introduce several contexts to illustrate the implications of humor in educational settings, healthcare environments, and organizational contexts.

An Individual Difference Perspective on Humor

It is funny (no pun intended) that people admit to so many personal inadequacies such as being tone deaf, having two left feet, being terrible with directions, but it is the rare person who admits to not having a sense of humor (Martin & Lefcourt, 1984). It seems that having a sense of humor is a prized personal trait (see chapter 5, "Understanding the Development of the Humor Assessment Instrument," which examines, in depth, the trait view of humor). Several researchers (Thorson, Powell, Sarmany-Schuller, & Hampes, 1997) claim that humor is associated with personal warmth and cheerfulness, optimism, assertiveness, and self-esteem. Clearly these are qualities one would hope to possess. Those who use humor effectively are perceived as more competent (Graham, Papa, & Brooks, 1992), credible (Wrench & Punyanunt-Carter, 2005), and attractive (Wanzer et al., 1996). Adding to the list, those who use humor experience less stress (Cann & Etzel, 2008; Miczo, 2004), are less lonely (Miczo, 2004; Wanzer et al., 1996), have higher self-esteem (Kuiper & Martin, 1993), have more decoding ability (i.e., conversational and nonverbal sensitivity), experience less receiver apprehension (Merolla, 2006), and are more communicatively flexible (Wanzer, Booth-Butterfield, & Booth-Butterfield, 1995). In fact, Fisher and Fisher (1983) found that those who use humor are above average in intelligence and creativity. One could easily conclude that personal success is closely associated with having a sense of humor and using it. Most would agree, few individual predispositions offer so many personal rewards.

But the reality is some people are funny and some are not! Indeed, there are individual differences in regard to one's ability to produce and appreciate humor. Booth-Butterfield and Booth-Butterfield (1991) conceptualize humor as a result of one's information processing abilities. They view humor as a personal predisposition, an individual difference variable. They believe the ability to use humor effectively is a highly honed skill. Chances are you know someone who excels in conversation, is dynamic, charms anyone they come in contact with, and generally seems to have a good command of their interpersonal interactions. It is likely this person uses humor effectively, as well. On the other hand, you also know someone who struggles interpersonally, is serious to a fault, and is, unfortunately, humorless. No judgment is made about which person is a better friend, employee, spouse, but like all individual differences, some are revered and others are not.

Classroom Implications of Humor

Wanzer and colleagues proposed a humor-learning relationship (1995, 1996), which means that teachers who use appropriate humor in the classroom enhance student learning. In fact, students support the humor-learning model and report they learn more from instructors who use humor in the classroom because they are responsive, immediate, flexible, adaptable, competent, and assertive. Their out-of-classroom communication is also enhanced because meaningful and personal conversations between students and teachers occur when a teacher is perceived as high in humor orientation (Aylor & Opplinger, 2003). Others support this contention (Dziegielewski, Jacinto, Laudadio, & Legg-Rodriguez, 2003) and contend that "humor can be used as a tool to engage students' minds" (p. 77). Chapter 14, "Influence of Teacher Humor on Student Learning," and chapter 15, "Graduate Advisor-Advisee Communication and Use of Interpersonal Humor," examine these findings in depth.

Health Care Implications of Humor

People use humor to cope (Wanzer, Booth-Butterfield, & Booth-Butterfield, 2005; Wanzer, Sparks, & Frymier, 2009) and provide comfort to others, especially those in distress. Successful aging and well-being have also been tied to humor use (Celso, Ebener, & Burkhead, 2003). The use of humor can also empower people so that they can better problem- solve (Bippus, 2000). Humor is a central component of skillful comforting. Chapter 12, "Humor in Health Care," and chapter 13, "Humor and Laughter as Medicine: Physiological Impacts and Effects," explore these implications.

Organizational Implications of Humor

In 1960 Roy wrote "Banana Time," an exposé on how workers at a machine shop used humor and joking to make monotonous work more tolerable. The funny antics facilitated the development of social relationships and helped define in-group and out-group membership between coworkers. Since then, researchers have been fascinated with studying humor at work. Rizzo, Wanzer, and Booth-Butterfield (1999) revealed that managers who use humor have better relationships with their subordinates, report decreased stress in the workplace, while simultaneously increasing productivity. Campbell, Martin, and Wanzer (2001) determined that a supervisor's humor leads to employee satisfaction. Wanzer et al. (2005) extended this line of reasoning to hospitals and concluded that nurses who used humor were better equipped to cope with the stress of their jobs. Chapter 11, "Bucket Humor: The Significant Role of Humor Within Organizational Culture," examines the implications of humor in the organization in depth.

It is clear there are social, educational, health, and occupational benefits associated with humor use.

Contemporary Theories of Humor

American satirist and social critic H. L. Mencken reportedly said, "A professor must have a theory as a dog must have fleas." Scholars estimate that there are over 100 documented theories of humor, although many overlap (Graham et al., 1992; Gruner, 1997; Ziv, 1988). These theories have been categorized into several broad theoretical perspectives. In this section, we review four theoretical perspectives that have received the most attention by contemporary scholars: (a) *Arousal/Relief/Release Theories,* (b) *Psychoanalytic Theory,* (c) *Incongruity Theory,* and (d) *Superiority and Disparagement Theories.* The theoretical approaches to humor are useful in suggesting avenues for research and ways to understand how and why humor works. The theories and theoretical approaches have been popular at different times throughout history.

Interest in understanding what makes something humorous goes back to the Greek philosophers; however, contemporary interest in developing a testable theoretical understanding of the role and function of humor first appeared during the late 19th century (Goldstein, 1976, p. 104). As Goldstein (1976) suggests, interest in understanding humor from antiquity to about 1940 consisted of mainly observational studies conducted without the guidance of theory or with the goal of developing theory, which he labels the pretheoretical stage.

Consider the following scenario:

> The huge college freshman figured he'd try out for the football team. "Can you tackle?" asked the coach.
>
> "Watch this," said the freshman, who proceeded to run smack into a telephone pole, shattering it to splinters.
>
> "Wow," said the coach. "I'm impressed. Can you run?"
>
> "Of course I can run," said the freshman. He was off like a shot, and in just over nine seconds, he had run a 100-yard dash.
>
> "Great!" enthused the coach. "But can you pass a football?"

The freshman rolled his eyes, hesitated for a few seconds. "Well, sir," he said, "If I can swallow it, I can probably pass it."

When you finish laughing, reflect for a moment about why this banter between the athlete and his coach is humorous. Perhaps it is the absurdity of the athlete's thought process that made you smile or the incongruity between what the coach was asking and the freshman's response to the query, "Can you pass a football?" Maybe you felt a degree of intellectual superiority knowing you understood the coach's question and are not as dim witted as the athlete. Perchance you laughed because so-called "potty humor" is, according to psychoanalytical views, always a fun regression. You might have even found yourself "holding your breath" for a moment while the athlete pondered his options, then burst out laughing at his chosen response. If any or all of these reactions were true for you, you have just experienced several of the theoretical foundations that best describe why something is funny.

In an effort to understand the origins of humor and laughter, theorists have developed many theories. Let's start at the beginning, the first theory is ... *stop* ... *wait* ... did you just gasp at the thought that we were actually going to enumerate each theory starting with the first? If so, you will be relieved to know this was just an attempt to illustrate the relief aspects of humor. You are now free to exhale and smile, safe in the knowledge that we were merely joking! Okay, enough jesting, rest assured we will only focus on the most prominent theories of humor which include arousal/relief/release theories, the psychoanalytic perspective, incongruity theory, and superiority and disparagement theories.

1 Arousal/Relief/Release Theories

Arousal/relief/release theories of humor received much attention during the 1960s and 1970s, corresponding with the interest in the psychology of emotions. The energy-release theory of laughter is traced to the ideas of 19th-century writer Herbert Spencer. This perspective of humor proposes that "laughter is a release of repressed or unused energy" (Graham et al., 1992, p. 162) and that "anxious feelings and built-up tensions are released through humor response" (Graham et al., 1992, p. 166). Arousal theories focus on the role of psychological and physiological arousal in the humor process (Martin, 2007, p.58).

In this chapter we use the terms humor and laughter interchangeably; however, laughter is the manifestation of humor and this distinction is especially salient for arousal theories. A reduction in arousal is welcome and pleasurable, and laughter is the behavioral response. Morreall (1983) suggests that some humor theorists have classified laughter as an emotion connected with glee, scorn, and giddiness (pp. 2–3) and, like other emotions (e.g., fear, anger), is related to increased arousal. The problem with tying laughter to humor is that the arousal theory does not distinguish between humorous and nonhumorous laughter. We have all had the experience of feigning laughter when we could have just as easily cried or screamed.

Robinson (1991) suggests that relief or release from arousal-provoking stimuli can take several forms. The relief can be an escape from reality or reason (a cognitive escape), or from anxiety, fear, anger, or embarrassment (an emotional escape), or the relief might be the result of nervous energy (a physical escape). You may have heard the expression that laughter is a good way to "blow off steam" and relieve stress. Perhaps you have even heard the expression "comic relief" (which was also the title of a series of HBO benefit concerts hosted by comedians Whoopi Goldberg, Robin Williams, and Billy Crystal). Comic relief is conceptualized as a relief from tension by the introduction of something humorous or funny. You may have heard the saying "Laughter is the best medicine." It suggests we often use humor to relieve the stress and tension of everyday life. Perhaps you can relate to this scenario. You come home after a difficult day at school or work, turn on the TV, and watch an episode of one of your favorite sitcoms such as *Family Guy, Modern Family, Two and a Half Men,* or a rerun of *Seinfeld.* Even though you may have seen the episode a few times (and for *Seinfeld,* perhaps dozens of times!), you watch it and still laugh. Afterward, you feel less stressed and may even experience a sense of relief from the tensions of the day. The bottom line is that relief theory says "that with laughter comes relief."[3]

One arousal theory developed by Berlyne (1972) argued for the "inverted-U relationship" between physiological arousal and pleasure. According to this theory, "the greatest pleasure is associated with a moderate amount of arousal, whereas too little, or too much, arousal is unpleasant" (Martin, 2007, p. 58). An "arousal jag mechanism" is suggested, which argues that when arousal is elevated beyond an optimal level, it becomes a negative. Thus, when a joke or funny story is told, arousal increases. When the punch line of a joke or story is delivered it causes the arousal level to be reduced, and the listeners' arousal is brought to a pleasurable level once again. We feel a sense of relief at the end of the joke or story, such as "opening a safety valve on a steam pipe" (Lynch, 2002, p. 427). Thus, Berlyne (1972) conceptualized laughter as a method of releasing excess arousal to an "optimal level." Some movies employ relief theory as a way to induce a humorous reaction from audiences. It has been suggested that the character of James Bond is notorious in the use of quips and one-liners delivered in these movies to relieve audience tension after some tense moments. For example, after throwing a villain out of an airplane in flight, Bond utters, "Have a nice flight," and the audiences groan and their built-up tension is released.[4]

While little empirical support has been found for Berlyne's inverted-U relationship between arousal and pleasure, there has been "consistent support for the idea that humor is associated with increased autonomic arousal and that increases in arousal, regardless of their source, can increase the subsequent emotional enjoyment of humor" (Martin, 2007, p. 62).

2 Psychoanalytic Theory

The psychoanalytic theory is attributed to Sigmund Freud (1905/1960). In his book *Jokes and Their Relation to the Unconscious* (1905), Freud refined Spencer's Arousal/Relief/Release Theory and proposed that humor and laughter are the result of repressed feelings, particularly sexual tensions. Freud thought that humor and laughter permitted individuals to deal with nervous energy and social taboos such as sexuality, death, fear, embarrassment, and aggression. An underlying premise of Freud's theory of humor rests on his belief that the transition from seriousness to non-seriousness produced a net economic savings in thought and this consequent savings is released in laughter. Not surprisingly, Freud's theory features psychological and physiological domains of humor, believing that humor and laughter are the result of repressed feelings, particularly sexual tensions. Freud thought of humor as "liberating" (Dziegielewski et al., 2003, p. 79) because one is permitted a pleasurable delight through a sanctioned means of expressing (i.e., the joke) a non-sanctioned emotion (e.g., aggression, libidinous thoughts).

Consider the following statement offered by a young woman about her recently deceased grandfather's death:

> *"When I die, I want to go peacefully like my Grandfather did, in his sleep—not screaming, like the passengers in his car."*

Anonymous

By most standards, making light of the untimely deaths of innocent people is unthinkable and morally reprehensible. However, under the guise of humor we are temporarily permitted to indulge ourselves and laugh. In other words, we buy a bit of license and momentary reprieve from socially appropriate behavior when we express our repression in tension-relieving laughter and humor (McGhee, 1979). So go ahead, smile, Freud would encourage you to liberate yourself and laugh at the young woman's depiction of her grandfather's peaceful death.

Characteristically Freudian, a joke was effective when it allowed for the expression of some repressed sexual or aggressive impulse. This is again evidenced in the following example taken from McGhee (1979, p. 9):

> Mr. Brown: "This is disgusting. I just found out that the superintendent has made love to every woman in this building except one."

> Mrs. Brown: "Oh, it must be that stuck-up Mrs. Johnson on the third floor."

In this example, both the sexual nature of the joke is evident (clearly the wife is also one of the residents who has had relations with the superintendent) as well as the stupidity of the wife who has inadvertently just disclosed her extramarital liaison (Martin, 2007, p. 34).

For Freud, humor also occurs in stressful or aversive situations, and is seen as the ability to laugh at one's own limitations and errors. Today, we might refer to this as self-deprecating humor, which we discuss later in this chapter when we introduce superiority/disparagement theories. The psychoanalytic approach to humor dominated research during the first half of the 20th century. But like Freudian theory in general, "it has largely been abandoned by empirical researchers since the 1980s" (Martin, 2007, p. 42).

During the mid 1960s, another phase of humor research began that focused on the cognitive foundations of humor. With the rise of cognitive approaches to psychology in the 1970s came interest in the cognitively oriented incongruity theories of humor. The cognitive approach to understanding humor and its origins and effects continues to be the dominant approach to the development of theories of humor through the 21st century. The next theoretical approach to understanding humor, incongruity theory, grounds itself in the cognitive approach which emphasizes the mental, intellectual, or cognitive components of humor (Shade, 1996).

3 Incongruity Theory

Incongruity theory focuses on the cognitive process required to interpret, comprehend, and appreciate a humorous stimulus. The theory suggests that when two highly disparate ideas or entities are juxtaposed, it results in humor (Gruner, 1997, p. 24). Returning to the notion of the oxymoron introduced earlier, let's consider the oxymoron "jumbo shrimp." To understand the humor in this phrase requires knowledge of the meaning of the words "jumbo" and "shrimp." The recognition that one is the opposite of the other and the appreciation of this absurd pairing provokes a humorous response (Blumenfeld, 1986). Other oxymorons such as "essential luxury," "government efficiency," "pretty ugly," "working vacation," "insanely normal," and "slight hernia" also underscore incongruity (if you have ever had a hernia you will quickly understand that there is no such thing as a "slight" one, they all hurt!) and could also be considered humorous.

Incongruity, in itself, is a violation of an expectation. Applied to humor, the reason something is funny is because of the discovery of an inconsistency and a contradiction (Berger, 1976; Schopenhauer, 1896). Much of humor is inherently ambiguous, which makes it a fairly sophisticated form of communication (Bippus, 2000). The original incongruity theory, primarily attributed to Berlyne (1969), has been modified to include a resolution component, which results in a two-step endeavor. First, the incongruity is recognized, and second, mindful resolution of the incongruity is required to properly interpret the stimulus and record it as folly (LaFave, Haddad, & Maesen, 1976). In essence, one must first "get" the joke (i.e., humorous stimulus), and resolution occurs when the incongruity is revealed. Returning to the athlete and the coach's conversation, we can see how incongruity best characterizes the coach's intended meaning and the athlete's interpreted meaning.

Incongruity theories of humor focus on cognition with less attention to the social and emotional aspects of humor. The perception of incongruity is the crucial determinant of whether something is humorous; things that we consider funny are surprising, unusual, or different from the norm (Martin, 2007, p. 63). "Humor occurs when there is a mismatch or clash between our sensory perceptions of something and our abstract knowledge or concepts about that thing" (ibid., p. 63). For example, the *Stayfree* brand of feminine hygiene products conducted an advertising campaign in Canada called "A Date with Stayfree." In their video spots, a series of attractive, shirtless, and obviously very masculine men were shown holding a package of maxi pads and touting the beauty of the product. Clearly, there is unexpectedness and incongruity in the image of masculine men promoting this clearly feminine product. This incongruity thus becomes the basis for the humor in the ads.

This bit of humor is also grounded in incongruity theory:

> A lady went into a clothing store and asked, "May I try on that dress in the window?" "Well," the sales clerk said doubtfully, "don't you think it would be better to use the dressing room?" (as cited in Martin, 2007, p. 64).

In this joke, the punch line is incongruous because it does not seem to follow from the first part of the joke. In this case, the funniness of the joke depends on the unexpectedness or surprise of the punch line.

To date, research generally supports the idea that "incongruity of some type is an essential element of humor" (Martin, 2007, p. 72). However, current thinking suggests that rather than being surprising, incongruity is actually *expected* in humor, and a lack of incongruity would be surprising. According to Martin (2007), "Although incongruity theories and other cognitive approaches make important contributions to the study of humor, it is important to note that they do not adequately account for all aspects of humor" (p. 74).

4 Superiority/Disparagement Theories

While incongruity theory is cognitively rooted, superiority and its close relative, disparagement theory, is an affective–socially based perspective (Berlyne, 1969). Superiority/disparagement theories contend that humor is the manifestation of our joy at the inadequacy of others (Zillmann, 1983). Some believe that part of the human condition is to revel in feeling superior to others. This is not a new theory and, indeed, superiority is the oldest theory of humor. Experts trace the origin to Plato and Aristotle; both considered superiority theorists, as they spoke of the human desire to triumph at the weakness and limitations of others.

Think for a moment about the following excerpt from a college classroom:

> One day a college psychology professor was greeting his new college class.
>
> He stood up in front of the class and said, "Would everyone who thinks he or she is stupid please stand up?"
>
> After a minute or so of silence, a young man stood up.
>
> "Well, hello there, sir. So you actually think you're a moron?" the professor asked.
>
> The kid replied, "No sir, I just didn't want to see you standing there all by yourself."
>
> www.free-jokes-online.com/jokes/are_you_stupid.html

If you laughed at the conversation between the professor and the student, chances are you felt that the professor was deserving of the insult and the student merely responding appropriately to the initial put-down. A derivative of superiority theory, termed dispositional theory, suggests that if the target of the humor deserves the disparagement, in this case the professor, then the insult is warranted and appreciation in the form of humor is experienced. This theory adds a relational element to our evaluation of humor as it features how we feel about the target of the joke (Zillmann & Cantor, 1976). The relationship between the joke teller and the butt of the joke is important because it influences whether the communication is humor or verbal aggression. Simply put, it is funny when our enemies are disparaged but it is not funny when a friend is targeted. Unlike incongruity theory, the superiority perspective suggests that humor appreciation emanates not only in the message, but also in our affective response to the target of the humor. In effect, something is funny only if the right person is disparaged. Returning to our friends in the classroom, our guess is that students tried very hard to stifle their laughter.

One of the biggest proponents of the incongruity approach to humor is Gruner (1997), who views humor as a type of "playful aggression." Gruner suggests that humor is a form of play like in a game, competition, or contest, where there are winners and losers. Indeed, Gruner (1978) suggests that the laughter of superiority actually began with early humans, even before language developed. According to Gruner (1997), "laughing equals winning" (p. 8). Gruner bases his theory of humor on the assumption that the predisposition for competitiveness and aggressiveness was essential in the survival of the human species (Martin, 2007, p. 45). Humor, from a superiority perspective, is characteristically aggressive communication and includes arguing and verbal aggression (Infante & Wigley, 1986; Rancer & Avtgis, 2006). With the evolution of language, people could make fun of others with words rather than with physical aggression. This form of humor is evident in slapstick, practical jokes (evidenced in the TV program *Punk'd*), laughing at others' clumsiness and verbal mistakes, and jokes that make fun of individuals' ethnicity or occupation (note the plethora of jokes about lawyers such as, Why won't sharks attack lawyers? Professional courtesy.[5]). The competitive nature of humor is evident in contests in which people attempt to outdo one another with exchanges of clever, biting, and verbally aggressive wordplay. You can see evidence of this type of humor in MTV's program, *Yo Mamma,* in which contestants try to one-up each other with often vicious but humorous putdowns, the winner being selected on the basis of whose humor was the most biting and clever. One of the putdowns heard on the program, and we will share the less offensive ones, goes something like, Your mamma's so old, the fire department's on standby when you light her birthday candles, and Your mamma's so dumb she tripped over the cordless phone. Gruner (1997, p. 136) provides a milder example of this type of competitive exchange:

Jill: This coffee tastes like mud.

Jane: That fits. It was ground today.

Jill: Well, it can't perk me up this morning.

Jane: That's because you're such a drip.

Jill: Cracks like that could make me dislike you in an instant.

Jane: Oh, simmer down. You're boiling over.

Jane: Sometimes I feel like decaffeinating you.

According to Gruner, all humor, no matter how seemingly benign, has a winner and a loser. He argues that all humor is based on aggression. Even self-deprecating humor can be explained by superiority humor, "[W]e can momentarily feel superior *to ourselves.* We can recall and laugh at our own past or present misfortunes, mistakes, and embarrassments because they are behind us, and we are now much better off" (Gruner, 1997, p. 13). Research exploring humor from this disparagement perspective suggests that humor "elevates a person above the target of humor" (Graham et al., 1992, p. 162).

Professional comedians use self-deprecating jokes to amuse us and leave us feeling superior to them. Advertisers often employ what at first may appear to be self-deprecating messages, but are really a clever play on words. For example, a pest control company has used the slogan, "When you think of pests, think of us." A carpet manufacturer has used "Eight million people walked all over us. And they don't even know our name." And a Denver, Colorado–based pizzeria created a large billboard that read, "We've never had to change our recipe, because it never sucked" in a veiled reference to a national pizza chain who had altered both its sauce and crust recipes due to poor customer reviews.

Echoing Zillmann (1983), Graham et al. (1992) remind us that "[s]elf-disparagement may not increase an individual's appeal but it may help to minimize deprecation from others" (p. 165). Of course, the King of Self-Deprecation was the late, great actor and comedian Rodney Dangerfield.

His trademark was employing self-disparagement as the basis for his humor. Many of you may recall his signature line, "I get no respect!" Among some examples of his self-deprecating humor are the following:

> Last week, I went to my doctor. I told him, "Doc, every morning when I look in the bathroom mirror, I feel like throwing up, what's wrong with me?" He said, "I don't know but your eyesight is perfect."
>
> My mother had morning sickness … after I was born.
>
> When I was born, the doctor came into the waiting room and told my father, "We did everything we could … but he still pulled through."
>
> I tell you I get no respect. Why the last sweepstakes letter I received began with "You may already be a loser."
>
> Dangerfield, R. (2000)

Throughout the decades, we have seen comedians exchange insults, barbs, and other forms of aggressive humor among and between each other. For example, comic pairings such as Laurel and Hardy, The Three Stooges, Abbott and Costello, Burns and Allen, Sonny and Cher, and Rowan and Martin were known to exchange forms of disparagement and aggressive humor. Gruner even argues that if we eliminate aggression from humor, we eliminate humor altogether. Martin (2007) cautions that "while such aggressive uses of humor in coping may make us feel better, when directed at spouses, close friends, and family members, they can have a negative effect on the relationship" (p. 49). There is little doubt that aggressive elements play a part in many jokes and forms of humor. However, Martin (2007) suggests that superiority theories have been supplanted by incongruity theories.

A Union of Explanations

The theoretical perspectives of humor outlined in this chapter are not exhaustive, but they do represent the basis for the majority of humor research. Some scholars argue that aspects of each perspective are necessary for a comprehensive theory of humor. In other words, humor is the result of incongruity, feelings of superiority, relief, and a mechanism to share repressed feelings (Merolla, 2006). To explore this comprehensive view of humor, consider the following story.

> A new business was opening and one of the owner's friends wanted to send him flowers for the occasion. They arrived at the new business site and the owner read the card … "Rest in Peace." The owner was angry and called the florist to complain. After he had told the florist of the obvious mistake and how angry he was, the florist replied, "Sir, I'm really sorry for the mistake, but rather than getting angry, you should imagine this: Somewhere, there is a funeral taking place today, and they have flowers with a note saying, 'Congratulations on your new location!'"
>
> Anonymous

Let's examine how each of the aforementioned theories of humor contributes to our understanding of the humorousness of the preceding tale. First, one would have to understand the social conventions associated with opening a new business and honoring the dead to appreciate how the intended message and the received message produced an incongruous situation. The unfortunate predicament is further revealed when the florist implores the new business owner to consider how the family of the deceased feels about their loved one being "congratulated on their new location" instead of the gentle "rest in peace" sentiment. Superiority theory suggests that we might secretly enjoy another's quandary and shake our heads wondering how the florist could make such a consequential mistake. Perhaps you were mildly amused and your attention was piqued when you considered the flower mix-up. In effect, you were aroused by the story and the humorous predicament and you probably laughed out loud. Finally, laughing at death and other maladies can make them seem insignificant and less threatening. In sum, each theory juxtaposes the situation in a slightly different way, offering a nuanced and simultaneously interdependent view of why the story is funny.

CONCLUSION

Each of the theories of humor we have described has utility, given the constraints of the specific situation to which it may be applied. Today, according to Martin (2007), "cognitive theories tend to predominate" (p. 32). It is gratifying to see from this review that members of the communication discipline have been instrumental in advancing our understanding of humor. Indeed the study of humor remains a fruitful area of research for communication scholars. This is underscored by the research we have presented that has revealed the many functional outcomes associated with the use of humor across communication contexts.

At this time, however, we cannot say that there is one general theory that explains all of humor or laughter. There appears to be a movement away from "grand theories" that attempt to explain all aspects of humor, and a movement toward "minitheories" or what we might call "special theories" that attempt to discuss more narrow forms of humor such as teasing and irony (Martin, 2007, p. 32). In many ways this situation mirrors the status of contemporary communication theory. The communication discipline functions with two kinds of theories: style-specific and general. Style-specific, or "special" theories guide the actual practice of communication for specific groups of people who share a common vision. General theories describe aspects of communication common to many groups of people and are based on broad, generalizable regularities (Infante et al., 2010, pp. 75–76). At this point in the evolution of the communication discipline, we have many more style-specific (i.e., special) theories of communication than we do general theories. The same status appears to be evident regarding theories of humor (Lynch, 2002). As humor theorist Morreall (1983) suggests, "[W]e are still without an adequate general theory of laughter. The major difficulty here [in developing a general theory] is that we laugh in such diverse situations that it seems difficult, if not impossible, to come up with a single formula that will cover all case of laughter" (p. 1). And today, as Martin (2007) suggests, there are even fewer attempts to create a "grand" or general theory of humor than there is a trend toward the development of "smaller 'mini-theories' that focus on more circumscribed efforts (e.g., teasing, irony)" (p. 32).

While theories of humor will undoubtedly continue to proliferate, an economical interpretation was offered by LaFave et al. (1976), who succinctly concluded that humor is the result of an unexpected happiness (such as a feeling of superiority, relief, or arousal) as an outcome of apparent incongruity. Although we will not likely reach any definitive conclusion about which theory of humor is best or which theoretical combination is most provocative; we can safely and most assuredly claim that the study of humor is steeped in theory.

Reviewing this body of theory and research may have stimulated you, the reader, to begin your own research in this area. And who knows, in applying the knowledge reviewed, you might even be more successful in your many communication efforts.

Notes

1. *Online Etymology Dictionary*. Retrieved from Dictionary.com website dictionary. reference.com/browse/oxymoron

2. www.merriam-webster.com/dictionary

3. EzineArticles.com/?expert=Sterling_Barnes

4. Linda Ann Nickerson from helium.com/ items/337429-the-relief-theory-and-its-effect-on-humor

5. www.loadsofjokes.com/jokes/54.html

References

Apte, M. (1985). *Humor and laughter: An anthropological approach.* Ithaca, NY: Cornell University Press.

Aylor, B., & Opplinger, P. (2003). Out-of-class-communication and student perceptions of instructor humor orientation and socio-communicative style. *Communication Education, 52,* 122–134.

Berger, A. A. (1976). Anatomy of a joke. *Journal of Communication, 26,* 113–115.

Berlyne, D. E. (1969). Laughter, humor, and play. In G. Lindzey & E. Aronson (Eds.),*Handbook of social psychology* (2nd ed., Vol. 3). Reading, MA: Addison-Wesley.

Berlyne, D. E. (1972). Humor and its kin. In J. H. Goldstein & P. E. McGhee (Eds.), *The psychology of humor: Theoretical perspectives and empirical issues* (pp. 43–60). New York: Academic Press.

Bippus, A. M. (2000). Humor usage in comforting episodes: Factors predicting outcomes. *Western Journal of Communication, 64,* 359–384.

Blumenfeld, W. S. (1986). *Jumbo shrimp and other almost perfect oxymorons.* New York: Perigee.

Booth-Butterfield, M., & Booth-Butterfield, S. (1991). Individual differences in the communication of humorous messages. *Southern Communication Journal, 56,* 32–40.

Butzer, B., & Kuiper, N. A. (2008). Humor use in romantic relationships: The effects of relationship satisfaction and pleasant versus conflict situations. *Journal of Psychology: Interdisciplinary and Applied, 142,* 245–260.

Campbell, K. L., Martin, M. M., & Wanzer, M. B. (2001). Employee perceptions of manager humor orientation, assertiveness, responsiveness, approach/avoidance strategies, and satisfaction. *Communication Research Reports, 18,* 67–74.

Cann, A., & Etzel, K. C. (2008). Remembering and anticipating stressors: Positive personality mediates the relationship with sense of humor. *Humor: International Journal of Humor Research, 21,* 157–178.

Cann, A., Zapata, C. L., & Davis, H. B. (2009). Positive and negative styles of humor in communication: Evidence for the importance of considering both styles. *Communication Quarterly, 57,* 452–468.

Celso, B. G., Ebener, D. J., & Burkhead, E. J. (2003). Humor, coping, health status, and life satisfaction among older adults residing in assisted living facilities. *Aging and Mental Health, 7,* 438–445.

Dangerfield, R. (2000). *No Respect.* Mercury Records

Dangerfield, R. (2004). *It's Not Easy Bein' Me.* New York: Perennial Currents-HarperCollins.

Dziegielewski, S. F., Jacinto, G. A., Laudadio, A., & Legg-Rodriguez, L. (2003). Humor: An essential communication tool in therapy. *International Journal of Mental Health, 32,* 74–90.

Fisher, S., & Fisher, R. L. (1983). Personality and psychopathology in the comic. In P. E. McGhee & J. H. Goldstein (Eds.), *Handbook of humor research: Volume II Applied Studies* (p. 54). New York: Springer-Verlag.

Freud, S. (1960/1905). *Jokes and their relation to the unconscious* (J. Strachey, Trans.). New York: W. W. Norton.

Goldstein, J. H. (1976). Theoretical notes on humor. *Journal of Communication, 26,* 104–112.

Graham, E. E., Papa, M. J., & Brooks, G. P. (1992). Functions of humor in conversation: Conceptualization and measurement. *Western Journal of Communication, 56,* 161–183.

Graham, E. E., & Titsworth, S. (2009). Measurement in interpersonal communication. In R. B. Rubin, A. M. Rubin, E. E. Graham, E. M. Perse, & D. R. Seibold (Eds.), *Communication research measures II: A sourcebook* (pp. 76–93). New York: Routledge— Taylor & Francis.

Gruner, C. R. (1978). *Understanding laughter: The workings of wit and humor.* Chicago: Nelson-Hall.

Gruner, C. R. (1997). *The game of humor: A comprehensive theory of why we laugh.* New Brunswick, NJ: Transaction Publishers.

Infante, D. A., Rancer, A. S., & Avtgis, T. A. (2010). *Contemporary communication theory.* Dubuque, IA: Kendall-Hunt.

Infante, D. A., & Wigley, C. J. (1986). Verbal aggressiveness: An interpersonal model and measure. *Communication Monographs, 53,* 61–69.

Kuiper, N. A., & Martin, R. A. (1993). Humor and self-concept. *Humor: International Journal of Humor Research, 6,* 251–270.

LaFave, L., Haddad, J., & Maesen, W. A. (1976). Superiority, enhanced self-esteem, and perceived incongruity humour theory. In A. J. Chapman & H. C. Foote (Eds.), *Humour and laughter: Theory, research, and applications* (pp. 63–91). New York: John Wiley and Sons.

Lynch, O. H. (2002). Humorous communication: Finding a place for humor in communication research. *Communication Theory, 12,* 423–445.

Martin, R. A. (2007). *The psychology of humor: An integrative approach.* Burlington, MA: Elsevier Academic Press.

Martin, R. A., & Lefcourt, H. M. (1984). Situational humor response questionnaire: Quantitative measure of sense of humor. *Journal of Personality and Social Psychology, 47,* 145–155.

McGhee, P. E. (1979). *Humor, its origin and development.* San Francisco: W. H. Freeman.

Merolla, A. J. (2006). Decoding ability and humor production. *Communication Quarterly, 54,* 175–189.

Meyer, J. C. (2000). Humor as a double-edged sword: Four functions of humor in communication. *Communication Theory, 10,* 310–331.

Miczo, N. (2004). Humor ability, unwillingness to communicate, loneliness, and perceived stress: Testing a security theory. *Communication Studies, 55,* 209–226.

Morreall, J. (1983). *Taking laughter seriously.* Albany, NY: State University of New York Press.

Nabi, R. L., Moyer-Guse, E., & Byrne, S. (2007). All joking aside: A serious investigation into the persuasive effect of funny social issue messages. *Communication Monographs, 74,* 29–54.

Opplinger, P. A., & Sherblom, J. C. (1992). Humor: Incongruity, disparagement, and David Letterman. *Communication Research Reports, 9,* 99–108.

Priest, R. F., & Thein, M. T. (2003). Humor appreciation in marriage: Spousal similarity, assortative mating, and disaffection. *Humor: International Journal of Humor Research, 16,* 63–78.

Rancer, A. S., & Avtgis, T. A. (2006). *Argumentative and aggressive communication: Theory, research, and application.* Thousand Oaks, CA: SAGE.

Rizzo, B., Wanzer, M. B., & Booth-Butterfield, M. (1999). Individual differences in managers' use of humor: Subordinate perceptions of managers' humor orientation, effectiveness, and humor behaviors. *Communication Research Reports, 16,* 370–376.

Robinson, V. M. (1991). *Humor and the health professions,* 2nd Ed. Thorofare, NJ: Slack, Inc.

Roy, D. F. (1960). "Banana Time." Job satisfaction and informal interaction. *Human Organization, 18,* 158–168.

Schopenhauer, A. (1896). *The world as will and idea.* London: Kegan, Paul, Trench, and Trubner.

Shade, R. A. (1996). *License to laugh: Humor in the classroom.* Englewood, CO: Teacher Ideas Press.

Thorson, J. A., Powell, F. C., Sarmany-Schuller, I., & Hampes, W. P. (1997). Psychological health and sense of humor. *Journal of Clinical Psychology, 53,* 605–619.

Vangelisti, A. (1994). Messages that hurt. In W. R. Cupach & B. H. Spitzberg (Eds.), *The dark side of interpersonal communication* (pp. 53–82). Hillsdale, NJ: Lawrence Erlbaum Associates.

Wanzer, M. B., Booth-Butterfield, M., & Booth-Butterfield, S. (1995). The funny people: A source-orientation to the communication of humor. *Communication Quarterly, 43,* 142–154.

Wanzer, M. B., Booth-Butterfield, M., & Booth-Butterfield, S. (1996). Are funny people popular? An examination of Humor Orientation, loneliness, and social attraction. *Communication Quarterly, 44,* 42–52.

Wanzer, M. B., Booth-Butterfield, M., & Booth-Butterfield, S. (2005). 'If we didn't use humor, we'd cry': Humorous coping communication in healthcare settings. *Journal of Health Communication, 10,* 105–125.

Wanzer, M. B., Sparks, L., & Frymier, A. B. (2009). Humorous communication within the lives of older adults: The relationships among humor, coping efficacy, age, and life satisfaction. *Health Communication, 24,* 1–9.

Wrench, J., & Punyanunt-Carter, N. M. (2005). Advisor-advisee communication two: The influence of verbal aggression and humor assessment on advisee perception of advisor credibility and affective learning. *Communication Research Reports, 22,* 303–313.

Young, S. L., & Bippus, A. M. (2001). Does it make a difference if they hurt you in a funny way?: Humorously and non-humorously phrased hurtful messages in personal relationships. *Communication Quarterly, 49,* 35–52.

Zillmann, D. (1983). Disparagement humor. In P. E. McGhee & J. H. Goldstein (Eds.), *Handbook of humor research: Basic issues* (Vol. 1, pp. 85–108). New York: Springer-Verlag.

Zillmann, D., & Cantor, J. (1976). A disposition theory of humour and mirth. In A. J. Chapman & H. C. Fout (Eds.), *Humour and laughter: Theory, research, and applications* (pp. 93–115). New York: John Wiley and Sons.

Ziv, A. (1988). Introduction. In A. Ziv (Ed.), *National styles of humor* (pp. vii–xiii). New York: Greenwood Press.

Ziv, A. (2010). The social function of humor in interpersonal relationships. *Symposium: Global Laughter, SOC, 47,* 11–18.

CHAPTER 2
HUMOR FUNCTIONS IN COMMUNICATION

John C. Meyer
University of Southern Mississippi

Among the first qualities we look for when meeting another person is a sense of humor. Understanding a person's response to humor helps in learning the person's perspectives on the world. Thus, on first meeting, one is tempted to test the relationship by using humor. Shared humor builds one's confidence in and understanding of the other, prompting further comfortable communication. This key function of seeking similarities or commonalities becomes humor's most common purpose in its enactment through communication. Mutual norms for communication and shared perspectives on issues discussed emerge. Such sharing through communication with humor fulfills a basic need for uncertainty reduction (Berger & Bradac, 1982).

A public speaker is no different; often the speaker makes jokes early on to ingratiate him- or herself with an audience. A perception of common understanding through humor can unite speakers with audiences. Relevant humor shows an audience that its members are appreciated by the speaker, and gets them involved. Successful humor relaxes both speaker and audience, and makes both more open to further interaction. The challenge of invoking humor one hopes to share with an audience may be rewarded by an extra level of comfort with and acceptance by that audience. Laughing together with a speaker shows an alliance on some level with that speaker.

Humor use thus promotes a "sharedness" that enhances relationships and further interaction. Yet the purposes or functions that humor serves in communication range further than simple unifying ingratiation. Audiences also appreciate the "whipsaw" of a sudden memorable quip in a debate, and will laugh at some jokes ridiculing others—or even themselves or their own group. Humor may unify one group at the expense of dividing from or alienating some others. Gruner (1997) suggested that all humor stems from one party's superiority over another—so some "gotcha" must inhere in humor. The playful element of humor suggests a lack of commitment to information conveyed humorously (Raskin, 1985). Humor may enhance relationships or mask an attack—or do both at the same time (Mills & Babrow, 2003). The desirable sharing accomplished through humor can be mitigated by drama, conflict, or opposition, also expressed through humor.

Humor in communication, as with any message, not only serves to transmit information or share meaning but also engages a relationship among those exposed to it. Humor thus may communicate multiple meanings and serve multiple communication purposes at once. Attempts to understand the purposes or functions of humor in communication generally start with a basic division: Humor unites or divides (Meyer, 1990, 2000). Humor functions range on a continuum from unifying to dividing, yet the unifying functions are often found most rewarding, reducing focus on the more divisive functions. The former enthrall and motivate communicators to proceed. The latter, however, can insult or infuriate others and redefine social boundaries. A more detailed exploration of the functions of humor in communication thus proves useful.

HUMOR IN RELATIONSHIPS

One may certainly ask for more details: Through what means does humor unite or divide? What creates differences in humor functions? More specific functions of humor have been clarified through research over the years. Basic conversational functions occur through the invocation of humor's most vocal marker, laughter: It indicates a switch of conversational turns, it shows how one should receive a comment, it shows how a comment was taken by the other party, it seeks further elaboration of a point, and as already explored here, it shows unity in the relationship

(O'Donnell-Trujillo & Adams, 1983). As a conversational tool, then, humor clarifies on a "micro" or conversational level what one said, what meaning was intended, and what meaning was received.

Other overarching topical and relational functions have emerged. With shared humor taking for granted some shared knowledge or scripts as background to the message, it always has a nonserious or "nonbona fide" element to its communication (Raskin, 1985). One is not committed to the truth of one's statements when invoking humor—though what is said could well be true. Humor has critiqued or mocked in ways where one can then say, "I was only joking," to another trying to take one's remarks seriously. One can critique a friend in a playful tone, simultaneously making a (negative) point and reinforcing a (positive) relationship (Mills & Babrow, 2003). Humor in communication certainly manages to "say something" about the relationship or communication itself, giving humor a component of metacommunication (Berger, 1995).

HUMOR IN PERSUASION

Persons sharing humor seem to be "on the same page" in initial understanding of a given event or issue. That commonality suggests that mutual appreciation of humor can make each sharing party more persuadable by the other. The shared commonality reduces one's uncertainty about communication with the other and increases one's comfort level. The sense of being entertained by humor with another can lower people's usual defenses against persuasion as they are necessarily distracted by humor appreciation (Petty & Brock, 1981). One is busy laughing and appreciating a humorous perspective, all the while a persuasive message may successfully alter one's views. Familiar or agreeable opinions expressed humorously may reinforce one's own opinion, while laughing at a well-phrased oppositional statement opens the mind to at least listen to and entertain divergent views.

Understanding humor requires understanding multiple perspectives on an issue. To perceive humor, one must have a sense of moral right or expected pattern and a conception of a violation of that expectation in mind simultaneously (Veatch, 1998). Such multiple perspectives on an issue may lead one to reconsider opinions or behaviors on that issue. Humor requires—and perhaps elicits—a sense of objectivity about an issue to appreciate it (Grimes, 1955). High ego-involvement in an issue leads one to accept few nonbona fide messages about it, making humor appreciation less likely. If humor appreciation lowers the ego-involvement of the audience in a topic, changing minds is easier (Sherif, Sherif, & Nebergall, 1965). A danger to persuasion appears, in that humor at the expense of a topic that receivers are ego-involved in results in more defensive reactions without appreciation of the humor (Futch & Edwards, 1999). But if people can joke about a topic, they become less attached to it and can at least entertain more objectivity. Rationality and objectivity go hand in hand, and humorous messages promoting more objectivity through laughing at an issue may lead to persuasion through rational appeals. Incongruity from humor can help receivers see a new perspective on the topic—the one they were surprised by along with the one they had been attached to. Humor can memorably introduce or reinforce consideration of a perspective by incongruity (Burke, 1984). Using humor in communication successfully may open receivers to other perspectives on an issue, thus facilitating persuasion.

One humor-using persuader who provided a focus for research was President Ronald Reagan. In his day, Reagan sought to use enough humor for persuasion that authors collected funny stories and quips from his speeches. He could persuade about many controversial topics while maintaining a notably high level of goodwill from the public. He was well-thought-of even by many who disagreed with him; his use of humor seemed an essential tool to help him remain so. Humor could keep people entertained on one level, and perhaps persuade them on another level. Multiple studies through the years have shown that using humor can bolster speaker credibility with audiences and hold their attention (Duncan & Nelson, 1985; Gruner, 1967, 1970). Reagan would find a way to tell a story or tell a joke that would reach out to his audiences and show them that he could relate to their lives. By adding this element of entertainment for audiences, Reagan successfully bolstered his credibility.

In addition, however, Reagan would find a way to mock "inferior" politicians who were favoring all sorts of ridiculous measures, persuasively uniting his audience with him in opposition to "them." Reagan thus enacted three key strategies involving humor: boosted his credibility through audience goodwill toward him, entertained the audience with memorable quips and stories to make persuasive points, and staged a "jolly rebellion" against his government opponents without becoming overly negative. Thus, humor was his "velvet weapon" (Meyer, 1990). Politicians since that time have tried to use humor as effectively, or have suffered in comparison. It seems expectations for humor's necessity as a boost to communicate influence have never been higher.

FOUR KEY SOCIAL FUNCTIONS OF HUMOR

Research has pinpointed four key functions of humor: identification, clarification, enforcement, and differentiation (Meyer, 2000). Identification and clarification fall on the unity side of the continuum, as identification focuses on the shared script or expectations of both communicators. The clarification function starkly reveals a perspective through a humorous remark. Enforcement and differentiation fall, contrarily, on the division side of the humor continuum. Enforcement humor highlights social norm violations or a person's missing knowledge, while differentiation humor places in dramatic contrast another party through putdowns. These four functions form a continuum from "most unifying" to "most dividing" uses of humor. Unifying functions provide primarily an interpersonal bond, while the dividing functions critique or establish social boundaries through humor.

Identification

The strongest unifying function of humor, identification occurs with messages that invoke and stress shared context or meaning. Humor shows that some key aspect of the topic is shared among communicators. A "truth" is pointed out that communicating parties instantly can see and share. Inside jokes that refer to shared experiences often serve this humor function. The interpersonal bond is reinforced through shared humor. One instance of humor potentially shared by all email users who wanted to thank all friends and loved ones for the educational emails over the years expressed ...

> Thanks to you, I no longer have any savings because I gave it to a sick girl (Penny Brown) who is about to die in the hospital for the 1,387,258th time. ... and I no

longer have any money at all, but that will change once I receive the $15,000 that Bill Gates/Microsoft and AOL are sending me for participating in their special email program.

Most people who use email have received messages erroneously informing us of similar information like that, and sharing such stories allows us to relate and laugh together about the experience.

Group cohesiveness also grows through identification humor (Graham, Papa, & Brooks, 1992). Through the crucial process where communication reduces uncertainty about others, humor use often leads dramatically to identification. When others in a group react to humor similarly as oneself, the self experiences the reward of being "in the know" and sharing that experience. Older readers (or even those familiar with issues that older people face) may share appreciation of the following account:

> I feel like my body has gotten totally out of shape, so I got my doctor's permission to join a fitness club and start exercising. I decided to take an aerobics class for seniors. I bent, twisted, gyrated, jumped up and down, and perspired for an hour. But, by the time I got my leotards on, the class was over.

Humor puts to use shared scripts that reinforce shared values among communicators through enhancing mutual understanding and likely resulting in laughter (Meyer, 1997). Humor serves a powerful function by integrating communicators through identification with a captured experience or issue stance, reducing uncertainty and tensions while integrating communicators into a stronger group.

For public speakers, identification humor builds credibility (Gruner, 1985; Malone, 1980). An interpersonal commonality becomes clear between speaker and audience that enhances attention. Speakers may invoke self-deprecatory humor to relate to audiences by showing a shared humanity and interest in the same values (Chapel, 1978). Such sharing reduces audience uncertainty and ambivalence. Specific information about the audience is most powerful to invoke in such instances, but some examples could be used with many audiences: "I wondered why the baseball kept getting bigger," intoned one speaker. "Then it hit me." (Such a speaker starts with a simple question of perception, with the answer to the question resulting from a double-meaning pun most audiences can identify with both ways—being "hit" by a ball or by an idea, respectively.) Another related that "I totally take back all those times I didn't want to nap when I was younger." (Most audiences can relate to being impatient with forced naps as a child but recently wanting naps at times now unavailable for adults.) Effective users of identification humor place themselves and the audience on the same social level with such shared experiences. The relief experienced through such tension reduction can enamor an audience with the speaker and perhaps with the message as well.

Clarification

A slightly less unifying, somewhat more "edgy" humor function, clarification humor encapsulates an opinion or belief in a sharp phrase or anecdote. As the humor captures attention and stimulates memory, receivers recall the position advocated with extra clarity (Goldstein, 1976; Gruner, 1967). These days, such a quip may receive extra play through mass media. In the past, newspapers, magazines, or *Reader's Digest* would pick them up, and such witticisms could serve as a sound bite on the radio or television news. Now they can be passed around via email or by views on YouTube. Some clarification of norms can be provided by children (even if unintended), as when some seven-year-old children were asked, "What do you think of beer?" One boy replied, "I think beer must be good. My dad says the more beer he drinks, the prettier my mom gets." Another social norm is clarified when talking to a young person, warning that "if you think your teacher is tough, wait till you get a boss." Crisp, pointed comments thus reinforce a commonly experienced social norm.

When the emphasis of the remark focuses on the expected norm rather than a perceived violation of such a norm, the humor clarifies beliefs or social norms. In the workplace, for instance, humorous remarks or teases have long been explored as responses to receiving new information. Humor use clarifies how a group will respond to potential change (Ullian, 1976). Discomfort and uncertainty about change can be channeled through remarks that make light of the need for altering routines or the social order. Laughing together at such remarks reinforces norms and social roles—or makes their ordered alteration more possible by stressing that the background norms and expectations at that workplace still endure. Such humor in the workplace may unite everyone around the idea that "we can cope with this, too," at the very least.

Similarly, errors and mistakes in messages can spark humor. Messages seeking to transmit information that go awry can then actually reinforce their meaning through humor. Such a message becomes more noticed than it otherwise might have been. Messages that humorously violate work norms may thus reinforce them, as regarding bill-paying: "If you think nobody cares, try missing a couple of payments," as well as the work ethic itself: "Hard work pays off in the future. Laziness pays off now." The incongruity of a message's violation of expectations makes it stand out all the more due to its error, yet its intended message is implied. The expected pattern of messages is reinforced by laughter as an "exception" to the norm or rule.

Key to the clarification function is that one can memorably encompass a position on an issue through a humorous remark. Rapier wit can thus help persuade through a memorable quip or one-liner. Humor allows a sudden and dramatic clash of a perceived violation with an expected norm, with speaker and audience sharing such a norm and presuming that it will emerge triumphant after the interaction. Through the years, public personalities have built their fame through clarifying one-liners or anecdotes. Writers such as H. L. Mencken and comedians such as Will Rogers built their writing and speaking careers largely on such wit. President Reagan (1976), for instance, once noted that "bureaucracy has a built-in instinct for preservation and reproduction of its own kind. A federal program, once started, is the nearest thing to eternal life you'll ever see on this earth." He would also tell humorous stories to memorably make campaign points.

Power seems inherent in the clarification function as its use can entertain audiences and set them up to be persuaded at the same time. Remarks like "I had never thought of it that way" or "that's so true" that follow such humor may make receivers open-minded enough for persuasion (Grimes, 1955). Clarification lets receivers suddenly think about a topic differently, as when a little boy once asked his father, "Daddy, how much does it cost to get married?" The father replied, "I don't know son, I'm still paying." The worth of marriage was also questioned by the attempted humorous remark noting that "marriage is the triumph of imagination over intelligence." Suddenly, one thinks of marriage using a different value-set; likely reinforcing existing beliefs about marriage, but perhaps opening up a new line of reasoning about it. A different view of the effects of aging may stem from an interview with a 104-year-old woman, who was asked, "And what do you think is the best thing about being 104?" She simply replied, "No peer pressure." A sudden, different way to consider advanced age is presented. Humor's power to memorably make a point, generally short of teasing or attacking, is encapsulated in the clarification function.

Enforcement

Moving toward the more divisive end of the humor function continuum, enforcement humor provides for the potentially friendly criticism of one violating social expectations. Similar to the clarification function in that one's position can be made clear through humor, this function adds a critical or even attacking element to it. Such a function is often home to the tease. This humor "calls to account" a person or group found to be off an expected track. A noted incongruity now needs correction. Children, once again, may be teased or wind up teasing in the manner of enforcement. To return to the seven-year-old children who were asked, "What do you think of beer?" Another boy responded, "My Mom and Dad both like beer. My Mom gets funny when she drinks it and takes her top off at parties, but Dad doesn't think this is very funny." In this instance, the humor comes from a violation of a serious social norm that would often be considered unacceptable. As a unique violation, however, the humor serves as a reminder of the norm and the act that needs correcting.

Duncan (1962) showed that humor enforces social norms through "discipline by laughter." The desire not to be the subject of humor or jokes can be strong, and people take pains to avoid it. Thus, being teased about something lets that person and witnesses know that such divergences from the norm will be noted, pointed out, and perhaps ridiculed. Taking steps to avoid this allows the strengthening of social norms as people conform with more zeal. Consider the following instance of humor involving a bit of "idiocy" most would gladly avoid:

> A New York lawmaker called a travel agent and asked, "Do airlines put your physical description on your bag so they know whose luggage belongs to whom?" The travel agent said, "No. Why do you ask?" He replied, "Well, when I checked in with the airline, they put a tag on my luggage that said FAT, and I'm overweight. I think that's very rude." After putting him on hold for a minute while the laughing travel agent looked into it, the agent returned to the line and explained that the code for the Fresno, California airport is "FAT" for Fresno Air Terminal, and the airline was just putting a destination tag on his luggage.

Violations of several potential norms are invoked here, including taking one's own weight too seriously, taking insult where none was meant, and invoking one's power to protest an attack on one that never really took place. People can read or hear such a story and, in understanding the humor, also understand the social norms needing conformity to avoid such an account being made of them.

Alternatively, humor serves as a "safety valve" for processing social norm violations through laughter, and thus strengthens the effectiveness of norms. As with the royal fool through the ages who could mock the king and social convention with impunity, while others serious about such violations could be banished or killed, people violate norms for the sake of humor. The source of the humor comes from contradicting norms that many would never seriously consider removing or altering. The attention and laughter that such violations receive reinforce the notion that here is an important social norm that should *not* be changed. After all, if the norm were trivial or of little concern, violating it would not be a noteworthy event. Violations of a norm that matters, however, prove to be funny because the norm in fact *does* matter.

Teasing serves to gently correct while maintaining some level of identification with another party (Alberts, Kellar-Gunther, & Corman, 1996; Graham, Papa, & Brooks, 1992; Young & Bippus, 2001). Enough contact has preceded the interaction that shared norms make possible mutual understanding of humor "scripts"—though knowledge of what leads to the humor may vary. One is familiar enough with relational norms to understand a violation. One may laugh at a group member who forgot something important, or at the ignorance of an outsider to the group, or a child still learning about social expectations and basic knowledge. For instance, a teacher was reading the story of the *Three Little Pigs* to her class.

> She came to the part of the story where the first pig was trying to gather the building materials for his home. She read, "And so the pig went up to the man with the wheelbarrow full of straw and said: 'Pardon me sir, but may I have some of that straw to build my house?'" The teacher paused, and then asked the class: "And what do you think the man said?" With the literalness of many six-year-olds, one little boy raised his hand and said very matter-of-factly, "I think the man would have said, 'Well, I'll be damned!! A talking pig!'" The teacher had to leave the room.

Actual malice may not be present in such laughter, but the humor clearly suggests that the person targeted does need to learn. Most understand that in children's stories, some aspects of normal reality are suspended for the sake of the story. That particular child would eventually need to learn that norm.

Humor serving the enforcement function stresses the violation of the norm, indicating that it may be funny for now but needs to be corrected. Teasing has little effect if no (social) *difference* will be made by acting or appearing differently. The message often becomes clear: This is a funny violation, but it is funny because it *is* a violation, so correct it! Those unable to correct the condition often must adjust to continual teasing for being, somehow, outside the social norm.

Differentiation

Contrasting one group or individual dramatically opposed to another, differentiation serves as the most divisive function of humor. A communicator may ridicule another speaker or group by drawing a memorable distinction between them. One party is clearly laughed at by those laughing with the humorous messenger. Those who perceive the humor in such remarks understand the social divisions referred to. Differentiation humor exposes social alliances and divisions. Perhaps the easiest and most universal division one may encounter through such humor is between the sexes, as in this story:

> In the hospital the relatives gathered in the waiting room, where a family member lay gravely ill. Finally, the doctor came in looking tired and somber, "I'm afraid I'm the bearer of bad news," he said as he surveyed the worried faces. "The only hope left for your loved one at this time is a brain transplant. It's an experimental procedure, very risky, but it is the only hope. Insurance will cover the procedure, but you will have to pay for the brain." The family members sat silent as they absorbed the news. After a time, someone asked, "How much will a brain cost?" The doctor

quickly responded, "$5,000 for a male brain; $200 for a female brain." The moment turned awkward. Some of the men actually had to try not to smile, avoiding eye contact with the women. A man, unable to control his curiosity, finally blurted out the question everyone wanted to ask, "Why is the male brain so much more than a female brain?" The doctor smiled at the childish innocence and explained to the entire group, "It's just standard pricing procedure. We have to price the female brains a lot lower because they've been used."

Not only is the target of the humor uncertain at first, but the sudden final line dramatically puts down "the other" gender.

Ridicule may serve unity as well as division as it reinforces political alliance among one group's members by highlighting contradictions with and differences from others (Schutz, 1977). Research suggests that jokes disparaging a disliked group are funnier to receivers than those disparaging a liked group (Goldstein, 1976). Humor can elicit the sense one has of belonging to a "good group" or of being a "good person," as opposed to those others who are funny due to ignorance or malevolence. The contrast of those others with one's own success leads to an experience of humor.

Even a hint of disagreement with a power structure or authority expressed through humor may arouse interest in an audience through potential conflict. People love drama, after all, and humor cloaks natural human conflict in an aura of goodwill, at least between humor senders and receivers. Joking about the boss, or the corporate executives, or the administrators, or a political group perceived as oppressive sparks high levels of enjoyment. One can "rebel" through humor and perhaps escape serious consequences, while showing a powerful sense of sharedness with those who feel similarly.

Putting opponents or those outside of desired social norms in their place through mockery—showing that they believe in or do ridiculous things—has long been a staple of comedy. Comedians ridicule individual "idiots," misled social groups, or even particular audience members. Politicians have long used narrative to scorn through satire and put down through buffoonery those they oppose. One of Cicero's key persuasive tools in defending ancient Roman citizens was to ridicule their accusers through humor (Volpe, 1977). President Abraham Lincoln developed comic storytelling into a major source of argument and evidence (Schutz, 1977). He could use ridicule as a powerful rhetorical weapon as he delighted in pointing out the ignorance to the consequences of their arguments of his proslavery opponents. President Reagan would encapsulate his differences with his opponent in turns of phrase like "If the President wants a definition of recession, I'll give him one. Recession is when your neighbor loses his job, depression is when you lose yours, and recovery will be when Jimmy Carter loses his" (Boller, 1982, p. 354).

As potentially the harshest function of humor, receivers who recognize divisive humor may be familiar with the subject while expected to completely disagree with the humor's target. The senses of conformity to norms and experiencing their violation are drawn in highly dramatic contrast through differentiation. This humor function has been viewed most prominently through hundreds of years, as "superiority" has long been viewed as a key element of humor (Gruner, 1997) and humor was viewed as in bad taste in many eras as flouting social convention (Morreall, 1983). Differences between groups and hierarchical levels spawn violations of expectations (Burke, 1984), which can be focused on through humor. Social groups and hierarchies are thus laid out, explored, and reified through humor use. Differentiation humor sets up and reinforces social boundaries.

PARADOXES IN HUMOR FUNCTIONS

The paradoxical nature of humor—as it both unites and divides—can be explained by its elements occurring simultaneously. The mental flash that results in an experience of humor assimilates several cognitive factors in an instant. Veatch (1998) suggested that to experience humor, one must hold a sense of a moral order or pattern, and a sense of its violation in mind at the same time. Both perceptions must be present simultaneously for humor to be experienced. Thus, if one is not aware of a consistent pattern, one cannot understand a violation of it to experience it as funny. Similarly, if a violation of expectations is so severe or dangerous in implications that high stress results, then experiencing humor is unlikely due to anger, fear, and concern for serious consequences outweighing the sense of an ongoing stable pattern or norm. The simultaneous presence of the norm and its violation in mind make possible humor, and in turn its functions leading to possible unity, persuasion, or division.

Humor's function is theoretically determined by whichever element the humor use focuses on. Main attention on the expected pattern, moral order, and related social norms, or conversely, on a norm violation determines the communication's place on the function continuum. Humor can thus stress the expected pattern and its underlying solidity—serving the identification and clarification functions—or it can stress the violation of the moral order in service to the enforcement or differentiation function. Both cognitions must be in mind to experience humor, but the focus of communication and its context focus more strongly on one or the other. Unification humor focuses primarily on the shared norm being important, solid, and unchanging, reinforcing the identification function. Some sense of temporary violation of a solid social norm characterizes the clarification function. A stronger focus on the pattern violation as problematic characterizes the enforcement function, while differentiation regards the violation of expectations as funny but not tolerable in serious situations. Thus, two key functions of humor serve to socially unite, two to socially divide, and the context and participants determine what elements are emphasized as humor emerges and which function will follow.

DISCUSSION AND CONCLUSION

Humor occurs in the mind as a cognitive, even unconscious experience (Apte, 1985). Scholars have suggested that perception of a potential humorous event precedes a judgment phase where one experiences humor and perhaps expresses it (Leventhal & Cupchik, 1976). The "mechanics" of humor in the mind may remain mysterious, but their manifestations in terms of function in communication can be usefully categorized and applied by communicators. People certainly think about how to use humor and enjoy it in others' messages.

Humor's tendency to unite or divide elicits the difficulties one finds with using humor in communication: the joke that did not work because the audience did not "get it" (did not understand what pattern might be referred to, or the humor script); the story that the audience takes so "seriously" that they see no solid pattern but only a dangerous violation; the humor that puts down someone the receiver values or likes and makes the violation seem far too severe to laugh at; or the humorous remark that seemed to fail because the audience found it trivial—a minor "blip" in a pattern of life. Humor may dramatically reinforce a communicator's success through identification with an audience or clarification of a point. It can also spell a failure to communicate as shared values and social expectations are not evident in the attempt at humor. Humor thus does illuminate social groups and orders as those who laugh together show some unity and shared understanding, while those who do not do so differ in key ways.

Humor, it seems, can serve as a social manipulation tool. Martineau (1972) described how humor could unite groups and divide one group's members from others. His sociological model suggested that humor within and between group members could fortify group unity, or cause conflict and divide or reorganize relationships among members or groups. "Those who laugh together, stay together," one dares to say. Charting shared humor will likely result in clear markers of social groups and hierarchical levels. Getting others to laugh or having them refuse to do so sends clear messages going forward about the social organization that people perceive.

One cannot know humor's ultimate function unless one focuses on its receiver and its context. Humorous incidents are judged based on both affective and cognitive information, so that experience and situation are involved in the presence of humor (Leventhal & Cupchik, 1976). Humor meant by its producer to unify, for instance, might be considered the height of differentiation to an offended party. Also, a basic choice is made by both senders and receivers of humor whether to experience humor or not (Attardo & Raskin, 1993). Humorous messages, taken in a "bona fide" spirit, may communicate basic information only or simply nonsense without the perception of humor (Raskin, 1985). The nonbona fide playful aspect of humor is key to experiencing the mental duality that allows its experience. Depending on the context of the situation, though, one may choose to "play" or not.

Humor leads to enough useful and practical communicative consequences that its use, while treacherous, will continue to be found worthwhile. Its dramatic means of unifying and laying ground for persuasion of audiences suggest that it is a powerful communication tool. So, practically speaking, does its regular use or appreciation affect how we perceive other people—and our desire to develop relationships with and be influenced by them. Prosocial behaviors involving humor, for instance, increase compliance-gaining in the college classroom (Punyanunt, 2000). Negative humor that puts down an audience or its members serves, not surprisingly, to decrease the credibility or persuasiveness of the message (Frymier, Wanzer, & Wojtaszczyk, 2008). So an effective use of humor can dramatize one's conflicts with others, as well as reinforce bonds and shared meaning with one's audience.

Clear practical functions of humor in communication emerge, then, along with the ineffable mystery of the humor experience. The basic question of how or why individuals take a comic perspective rather than a tragic perspective on a situation remains to be further explored. Ego-involvement and perceived impact of an issue on the self no doubt play some role (Sherif, Sherif, & Nebergall, 1965), but so do other aspects of personality, context, and situation. So often, the latter factors are crucial and spoil the neat, efficient categories one may set up in communication. Yet a perspective of humor functions laid out on their continuum from highly uniting with identification and clarification functions to enforcement and the highly divisive differentiation function lets communicators know what kind of humor they may try to employ—along with what kind of function the humor may eventually serve for hearers of the message.

References

Alberts, J. K., Kellar-Gunther, Y., & Corman, S. R. (1996). That's not funny: Understanding recipients' responses to teasing. *Western Journal of Communication, 60,* 337–357.

Apte, M. (1985). *Humor and laughter: An anthropological approach.* Ithaca, NY: Cornell University Press.

Attardo, S., & Raskin, V. (1993). *The general theory of verbal humor.* Berlin: Mouton de Gruyter.

Berger, A. A. (1995). *Blind men and elephants: Perspectives on humor.* New Brunswick, NJ: Transaction.

Berger, C. R., & Bradac, J. J. (1982). *Language and social knowledge: Uncertainty in interpersonal relations.* London: Arnold.

Boller, P. F., Jr. (1982). *Presidential anecdotes.* New York: Penguin Books.

Burke, K. (1984/1934). *Permanence and change.* Los Angeles: University of California Press.

Chapel, G. W. (1978). Humor in the White House: An interview with presidential speechwriter Robert Orben. *Communication Quarterly, 26,* 44–49.

Duncan, C. P., & Nelson, J. E. (1985). Effects of humor in a radio advertising experiment. *Journal of Advertising, 14,* 33–40.

Duncan, H. D. (1962). *Communication and social order.* New York: Bedminster.

Frymier, A. B., Wanzer, M. B., & Wojtaszczyk, A. M. (2008). Assessing students' perceptions of inappropriate and appropriate teacher humor. *Communication Education, 57,* 266–288.

Futch, A., & Edwards, R. (1999). The effects of sense of humor, defensiveness, and gender on the interpretation of ambiguous messages. *Communication Quarterly, 47,* 80–97.

Goldstein, J. H. (1976). Theoretical notes on humor. *Journal of Communication, 26,* 104–112.

Graham, E. E., Papa, M. J., & Brooks, G. P. (1992). Functions of humor in conversation: Conceptualization and measurement. *Western Journal of Communication, 56,* 161–183.

Grimes, W. (1955). The mirth experience in public address. *Speech Monographs, 22,* 243–255.

Gruner, C. R. (1967). Effect of humor on speaker ethos and audience information gain. *Journal of Communication, 17,* 228–233.

Gruner, C. R. (1970). The effect of humor in dull and interesting informative speeches. *Central States Speech Journal, 21,* 160–166.

Gruner, C. R. (1985). Advice to the beginning speaker on using humor—What research tells us. *Communication Education, 34,* 142–147.

Gruner, C. R. (1997). *The game of humor: A comprehensive theory of why we laugh.* New Brunswick, NJ: Transaction.

Leventhal, H., & Cupchik, G. C. (1976). A process model of humor judgment. *Journal of Communication, 26,* 190–205.

Malone, P. B. (1980). Humor: A double-edged tool for today's managers. *Academy of Management Review, 5,* 357–360.

Martineau, W. H. (1972). A model of the social functions of humor. In J. H. Goldstein & P. E. McGhee (Eds.), *The psychology of humor* (pp. 101–125). New York: Academic Press.

Meyer, J. (1990). Ronald Reagan and humor: A politician's velvet weapon. *Communication Studies, 41,* 76–88.

Meyer, J. C. (1997). Humor in member narratives: Uniting and dividing at work. *Western Journal of Communication, 61,* 188–208.

Meyer, J. C. (2000). Humor as a double-edged sword: Four functions of humor in communication. *Communication Theory, 10,* 310–331.

Mills, C. B., & Babrow, A. S. (2003). Teasing as a means of social influence. *Southern Communication Journal, 68,* 273–286.

Morreall, J. (1983). *Taking laughter seriously.* Albany: State University of New York Press.

O-Donnell-Trujillo, N., & Adams, K. (1983). Heheh in conversation: Some coordinating accomplishments of laughter. *Western Journal of Speech, 47,* 175–191.

Petty, R. E., & Brock, T. C. (1981). Thought disruption and persuasion: Assessing the validity of attitude change experiments. In R. E. Petty, T. M. Ostrom, & T. C. Brock (Eds.), *Cognitive responses in persuasion* (pp. 55–79). Hillsdale, NJ: Lawrence Erlbaum.

Punyanunt, N. M. (2000). The effects of humor on perceptions of compliance-gaining in the college classroom. *Communication Research Reports, 17,* 30–38.

Raskin, V. (1985). *Semantic mechanisms of humor.* Boston: Reidel.

Reagan, R. (1976, January 15). [Audio tape transcribed by author.] Campaign appearance in Keane, NH.

Schutz, C. E. (1977). *Political humor.* London: Associated Presses.

Sherif, C. W., Sherif, M., & Nebergall, R. E. (1965). *Attitude and attitude change: The social judgment-involvement approach.* Philadelphia: W. B. Saunders.

Ullian, J. A. (1976). Joking at work. *Journal of Communication, 26,* 129–133.

Veatch, T. C. (1998). A theory of humor. *Humor: International Journal of Humor Research, 11,* 161–216.

Volpe, M. (1977). The persuasive force of humor: Cicero's defense of Caelius. *Quarterly Journal of Speech, 63,* 311–323.

Young, S. L., & Bippus, A. M. (2001). Does it make a difference if they hurt you in a funny way? Humorously and non-humorously phrased hurtful messages in personal relationships. *Communication Quarterly, 49,* 35–52.

CHAPTER 3

HUMOR AND MESSAGE PRODUCTION

Nathan Miczo
Western Illinois University

HUMOR AND MESSAGE PRODUCTION

If laughter is the best medicine, then we ought to devote as much attention to the doctors and pharmacists of wit as we do to the ailments that give rise to the prescription. Interest in the sense of humor is longstanding, and investigations vis-à-vis the field of communication are no exception. Humor-related research ranges from the public communication setting (Gruner, 1985) to the interpersonal (Graham, Papa, & Brooks, 1992). The communication discipline also parallels other fields in the relative neglect of humor production compared to humor comprehension and appreciation. Evidence that this situation is changing, however, can be gleaned from research on humor orientation as an individual difference variable (Booth-Butterfield & Booth-Butterfield, 1991) and the security theory of humor (Miczo, 2004; Miczo, Averbeck, & Mariani, 2009), which attempts to explain underlying differences in humor production abilities. Concomitantly, the field of communication continues to witness advances in our understanding of message production, particularly with the development and refinement of the goals-plans-action (GPA) framework (Dillard, 1990, 1997). It is a propitious time, therefore, to pose the question: What can the field of communication bring to the study of humor production? The converse of this question is also of interest: What can a confrontation with humor bring to our understanding of how communicators produce messages? This chapter proceeds by first exploring issues in the conceptualization of humor and then addressing those issues with concepts and constructs from the area of message production. We can begin by conceptually disentangling three constructs: laughter, humor appreciation, and humor production.

CONCEPTUALIZATION OF HUMOR

Laughter

Laughter is a nonverbal vocalization that predates the development of speech both phylogenetically and ontogenetically. A laugh-like vocalization with open mouth display is evident in genetically similar primate species, typically occurring during periods of rough-and-tumble play or mock aggression (Morreall, 2009; Provine, 2000). Ontogenetically, Sroufe and Waters (1976) found that laughter appears in infants at around four months old, often elicited by stimuli that is "physically vigorous" (p. 178). Rothbart (1973) suggested that this stimulation must remain within tolerable arousal levels and that laughter therefore serves as a safety signal to the caretaker. Further, laughter produces physiological effects on the body. Fry (1994) suggested a two-step procedure of stimulation and relaxation. In the stimulation phase, heart rate and blood pressure increase, immune function is enhanced, and there is an overall jump in alertness. The relaxation, or refractory, phase involves a shorter, more rapid drop in heart rate, blood pressure, and muscle activity. Laughter is also highly contagious (Provine, 1992), accounting for the fact that individuals are more likely to laugh when in the presence of others than by themselves (Devereux & Ginsburg, 2001; Martin & Gray, 1996). Taken together, these lines of evidence have resulted in formulations of laughter as a safety signal, sending the message that all is well. Hayworth (1928) noted that the tension and arousal jag that precedes laughter is similar to the body's preparation for action in the fight-or-flight response. If the threat turned out to be not a threat, laughter would provide a mechanism for the rapid release of that tension and subsequent state of relaxation. Further, the contagiousness of laughter as a vocal signal would allow the group to relax even if they were not able to see each other directly. Morreall (2009) makes a similar argument and then proposes how individuals might have attempted to reproduce the conditions of laughter because of its pleasurable effects.

This brief foray into the dynamics of laughter is necessary for two reasons. First, as Morreall (2009) noted, humor production is shaped by the conditions that give rise to laughter. Second, laughter itself plays predictable roles in relation to humor production. There are observable differences between different types of laughter, and between laughter and other vocalizations (Bachorowski & Owren, 2001). Further, although people can laugh suddenly or so vociferously that it disrupts the flow of interaction, it is more typical that laughter is subordinated to speech (Provine, 2000). O'Donnell-Trujillo and Adams (1983) suggested five coordinating functions of laughter in conversation. For speakers, laughter could signal the end of a speaking turn as well as indicating how to hear an utterance (i.e., as something funny or not to be taken seriously); listeners could use laughter as an invitation to elaborate or to indicate how an utterance was heard; finally, mutual laughter can be a resource for affiliation insofar as it signals agreement about the status of something as laughable. Provine's (1993) naturalistic study of "small groups, usually pairs" (p. 292) found that speakers often laughed more than hearers at their own comments. Glenn (2003) reports a similar pattern for two-party conversations, but notes that in multiparty groups, speakers rarely laugh first. He suggests that a bias against self-praise is operating in multiparty groups, but that rule is relaxed in dyadic humor because both parties must laugh if there is to be shared laughter.

Humor Appreciation

Humor appreciation refers to the capacity to enjoy humor. Laughter is the most visible expression of this enjoyment, and the pleasurable feelings accompanying laughter have been variously labeled amusement (Morreall, 2009), mirth, and the feeling of nonseriousness (Chafe, 2007). Chafe described nonseriousness as "a reaction to situations it would be counterproductive to take seriously, with the result that they are rejected as candidates for inclusion in one's repertoire of knowledge about the way the world is" (p. 13). Morreall proposes a four-component sequence of emotions that begins as (1) beliefs and desires motivate (2) physiological changes that lead to (3) adaptive action and (4) the person's awareness of these changes constitute the feelings of emotions (p. 28). Anger or fear, for example, are prompted by a belief that something is a threat, which gives rise to bodily reactions indicative of a fight-or-flight mode, and subsequent adaptive action (i.e., fighting or running away). According to Morreall, the feelings aroused by laughter should not be considered emotions. He argued that since the objects of amusement are not real, and therefore "rejected as candidates" (Chafe, 2007, p. 13) for worldly knowledge, they do not require beliefs or desires. Further, emotions concern practical engagement in the here and now, while the effects of amusement actually work to disengage us from practical concerns.

One might counter Morreall (2009) by arguing that objects that cross one's path or that are brought up in conversation require an appraisal for relevance, even if they are appraised as nonserious. In their stress and coping paradigm, Lazarus and Folkman (1984) briefly discuss benign-positive appraisals, which are characterized by pleasurable emotions. Additionally, laughter as a response to a benign-positive appraisal does involve physiological changes, as noted above. Finally, the incapacitation as a result of laughter's bodily effects can be adaptive if it prevents individuals from fleeing or attacking in situations where it would be "counterproductive to take [such action] seriously" (Chafe, 2007, p. 13). If emotional expressions are as much about interpersonal communication as internal experience (Andersen & Guerrero, 1998), then the contagiousness of laughter, the open mouth display, and the bodily incapacitation serve affinity-seeking and promoting functions. If the feelings that accompany laughter are emotions, then they fall within the purview of the communication of emotional messages. Following Burleson and Planalp (2000), amusement as an affective state can influence the production of subsequent messages, laughter and smiling can themselves be the content of messages, and humorous statements can be employed to manage the emotions of others.

There is more to humor appreciation than feelings of amusement, however. Carrell (1997) proposed a two-component model of humor appreciation. The first step is joke competence, which is "an audience's ability to recognize/determine that a text is a joke" (p. 176). In the second step, humor competence, the message "is processed by the audience for its amusement value" (p. 177). Drawing on both Carrell (1997) and Hay (2001), Bell (2007) further distinguishes between understanding and appreciation within the construct of humor competence, and then adds agreement as a final step. Bell's proposal for humor competence as a social construct directs our attention to humor's complexity. That is, a person may fail to recognize that a text is a joke, or the person may recognize the form of a joke without understanding its content. Even here, a person may laugh because he/she realizes a joke has been told or because others are laughing, even if the person does not know what others are laughing about. Additionally, a person might appreciate the humor but suppress laughter because it seems inappropriate to the context. Finally, a person might understand and agree with the sentiment expressed in the humor, but fail to laugh because he/she does not appreciate that the sentiment was expressed humorously. The complexity of the humor appreciation process highlights the difficulties of defining humor production as simply that which makes one laugh.

Humor Production

Humor production concerns the ability to produce humorous messages. Before advancing to a discussion of humorous messages, it is necessary to distinguish two senses of what it means to produce humor. Provine (2000) contrasts a stand-up comedy model and a conversational laughter model by noting three differences: (1) stand-up comedy is based on joke-telling whereas everyday humor involves few instances of pre-scripted joke forms; (2) the comedian is physically and socially removed from the audience, while in conversational humor there is "intimate contact and interaction" (p. 43); (3) comedians typically talk without laughing, while in everyday humor speakers often laugh more than hearers (but see Glenn, 2003, for an alternative view). Morreall (2009) draws a similar distinction between the joke teller and the wit: (1) "the joke teller is a performer but not a creator of humor, while the wit both creates and performs humor" (p. 84); (2) the joke teller is limited by his/her repertoire of remembered jokes, while the wit can potentially create humor on the spot and/or from his/her own experiences; and (3) jokes interrupt the flow of conversation, while wit contributes to and furthers the flow of conversation. While recognizing that a certain amount of timing and delivery skill is involved in the performance of jokes, in this chapter I am principally concerned with the wit. Mirroring Bell's (2007) formulation presented earlier, we can posit the wit as someone who has the ability to first recognize the opportunity for humor in a situation and can then enact the humor in such a way that it has amusement value for the audience.

Humorous messages can be defined as messages designed to produce amusement by inducing a cognitive shift in a playful context. We have already discussed amusement as the enjoyable feeling at the heart of humor appreciation. The concept of a cognitive shift (Latta, 1998) can be understood by discussing the notion of incongruity. Although incongruity theory remains one of the three big theories of humor and laughter (along with superiority theories and relief theories, Morreall, 1983), many humor scholars today incorporate the idea as part of the definition of humor. The basic idea of incongruity is that we form schemas about the world that help orient and guide us in our everyday environments. These knowledge structures are often understood as being composed of images and linguistic concepts linked in interconnected webs of association (i.e., associative networks) (Carlston & Smith, 1996). At times, we perceive or encounter something incongruous, or at odds, with what our schemas lead us to expect in that situation. When that incongruity amuses us, we have humor. Various terms have been proposed to capture this juxtaposition of elements, such as appropriate incongruity (Oring, 1992), script opposition (Raskin, 1985), deviations from norms (Archakis & Tsakona, 2005), or violations of expectations (Meyer, 2000). Attardo's (2001) general theory of verbal humor (GTVH) represents an attempt to analyze humor by directing attention to six knowledge resources: (1) script opposition, the two schemas or scripts that are the basis of the humor, (2) logical mechanism, the mental operations necessary to understand the opposition, (3) the situation, or what the humor is about, (4) the target(s) or butt of the humor, (5) the narrative strategy or form of the humor, and (6) the language or exact wording used to enact the humor. Although Attardo focused on jokes and texts, the GTVH has been used to examine conversational data (Archakis & Tsakona, 2005) as well as expanded to examine the verbal and nonverbal behaviors of an Italian film star (Canestrari, 2010).

Incongruity gives rise to a cognitive shift as receivers oscillate from one script/schema to another. It is readily apparent that many times things occur that violate our expectations and we appraise the incongruity as requiring some kind of active response on our part. For example, if we round a corner and find ourselves confronting a bear, the situation may be unexpected but our appraisal is likely to result in fear and a subsequent instinct to flee. In humor, the appraisal is benign-positive, and so we are free to relax and enjoy the cognitive shift (e.g., we round the corner and find ourselves confronting a person in a Smokey the Bear costume). Humor producers, therefore, must not only enact a message that hinges on an incongruity, but they must also convey that message in such a way that the metamessage of safety and security is also conveyed. These metamessages have been referred to as play frames (Goffman, 1974, 1986) or contextualization cues (Lytra, 2007). Formulating play frames can be done verbally, as with joke-prefacing devices (Cashion, Cody, & Erickson, 1987), such as "I've got a joke for you," nicknames, or word/phrase repetition. Nonverbal cues also provide a rich array of means by which a humorist can convey the metamessage "this is not serious." It was pointed out earlier that in dyadic conversation, speakers often laugh at their own statements first, to signal to the hearer how to hear an utterance. Other cues include changes in volume, pitch, or rhythm, clapping, dialect, or blank face (Bell, 2007; Lytra, 2007). The need to frame humorous messages with contextualization cues directs our attention to something about humor production skills. To make others laugh, humorists must subordinate their own laughter to their speech. It has already been pointed out that they often do suppress their amusement until the thought has been expressed or the reaction of the hearer becomes evident. This is part of the timing and delivery of humor, but it may also speak to why measures of humor appreciation and humor production are often only moderately correlated. That is, the wit has to control the appreciation of humor in one's self to enact it for others.

Delving into the definition of humor has brought to light the important issue of playfulness. The need for wits to construct a play frame when enacting humor should not be taken to imply that all humor is playful. Humor can be serious (i.e., the opposite of playful), but even in serious humor the communicator must still couch the message in play frames. Playfulness is therefore implicated in humor, but caveats are in order. Humor and play overlap but they are not the same. Play can be characterized as a paratelic activity (Miller, 1973). It involves a switch from a serious, goal-directed mode of activity to one in which goal orientation is suspended. In play, an activity is undertaken and continued for the intrinsic gratification it provides. Play is often characterized by "inefficiencies in behavior and self-imposed obstacles" (Miczo, 2004, p. 210) to prolong the performance itself. Children, for example, stop playing when play ceases to be fun. We implicitly recognize this "essence of play" when we frown on someone who plays only to win. One of the prerequisites of play, however, is that other needs are not pressing (Gosso, Otta, Morais, Ribeiro, & Bussab, 2005). Playful humor, therefore, is play that is intended to amuse. The engagement and intrinsic gratification of play can produce a feeling of flow in virtually any activity, but not all flow experiences will produce amusement and joy. It may be a general principle that as the seriousness of play increases, the fun and amusement decrease. Conversely, the more the activity is enjoyed for its own sake, the more fun, amusing, and humorous it is. As adults' cognitive abilities develop and/or their proclivity for more physically vigorous forms of play diminishes, they ought to find playing with words and concepts more enjoyable.

Broadly speaking, then, humor can be playful or it can be serious. In both cases, it must be enacted through the use of a play frame. There are several reasons why a communicator might wish to use humor to craft a serious message, such as to soften the blow of a critical message, to protect the face of one or both interlocutors, or to take advantage of humor's deniability. In these cases, it is doubtful that the sender intended the primary purpose of the message to amuse. Rather, the sender is probably concerned that the message be interpreted "correctly" (e.g., Attardo's concept of relevant inappropriateness with regard to irony). If the message is not intended to amuse, is it still humor? Adopting a message perspective, we can say that a message that turns on opposed scripts and enacts play frames in its presentation is a humorous message; the distinction between playful and serious humor adds further refinement to our understanding of how humor is utilized by communicators.

While the playful–serious distinction centers around the intentions of the humorist, another popular approach is to examine the functions that humor serves, both interactionally and relationally. It is beyond the scope of this chapter to examine the many functional typologies that have been proposed. Many of those typologies, however, either include or can be reduced to two overarching functions, a positive one and a negative one. The positive function of humor concerns its affiliative potential and includes such forms as reducing tension and conflict (Ziv, 1984), garnering social support (Lefcourt, 2001), and providing perspective on life's problems (Hyers, 1996). The negative function of humor covers its capacity to separate or distance people from each other, including such uses as expressing hostile feelings (Graham, Papa, & Brooks, 1992), enforcing group norms (Alexander, 1986), and enhancing feelings of superiority over others (Gruner, 1997).

Meyer (2000) proposed four rhetorical functions of humorous communication. The first, *identification*, involves creating a bond between speaker and audience to build support and increase credibility and cohesiveness. With *clarification*, speakers condense their views into memorable phrases or anecdotes, while also commenting on unexpected or inappropriate behavior without being critical of audience members. *Enforcement* allows speakers to criticize or ridicule audience members concerning a member's violation of normative behavior. *Differentiation* emphasizes contrast between speakers and opponent(s), or between the speaker's group and another group. Meyer argued that these four functions could be collapsed into two more fundamental functions: unification and division. Humor that draws the speaker and audience together (identification and clarification) serves a unifying function, while humor that creates distinctions between the speaker and another person/group (enforcement and differentiation) serves a divisive function.

PRODUCTION OF HUMOROUS MESSAGES

It has become virtually axiomatic that all communication is goal driven. Given that premise, goals have become an important starting point for understanding why individuals produce messages. In particular, Dillard (1990, 1997) has advanced the understanding of message production by proposing the goals-plans-action (GPA) framework. In this model, goals are desired end states that individuals strive to bring about; that desire gives rise to a planning process, wherein communicators evaluate various means for reaching their goal in order to formulate a plan; that plan is then put into effect via action. Dillard further distinguishes between primary and secondary goals. A primary goal is the organizing goal; it defines what the interaction is about. Although early research assumed the primary goal was always an influence goal, more recent formulations stipulate that the primary goal can shift once interaction gets under way, so that the primary goal defines what a communicator is striving to bring about at the moment (Dillard & Schrader, 1998; Wilson, 2002). Secondary goals are recurrent considerations that typically shape or constrain primary goal pursuit. Although there is no single set of secondary goals, many approaches include such goals as concern for self, concern for partner, concern for the relationship, and concern for managing the interaction (Wilson, 2002).

Dillard (1997) proposed a number of questions concerning the goal construct, and two questions in particular are relevant to humor. One is the issue of whether goals must be present in conscious awareness, and the other is the question concerning the nature of the hierarchical organization of goals. In raising the issue of consciousness, Dillard suggested three possibilities. The *inside-only* perspective contends that goals necessarily reside in consciousness. The *outside-in* approach argues that goals begin outside of conscious awareness but that they can be brought to awareness by effortful attention. Finally, the *inside-out* perspective posits that goals originate in consciousness, but via repetition and overlearning they gradually drift out of awareness. The second issue concerns goal hierarchy, and Dillard proposes two possibilities. The *consummatory* approach involves a two-step hierarchy of consummate goals (ultimate objectives) and contributory goals (all behaviors necessary to reach objectives). The *levels* perspective advances as many levels as are needed conceptually. Generally speaking, a levels approach is organized around a temporal dimension; that is, more abstract goals tend to be further out temporally, while more concrete goals that are nearer in time tend to require a number of more definite actions.

In applying the GPA model to humor production, the first thing that is evident is that serious, or bona fide communication, humor fits easily into its framework. Serious humor is telic, or goal-oriented, by definition; that is, the communicator has a point that he/she wants to get across, considers multiple, sometimes conflicting concerns, formulates a plan for getting the point across, and then speaks. Young and Bippus (2001) advanced a similar argument in examining humor and hurtful messages. They noted that the person using humor may be attempting to appear as more benign or more face-saving when uttering a hurtful message, though receivers may see things otherwise. Their results confirmed that humorously phrased messages were perceived as less hurtful, though certain categories were perceived as more intentionally hurtful. Bippus (2003) examined the role of humor in conflict and found that receivers were able to distinguish between humor directed toward the speaker's own needs and humor that considered the receiver. Humor that was more partner concerned was related to more positive conflict outcomes. Finally, research on comforting (Bippus, 2000) reveals that humor can also help ease another's distress. Taken together, these studies suggest that humor is a common way to accomplish social goals.

Playful humor, on the other hand, presents a challenge for the GPA framework. One could adopt Berger's (1997) assertion that "people sometimes seek to interact with others simply for the sake of talking with someone, which is itself a goal" (p. 13). Or, one could cite Kellermann's (1992) argument that communication is purposive, and therefore, the mere act of communicating is goal-driven even if there is no goal at stake. Rather than fall back to one of these positions, I would like to address the challenge posed by a paratelic humorous mode of communication. Confronting such a challenge has the potential to enhance our understanding of message production processes more generally.

To begin, we can conceive of consciousness dimensionally. One end of this dimension is bounded by full conscious awareness, while the other describes fully unconscious motives. Somewhere along this dimension is a threshold; most likely this threshold varies from person to person but is also fluid according to physiological and situational factors. In goal-driven interactions, we have some definite point in mind that we want to get across and that point has to be fully conscious to have organizing power. We also have a host of secondary concerns that impact how we want to get that point across. Many of these considerations reflect habitual concerns for self and partner face, as well as relational maintenance and so they most likely hover somewhere around the threshold. If necessary, we could articulate them; however, we may not often need to be fully aware of them. At a level below that, sunk deeper into the unconscious are a host of overlearned rules for conversation and discourse competence. These would be more difficult to bring to awareness, but not impossible. For example, a communicator might be unaware that he/she routinely interrupts others during conversation, but if this were pointed out by others, that person would presumably be able to become more cognizant of the tendency. At the lowest level of the dimension are needs and motives that are unconscious and may even be difficult for others to notice because they would require a high degree of familiarity with our communication patterns across a variety of contexts. Notice that this is a levels perspective, but it is more like an inverse levels perspective. That is, as one travels up toward consciousness, one arrives at the immediate interactional context.

Conceptually speaking, being in a playful mode means foregoing any definite aim or pursuit. There is no primary goal in consciousness. Insofar as fantasy and imagination are given free rein, play allows one to range along those deeper levels of the consciousness dimension. Roles may be reversed; for example, the child gets the better of the parent. Relationships become more negotiable and one can become something one is not. And of course, words can be played with, given new meaning, or no meaning whatsoever. Playful humor operates in just this way. As a form of play, it involves relaxing the consciousness threshold and giving full rein to the imagination. As a form of humor, it still involves incongruities that are amusing. Recall that in the conversational humor model, humor often arises from the interaction itself. In other words, interactants are having a conversation and something funny occurs to one of the participants. Most often, this is something about the situation or the partner, so it means the focus has shifted to what would normally be a more secondary concern. Humor can also arise from the conversation itself, the words spoken or the topic being discussed. That is, something from the deeper level of discourse competence suddenly grabs one's attention. Notice, one has to be willing to let go of the primary goal to entertain the shift and one must further decide whether to express the thought as a humorous utterance. As Morreall (2009) argued, humor involves a disengagement from the practical, goal-driven aspect of the conversation. Contrary to his argument, this does not mean one is disengaged from the here and now, but rather, one becomes engaged with the process of communicating itself, at the content and/or relational level. This formulation is therefore consistent with the definition of humor advanced earlier.

In addition to the GPA model, other approaches to message production can also shed light on humor production. Second-generation action assembly theory (AAT2) (Greene, 1997) provides one such means. A central feature of AAT2 is the procedural record, which is a cognitive structure consisting of nodes and links; more specifically, these records contain information about behavior as well as the constellation of features associated with that behavior, such as outcomes, situations, and persons. Procedural records that have been frequently and consistently activated together may form unitized assemblies, such that the activation of one record spreads quickly and automatically to the other(s). From moment to moment, every node is in some state of activation. Perceptions of the environment will cause some nodes to activate beyond a threshold and spread activation to other nodes or records. However, activation is short-lived. To offset the rapid decay of activated records, AAT2 introduces the idea of the coalition. A coalition is a momentary assemblage of activated behavioral features that could be said to "fit together" (p. 159). The fact that activation can spread along unexpected pathways explains the creative nature of moment-to-moment communication; the existence of coalitions captures our ability to focus our attention for a time while the inevitable decay process also suggests why attention wanders.

AAT2 might be used to explain humor production in the following manner: In conversation, our partner says something and that word or phrase activates relevant procedural records. Insofar as many words have multiple meanings or associations, another set of procedural records are simultaneously activated. In and of themselves, these opposed scripts are not necessarily amusing; therefore, it is clear that additional factors, either executive processes or procedural records for enacting humor, would also need to be present and accessible to the person. Such an explanation is consistent with the construct of humor orientation (HO) (Booth-Butterfield & Booth-Butterfield, 1991). In their original research on HO, Booth-Butterfield and Booth-Butterfield found that high HO individuals reported they used humor in more situations and used more types of humor compared to low HO individuals. Further, they reported that their humor was more spontaneous than planned. These findings are consistent with the idea that humorists have developed unitized assemblies for contextualization cues and humor forms that are readily accessible because they are frequently enacted.

Admittedly, there is a difference between planned humor and elaborated humor; this distinction can be highlighted by using AAT2 concepts to explain a study by Kozbelt and Nishioka (2010). These researchers were interested in the idea that humor production was associated with a flash of insight, as suggested by approaches emphasizing suddenness in humor, or the "Aha" moment.

To test this, participants viewed photographs of everyday social situations and were instructed to devise funny captions to go along with each one (20 photographs total). They were given a minute to think about a funny response before the screen began flashing as a warning and they were instructed to "pick the first caption that came to mind that they thought was acceptably funny" (p. 388). And, if they thought of multiple captions, to pick the one that was funniest. They were then instructed to type it in and click a Submit button. The computer recorded the time between presentation of the photo and the onset of typing (pre-typing time), and the time from onset of typing to clicking the Submit button (typing time). Captions were then rated for funniness by judges. Contrary to the insight explanation, there were small but positive correlations between funniness and both typing time and total time. Insight, however, would have been better assessed by having participants type in the first thing that occurred to them and then having these captions rated for funniness. In AAT2 terms, one would expect that even funny people would need time to assemble the funniest response possible as they sorted through various procedural records and/or unitized assemblies. This could account for the not uncommon phenomena of having the perfect humorous comeback two or three turns after it would have been discourse relevant. In playful conversations, one might still be able to work it in because rules for relevance have been suspended.

It remains to be explored why a humorist would enact one form of humor over another. Meyer (2000) suggested that the difference between unification and division humor is which aspect of a violation is emphasized. In unification humor, what is stressed is the "overall normality of the situation, providing reassurance while noting some humorous divergence from that normality" (p. 325). In division humor, "it is the violation that is stressed over the normality" (p. 326) and the violation and/or the violator needs to be corrected or otherwise brought into line. Memorable messages provide a mechanism for accounting for the use of divisive, or aggressive, humor. Memorable messages "frequently reflect rules of what should or should not be done" (Honeycutt & Cantrill, 2001, p. 37). Although early work on the construct was mostly descriptive, Smith and Ellis (2001) applied a control theory explanation to account for how memorable messages work. Control theory is a broad approach explaining how a negative feedback loop operates to keep a system within desired parameters. In the Smith and Ellis approach, memorable messages basically work as negative feedback. That is, when my behavior falls below what I expect from myself based on personalized or idealized standards of conduct, recall of a memorable message prompts me to bring my behavior back into line with expectations. Although they applied their approach to self-focused messages, there is no reason to believe that memorable messages couldn't be applied to the evaluation of others' behaviors. Thus, when you or your behavior falls outside the parameters of what I expect or desire, recall of a memorable message might prompt me to emphasize the violation and the concomitant unacceptability of your behavior (or you yourself). Phrasing it humorously allows me to minimize face threat, or potential relational damage, while also possibly avoiding conflict and/or direct discussion of the transgression.

A cognitive mechanism that might account for affiliative or unifying humor is imagined interactions. Imagined interactions are social cognitive processes "whereby actors imagine and therefore indirectly experience themselves in anticipated and/or past communicative encounters with others" (Honeycutt, 2003, p. 2). When we engage in imagined interactions with someone, we not only access procedural records for the person and the topic of talk, but also records for how to "do" conversation itself. Honeycutt and Brown (1998) found a positive relationship between HO and use of imagined interactions to rehearse jokes (rather than plan them), so it may be that affiliative humorists spend more time thinking humorously, cultivating a humorous outlook on life that facilitates its use in conversation. The potential for misunderstanding and failed humor that are attendant risks of humor use means that trying out humor imaginatively before an utterance might increase its effectiveness. That is, the humorist could envision the potential response to humor and then proceed in a manner that would enhance, rather than harm, relational bonds. There is considerable evidence that individuals who use affiliative humor are more responsive and sensitive to conversational partners (Merolla, 2006; Miczo, Welter, & Norton, 2011; Wanzer, Booth-Butterfield, & Booth-Butterfield, 1995). In Meyer's (2000) framework, affiliative humor would involve online imagined interactions insofar as the humorist has to note a violation and then reframe the breach playfully (i.e., not seriously).

CONCLUSION

Whatever the medicinal values of laughter, it is clear not just any over-the-counter remedy will be effective in increasing one's ability to produce humor. One of the few attempts to design and evaluate a program to increase humor production and appreciation found only modest evidence of success (Nevo, Aharonson, & Klingman, 1998). There are also risks attendant on humor usage, including lowered ratings of intelligence (Bressler & Balshine, 2006) and not being taken seriously (Plester & Orams, 2008). To date, research on humor production has been hampered by underdeveloped models of how humorists produce messages. One of the goals of this chapter has been to suggest fruitful avenues of research toward that end. Understanding the social-cognitive mechanisms involved in producing different forms of humor will allow us to better design programs that have any hope of improving humor usage. On the other hand, humor poses some challenges for our current understanding of message production. In particular, the play element of humor is not easily reconciled with the assumption of goal-driven communication behavior. A secondary goal of this chapter has been to offer a means of *rapprochement* between these two areas of inquiry. Clearly, it is time to use the tools and concepts of message production to begin explaining the "pharmacology of humor."

References

Alexander, R. D. (1986). Ostracism and indirect reciprocity: The reproductive significance of humor. *Ethology and Sociobiology, 7,* 253–270.

Andersen, P. A., & Guerrero, L. K. (1998). Principles of communication and emotion in social interaction. In P. A. Andersen & L. K. Guerrero (Eds.), *Handbook of communication and emotion: Research, theory, applications, and contexts* (pp. 49–96). San Diego: Academic Press.

Archakis, A., & Tsakona, V. (2005). Analyzing conversational data in GTVH terms: A new approach to the issue of identity construction via humor. *Humor, 18,* 41–68.

Attardo, S. (2001). *Humorous texts: A semantic and pragmatic analysis.* Berlin: Mouton de Gruyter.

Bachorowski, J.-A., & Owren, M. J. (2001). Not all laughs are alike: Voiced but not unvoiced laughter readily elicits positive affect. *Psychological Science, 12,* 252–257.

Bell, N. D. (2007). Humor comprehension: Lessons learned from cross-cultural communication. *Humor, 20,* 367–387. doi:10.1515/HUMOR.2007.018

Berger, C. R. (1997). *Planning strategic interaction: Attaining goals through communicative action.* Mahwah, NJ: Lawrence Erlbaum.

Bippus, A. (2000). Humor usage in comforting episodes: Factors predicting outcomes. *Western Journal of Communication, 64,* 359–384.

Bippus, A. (2003). Humor motives, qualities, and reactions in recalled conflict episodes. *Western Journal of Communication, 67,* 413–426.

Booth-Butterfield, S., & Booth-Butterfield, M. (1991). Individual differences in the communication of humorous messages. *Southern Communication Journal, 56,* 205–218.

Bressler, E. R., & Balshine, S. (2006). The influence of humor on desirability. *Evolution and Human Behavior, 27,* 29–39. doi:10.1016/j.evolhumbehav.2005.06.002

Burleson, B. B., & Planalp, S. (2000). Producing emotion(al) messages. *Communication Theory, 10,* 221–250.

Canestrari, C. (2010). Meta-communicative signals and humorous verbal interchanges: A case study. *Humor, 23,* 327–349. doi:10.1515/HUMR.2010.015

Carlston, D. E., & Smith, E. R. (1996). Principles of mental representation. In E. T. Higgins & A. W. Kruglanski (Eds.), *Social psychology: Handbook of basic principles* (pp. 184–210). New York: Guilford Press.

Carrell, A. (1997). Joke competence and humor competence. *Humor, 10,* 173–185.

Cashion, J. L., Cody, M. J., & Erickson, K. V. (1987). You'll love this one… An exploration into joke-prefacing devices. *Journal of Language and Social Psychology, 5,* 303–312.

Chafe, W. (2007). *The importance of not being earnest: The feeling behind laughter and humor.* Amsterdam: John Benjamins Publishing Company.

Devereux, P. G., & Ginsburg, G. P. (2001). Sociality effects on the production of laughter. *The Journal of General Psychology, 128,* 227–240.

Dillard, J. P. (1990). A goal-driven model of interpersonal influence. In J. P. Dillard (Ed.), *Seeking compliance: The production of interpersonal influence messages* (pp. 41–56). Scottsdale, AZ: Gorsuch Scarisbrick Publishers.

Dillard, J. P. (1997). Explicating the goal construct: Tools for theorists. In J. O. Greene (Ed.), *Message production: Advances in communication theory* (pp. 47–69). Mahwah, NJ: Lawrence Erlbaum.

Dillard, J. P., & Schrader, D. C. (1998). On the utility of the goals-plans-action sequence. *Communication Studies, 49,* 300–304.

Fry, W. F. (1994). The biology of humor. *Humor, 7,* 111–126.

Glenn, P. (2003). *Laughter in interaction.* Cambridge, MA: Cambridge University Press.

Goffman, E. (1974/1986). *Frame analysis: An essay on the organization of experience.* Boston: Northeastern University Press.

Gosso, Y., Otta, E., Morais, M. de L. S. e., Ribeiro, F. J. L., & Bussab, V. S. R. (2005). Play in hunter-gatherer society. In A. D. Pellegrini & P. K. Smith (Eds.), *The nature of play: Great apes and humans* (pp. 213–253). New York: Guilford Press.

Graham, E. E., Papa, M. J., & Brooks, G. P. (1992). Functions of humor in conversation: Conceptualization and measurement. *Western Journal of Communication, 56,* 161–183.

Greene, J. O. (1997). A second generation action assembly theory. In J. O. Greene (Ed.), *Message production: Advances in communication theory* (pp. 151–170). Mahwah, NJ: Lawrence Erlbaum.

Gruner, C. R. (1985). Advice to the beginning speaker on using humor: What the research tells us. *Communication Education, 34,* 142–147.

Gruner, C. R. (1997). *The game of humor: A comprehensive theory of why we laugh.* New Brunswick, NJ: Transaction Publishers.

Hay, J. (2001). The pragmatics of humor support. *Humor, 14,* 55–82.

Hayworth, D. (1928). The social origin and function of laughter. *Psychological Review, 35,* 367–384.

Honeycutt, J. M. (2003). *Imagined interactions: Daydreaming about communication.* Cresskill, NJ: Hampton Press.

Honeycutt, J. M., & Brown, R. (1998). Did you hear the one about?: Typological and spousal differences in the planning of jokes and sense of humor in marriage. *Communication Quarterly, 46,* 342–352.

Honeycutt, J. M., & Cantrill, J. G. (2001). *Cognition, communication, and romantic relationships.* Mahwah, NJ: Lawrence Erlbaum.

Hyers, C. (1996). *The spirituality of comedy: Comic heroism in a tragic world.* New Brunswick, NJ: Transaction Publishers.

Kellermann, K. (1992). Communication: Inherently strategic and primarily automatic. *Communication Monographs, 59,* 288–300.

Kozbelt, A., & Nishioka, K. (2010). Humor comprehension, humor production, and insight: An exploratory study. *Humor, 23,* 375–401. doi:10.1515/HUMR.2010.017

Latta, R. L. (1998). *The basic humor process: A cognitive-shift theory and the case against incongruity.* Berlin: Mouton de Gruyter.

Lazarus, R. S., & Folkman, S. (1984). *Stress, appraisal, and coping.* New York: Springer Publishing Company.

Lefcourt, H. M. (2001). *Humor: The psychology of living buoyantly.* New York: Kluwer Academic/Plenum Publishers.

Lytra, V. (2007). Teasing in contact encounters: Frames, participant positions and responses. *Multilingua, 26,* 381–408. doi:10.1515/MULTI.2007.018

Martin, G. N., & Gray, C. D. (1996). The effects of audience laughter on men's and women's responses to humor. *The Journal of Social Psychology, 136,* 221–231.

Merolla, A. J. (2006). Decoding ability and humor production. *Communication Quarterly, 54,* 175–189. doi:10.1080/01463370600650886

Meyer, J. C. (2000). Humor as a double-edged sword: Four functions of humor in communication. *Communication Theory, 10,* 310–331.

Miczo, N. (2004). Humor ability, unwillingness to communicate, loneliness, and perceived stress: Testing a security theory. *Communication Studies, 55,* 209–226.

Miczo, N., Averbeck, J. M., & Mariani, T. (2009). Affiliative and aggressive humor, attachment dimensions, and interaction goals. *Communication Studies, 60,* 443–459. doi:10.1080/105110970903260301

Miczo, N., Welter, R. E., & Norton, H. E. (2011, April). Communication anxiety and cognitive competence as predictors of affiliative and aggressive humor. *Paper presented at the Central States Communication Association conference,* Milwaukee.

Miller, S. (1973). Ends, means, and galumphing: Some leitmotifs of play. *American Anthropologist, 75,* 87–98.

Morreall, J. (1983). *Taking laughter seriously.* Albany: State University of New York Press.

Morreall, J. (2009). *Comic relief: A comprehensive philosophy of humor.* Chichester, UK: Wiley-Blackwell.

Nevo, O., Aharonson, H., & Klingman, A. (1998). The development and evaluation of a systematic program for improving sense of humor. In W. Ruch (Ed.), *The sense of humor: Explorations of a personality characteristic* (pp. 385–404). Berlin: Mouton de Gruyter.

O'Donnell-Trujillo, N., & Adams, K. (1983). Heheh in conversation: Some coordinating accomplishments of laughter. *The Western Journal of Speech Communication, 47,* 175–191.

Oring, E. (1992). *Jokes and their relations.* Lexington: The University Press of Kentucky.

Plester, B., & Orams, M. (2008). Send in the clowns: The role of the joker in three New Zealand IT companies. *Humor, 21,* 253-281. doi:10.1515/HUMOR.2008.013

Provine, R. R. (1992). Contagious laughter: Laughter is a sufficient stimulus for laughs and smiles. *Bulletin of the Psychonomic Society, 30,* 1–4.

Provine, R. R. (1993). Laughter punctuates speech: Linguistic, social and gender contexts of laughter. *Ethology, 95,* 291–298.

Provine, R. R. (2000). *Laughter: A scientific investigation.* New York: Viking Press.

Raskin, V. (1985). *Semantic mechanisms of humor.* Dordrecht/Boston/Lancaster: D. Reidel.

Rothbart, M. K. (1973). Laughter in young children. *Psychological Bulletin, 80,* 247–256.

Smith, S. W., & Ellis, J. B. (2001). Memorable messages as guides to self-assessment of behavior: An initial investigation. *Communication Monographs, 68,* 154–168.

Sroufe, L. A., & Waters, E. (1976). The ontogenesis of smiling and laughter: A perspective on the organization of development in infancy. *Psychological Review, 83,* 173–189.

Wanzer, M., Booth-Butterfield, M., & Booth-Butterfield, S. (1995). The funny people: A source-orientation to the communication of humor. *Communication Quarterly, 43,* 142–154.

Wilson, S. R. (2002). *Seeking and resisting compliance: Why people say what they do when trying to influence others.* Thousand Oaks, CA: SAGE.

Young, S. L., & Bippus, A. M. (2001). Does it make a difference if they hurt you in a funny way? Humorously and non-humorously phrased hurtful messages in personal relationships. *Communication Quarterly, 49,* 35–52.

Ziv, A. (1984). *Personality and sense of humor.* New York: Spring Publishing Company.

CHAPTER 4

INTRODUCTION TO THE MEASUREMENT OF HUMOROUS COMMUNICATION

Melissa Bekelja Wanzer
Canisius College

Melanie Booth-Butterfield
West Virginia University

"I laughed so hard I was gasping for breath, my body was shaking, and tears were streaming down my face!" A statement such as this exemplifies the diverse channels and potential avenues for measuring humorous communication. We can assess humor through self-reports, through observable behavior, and even through physical changes. As with many communication phenomena, humor represents a rich opportunity for generating data, but also a great challenge in determining what those data mean and how best to measure humorous communication.

What exactly is humor? If you seek a definition of humor, you will find multiple descriptions. Humor can be conceptualized as an internal body fluid such as lymph or blood, a particular mood, a response to a message, an amusing object, or an active enactment of behaviors intended to obtain entertained responses. In this chapter we focus on measuring the active communication elements of humor: how humor is enacted and received in interactions (as opposed to a person's characteristic disposition or temperament, the act of indulging or "humoring" someone, or bodily fluids). According to Booth-Butterfield and Booth-Butterfield (1991) humor involves "intentional verbal and nonverbal messages and other forms of spontaneous behavior that elicit laughter, chuckling and taken to mean pleasure, delight and/or surprise, in the targeted receiver" (p. 206). This definition focuses on positive elements and intents; communication that is entertaining, enjoyable, and light-hearted. But recognizing that all humor might not be productive, other researchers (e.g. Martin, Puhlik-Doris, Larsen, Gray, & Weir, 2003) have extended the enactment of humor to focus on negative, or more maladaptive dimensions of humor—aggressive, self-defeating, and the like. It is important to consider both positive and negative humor, as well as received versus enacted humor, when addressing measurement issues in this chapter.

OVERVIEW

What gains in knowledge should accrue when we measure humor? There are a variety of types of outcomes associated with communication linked to humor, so our measurement needs to be based on what we hope to understand. For example, we may be interested in distal, indirect outcomes of humor in interactions (perceptions of teachers, effective coping) or we may focus on specific behaviors associated with responding and competent enactments of such humor (e.g., how long someone laughs in a particular incident or how effectively someone tells a joke). Often we gauge the affective components associated with humor, the feelings and emotions (attraction, embarrassment, anger, relief) associated with humor. Another major area of study is the perceived individual benefits of either enacting humor or amusement and laughter in response (how we cope using humor, functions of humorous communication). Each of these research goals would entail different approaches to measuring humor in communication.

Humor can be assessed with several methods: physiological, observed behaviors, and introspective survey/self-report. It should be noted that with humor-related communication, as with other psychological variables, these channels may not be highly correlated (e.g., Clevenger, 1959; Martin et al., 2003; Williams et al., 2002). It is imperative to determine which type(s) of measurement will address the outcomes of interest. For example, if one is examining medical benefits of laughter, physiological measurement would be most appropriate (e.g., Curtis, 1979). If you want to be able to visibly see how humor is experienced or the outcomes from humorous communication, then behavioral observations would be the best choice. For example, observed humor enactments were measured in Wanzer, Booth-Butterfield, and Booth-Butterfield (1995), to determine whether observers could distinguish performance of humor among high humor– and low humor–oriented individuals, and Graham, Papa, and Brooks (1992) used observation/coding of humor to validate the Uses of Humor Index (UHI). Observation of behavior tends to be more reliable if multiple people do the rating, and if they are trained in what to look for (Clevenger, 1959).

Most often humorous communication and its effects have been addressed through self-report—even if the self-report is on perceptions of a targeted person. Sometimes humor is measured within a dyad to examine the reciprocal effects, e.g., Maki, Booth-Butterfield, and McMullen (2012), Graham (1995). Often self- and other perceptions are included among the survey/self-report method (e.g., Rizzo, Wanzer, & Booth-Butterfield, 1999). Both qualitative and quantitative means of assessing humor have been undertaken, sometimes in the same project. For example, Holmes and Schnurr (2005) used ethnographic analyses of workplace humor and linked them with humor enactment rates (proportion of humor per 100 minutes in meetings) to describe the use of humor in various corporate departments.

This chapter discusses issues in measurement of humor and some of the primary measures of humor in both communication and psychology. To enhance clarity on this topic we begin by making an important distinction between source and receiver perspectives on humorous communication.

SOURCE AND RECEIVER APPROACHES IN HUMOR RESEARCH

One way to organize the extensive body of humor research conducted in fields such as communication and social psychology is to delineate among research that uses either a source or receiver approach or both. Receiver approaches to humor research typically examine the effects of humor exposure on study participants (Wanzer et al., 1995). For example, in the field of communication numerous researchers have studied the impact of humor on different types of audiences (public speaking, mass media, instructional) looking for effects on persuasion, learning, credibility, motivation, and enjoyment of content (Bryant, Brown, Silberg, & Elliot, 1981; Bryant, Comisky, & Zillmann, 1979; Bryant, Crane, Comisky, & Zillman, 1980; Bryant & Zillmann, 1988; Downs, Javidi, & Nussbaum, 1988; Gorham & Christophel, 1990; Grimes, 1955; Gruner, 1964, 1965, 1966; Houser, Cowan, & West, 2007; Lieberman, Neuendorf, Denny, Skalski, & Wang, 2009; Madden & Weinberger, 1982). Much of this scholarship has highlighted the positive effects of humor and illustrated how exposure to humorous content contributed to increases in receivers' persuasability, influence, motivation, and learning as well as increased enjoyment of subject matter in public presentations and in the media.

A second area of communication research has explored the goals that communicators accomplish by utilizing humorous communication (Graham, 1988; Graham & Rubin, 1987; Graham et al., 1992). This research focuses on what communicators achieve when they employ humorous messages in their relationships. Research by Graham et al. (1992) indicated that, in general, individuals often use humor to express positive and negative affect or to share information with others (i.e., expressiveness).

More recently, communication researchers have explored the effects of humor use in specific interpersonal situations such as comforting and conflict episodes. Bippus (2000) found that all of her study participants could recall a time when someone used humor as part of comforting communication. Those participants indicated the quality of the humorous communication was salient and that it greatly influenced the perceived effectiveness of the comforting messages. Not surprisingly, participants evaluated humorous messages that were well-timed and funny as the most successful examples of comforting communication (Bippus, 2000). Along the same lines, Bippus (2003) studied factors affecting how humorous messages are perceived during conflict episodes. She found that study participants' "attributions about the speaker's reasons for using humor, and their perceptions of the characteristics of the humorous messages themselves, were most strongly correlated with the outcomes of the conflict as perceived by the recipient of the humor" (Bippus, 2003, p. 422). Such research indicates that sources often incorporate humor to achieve specific interpersonal goals.

Much of the humor research from fields such as communication studies and social psychology has been from a receiver-oriented approach. Researchers have measured sense of humor from a humor appreciation perspective (Martin & Lefcourt, 1984), personality correlates of sense of humor (Goodchilds, 1959; Smith & Goodchilds, 1963) and the effects of humor exposure on behavior and perceptions of receivers (Gruner, 1967, 1976).

While this is certainly not a comprehensive list of the humor research conducted from a receiver perspective, it does shed light on some of the apparent trends in humor measurement. Indeed, "social science researchers in general and communication researchers in particular, have focused their efforts on the communication of humor from a receiver perspective" (Wanzer et al., 1995, p. 143).

A second, consistent observation of this scholarship is that humor is viewed as a generally positive attribute in communication that generally produces favorable impressions in receivers. While some research has observed negative elements or aspects of humor production (i.e., teasing research) (see for example, Conoley, Herschberger, Gonzalez, Rinker, & Crowley, 2007; DiCioccio, 2008; Gaidos, 2009; Kline & Guinsler, 2007; Madlock & Booth-Butterfield, 2008), a more substantial body of work highlights the merits of humor (see for example, McRoberts & Larsen-Casselton, 2006).

With the development of the Humor Orientation scale (hereafter referred to as HO) by Booth-Butterfield and Booth-Butterfield (1991), researchers began to investigate individual differences in humor production. For example, Wanzer et al. (1995) added validation for the HO measure and presented a case for researchers to study humor from a source perspective.

A source approach to the study of humor is important to researchers for a number of reasons. A source orientation indicates that a substantial portion of social humor is discursively generated and intentional. From this perspective, communication researchers can focus on the communicatively complex ways that sources encode and enact humorous messages, in addition to the outcomes or effects of humor use. Some research indicates humor is an important facet of communication competence (Duran, 1983, 1992; Wanzer et al., 1995).

Research conducted from a source orientation has shed light on how individuals differ in their abilities and propensities to enact humorous behaviors. For example, we know that individuals who employ humorous communication more frequently are more communicatively competent (Wanzer et al., 1995), viewed as more socially attractive (Wanzer, Booth-Butterfield, & Booth-Butterfield, 1996), less lonely (Wanzer et al., 1996), use humor to cope with stress and, as a result report greater coping efficacy (Wanzer, Sparks, & Frymier, 2009). Research using nurses, college students, aging adults, and even grieving adults (Booth-Butterfield, Wanzer, Krezmien,

& Wiel, 2010) indicates that higher humor–oriented individuals report greater coping efficacy. This body of research indicates that sources seem to benefit both intrapersonally and interpersonally from enacting humorous messages. From a communication perspective, this scholarship illustrates the intrapersonal and interpersonal merits of humor production; this is clearly distinguished from a receiver orientation.

SELECTION OF MEASURES OF HUMOR

Just as there are over 100 humor theories in existence (Foot & McCreaddie, 2006), there are numerous humor measures; however, only a small number of these are utilized by research teams. Measures discussed in this chapter were selected for inclusion based on several criteria. First, the humor measure was created by an individual with some apparent knowledge of scale development. Importantly, the creator of the scale addressed issues of scale reliability and validity in the original manuscript, explaining scale development processes. Next, the measure was originally published in a peer-reviewed journal, thus offering heightened credibility. A third criterion for inclusion was that the scale has been used by researchers other than those who developed the scales. It is important to examine how the scale performed and scrutinize whether the scale offers a reliable and valid assessment of the constructs it measures. Finally, the measures included in this chapter are widely accessible and available for other researchers to implement.

In the next section, we summarize some of the seminal work on humor measures conducted in the fields of communication and social psychology.

MEASURES FROM THE FIELD OF COMMUNICATION

There are relatively few humor measures developed within the field of communication, but we overview several of the primary examples.

The Humor Orientation scale is a 17-item, Likert-type scale measure of one's predisposition to enact humor successfully across a variety of contexts (Booth-Butterfield & Booth-Butterfield, 1991). It typically exhibits internal reliability above 0.85. Items reference different ways individuals tend to try to be funny; from telling jokes and stories to general assessments of "funniness." The HO scale has been reliably adapted as an other-report or perceived HO, as well as self-report measure (e.g., Campbell, Martin, & Wanzer, 2001; Rizzo et al., 1999; Wanzer & Frymier, 1999). It should be noted that the HO measures predominantly humor enacted for prosocial purposes. Recent research indicates that HO correlates most strongly with the positive types of humor styles, rather than the negative types of humor (Cann, Zapata, & Davis, 2009). (For a more complete description, see Graham, 2009). This propensity towards more prosocial humor use may explain why individuals rated as higher in HO are perceived as better managers (Campbell et al., 2001) and instructors (Wanzer & Frymier, 1999).

A more functional or motives-based approach to humorous communication was taken by Graham et al. (1992) in the Uses of Humor Index (UHI). This scale underwent extensive validation to determine construct and convergent validity. The UHI contains 11 items, on a five-point Likert-type scale, assessing the ways people use humor to accomplish goals in communication interactions. This scale includes three dimensions in using humor: positive affect (e.g., develop friendships), expressiveness (e.g., disclosing difficult information), and negative affect (e.g., put others in their place). The internal reliability for this scale is typically approximately 0.72. Martin and Gayle (1999) used the UHI to explore how organizational leaders use humor and whether such use was related to communicator style. They found that organizational leaders reported using more prosocial than antisocial types of humor and that dramatic and animated communicator styles predicted the use of this humor.

Recognizing that not all humor attempts may be useful or productive, Frymier, Wanzer, and Wojtaszczyk (2008) developed a scale addressing appropriate and inappropriate use of humor by teachers. This 41-item Teacher Humor Scale (THS) was based on a previous inductively derived typology of students' perceptions (Wanzer, Frymier, Wojtaszczyk, & Smith, 2006), and underwent validity testing, which revealed a linkage with perceived competence, one's own HO, and nonverbal immediacy. The THS contains five dimensions of teacher humorous communication: Other Disparaging Humor, Related Humor, Unrelated Humor, Offensive Humor, and Self-Disparaging Humor. Responses are based on a five-point scale from Very Inappropriate to Very Appropriate, and each dimension demonstrates internal reliability of 0.80 or higher. This measure was used recently to examine the relationship between student perceptions of instructor humor and learning and to provide preliminary empirical support for the Instructional Humor Processing Theory (IHPT) (Wanzer, Frymier, & Irwin, 2010). As predicted by IHPT, instructors' use of appropriate humor (e.g., Related Humor) correlated positively with student reports of learning.

The Humor Assessment Instrument (HA) (Richmond, 1999) was initially published in a textbook and did not receive blind peer review in the publication process. However, it has been used successfully in subsequent research (e.g., Wrench & McCroskey, 2001). The Humor Assessment Instrument correlates at 0.51 with the HO scale, suggesting substantial overlap. A more complete discussion of the HA measure appears in chapter 5.

While not a specific "scale" per se, the assessment of humorous actions, through both verbal and nonverbal channels, has been structured into a coherent measure. Booth-Butterfield and Booth-Butterfield (1991) and Wanzer, Booth-Butterfield, and Booth-Butterfield (2005) identified nine distinct categories for humor production: low humor (e.g., acting stupid or silly), nonverbal mannerisms (e.g., funny gestures, facial displays, vocalics), impersonation (e.g., mimicking a character, action, or situation), language/word play (e.g., witty or clever use of verbal communication), other orientation (e.g., including and adapting to an audience), expressiveness/general humor (e.g., making light of situations), laughter (i.e., overt mirth, giggling), use of props (e.g., the use of objects or tools to create humor), and seeking out others (i.e., finding someone else who is humorous to entertain). Although not all people employ the full array of humor-related behaviors, more humor-oriented people use a wider range. Additionally, these nine categories are congruent with typologies derived from other research (e.g., Buijzen & Valkenburg, 2004) and can provide a framework within which to further examine common humor enactments.

MEASURES FROM THE FIELD OF SOCIAL PSYCHOLOGY

Social psychologists have studied humor extensively and some might argue that they have conducted the lion's share of research on humor measures. Martin (2007) describes the study of sense of humor as a personality trait as "one of the most active areas of research in the psychology of humor" (p. 192). Over the last few decades, a number of measures have emerged that were designed to test different components of this construct. Not surprisingly, many of these measures have been used to study the relationship between sense of humor (hereafter referred to as SOH) and mental health (Martin, 2007). We would be remiss to not discuss psychological measures as they have important conceptual and research implications for humor research conducted in communication studies. Many of these scales measure sense of humor; however, conceptualizations of SOH differ dramatically from one study to the next, and this potentially problematic issue is addressed, as well.

Early on, the term "sense of humor" referred to one's general appreciation of humor (Martin, 2007). Over the years, this broad and ambiguous conceptualization of SOH has been redefined significantly. For example, in an attempt to refine the term, Eysenck (1972) advanced three equally important meanings associated with SOH: qualitative meaning (i.e., laughing at and appreciating similar objects), quantitative meaning (i.e., frequency of laughter and smiling), and productive meaning (i.e., extent to which the individual produces humorous content). Others have expanded on this conceptualization of SOH and have addressed the myriad ways that individuals differ in SOH (see for example, Babad, 1974; Hehl & Ruch, 1985).

Working from extant research, Martin (2007) describes SOH as a habitual behavior pattern, an ability, a temperament trait, an aesthetic response, an attitude, a world view, or a coping mechanism (p. 194). The way SOH is conceptualized (i.e., production versus appreciation) determines the type of approach (i.e., source, receiver, or both) and, ultimately, the type of humor measure used in research. The next sections summarize humor appreciation measures, Q-sort measures, ability measures, and self-report measures of humor.

HUMOR APPRECIATION MEASURES

Early research in social psychology adopted a receiver-oriented approach and often studied patterns in personality by exposing individuals to different types of humorous stimuli (i.e., sexual, aggressive, nonsense, etc.) and then correlating study participants' humor appreciation and responses with personality traits (see for example, Grziwok & Scodel, 1956; Hammes & Wiggins, 1962; Wilson & Patterson, 1969). According to Martin (2003), humorous stimuli are typically "grouped into various categories (e.g., innocent, aggressive, sexual) on the basis of either a priori judgments of the researchers or factor analytic procedures" (p. 319). Research conducted during this time period examined whether appreciation of certain types of humor, e.g., aggressive humor, and responding positively to them, was correlated with specific personality tendencies (Martin, 2003).

O'Connell (1960) adopted a psychoanalytic perspective to develop the Wit and Humor Appreciation Test (WHAT) and examine the relationship between study participants' appreciation of certain types of humor and mental health. The WHAT includes 30 jokes selected by clinical psychologists to illustrate hostile wit, nonsense wit, and Freudian humor (i.e., self-disparaging humor or humor attempts that involve cathartic release of stress). Ten jokes were placed into each of the three different humor categories. In the original research, study participants were exposed to either a stressful or nonstressful situation and then asked to evaluate their appreciation of the three types of humor. In addition, researchers examined whether individual differences such as mental adjustment and sex affected evaluations of different types of humor. Mental adjustment was assessed using a measure that calculated discrepancies between study participants' self-concept reports and ideal self-reports. As predicted, males appreciated hostile wit more than females did and poorly adjusted individuals were more likely to employ hostile wit than well-adjusted individuals (O'Connell, 1960). The researchers concluded that, in general, well-adjusted individuals seem to have a better overall appreciation of humor than poorly adjusted individuals.

This early research was plagued with a number of methodological flaws; the most important one was the lack of rigorous manipulation checks of humorous content. That is, they did not empirically evaluate the classifications of their different types of humor (Martin, 2007). The apparent problems with early humor appreciation tests prevent researchers from comparing results across different studies.

Another problem with early measures of humor was that they typically only tapped into a relatively small portion of the humor that individuals naturally encounter in their everyday lives (i.e., canned jokes and cartoons, see, for example O'Connell, 1960) (Martin, 2007). In addition, these measures assessed study participants' appreciation or enjoyment of humor, not their ability to spontaneously produce humor. Some of the seminal self-report SOH measures attempted to address these shortcomings.

Q-SORT TECHNIQUE FOR MEASURING HUMOR

Another form of assessing SOH is the Humorous Behavior Q-sort Deck (HBQD). This measure differs from previous SOH scales because it incorporates a significant number of behaviors associated with SOH (Craik, Lampert, & Nelson, 1996). The HBQD is a measure that attempts to provide a description of an individual's style of humor by focusing on a range of humorous behaviors (Craik et al., 1996). A total of 456 participants filled out the HBQD, a self-report measure designed to create an accurate depiction of an individual's humor style. The measure includes 100 statements that describe a variety of types of humorous enactments. To create the HBQD, the researchers conducted a thorough survey of theoretical and empirical scholarship in psychology on humor.

Unlike traditional self-report paper and pencil measures, respondents were asked to describe their day-to-day humor use by sorting the 100 HBQD statements into nine categories. When sorting the descriptive statements, respondents were asked to contemplate whether the behavior was 1 (Very Uncharacteristic), 5 (Neutral), or 9 (Very Characteristic) of their day-to-day behavior. Importantly, items on the HBQD can be assessed by the individual completing the measure, peers, or trained coders.

Sample items on the HBQD include "spoils jokes by laughing before finishing them," "enhances humorous impact with a deft sense of timing," and "appreciates the humorous potential of persons and situations." Researchers conducted factor analysis of the self-descriptive Q-sorts of university students and identified five styles of humorous conduct. These five factors were described as socially warm versus cold, reflective versus boorish, competent versus inept, earthy versus repressed, and benign versus mean spirited. Some research indicates that this method is both reliable and valid (Craik & Ware, 1998). Martin (2003) argues that this method "holds promise for the study of individual differences in humor using observational rather than a self-report methodology" (p. 320). Importantly, this research attempts to shed light on the different ways individuals enact humorous messages and how these messages are perceived by others.

ABILITY MEASURES OF HUMOR

Researchers have also measured study participants' ability to produce humorous content. These researchers approached humor production as an ability that is similar to other abilities such as creativity and intelligence (Martin, 2003). Lefcourt and Martin (1986) had study participants develop humorous monologues that were then rated based on their funniness by trained judges. Similarly, Kohler and Ruch (1996) had study participants complete cartoon punch lines to determine variability in study participants' ability to create humor.

Feingold developed a joke memory test. Feingold's (1982) joke memory test is a 32-item measure that includes a number of open-ended statements that participants must complete. Feingold extrapolated well-known joke fragments such as "Take my wife, _____." Correct answers are scored on a strict protocol provided by Feingold (1982). The standard instructions provide the respondent with as much time as needed to complete all the messages. According to Feingold this scale measures a person's SOH via one's ability to complete joke fragments. However, a criticism of this measure is that it assesses an individual's joke-memory (Wanzer et al., 1995). In addition, the 1982 measure contains jokes that are quite antiquated, which makes the task difficult and potentially invalid for current college students.

Feingold and Mazzella (1991) conducted subsequent research that explored sense of humor as an aptitude or skill. To study the relationship between psychometric intelligence and humor ability, 59 undergraduates completed various humor tests; e.g., tests of humor memory (see Feingold, 1982 measure) and tests of humor cognition. Study participants completed intelligence, verbal ability, and humor tests as well as humor comprehension measures. The primary goal in this research was to determine whether humor ability differs from intelligence and verbal abilities. Results indicate that humor ability indeed differs from other types of communication abilities such as verbal competence and intelligence.

SELF-REPORT MEASURES OF SENSE OF HUMOR

The first self-report SOH measure was developed by Svebak (1974). Svebak conceived SOH as being composed of three dimensions: metamessage sensitivity (being able to view hidden messages), personal liking or affinity toward humorous content, and emotional permissibility or the inclination to laugh. The Sense of Humor Questionnaire (SHQ) is a 21-item Likert-type measure with seven items for each of the three primary dimensions. For each of the 21 items, individuals are asked to indicate to what extent the item is descriptive of them (4-point Likert-type scale).

According to Martin (2007) early research found moderate correlations between the metamessage and liking dimensions and no correlation between the liking and emotional expressiveness dimensions. Because there are reliability and validity issues with the emotional expressiveness dimension, researchers primarily use the metamessage and liking measures. Svebak (1974) created a six-item version (SHQ-6) of his original SOH scale and distributed it to 1,000 study participants. His data indicated that the scale had acceptable reliability.

Martin and Lefcourt (1984) developed the Situational Humor Response Questionnaire (SHRQ) to study the stress-moderating effects of SOH. Building on Svebak's seminal work on SOH, this measure conceptualizes SOH based on the emotional expressiveness dimension of the SHQ. More specifically, this 18-item scale measures the extent to which individuals react to different real life situations with laughter, smiles, and general amusement. The researchers adopted a receiver-oriented approach in their conceptualization of the SHRQ and focused on the extent to which individuals are able to appreciate or find humor in potentially stress-inducing situations.

The SHRQ has been used extensively (see, for example, Lefcourt & Martin, 1986; Lourey & McLachlan, 2003; Wanzer et al., 1995) and has achieved acceptable internal consistency and test-retest reliability (Martin, 2007). Extant research supports the validity of the SHRQ (Lefcourt & Martin, 1986; Martin 1996, 2007), and people who score high on the SHRQ also score higher on the Humor Orientation scale (Wanzer et al., 1995). Lefcourt and Martin (1986) note that males and females score similarly on the SHRQ and that scores on the SHRQ are not correlated with social desirability measures; thus offering some indication of the scale's discriminant validity.

While this scale certainly has its strengths and has been used repeatedly to measure SOH, it is not without pitfalls. The SHRQ focuses primarily on reactions to situations in the form of laughter and smiling; there is no attention to the discursive or humor-producing elements of SOH. Indeed, Martin (2007) and others (Thorson, 1990) point out the apparent shortcomings of this measure. The scenarios presented in the SHRQ were originally created for college student populations and may not work for noncollege samples. In addition, the scenarios may not be perceived as the scale authors originally intended because they are dated and designed for a fairly homogeneous sample (lacking in diversity in age, race, education, etc.). An example of a scenario from the scale is: "If you were shopping by yourself in a distant city and unexpectedly saw an acquaintance from school (or work) how would you respond?" Study participants would then choose from the following responses to this situation: (a) I would probably not have bothered to speak to the person, (b) I would have talked to the person but wouldn't have shown much humor, (c) I would have found something to smile about in talking with him or her, (d) I would have found something to laugh about with the person, (e) I would have laughed heartily with the person (Martin & Lefcourt, 1984, p. 148).

Thorson and Powell (1993) developed the Multidimensional Sense of Humor Scale (MSHS) to address their concerns with the SHQ and the SHRQ (Martin & Lefcourt, 1984; Svebak, 1974). They argued that earlier SOH measures were flawed because they failed to acknowledge the multidimensional nature of SOH.

The original version of the MSHS is a 29-item Likert-type measure that includes four factors associated with SOH. Twelve items assess respondents' ability to generate humorous messages. A sample item included in the factor labeled *humor production* is "Other people tell me that I say funny things." Eight items are included in the second factor labeled *attitudes toward humor*. Items included in the second factor measured respondents' attitudes toward humor; a sample item was "I like a good joke." The third factor, labeled *coping with humor,* included 6 items that measured respondents' propensity to use humor to cope with stressful situations. A sample item was "Humor helps me cope." The fourth factor of the MSHS, labeled *humor appreciation,* included 3 items that measured respondents' use of humor to achieve interpersonal goals. A sample item included in this factor was "Things go better with humor."

After administering the original 29-item four-factor scale to 234 respondents (age range 18 to 67) and using principal components factor analysis to determine the scale factor structure, a 24-item scale emerged. The 24-item scale achieved a coefficient alpha of 0.926, and measured the following areas of SOH: humor production and social uses of humor (11 items), coping humor (7 items), humor appreciation (2 items), and attitudes toward humor (4). The 24-item version of the MSHS has been used to measure the relationship between SOH and the tendency to worry (Kelly, 2002). In addition, Thorson and colleagues investigated differences in male and female and blacks and whites in scores on the MSHS (Thorson, Powell, & Samuel, 2001). This scale has also been used on samples outside the United States to learn more about cultural differences in SOH (Ho, Chik, & Thorson, 2008). The scale was recently revised, translated into Chinese, and administered to 289 undergraduate Chinese students (Ho et al., 2008). The Chinese version of the scale achieved acceptable reliability and the four-factor structure was retained. It should be noted that this measure constitutes a hybrid approach to the study of humor, incorporating several varying perspectives.

Not surprisingly, researchers from social psychology have had a long-standing interest in how humor is used to moderate negative emotions such as stress and anxiety. Martin and Lefcourt (1983) designed the Coping Humor Scale (CHS) to further pursue their research interests in humor and coping. Rather than measuring SOH from a broader framework, this scale assessed how individuals use humor to manage stressful situations. This seven-item Likert-type scale includes items such as "I often lose my sense of humor when I am having problems" (reverse scored) and "I have often found that my problems have been greatly reduced when I tried to find something funny in them." This measure has demonstrated "marginally acceptable internal consistency and acceptable test-retest reliability" (Martin, 2007, p. 210).

According to Martin (2007), there is adequate support for the construct validity of the CHS (see, for example, Lefcourt & Martin, 1986). Indeed, peer ratings of individuals who score high on the CHS indicate that they typically use humor to cope with stress and are able to laugh easily at themselves (Lefcourt & Martin, 1986; Martin, 1996). This scale has been used frequently to measure the relationship between individual differences and the use of humor as a coping strategy (Chen & Martin, 2007; Oguz & Yuksel, 2010). More recently, Oguz and Yuksel (2010) used the CHS to draw comparisons between Turkish college students and Western college students and found that Turkish students scored lower than Western students did. Turkish students who scored higher on the CHS were generally happier than those scoring lower on the CHS. While this scale has been used to study the relationship between humor and coping, it does have psychometric limitations related to its internal consistency (alpha coefficient = 0.61 with corrected item-total correlations ranging from 0.11 to 0.54, see Martin & Lefcourt, 1983, p. 1316).

Until Martin and his colleagues created the Humor Styles Questionnaire in 2003, the majority of humor measures created to study the relationship between humor and mental health "were based on the assumption that a sense of humor is inherently beneficial to health and well-being"

(Martin, 2007 p. 210). To address an apparent conceptual gap, Martin worked with his graduate students to create a measure that tapped into both adaptive and maladaptive types of humor. This scale focuses less on how people react to different types of situations by using humor and laughter and more on how individuals spontaneously produce humor during social interaction. The Humor Styles Questionnaire (HSQ) assesses how and why individuals use humor in their daily lives. The items measure how individuals discursively produce humor during social interactions and employ humor as a means of coping communication.

To develop the SHQ, Martin and colleagues examined extant conceptual and theoretical literature that explored both the positive and negative functions of humor during social interaction. They identified four dimensions or styles of humor use, which they labeled: affiliative, self-enhancing, aggressive, and self-defeating. Affiliative and self-enhancing humor styles are identified as adaptive, positive, or healthy types of humor. Alternatively, aggressive and self-defeating humor styles are viewed as maladaptive, negative, or unhealthy styles of humor. Self-enhancing humor involves using humor to manage situations and people while an affiliative humor style involves using humor as a way to relate effectively to others. The researchers predicted that individuals who enact these particular styles reap a variety of personal (i.e., well-being) and social benefits (greater social support). Aggressive humor involves demeaning and harming others in an attempt to be funny, while self-disparaging humor entails self-attacks to elicit laughter. The researchers predicted that frequent use of these types of humor would be associated with greater depression and poor mental health.

The researchers set out to create a self-report measure that would tap into the four styles of humor. They started out with a total of 111 Likert-type items that assessed one of the four humor styles. The final iteration of the scale includes 8 items that tap into each of the four dimensions of humor. The four independent, 8-item scales achieved adequate scale reliabilities that ranged from 0.77 to 0.81 with test-retest reliabilities ranging from 0.80 to 0.85. Martin and colleagues (2003) describe the HSQ dimensions as somewhat related; however, correlations for the four dimensions were weak enough to indicate that the four miniscales tap into conceptually different styles of humor production.

Martin and colleagues (2003) found that scores on the two positive styles of humor were strongly associated with scores on other positive indicators of psychological health such as self-esteem, positive emotion, and social support. Conversely, individuals scoring higher on the two positive humor style measures were also less likely to be depressed or anxious. Along the same lines, individuals who scored higher on the aggressive humor style measure were more likely to be hostile and aggressive. Individuals scoring higher on the self-defeating humor measure were more likely to be depressed, anxious, and hostile. The researchers also found that males were more likely to report aggressive and self-defeating humor styles than were females (Martin et al., 2003).

The HSQ has been used extensively to study the way people use humor during conversations. Researchers have translated the HSQ into several languages and there appears to be some evidence for the scale's validity. Some research indicates that peer ratings of individuals that completed the HSQ were similar to study participants' self-reports (Martin et al., 2003).

UNIQUE, RESEARCHER-ADAPTED, OR SHORTENED SCALES

There are numerous examples of humor-related measurements that have been used essentially one time, in specific research. At times humor is used as a manipulation, such as Young and Bippus' (2001) work in which they instructed respondents to recall either a humorous or nonhumorous episode. When humor is employed as an outcome variable, these types of implementations constitute measures or assessment of humor that may be useful and perform well in that study, but they are not widely adapted, validated, or implemented by other research teams. For example, Frymier et al. (2008) adapted the HO scale to reflect perceived teachers' humorous behaviors. This nine-item scale exhibited a reliability of 0.92 and eliminated self-analysis items such as "I can easily remember jokes or stories."

CONTENT/TEXTUAL ANALYSIS

Humorous communication is, at times, analyzed by how it appears in text or pictures. Norrick (2010) examined laughter that occurs prior to punch lines in various conversational texts, finding that much laughter is interpersonally supportive, and actually sets up the later-occurring story punch line. Lloyd (2007) presented a text and pictorial analysis of a regular joke competition in New Zealand specifically involving penises. Buijzen and Valkenburg (2004) content-coded diverse categories of humor used in televisions commercials aimed at various age groups and male vs. female viewers. They analyzed how types/categories of humor vary in complexity and are aimed differently depending on the targeted audience.

ETHNOMETHODOLOGY

Ethnomethodological approaches embed the researchers in the targeted context or interactions to examine naturally occurring humor and responses. For example, Scholl and Ragan (2003) analyzed humorous interactions within specialized, humor-oriented, health-related units in a rehabilitation facility. They noted that humor created a more positive, happy context and facilitated the spontaneous building of mirth among the patients. Such descriptive analyses add to our understanding of diverse elements within humorous contexts, enactments, and outcomes.

PERCEIVED "FUNNINESS" RATINGS

A simple, direct, and valid way to measure humor is individual ratings of how amusing, entertaining, or funny something is. These is sometimes a single item that asks how humorous a target (whether human, written, or technical) appears to be on a multilevel scale [1 = Not At All Funny to 10 = Extremely Funny]. For example, Wanzer et al. (1995) employed a brief six-item funniness scale to gauge presenters' joke-telling. Such measures are easy to use and may provide an accurate depiction of others' humor abilities.

CURRENT ASSESSMENT AND NEW DIRECTIONS FOR HUMOR MEASURES

Indeed, there appear to be a number of reliable and valid humor measures available for researchers. However, there are certainly areas where researchers can contribute to the development of humor measurement. For example, assessments that measure children's use of humor are needed. These tools would address whether some children are funnier than others and, perhaps, whether children, like adults, use humorous messages to achieve goals.

While there is certainly scholarship available on how children develop their ability to enact humor (see, for example, McGhee 1971, 1979), there is less research on how to systematically measure children's humor production. Communication researchers are uniquely qualified to examine how humor use varies across the lifespan. Others have already studied how children's humor use changes over time. For example, Socha and Kelly (1994) studied children's use of humor and impression management, gender differences, and target differences, and noted changes over time from prosocial to antisocial humor use. As children aged, they were more likely to enact antisocial humorous messages with their peer groups. Others, such as Kotthoff (2006), describe playfulness and teasing communication among even very young children. Many perspectives on children's use of humor have come from a clinical perspective. For example, Peller (1956) noted that children seem to use humor when they feel guilty and want to avoid consequences. McGhee (2002) takes a social-developmental view and indicates that even parents often observe predispositional differences in humorous communication among their children, as further delineated and measured by Booth-Butterfield, Wanzer, Birmingham, and Booth-Butterfield (2011). More stringent empirical work is needed in this area to systematically explore how and why children enact humor in their interactions.

Another area of study includes building the skill of humor communication. Perhaps measures can be created to address humor competence or the ability of sources to enact humor messages that are perceived by receivers as appropriate and effective. Can individuals improve their ability to enact humorous messages over time? For example, transforming low HOs into high HOs may be unlikely because HO is a personality trait that builds over a lifetime. However, as with many other communication skills, the behaviors involved with enacting humor can be improved with training, practice, and positive reinforcement (Clark al., 1998; McIlheran, 2006; Rancer, Whitecap, Kosberg, & Avtgis, 1997; Wigley, 2008). People can become more competent in communicating humor by increasing their knowledge base of what contributes to good humorous messages and improving their behavioral skill in enacting humor correctly through repetition. Currently, little empirical research exists that addresses humor skill development over time. Perhaps there is little research available on humor skill development over time because there are no measures that assess a source's ability to disseminate humor competently.

There also is a need to study humorous communication at a more micro level to understand precisely what makes something funny, or how it is communicated on a meticulous level. Such study might entail experiments comparing appropriate use of humor (e.g., related, self-disparaging) with inappropriate (e.g., offensive, disparaging others) use of humor. Additional closely coded studies of specific behaviors that differentiate funny from nonfunny enactments could increase the specificity of our knowledge of humor enactment. Such research would involve detailed examination of pausing effects, intonations, duration, and potentially physiological measures such as electromyographic readings (e.g., Cacioppo, Petty, Losch, & Kim, 2008) to determine which facial muscles are activated in humor enactments. New research also is beginning to examine the debilitating effects brain damage has specifically on humor enactments and the processing of humor (Heath & Blonder, 2005).

Finally, what elicits humor and amuses people certainly differs from culture to culture. However, it seems reasonable that within any culture, individuals are funny (or not). That is, regardless of an individual's ethnic background or nationality, it is likely that some citizens are better at creating humor than others. Therefore, cross-cultural comparisons of the skill and propensity to enact humorous communication are needed.

CONCLUSION: TAKE-AWAY POINTS

There are several major points we want to emphasize in closing—"take-away points," if you will. First, it is important for scholars to carefully delineate source versus receiver approaches to avoid confusion in understanding humor results. Whether the humor is elicited by a source or appreciated by a receiver needs to be clear throughout our work.

Second, when studying sense of humor, researchers must clearly articulate how the construct is defined, because there are numerous conceptualizations available. The way SOH is defined, i.e., appreciation of humor versus humor production, dictates the type of measure to be appropriately used.

We have to recognize that much more work is yet to be done on all forms of humor, but especially measuring humorous communication from observational and physiological approaches. Little has been published on humor using these more concrete assessments. Part of this effort could entail the competent use of humor and how skills may be built. Of course, the first order of business for research on humor competence is to determine what this entails in the widest possible context.

As a needed area of future study, humor researchers should consider developing self-report measures that can be used to study the communicatively complex ways that children encode and enact humor. These measures should address both prosocial and antisocial use of humor. Such measures could help researchers and practitioners understand how children's use of prosocial and antisocial humor impacts their social development and overall adjustment.

Finally, and perhaps most importantly, there are currently several valid instruments to measure self-reports of humor-related communication. They have been scrutinized and validated, but each may measure somewhat different aspects of humor. Therefore, researchers need to carefully align measures with specific research questions and hypotheses.

References

Babad, E. Y. (1974). A multi-method approach to the assessment of humor: A critical look at humor tests. *Journal of Personality, 42,* 618–631.

Bippus, A. (2000). Humor usage in comforting episodes: Factors predicting outcomes. *Western Journal of Communication, 64,* 359–384.

Bippus, A. (2003). Humor motives, qualities, and reactions in recalled conflict episodes. *Western Journal of Communication, 67,* 413–426.

Booth-Butterfield, M., Wanzer, M., Birmingham, M., & Booth-Butterfield, S. (2011). Children's humor enactment: Examining Parents' Perceptions *Paper presented at the annual conference of the International Communication Association,* Boston.

Booth-Butterfield, M., Wanzer, M. B., Krezmien, E., & Wiel, N. (2010). Humorous communication during bereavement: Intrapersonal and interpersonal emotion management strategies. *Paper presented at the National Communication Association Convention,* San Francisco.

Booth-Butterfield, S., & Booth-Butterfield, M. (1991). The communication of humor in everyday life. *Southern Communication Journal, 56,* 205–218.

Bryant, J., Brown, D., Silberberg, A., & Elliot, S. (1981). Effects of humorous illustrations in college textbooks. *Human Communication Research, 8,* 43-57.

Bryant, J., Comisky, P., & Zillmann, D. (1979). Teachers' humor in the college classroom. *Communication Education, 28,* 110–118.

Bryant, J., Crane, J. S., Comisky, P. W., & Zillmann, D. (1980). Relationship between college teachers' use of humor in the classroom and students' evaluations of their teachers. *Journal of Educational Psychology, 72,* 511–519.

Bryant, J., & Zillmann, D. (1988). Using humor to promote learning in the classroom. *Journal of Children in Contemporary Society, 20,* 49–78.

Buijzen, M., & Valkenburg, P. (2004). Developing a typology of humor in audiovisual media. *Media Psychology, 6,* 147–167.

Cacioppo, J., Petty, R., Losch, M., & Kim, H. (2008). Electromyographic activity over facial muscle regions can differentiate the valence and intensity of affective reactions. In R. Fazio & R. Petty (Eds.), *Attitudes: Their structure, function, and consequences* (pp. 69–83). New York: Psychology Press.

Campbell, K. L., Martin, M. M., & Wanzer, M. B. (2001) Employee perceptions of manager humor orientation, assertiveness, responsiveness, approach/avoidance strategies, and satisfaction. *Communication Research Reports, 18*(1), 67-74.

Cann, A., Zapata, C., & Davis, H. (2009). Positive and negative styles of humor in communication: Evidence for the importance of considering both styles. *Communication Quarterly, 57,* 452–468.

Chen, G. H., & Martin, R. A. (2007). A comparison of humor styles, coping humor, and mental health between Chinese and Canadian university students. *Humor: International Journal of Humor Research, 20,* 215-234.

Clark, N., Gong, M., Schork, A., Evans, D., Roloff, D., Hurwitz, M., Maiman, L., & Mellins, R. (1998). Impact of education for physicians on patient outcomes. *Pediatrics, 5,* 831-836.

Clevenger, T. (1959). A synthesis of experimental research in stage fright. *Quarterly Journal of Speech, 45,* 134–145.

Conoley, C., Herschberger, M., Gonzalez, L., Rinker, S., & Crowley, A. K. (2007). Responding to interpersonal teasing. *Journal of Emotional Abuse, 7,* 27–41.

Craik, K. H., Lampert, M. D., & Nelson, A. J. (1996). Sense of humor and styles of everyday humorous conduct. *Humor: International Journal of Humor Research, 9,* 273–302.

Craik, K. H., & Ware, A. P. (1998). Humor and personality in everyday life. In W. Ruch (Ed.), *The sense of humor: Explorations of a personality characteristic* (pp. 63–94). Berlin, Germany: Walter de Gruyter.

Curtis, G. (1979). Psychoendocrine stress response: Steroid and peptide hormones. In B. Stoll (Ed.), *Mind and cancer prognosis* (pp. 61–72). Chichester, UK: John Wiley & Sons.

DiCioccio, R. L. (2008). The development and validation of the teasing communication scale. *Human Communication, 11,* 261–278.

Downs, V.C., Javidi, M.M., & Nussbaum, J.F. (1988). An analysis of teachers' verbal communication within the college classroom: Use of humor, self-disclosure, and narratives. *Communication Education, 37,* 127-141.

Duran, R. (1983). Communicative adaptability: A measure of social communicative competence. *Communication Quarterly, 31,* 320–326.

Duran, R. (1992). Communicative adaptability: A review of conceptualization and measurement. *Communication Quarterly, 40,* 253–268.

Eysenck, H. J. (1972). Forward. In J. H. Goldstein & P. E. McGhee (Eds.), *The psychology of humor: Theoretical perspectives and empirical issues* (pp. xii–xvii). New York: Academic Press.

Feingold, A. (1982). Measuring humor: A pilot study. *Perceptual & Motor Skills, 54,* 986.

Feingold, A., & Mazzella, R. (1991). Psychometric intelligence and verbal humor ability. *Personality and Individual Differences, 12,* 427–435.

Foot, H., & McCreaddie, M. (2006). Humour and laughter. In O. Hargie (Ed.), *The Handbook of Communication Skills* (pp. 293–322). New York: Routledge.

Frymier, A., Wanzer, M., & Wojtaszczyk, A. (2008). Assessing students' perceptions of inappropriate and appropriate teacher humor. *Communication Education, 57,* 266–288.

Gaidos, S. (2009). When humor humiliates. *Science News, 176,* 18–22.

Goodchilds, J. (1959). Effects of being witty on position in the social structure of the small group. *Sociometry, 22,* 159–166.

Goodchilds, J., & Smith, E. (1964). The wit and his group. *Human Relations, 17,* 21–31.

Gorham, J., & Christophel, D. M. (1990). The relationship of teachers' use of humor in the classroom to immediacy and student learning. *Communication Education, 39,* 46–62.

Graham, E. (1988, November). An index for measuring humor motives: A functional approach. *Paper presented at the Annual Speech Communication Association,* New Orleans.

Graham, E. (1995). The involvement of sense of humor in developing social relationships. *Communication Reports, 8,* 158–169.

Graham, E. E. (2009). Humor Orientation Scale. In R. Rubin, A. Rubin, E. Graham, E. Perse, & D. Seibold (Eds.), *Communication research measures II: A sourcebook* (Vol. 2, pp. 158–163). New York: Routledge Taylor & Francis.

Graham, E., Papa, M., & Brooks, G. (1992). Functions of humor in conversations: Conceptualization and measurement. *Western Journal of Communication, 56,* 161–183.

Graham, E., & Rubin, R. (1987, November). The involvement of humor in the development of social relationships. *Paper presented at the annual convention of the Speech Communication Association,* Boston.

Grimes, H. (1955). A theory of humor for public address. *Speech Monographs, 22,* 217–226.

Gruner, C. R. (1964). An experimental study of the effectiveness of oral satire in modifying attitude. *Speech Monographs, 41,* 231–232.

Gruner, C. R. (1965). An experimental study of satire as persuasion. *Speech Monographs, 32,* 149–154.

Gruner, C. R. (1966). A further experimental study of satire as persuasion. *Speech Monographs, 33,* 184–185.

Gruner, C. R. (1967). Effect of humor on speaker ethos and audience information gain. *Journal of Communication, 17,* 228-233.

Gruner, C.R. (1976). Wit and humour in mass communication. In A. J. Chapman & H. C Foot (Eds.) *Humor and laughter: Theory, research, and applications* (pp. 287-311). London: John Wiley & Sons.

Gruner, C. R. (1997). *The game of humor.* New Brunswick, NJ: Transaction Books.

Grziwok, R., & Scodel, A. (1956). Some psychological correlates of humor preferences. *Journal of Consulting Psychology, 20,* 42.

Hammes, J. A., & Wiggins, S. L. (1962). Manifest anxiety and appreciation of humor involving emotional content. *Perceptual & Motor Skills, 14,* 291–294.

Heath, R. L., & Blonder, L. X. (2005). Spontaneous humor among right hemisphere stroke survivors. *Brain and Language, 93,* 267–276.

Hehl, F. J., & Ruch, W. (1985). The location of sense of humor within comprehensive personality spaces: An exploratory study. *Personality & Individual Differences, 6,* 703–715.

Ho, S. K., Chik, M. P., & Thorson, J. A. (2008). Psychometric study of a Chinese version of the Multidimensional Sense of Humor Scale. *North American Journal of Psychology, 10,* 425–433.

Holmes, J., & Schnurr, S. (2005). Politeness, humor and gender in the workplace: Negotiating norms and identifying contestation. *Journal of Politeness Research, 1,* 121–149.

Houser, M. L., Cowan, R. L., & West, D. A. (2007). Investigating a new frontier: Instructor communication behavior in CD Rom texts—Do traditionally positive behaviors translate into this new environment? *Communication Quarterly, 55,* 19–38.

Kelly, W. E. (2002). An investigation of worry and sense of humor. *Journal of Psychology, 136,* 657-666.

Kline, S., & Guinsler, N. (2007). Risk or rapport? The use of teasing and self-directed humor among men and women members of an online illness community. *Presented at the National Communication Association,* Chicago.

Kohler, G., & Ruch, W. (1996). Sources of variance in current sense of humor inventories. How much substance, how much method variance? *Humor: International Journal of Humor Research, 9,* 363-397.

Kotthoff, H. (2006). Let's have a joke! Children's joking and humor; some age and intercultural differences. *Television, 19,* 10-14.

Lefcourt, H. M., & Martin, R. A. (1986). *Humor and life stress: Antidote to adversity.* New York: Springer-Verlag.

Lieberman, E. A., Neuendorf, K. A., Denny, J., Skalski, P. D., & Wang, J. (2009). The language of laughter: A qualitative/quantitative fusion examining television narrative as humor. *Journal of Broadcasting and Electronic Media, 53,* 497–514.

Lloyd, M. (2007). Rear gunners and troubled privates: Wordplay in a dick joke competition. *Journal of Sociolinguistics, 11,* 5–23.

Lourey, E., & McLachlan, A. (2003). Elements of sensation seeking and their relationship with two aspects of humour appreciation-perceived funniness and overt expression. *Personality & Individual Differences, 35,* 277-287.

Madden, T. J., & Weinberger, M. G. (1982). The effects of humor on attention in magazine advertising. *Journal of Advertising, 11,* 8–14.

Madlock, P., & Booth-Butterfield, M. (2008). Hurtful teasing between romantic couples: The truth in disguise? *Paper presented at the National Communication Association,* San Diego.

Maki, S., Booth-Butterfield, M., & McMullen, A. (2012). Does our humor affect us?: An examination of a dyad's Humor Orientation. *Communication Quarterly.*

Martin, D. M., & Gayle, B. M. (1999). It isn't a matter of just being funny: Humor production by organizational leaders. *Communication Research Reports, 16,* 72-80.

Martin, R. A. (2003). Sense of humor. In S. J. Lopez & C. R. Snyder (Eds.), *Positive psychological assessment: A handbook of models and measures* (pp. 313–326). Washington DC: American Psychological Association.

Martin, R. A. (1996). The Situational Humor Response Questionnaire (SHRQ) and Coping Humor Scale (CHS): A decade of research findings. *Humor: International Journal of Humor Research, 9,* 251-272.

Martin, R. A. (2007). *The Psychology of Humor: An Integrative Approach.* Boston: Elsevier.

Martin, R. A., & Lefcourt, H. M. (1983). Sense of humor as a moderator of the relation between stressors and moods. *Journal of Personality & Social Psychology, 45,* 1313–1324.

Martin, R. A., & Lefcourt, H. M. (1984). Situational Humor Response Questionnaire: Quantitative measure of a sense of humor. *Journal of Personality & Social Psychology, 47*, 145–155.

Martin, R. A., Puhlik-Doris, P., Larsen, G., Gray, J., & Weir, K. (2003). Individual differences in uses of humor and their relation to psychological well-being. *Journal of Research in Personality, 37*, 48–75.

McGhee, P. E. (1971). Cognitive development and children's comprehension of humor. *Child Development, 42*, 123–138.

McGhee, P. E. (1979). *Humour: Its origin and development.* San Francisco: W. H. Freeman.

McGhee, P. E. (2002). *Understanding and Promoting the Development of Children's Humor.* NY: Kendall/Hunt.

McIlheran, J. (2006). The use of humor in corporate communication. *Corporate Communications, 11*, 267-274.

McRoberts, D., & Larsen-Casselton, C. (2006). Humor in public address, health care and the workplace: Summarizing humor's use using meta-analysis. *North Dakota Speech and Theatre Journal*, 26–33.

Norrick, N. (2010). Laughter before the punch line during the performance of narrative jokes in conversation. *Text and Talk, 30–31*, 75–95.

O'Connell, W. E. (1960). The adaptive functions of wit and humor. *Journal of Abnormal and Social Psychology, 61*, 263–270.

Oguz-Duran, N., & Yuksel, A. (2010). The effects of coping humor and gender on college adjustment in Turkish freshman. *Education, 130*, 470-478.

Rancer, A., Whitecap, V., Kosberg, R., & Avtgis, T. (1997). Testing the efficacy of a communication training program to increase argumentativeness and argumentative behavior in adolescents. *Communication Education, 46*, 273-286.

Peller, L.E. (1956). Review. *Children's humor. A psychological analysis,* by M.Wolfenstein. Glencoe, Illinois: The Free Press, 1954. *Psychoanalysis Quarterly, 25*:106-108.

Richmond, V. (1999). The Richmond Humor Assessment instrument. In V. P. Richmond & M. Hickson (Eds.), *Going public: A guide to public talk.* Boston: Allyn & Bacon.

Rizzo, B., Wanzer, M. B., & Booth-Butterfield, M. (1999). Individual differences in managers' use of humor: Subordinate perceptions of managers' humor orientation, effectiveness, and humor behaviors. *Communication Research Reports, 16*(4), 370-376.

Scholl, J., & Ragan, S. (2003). The use of humor in promoting positive provider-patient interactions in a hospital rehabilitation unit. *Health Communication, 15*, 319–330.

Smith, E., & Goodchilds, J. (1963). The wit in large and small established groups. *Psychological Reports, 13*, 273–274.

Socha, T. J., & Kelly, B. (1994). Children making 'fun': Humorous communication, impression management, and moral development. *Child Study Journal, 24*, 237–252.

Svebak, S. (1974). Revised questionnaire on the sense of humor. *Scandinavian Journal of Psychology, 15*, 328–331.

Thorson, J. A. (1990). Is propensity to laugh equivalent to sense of humor? *Psychological Reports, 66,* 737–738.

Thorson, J. A., & Powell, F. C. (1993). Sense of humor and dimensions of personality. *Journal of Clinical Psychology, 49,* 799–809.

Thorson, J. A., Powell, F. C., & Samuel, V. (2001). Sense of humor in black and white. *North American Journal of Psychology, 3,* 1–11.

Wanzer, M., Booth-Butterfield, M., & Booth-Butterfield, S. (1995). The funny people: A source-orientation to the communication of humor. *Communication Quarterly, 43,* 142–154.

Wanzer, M., Booth-Butterfield, M., & Booth-Butterfield, S. (1996). Are funny people more popular: The relationship of humor orientation, loneliness, and social attraction. *Communication Quarterly, 44,* 42–52.

Wanzer, M., Booth-Butterfield, M., & Booth-Butterfield, S. (2005). 'If we didn't use humor we'd cry': Use of humor as coping in healthcare. *Journal of Health Communication, 10,* 105–125.

Wanzer, M. B., & Frymier, A. B. (1999). The relationship between student perceptions of instructor humor and student's reports of learning. *Communication Education, 48,* 48–62.

Wanzer, M. B., Frymier, A. B., & Irwin, B. (2010). An explanation of the relationship between teacher humor and student learning: Instructional Humor Processing Theory. *Paper accepted to the Eastern Communication Association Conference,* Philadelphia.

Wanzer, M. B., Frymier, A. B., Wojtaszczyk, A., & Smith, T. (2006). Appropriate and inappropriate uses of humor by teachers. *Communication Education, 55,* 178–196.

Wanzer, M. B., Sparks, L., & Frymier, A. B. (2009). Humorous communication within the lives of older adults: The relationships among humor, coping efficacy, age, and life satisfaction. *Health Communication, 24,* 128–136.

Wigley, C. (2008). Verbal aggression interventions: What should be done? *Communication Monographs, 75,* 339–350.

Williams, P., Colder, C., Lane, J., McCaskill, C., Feinglos, M., & Surwit, R. (2002). Examination of the neuroticism-symptom reporting relationship in people with Type 2 diabetes. *Personality and Social Psychology Bulletin, 28,* 1015–1025.

Wilson, G. D., & Patterson, J. R. (1969). Conservatism as a predictor of humor preferences. *Journal of Consulting & Clinical Psychology, 33,* 271–274.

Wrench, J. S., & McCroskey, J. C. (2001). A temperamental understanding of humor communication and exhilarability. *Communication Quarterly, 49,* 142-159.

Young, S., & Bippus, S. (2001). Does it make a difference if they hurt you in a funny way? Humorously and non-humorously phrased hurtful messages in personal relationships, *Communication Quarterly, 49,* 35–52.

CHAPTER 5

UNDERSTANDING THE DEVELOPMENT OF THE HUMOR ASSESSMENT INSTRUMENT

Virginia Peck Richmond
University of Alabama at Birmingham

Jason S. Wrench
State University of New York at New Paltz

The first steps in the path of discovery, and the first approximate measures, are those which add most to the existing knowledge of mankind.

Charles Babbage (1830)

First and foremost, measurement is hard. Numerous books have written on the subject of effective measurement in both the physical sciences and the social sciences (e.g., Converse & Presser, 1986; DeVellis, 1991; Salkind, 2006). Sir Herman Bondi (1965) went so far as to say, "We find no sense in talking about something unless we specify how we measure it; a definition by the method of measuring a quantity is the one sure way of avoiding talking nonsense." In the field of communication studies, there have been countless numbers of measures created to help us understand human communication. In fact, Wrench, Jowi, and Goodboy (2010) catalogued over 520 different measures in various communication journals dating back to the 1940s. This chapter first summarizes the development of and research related to the impetus for the Humor Assessment Measure—the Humor Orientation Scale. Then, we examine the development of the Humor Assessment instrument.

THE DEVELOPMENT OF THE HUMOR ORIENTATION SCALE

In 1991 Booth-Butterfield and Booth-Butterfield created the Humor Orientation (HO) scale, consisting of a "list of statements that directly reference the communicative use of humor in interpersonal situations" (p. 208). The HO has been applied in a variety of communication contexts: in health care industry (Wanzer, Booth-Butterfield, & Booth-Butterfield, 1996b, 2005; Wrench & Booth-Butterfield, 2003), in romantic relationships (Honeycutt & Brown, 1998), in organizational communication (Avtgis & Taber, 2006; Campbell, Martin, & Wanzer, 2001; Rizzo, Wanzer, & Booth-Butterfield, 1999), intercultural communication (Miczo & Welter, 2006), and in the classroom environment (Aylor & Oppliger, 2003; Frymier, Wanzer, & Wojtaszczyk, 2008; Jones, 2006; Punyanunt, 2000; Wanzer & Frymier, 1999a). Furthermore, a substantial research agenda has definitely shown that an individual's humor orientation should be considered a communication trait (Merolla, 2006; Wanzer, Booth-Butterfield, & Booth-Butterfield, 1995, 1996a, 2007).

ORIGIN OF THE HUMOR ASSESSMENT INSTRUMENT

Let's start by saying that we never intended to develop another measure of humor. In fact, measurement development was the furthest thing from our minds when we crafted the original study. The origin of the development of the Humor Assessment instrument started in fall 1999. Jason Wrench, then a first-year doctoral student at West Virginia University, took a course in instructional communication with Virginia Richmond. Wrench was required to create and conduct a research study examining some facet of instructional communication and he become interested in the area of humor during his Master's program at Texas Tech University. Richmond approved Wrench's study on humor in the instructional context.

The original study set out to examine a series of variables found to be important in the instructional context: affective learning, nonverbal immediacy, cognitive learning, student motivation, teacher use of behavioral alteration techniques and messages, teacher credibility, teacher verbal aggression, and teacher humor orientation. Before collecting data, Wrench and Richmond conferred with McCroskey about the study for additional expert counsel. McCroskey first questioned the validity of humor orientation as a communication trait. McCroskey's argument stemmed from a basic analysis of items on the Humor Orientation Scale. Wrench and Richmond appraised the potential of the HO scale as operationalizing humor for his study. They were concerned that the HO items appeared to have validity issues.

When Booth-Butterfield and Booth-Butterfield (1991) created the HO Scale, they designed a measure that they claimed examined the extent to which an individual used humor in interpersonal encounters. However, only 6 of the 17 items address humor as a general communicative trait (e.g., "Being funny is a natural communication style with me," "I use humor to communicate in a variety of situations," etc.). The other 11 items ask questions about an individual's ability to tell jokes or humorous stories (e.g., "People usually laugh when I tell jokes or funny stories," "People don't seem to pay close attention when I tell a joke," etc.). Thus our concern lay with using a humor measure that encompassed predominately verbal humor use; specifically, only jokes or humorous stories.

Fundamentally, a scale that purports to measure how humans use humor in an interpersonal context should measure a large range of humor production. The notion that there are multiple types of humor (beyond jokes and storytelling) is widely seen in the humor literature. Figure 1 lists selected typologies of types of humorous messages. This list of typologies provides a representative range of research drawn from social psychology (Martin, Puhlik-Doris, Larsen, Gray, & Weir, 2003), instructional communication (Bryant, Comisky, & Zillmann, 1979; Downs, Javidi, & Nussbaum, 1988; Gorham, & Christophel, 1990; Neuliep, 1991; Wanzer & Frymier, 199b), and mediated communication (Buijzen & Valkenburg, 2004). In each of these communicative contexts, researchers found a range of communicative strategies that individuals can employ to be seen as humorous. Although some controversy arises over the creation of these typologies (Gruner, 1991), every few years a new academic typology surfaces that attempts to catalog or examine the types of humor by humans. Although joking and humorous storytelling are important techniques of conveying humorous messages, they are a small segment of these. As such, the HO Scale did not meet our basic requirements for content validity in the range of humor in interpersonal interactions.

FIGURE 1 TYPOLOGIES OF HUMOR

Bryant, Comisky, & Zillmann (1979)

I. Humor Categories

  A. Joke

  B. Riddle

  C. Pun

  D. Funny story

  E. Humorous comment

  F. Other

II. Spontaneity of Humor

  A. Prepared

  B. Spontaneous

  C. Indeterminable

III. Impact on Education

  A. Distracted from the educational point

  B. Neither distracted from nor contributed to the educational point

  C. Contributed to the educational point

IV. Relevance

    A. Not at all related

    B. Moderately related

    C. Extremely related

V. Other Factors

    A. Sexual

        1. Nonsexual hostile

        2. Sexual nonhostile

        3. Sexual hostile (put-downs with sexual content)

    B. Originator

        1. Instructor

        2. Student

        3. Other character

    C. Victim impact

        1. Self-disparagement

        2. Student disparagement

        3. Other disparagement

Buijzen & Valkenburg (2004)

I. Slapstick Humor

    A. Slapstick

    B. Peculiar Face

    C. Peculiar Voice

    D. Coincidence

    E. Clumsiness

    F. Stereotype

    G. Ridicule

    H. Malicious Pleasure

    I. Repartee

II. Surprise

    A. Conceptual Surprise

    B. Visual Surprise

    C. Transformation

    D. Exaggeration

III. Irony

    A. Irony

    B. Sarcasm

    C. Embarrassment

    D. Puns

    E. Scale

IV. Clownish Humor

    A. Clownish Behavior

    B. Anthropomorphism

    C. Speed

    D. Chase

V. Satire

    A. Satire

    B. Irreverent Behavior

    C. Outwitting

    D. Peculiar Music

VI. Misunderstanding

    A. Misunderstanding

    B. Ignorance

    C. Disappointment

    D. Peculiar Sound

VII. Parody

    A. Parody

    B. Bombast

    C. Rigidity

    D. Absurdity

    E. Infantilism

VIII. Miscellaneous

    A. Imitation

    B. Impersonation

    C. Eccentricity

    D. Sexual Allusion

    E. Repetition

    F. Grotesque Appearance

Downs, Javidi, & Nussbaum (1988)

I. Play Offs

    A. Self

    B. Students

    C. Others Not in Class

    D. Course Material

    E. Other

II. Purpose

    A. Relevant to Course

    B. Not relevant to Course

Gorham & Christophel (1990)

I. Brief comment about a student

II. Brief comment about a whole class

III. Brief comment about the university, department, or state

IV. Brief comment about national or world events, famous personalities, or popular culture

V. Brief comment related to a topic, subject, or class procedure

VI. Self-deprecating comment

VII. Personal anecdote or story related to the content

VIII. Personal anecdote or story not related to the content

IX. General anecdote related to content

X. General anecdote not related to content

XI. Joke

XII. Nonverbal humor

XIII. Other

Martin, Puhlik-Doris, Larsen, Gray, & Weir (2003)

I. Affiliative Humor

II. Self-Enhancing humor

III. Aggressive Humor

IV. Self-Defeating Humor

Neuliep (1991)

I. Teacher-Targeted Humor

    A. Humorous teacher self-disclosure that is content related

    B. Humorous teacher self-disclosure that is not content related

    C. Humorous teacher self-disclosure that is embarrassing

    D. Teacher role plays a humorous character related to class content

    E. Teacher role plays a humorous character not related to class content

    F. Teacher uses self-deprecating humor

II. Student-Targeted Humor

    A. Teacher makes a joke out of a student's error or mistake

    B. Teacher mildly insults a student in a friendly manner

    C. Teacher teases a student in a friendly manner

    D. Teacher has a student role play something that is humorous

III. Untargeted Humor

    A. Teacher points out an incongruity or awkward comparison

    B. Teacher tells a joke

    C. Teacher uses a play on words or pun

    D. Teacher engages in witty interaction, uses exaggerated analogies, or "BSes" with students

IV. External Source Humor

    A. Teacher relates a humorous event in history

    B. Teacher brings in an example of something humorous created by another person (e.g., cartoon, incident on TV, or other tangible product) related to the content

    C. Teacher brings in an example of something humorous created by another person (e.g., cartoon, incident on TV, or other tangible product) not related to the content

    D. Teacher demonstrates a natural phenomenon that students find humorous

V. Nonverbal Humor

    A. Teacher makes a funny face to the class

    B. Teacher uses her or his body to elicit a humorous response

Wanzer & Frymier (1999a)

  I. Appropriate

    A. Content-Related Humor

    B. Humor Not Related to Content

    C. Impersonation

    D. Nonverbal Behaviors

    E. Disparaging Humor

    F. Humorous Props

    G. Sarcasm

    H. Unintentional Humor

II. Inappropriate

    A. Making Fun of a Student

    B. Humor-Based Stereotypes

    C. Failed Humor

    D. Sexual Humor

    E. Irrelevant Humor

    F. Sarcasm

    G. Swearing

    H. Joking About Serious Issues

    I. Personal Humor (inside jokes)

    J. Sick humor

A different validity complication with the HO Scale was noted that further accounted for the specificity of the range in the HO Scale (Wrench & Richmond, 2004). According to Bryant (2000), content validity "concerns the degree to which an instrument assesses all relevant aspects of the conceptual or behavioral domain that the instrument is intended to measure, or how thoroughly it samples the relevant target domain" (p. 104). Booth-Butterfield and Booth-Butterfield (1991) only imply a definition of humor, operationalizing primarily with joke telling, humorous storytelling, and perceptions of others' perceptions about one's humor efficacy. The HO instrument culminates as a great measure of two types of humor—joke telling and humorous storytelling—in interpersonal interactions, but we believe it falls short of being a global measure of the use of humor in interpersonal relationships.

INTRODUCING THE HUMOR ASSESSMENT

After acknowledging validity concerns associated with the HO scale, Richmond modified the scale to measure a more general use of humor in interpersonal encounters. After a handful of revisions, the Humor Assessment Instrument was created. Tables 1 and 2 present two versions of the Humor Assessment instrument used to test and validate its psychodynamic properties. Table 1 contains the self-report version of the humor assessment, which is used to measure an individual's trait use of humor in interpersonal interactions. Table 2 contains the other report version of the humor assessment, which is used to measure a targeted communicator's perceived use of humor in interpersonal interactions.

TABLE 1: HUMOR ASSESSMENT SELF-REPORT

Directions: The following statements apply to how people communicate humor when relating to others. Indicate the degree to which each of these statements applies to you by filling in the number of your response in the blank before each item:

Strongly Disagree	Disagree	Neutral	Agree	Strongly Agree
1	2	3	4	5

_____ 1. I regularly communicate with others by joking with them.

_____ 2. People usually laugh when I make a humorous remark.

_____ 3. I am not funny or humorous.

_____ 4. I can be amusing or humorous without having to tell a joke.

_____ 5. Being humorous is a natural communication orientation for me.

_____ 6. I cannot relate an amusing idea well.

_____ 7. My friends would say that I am a humorous or funny person.

_____ 8. People don't seem to pay close attention when I am being funny.

_____ 9. Even funny ideas and stories seem dull when I tell them.

_____ 10. I can easily relate funny or humorous ideas to others.

_____ 11. I would say that I am not a humorous person.

_____ 12. I cannot be funny, even when asked to do so.

_____ 13. I relate amusing stories, jokes, and funny things very well to others.

_____ 14. Of all the people I know, I am one of the "least" amusing or funny persons.

_____ 15. I use humor to communicate in a variety of situations.

_____ 16. On a regular basis, I do not communicate with others by being humorous or entertaining.

SCORING: To compute your scores follow the instructions below:

1. How to Score:
   Step 1: Add scores for items 1, 2, 4, 5, 7, 10, 13, & 15.
   Step 2: Add scores for items 3, 6, 8, 9, 11, 12, 14, & 16.
   Step 3: Add 48 to Step 1.
   Step 4: Subtract the score for Step 2 from the score for Step 3.

Source: Wrench, J. S., & Richmond, V. P. (2004). Understanding the psychometric properties of the Humor Assessment instrument through an analysis of the relationships between teacher humor assessment and instructional communication variables in the college classroom. *Communication Research Reports, 21,* 92–103. Reprinted by permission of Taylor & Francis Group

TABLE 2: HUMOR ASSESSMENT OTHER-REPORT

Directions: The following statements apply to how target communicator could communicate using humor while interacting with others. Indicate the degree to which each of these statements applies to the target communicator by filling in the number of the your response in the blank before each item:

Strongly Disagree	Disagree	Neutral	Agree	Strongly Agree
1	2	3	4	5

_____ **1.** Target communicator regularly communicates with others by joking with them.

_____ **2.** People usually laugh when the target communicator makes a humorous remark.

_____ **3.** Target communicator is not funny or humorous.

_____ **4.** Target communicator can be amusing or humorous without having to tell a joke.

_____ **5.** Being humorous is a natural communication orientation for the target communicator.

_____ **6.** Target communicator cannot relate an amusing idea well.

_____ **7.** My friends would say that the target communicator is a humorous or funny person.

_____ **8.** People don't seem to pay close attention when the target communicator is being funny.

_____ **9.** Even funny ideas and stories seem dull when the target communicator tells them.

_____**10.** Target communicator easily relates funny or humorous ideas to other people.

_____**11.** I would say that the target communicator is not a humorous person.

_____**12.** Target communicator cannot be funny, even when asked to do so.

_____**13.** Target communicator relates amusing stories, jokes, and funny things very well to others.

_____**14.** Of all the people I know, the target communicator is one of the "least" amusing or funny people.

_____**15.** Target communicator uses humor to communicate in a variety of situations.

_____**16.** On a regular basis, the target communicator does not communicate with others by being humorous or entertaining.

SCORING: To compute your scores follow the instructions below:

1. How to Score:
   Step 1: Add scores for items 1, 2, 4, 5, 7, 10, 13, & 15.
   Step 2: Add scores for items 3, 6, 8, 9, 11, 12, 14, & 16.
   Step 3: Add 48 to Step 1.
   Step 4: Subtract the score for Step 2 from the score for Step 3.

Source: Wrench, J. S., & Richmond, V. P. (2004). Understanding the psychometric properties of the Humor Assessment instrument through an analysis of the relationships between teacher humor assessment and instructional communication variables in the college classroom. *Communication Research Reports, 21,* 92–103. Reprinted by permission of Taylor & Francis Group

Upon creation of the humor assessment instrument, Wrench and Richmond (2000) presented the results at the National Communication Association convention in Seattle. At this point, the study hit a huge hurdle that had not been answered in the original research study: Did we really need a new communication measure of humor? Although Wrench and Richmond (2000) had explained their criticisms of the Humor Orientation construct validity, we had not actually shown that our new measure, the Humor Assessment (HA) scale was distinctly different from the original measure, the HO scale. We quickly realized that we needed to determine that the HA scale actually did measure something different from humor orientation.

To ascertain if the different constructs argument Wrench and Richmond (2000) made held up under scientific scrutiny, Wrench and McCroskey (2001) set out to test both the humor assessment and humor orientation scales in light of biological factors (human temperament) and cultural factors (sense of humor). Wrench and McCroskey (2001) proposed that an individual's use of story- and joke telling were behaviors that would be exhibited by highly extraverted individuals and not by their senses of humor that are highly impacted by one's culture (McGhee, 1999). Conversely, Wrench and McCroskey hypothesized that a more general measure of humor that takes into account explicitly extraverted forms of humor (i.e., as operationalized by humor assessment) would be less impacted by one's sense of humor than by one's temperament.

The first hypothesis was that an individual's temperament would more greatly impact an individual's humor orientation than would one's humor assessment. Wrench and McCroskey (2001) employed Eysenck's (1998) 10-item measures of extraversion and neuroticism and Eysenck, Eysenck's, and Barret's (1985) 12-item measure of psychoticism. Eysenck's theory of human temperament purports that human genetics can be shown to directly impact three "supertraits." The supertraits were: (1) extraversion (the biologically based desire to be sociable, have stimulation around oneself, and easy-going nature); (2) neuroticism (the biologically based tendency toward mania [being very happy] and depression [being very sad]); and (3) psychoticism (the biologically based tendency to be tend to be a loner, unempathetic [uncaring about other people's emotions], and antisocial [violating social rules and norms]). In turn, these three supertraits help us understand how people actually behave. Research has consistently authenticated that these three supertraits are predictive of actual human behavior. Thus, using Eysenck's framework to understand the impact that human biology has on an individual's use of humor in interpersonal relationships is a solid approach. Wrench and McCrosky (2001) reported that both HA and HO correlated positively to the extraversion supertrait. However, the 21 percent difference in the amount of variance accounted for by extraversion was intriguing. Extraversion accounted for approximately 42 percent of an individual's HA; and about 63 percent of an individual's HO. That is, extraversion explains better a person's tendency for story- and joke telling than it does his or her holistic humor behavior. This finding was critical to establishing that the HA scale and HO scale measure distinct humor constructs.

The second factor Wrench and McCroskey (2001) wanted to ascertain was whether the humor assessment measure had a stronger cultural basis than the humor orientation scale. To determine the impact of culture on both measures, Wrench and McCroskey employed McGhee's (1999) Sense of Humor Scale (SHS). The SHS is designed to measure an individual's enjoyment of humor, tendency to laugh, use verbal humor, find humor in everyday life, ability to laugh at her- or himself, and use humor during times of stress. Though each smaller part can be examined separately, the measure itself tends to perform better when one apprehends all of the factors jointly as a global measure of one's sense of humor. An underlying essential construct of McGhee's (1999) perspective is that individuals can learn to be more humorous and see life through a more humorous lens. The primary way people learn many behaviors is through their interpersonal interactions, which are highly governed by one's culture. So seeing one's sense of humor as culturally driven based is practical. When one examines humorous artifacts from various cultures, the differences are commonly stark. Ultimately, Wrench and McCroskey (2001) found that sense of humor had a limited relationship to an individual's humor orientation, but that sense of humor moderately related to an individual's humor assessment.

Overall, the Wrench and McCroskey (2001) provided the necessary evidence that the Humor Assessment Instrument clearly measured an individual's use of humor in interpersonal encounters in a manner different from the Humor Orientation scale. Since the publication of these two foundational studies (Wrench & McCroskey, 2001; Wrench & Richmond, 2004) establishing HA, a number of unique research projects have emerged using the Humor Assessment measure.

THE HUMOR ASSESSMENT IN RESEARCH

With the publication of Wrench and McCroskey (2001) and Wrench and Richmond (2004), we have identified 11 studies using a variety of participant pools that have utilized the humor assessment measure in research. While many of these studies have been published or presented at conferences, others exist only as data sets collected by various research teams. Table 3 provides a general distinction between the 13 studies identified that used HA. This table provides the alpha reliabilities found for the humor assessment, along with sample types and size and purpose for using the measure conducted in each study. Alpha reliabilities have ranged from 0.85 to 0.96 in all of the studies ($M = 0.92$, $SD = 0.03$), which, according to Wrench, Thomas-Maddox, Richmond, and McCroskey (2008), indicates the measure has good to excellent reliability. While the bulk of the research conducted utilizing the humor assessment consisted of undergraduate students, research indicates that the measure is consistently reliable when non-undergraduate samples are utilized (0.95 for pharmaceutical sales representatives; 0.94 for religious followers' perceptions of a religious leader; and 0.96 for graduate advisee perceptions of their graduate advisor). Overall, across these 13 studies a total of 3,104 participants have completed the humor assessment.

TABLE 3: PSYCHOMETRIC PROPERTIES OF THE HUMOR ASSESSMENT INSTRUMENT

Authors	Alpha	Mean	Standard Deviation	N	Target of Measure	Sample
Hanger, Jack, & Willaman (2006)	0.85	50.95	9.61	191	Teacher's use of humor	Undergraduates
Hertz, Jaroff, Brush, & Golub (2009)	0.90	65.72	7.81	112	Participant use of humor	Undergraduates
Lumbatis, Hoskinson, Jones, Willhealm, & Lutz (2006)	0.89	63.90	8.46	278	Best friend's use of humor	Undergraduates

Stirling (2004)	Information not provided			455	Graduate teaching assistants	Undergraduates
Teven & Winters (2008)	0.95	Information Not Provided		55	Participant use of humor	Pharmaceutical sales representatives
Wrench (2001)	0.90	59.75	10.27	228	Participant use of humor	Undergraduates
Wrench & Brogan (2004)	0.92	57.66	10.22	155	Broadcasted teacher's use of humor	Undergraduates
Wrench, Brogan, Wrench, & McKean (2007)	0.94	63.25	10.50	180	Religious leader's use of humor	Religious followers (noncollege sample)
Wrench & Martin (2002)	0.92	56.36	9.88	305	Parent's humor assessment	Undergraduates
Wrench & McCroskey (2001)	0.89	63.20	8.84	225	Participant use of humor	Undergraduates
Wrench & Punyanunt-Carter (2008)	0.96	57.09	12.97	153	Graduate advisor's use of humor	Graduate advisees
Wrench & Richmond (2004)	0.95	53.93	13.71	448	Teacher's use of humor	Undergraduates
Wrench, Thomas-Maddox, Richmond, & McCroskey (2008)	0.91	62.06	9.82	319	Participant use of humor	Undergraduates

The final table in this chapter, Table 4, lists various correlations reported for the HA measure with a broad range of psychological and communication variables. The studies that have used the humor assessment range from studies focused on instructional communication to family communication. In all the studies, the one common, consistent factor is the prosocial and positive impact that an individual's humor assessment can have on their communication, communication with others, and communication outcomes. As with all research, some findings contradict each other (even when similar samples are utilized), but the basic message of the importance of using humor in our interpersonal interactions remains clear.

TABLE 4: CORRELATIONS OF THE HUMOR ASSESSMENT WITH OTHER VARIABLES[1]

Authors	N	r	p-value
Hanger, Jack, & Willaman (2006)			
Teacher misbehaviors			
Incompetence	197	−0.31	0.0005
Offensiveness	197	−0.41	0.0005
Insolence	195	−0.25	0.001
Attributions of teacher misbehaviors			
External attributions	194	0.31	0.0005
Internal attributions	194	−0.31	0.0005
Teacher apprehension test	194	−0.57	0.0005
Teacher credibility			
Competence	194	0.43	0.0005
Caring/goodwill	194	0.40	0.0005
Trustworthiness	193	0.45	0.0005
Classroom justice			
Distributive	196	0.39	0.0005
Procedural	196	0.42	0.0005
Interactional	194	0.40	0.0005
Hertz, Jaroff, Brush, & Golub (2009)			
Hypergender ideology	112	-0.16	0.09
Sarcasm			
Degree of sarcasm	112	0.29	0.002
Uses of sarcasm across communication contexts	111	0.21	0.03
Sociocommunicative orientation			
Assertiveness	112	0.12	0.21
Responsiveness	112	0.13	0.17
Communication competence	111	0.19	0.08
Lumbatis, Hoskinson, Jones, Willhealm, & Lutz (2006)			
General inventory of friendship inventory	278	0.25	0.0005
Communication satisfaction	278	0.49	0.0005

Trust	278	0.37	0.005
Temperament			
Extraversion	278	0.28	0.0005
Neuroticism	278	−0.16	0.007
Psychoticism	278	−0.12	0.04
Stirling (2004)			
Student misbehaviors	[2]	0.20	0.52
Cognitive learning		0.62	0.02
Graduate teaching assistant humor orientation		0.66	0.04
Teven & Winters (2008)			
Pharmaceutical representative's nonverbal immediacy		0.07	NS[3]
Pharmaceutical representative's adaptive selling		0.13	NS
Pharmaceutical representative's physical attractiveness		0.27	0.0005
Competence		0.00	NS
Caring		−0.21	NS
Responsiveness		0.09	NS
Machiavellianism		0.23	0.0005
Motivation to contact clients		−0.17	NS
Sales performance		−0.14	NS
Wrench (2001)			
Communication apprehension	228	−0.30	0.0005
Talkaholism	153	−0.03	0.68
Receiver apprehension	180	−0.37	0.0005
Temperament			
Extraversion	219	0.57	0.0005
Neuroticism	219	−0.25	0.0005
Psychoticism	219	−0.22	0.001
Family communication patterns			
Concept orientation	154	0.18	0.03
Socio orientation	152	−0.03	0.72
Communication competence	146	0.40	0.0005

Wrench & Brogan (2004)			
Perceived cognitive learning	154	0.34	0.0005
Student motivation	141	0.48	0.0005
Affective learning			
Affect toward teacher	141	0.51	0.0005
Affect toward content	153	0.31	0.0005
Likelihood of taking future courses in content area	154	0.31	0.0005
Likelihood of taking future courses with teacher	150	0.52	0.0005
Attitude toward distance education	143	0.23	0.00005
Teacher credibility			
Competence	151	0.50	0.0005
Caring/goodwill	153	0.50	0.0005
Trustworthiness	153	0.46	0.0005
Wrench, Brogan, Wrench, and McKean (2007)			
Liking of religious leader	237	0.58	0.0005
Satisfaction with religious climate	228	0.32	0.0005
Religious leader's sociocommunicative style			
Assertiveness	234	0.12	0.07
Responsiveness	235	0.50	0.0005
Religious leader uses of self-disclosure	221	0.41	0.0005
Religious leader credibility			
Competence	230	0.48	0.0005
Caring/goodwill	230	0.50	0.0005
Trustworthiness	233	0.45	0.0005
Communication satisfaction with religious leader	232	0.50	0.0005
Relationship satisfaction with religious leader	230	0.43	0.0005
Religious communication apprehension	231	−0.10	0.12
Religious maturity	202	0.25	0.0005
Wrench & Martin (2002)			
Family communication patterns	301	0.47	0.0005
Concept orientation	305	−0.21	0.0005
Socio orientation			

Adolescent conflict management strategies			
Nonconfrontational strategies	305	−0.14	0.0005
Solution-oriented strategies	305	0.29	0.0005
Control-oriented strategies	305	0.13	0.0005
Communication satisfaction with parent	301	0.44	0.0005
Wrench & McCroskey (2001)			
Sense of humor	225	0.18	0.005
Humor orientation	228	0.51	0.0005
Temperament			
Extraversion	224	0.42	0.0005
Neuroticism	224	−0.16	0.01
Psychoticism	224	−0.10	NS
State-trait cheerfulness index			
Cheerfulness	221	0.39	0.0005
Seriousness	221	−0.09	NS
Bad mood	221	−0.27	0.0005
Wrench & Punyanunt-Carter (2008)			
Relationship satisfaction with graduate advisor	149	0.51	0.0005
Graduate advisor's nonverbal immediacy	151	0.60	0.0005
Perceptions of mentoring from graduate advisor	151	0.49	0.0005
Social support from graduate advisor	144	0.48	0.0005
Wrench & Richmond (2004)			
Affective learning			
Affect toward content	439	0.28	0.0005
Affect toward teacher	440	0.52	0.0005
Teacher's nonverbal immediacy	446	0.46	0.0005
Cognitive learning	446	0.28	0.0005
Student motivation	446	0.24	0.0005
Teacher credibility			
Competence	432	0.39	0.0005
Caring/goodwill	432	0.37	0.0005
Trustworthiness	434	0.28	0.0005

Wrench, Thomas-Maddox, Richmond, & McCroskey (2008)			
Communication apprehension	311	−0.25	0.0005
Willingness to communicate	302	0.27	0.0005
Ethnocentrism	318	−0.32	0.0005
Sociocommunicative orientation			
Assertiveness	319	0.23	0.0005
Responsiveness	319	0.29	0.0005
Nonverbal immediacy	318	0.47	0.0005
Attitude toward higher education	309	0.38	0.0005
Belief that everyone should take public speaking in college	307	0.06	0.27

[1]The r value represents the correlation between the study variable listed and humor assessment.
[2]This information was not provided in the author's paper or publication.
[3]The information in the article indicated nonsignificance, but not at what level.

THE FUTURE OF THE HUMOR ASSESSMENT

The future of the humor assessment is being paved by countless researchers. As more researchers are exposed to the Humor Assessment measure, people are using the humor assessment in a variety of research contexts. In the future, we hope the humor assessment can be used in more studies and in a broader range of communication contexts. This increased utilization of the measure does not mean that there are not detractors. In a 2009 article by Cann, Zapata, and Davis, the authors argue that the Humor Assessment measure (as well as the Humor Orientation Scale) "do not differentiate between humor uses that can have negative as opposed to positive effects in interactions. Although all humor may evoke some humorous responses from at least some in an audience, negative forms of humor are accomplished at a social cost to the target of the humorous remark, and perhaps at a cost to the user" (p. 454). Admittedly, the humor assessment has not been used in a study where comparisons of an individual's use of humor and how others' perceive that individual's use of humor are similar or different. Stirling (2004) in her Master's thesis did examine graduate teaching assistants' humor orientation and their students' perceptions of graduate teaching assistants' humor assessments (basically mixing the two scales). Ultimately, graduate teaching assistants' humor orientations were positively related to student perceptions of the graduate teaching assistants' humor assessment, $r = 0.659$, $p = 0.041$. While Cann, Zapata, and Davis' concerns about the negative impact of inappropriate vs. appropriate humor or how an individual's sense of humor and whether others have the same sense of humor are clearly an issue in humor research, the benefits of using the humor assessment instrument are still clear.

References

Avtgis, T. A., & Taber, K. R. (2006). 'I laughed so hard my side hurts, or is that an ulcer?' The influence of work humor on job stress, job satisfaction, and burnout among print media employees. *Communication Research Reports, 23,* 13–18.

Aylor, B., & Oppliger, P. (2003). Out-of-class communication and student perceptions of instructor humor orientation and socio-communicative style. *Communication Education, 52,* 122–134. doi:10.1080/363452032000085090

Booth-Butterfield, M., & Booth-Butterfield, S. (1991). Individual differences in the communication of humorous messages. *Southern Communication Journal, 56,* 43–40.

Booth-Butterfield, M., Booth-Butterfield, S., & Wanzer, M. (2007). Funny students cope better: Patterns of humor enactment and coping effectiveness. *Communication Quarterly, 55,* 299–315. doi:10.1080/01463370701490232

Bryant, F. B. (2000). Assessing the validity of measurement. In L. G. Grimm & P. R. Yarnold (Eds.), *Reading and understanding more multivariate statistics* (pp. 99–146). Washington, DC: American Psychological Association.

Bryant, J., Comisky, P., & Zillmann, D. (1979). Teachers' humor in the classroom. *Communication Education, 28*(2), 110–118.

Buijzen, M., & Valkenburg, P. M. (2004). Developing a typology of humor in audiovisual media. *Media Psychology, 6,* 147–167.

Campbell, K. L., Martin, M. M., & Wanzer, M. B. (2001). Employee perceptions of manager humor orientation, assertiveness, responsiveness, approach/avoidance strategies, and satisfaction. *Communication Research Reports, 18,* 67–74.

Cann, A., Zapata, C. L., & Davis, H. B. (2009). Positive and negative styles of humor in communication: Evidence for the importance of considering both styles. *Communication Quarterly, 57,* 452–468.

Converse, J. M., & Presser, S. (1986). Survey questions: Handcrafting the standardized questionnaire. In M. S. Lewis-Black (Ed.), *Series: Quantitative applications in the social sciences—A Sage University paper: Vol. 63.* Newbury Park, CA: SAGE.

DeVellis, R. F. (1991). Scale development: Theory and applications. In L. Bickman & D. J. Rog (Eds.), *Applied social research methods series: Vol. 26.* Newbury Park, CA: SAGE.

Downs, V. C., Javidi, M., & Nussbaum, J. F. (1988). An analysis of teachers' verbal communication within the college classroom: Use of humor, self-disclosure, and narratives. *Communication Education, 37*(2), 127–41.

Eysenck, H. J. (1998). *Dimensions of personality.* New Brunswick: Transaction.

Eysenck, S. B., Eysenck, H. J., & Barrett, J. (1985). A revised version of the psychoticism scale. *Personality and Individual Differences, 6,* 21–29.

Frymier, A. B., Wanzer, M. B., & Wojtaszczyk, A. M. (2008). Assessing students' perceptions of inappropriate and appropriate teacher humor. *Communication Education, 57,* 266–288.

Gorham, J., & Christophel, D. M. (1990). The relationship of teachers' use of humor in the classroom to immediacy and student learning. *Communication Education, 39*(1), 46–62.

Gruner, C. R. (1991). On the impossibility of having a taxonomy of humor. *Paper presented at Ninth International Conference on Humor and Laughter,* Brock University, St. Catarines, Ontario.

Hanger, M., Jack, C., & Willaman, L. (2006). *The interrelationships among teacher misbehaviors, source credibility, and humor assessment.* Unpublished manuscript, School of Communication, Ohio University, Athens.

Hertz, M., Jaroff, H., Brush, E., & Golub, J. (2009). *Gender stereotypes: A hypergender ideology trait study.* Unpublished manuscript, Department of Communication and Media, SUNY New Paltz, New Paltz, NY.

Honeycutt, J. M., & Brown, R. (1998). Did you hear the one about?: Typological and spousal differences in the planning of jokes and sense of humor in marriage. *Communication Quarterly, 46,* 342–352.

Jones, R. L. (2006). *The effects of principals' humor orientation and principals' communication competence on principals' leadership effectiveness as perceived by teachers.* Unpublished dissertation. The University of Akron, Akron, OH.

Lumbatis, R., Hoskinson, C., Jones, J., Willhealm, L., & Lutz, K. (2006, April). Analysis of communication motives, temperamental predispositions, and companion humor orientation towards perceptions of best friendships. *Paper presented at the Eastern Communication Association's Convention,* Philadelphia.

Martin, R. A., Puhlik-Doris, P., Larsen, G., Gray, J., & Weir, K. (2003). Individual differences in uses of humor and their relation to psychological well-being: Development of the Humor Styles Questionnaire. *Journal of Research in Personality, 37,* 48–75.

McGhee, P. E. (1999). *Health, healing and the amuse system: Humor as survival training.* Dubuque, IA: Kendall Hunt.

Merolla, A. J. (2006). Decoding ability and humor production. *Communication Quarterly, 54,* 175–189.

Miczo, N., & Welter, R. E. (2006). Aggressive and affiliative humor: Relationships to aspects of intercultural communication. *Journal of Intercultural Communication Research, 35,* 61–77.

Neuliep, J. W. (1991). An examination of the content of high school teachers' humor in the classroom and the development of an inductively derived taxonomy of classroom humor. *Communication Education, 40*(4), 343–355.

Punyanunt, N. M. (2000). The effects of humor on perceptions of compliance-gaining in the college classroom. *Communication Research Reports, 17,* 30–38.

Rizzo, B. J., Wanzer, M. B., & Booth-Butterfield, M. (1999). Individual differences in managers' use of humor: Subordinate perceptions of managers' humor. *Communication Research Reports, 16,* 360–369.

Salkind, N. J. (2006). *Tests & measurement for people who (think they) hate tests & measurement.* Thousand Oaks, CA: SAGE.

Stirling, S. D. (2004). Graduate teaching assistants' use of humor in the college classroom and its impact on student behavior and learning. Unpublished Master's thesis. Texas Tech University, Lubbock.

Teven, J. J., & Winters, J. L. (2008). Pharmaceutical representatives' social influence behaviors and communication orientations: Relationships with adaptive selling and sales performance. *Human Communication, 10,* 465–486.

Wanzer, M., Booth-Butterfield, M., & Booth-Butterfield, S. (1996b, November). Combatting stress in the health-care setting: Analysis of humor orientation and perceived coping effectiveness. *Paper presented at the annual meeting of the Speech Communication Association,* San Diego.

Wanzer, M., Booth-Butterfield, M., & Booth-Butterfield, S. (2005). 'If we didn't use humor, we'd cry:' Humorous coping communication in health care settings. *Journal of Health Communication, 10,* 105–125.

Wanzer, M. B., Booth-Butterfield, M., & Booth-Butterfield, S. (1995). The funny people: A source-orientation to the communication of humor. *Communication Quarterly, 43,* 142–154.

Wanzer, M. B., Booth-Butterfield, M., & Booth-Butterfield, S. (1996a). Are funny people popular? An examination of humor orientation, loneliness, and social attraction. *Communication Quarterly, 44,* 42–52.

Wanzer, M. B., & Frymier, A. B. (1999a). The relationship between student perceptions of instructor humor and students' reports of learning. *Communication Education, 48,* 48–62.

Wanzer, M. B., & Frymier, A. B. (1999b, April). Being funny in the classroom: Appropriate and inappropriate humor behaviors. *Paper presented at the Eastern Communication Association's Convention,* Charleston, WV.

Wrench, J. S. (2001, April). Hand me downs: How family communication patterns and communication competence are impacted by temperament. *Paper presented at the Eastern Communication Association's Convention,* Portland, ME.

Wrench, J. S., & Booth-Butterfield, M. (2003). Increasing patient satisfaction and compliance: An examination of physician humor orientation, compliance-gaining strategies, and perceived credibility. *Communication Quarterly, 51,* 482–503.

Wrench, J. S., & Brogan, S. M. (2004). *The influence of broadcasted classrooms and student perceptions personal motivation and affect on perceptions of instructor credibility and nonverbal immediacy.* Unpublished manuscript, School of Communication, Ohio University-Eastern, St. Clairsville.

Wrench, J. S., Brogan, S. M., Wrench, J. D., & McKean, J. R. (2007, November). The relationship between religious followers' functional and relational goals and perceptions of religious leaders' use of instructional communication. *Paper presented at the National Communication Association's Convention,* Chicago.

Wrench, J. S., Jowi, D., & Goodboy, A. (2010). *The directory of communication related mental measures.* Washington, DC: National Communication Association.

Wrench, J. S., & McCroskey, J. C. (2001). A temperamental understanding of humor communication and exhilaratability. *Communication Quarterly, 49,* 142–159.

Wrench, J. S., McCroskey, J. C., & Richmond, V. P. (2008). *Human communication in everyday life: Explanations and applications.* Boston: Allyn & Bacon.

Wrench, J. S., & Punyanunt-Carter, N. M. (2008). The influence of graduate advisor use of interpersonal humor on graduate students. *The National Academic Advising Association (NACADA) Journal, 28,* 54–72.

Wrench, J. S., & Richmond, V. P. (2000, November). The relationships between teacher humor assessment and motivation, credibility, verbal aggression, affective learning, perceived learning, and learning loss. *Paper presented at the National Communication Association's Convention,* Seattle.

Wrench, J. S., & Richmond, V. P. (2004). Understanding the psychometric properties of the Humor Assessment instrument through an analysis of the relationships between teacher humor assessment and instructional communication variables in the college classroom. *Communication Research Reports, 21,* 92–103.

Wrench, J. S., Thomas-Maddox, C., Richmond, V. P., & McCroskey, J. C. (2008). *Quantitative methods for communication researchers: A hands on approach.* New York: Oxford University Press.

CHAPTER 6

HUMOR AS AGGRESSIVE COMMUNICATION

Rachel L. DiCioccio
University of Rhode Island

It is easy to recall those moments when hearing a funny joke or listening to an entertaining anecdote had us doubled over in hysterical laughter, a red face and wide smile presenting clear evidence of our amusement. Equally as memorable, however, are instances when a joke or comment has made us uncomfortable or even offended us. Amusement is replaced by embarrassment, and we are left feeling stung by a humorous remark. The paradoxical nature of humor is evident in our everyday interactions. Humor serves as a social tool that fosters positive feelings and encourages a sense of kinship, yet, it can also act as a demonstration of aggression. Just as the benefits of positive humor for individuals and their relationships are numerous, so, too, are the negative effects of aggressive humor. This chapter considers humor as a form of aggressive expression. The distinction between positive and negative forms of humor are reviewed, and three models that conceptualize humor are presented. Finally, the Model of Aggressive Communication is examined and a communication perspective for understanding aggressive humor is discussed.

The notion of aggressive humor is not new. Psychology scholars, most notably Freud, recognized and introduced the possible hostile nature of humor. Distinguishing between innocent and tendentious jokes, Freud (1960) characterized hostile humor as "disguised aggressiveness" (p. 129). He asserted that by using hostile jokes, one is able to evade the demonstration of overt aggression against another person. Freud (1960) argued that expressing hostile humor serves to release psychological tension and stifled aggressive impulses. Early attempts to conceptualize aggressive humor included the examination of individuals' recognition and evaluation of hostile cartoons (Byrne, 1956), sexual cartoon exposure and the reduction of aggression (Baron, 1978a), the cathartic effect of hostile jokes (Leak, 1974), the cathartic release of witnessing aggressive humor (Berkowitz, 1970), and exposure to hostile humor and the increase in overt aggression (Baron, 1978b). Such foundational studies solidified the early domain of aggressive humor, and set the stage for its continued examination. These studies laid the groundwork for new directions in the study of humor as aggressive communication.

MODELS OF HUMOR

Contemporary approaches to modeling humor recognize humor communication as a multidimensional concept. Selected approaches presented in this chapter include models of humor functions and humor styles. A third approach composed of research explicates the effects or outcomes related to humor, although offers less at a theoretical level and more at a taxonomical level. For this review, the humor models chosen represent the specific perspective, rather than comprising an exhaustive catalog.

Two functional humor models are representative of the functions category. First, Graham, Papa, and Brooks (1992) took a functional approach toward conceptualizing humor to better understand how and why people use humor. From an extensive review of humor theory and research, they identified 24 purposes for demonstrating humor. Positive purposes included such functions as: "8. To play with others (Baxter, 1990; Betcher, 1981, 1988; Cheatwood, 1983; Civikly, 1983, 1989); 10. To minimize anxiety (Bricker, 1980; Civikly, 1983, 1989; Smith & Powell, 1988); 13. To help others relax and feel comfortable (Civikly, 1983, 1989; Landy & Mettee, 1969; Smith & Powell, 1988); and 17. To increase liking by others (Civikly, 1983, 1989; Derks & Berkowitz, 1989; Goodchilds, 1959)" (p. 168). Negative functions included: "1. To transmit verbally aggressive messages (Berkowitz, 1970; Civikly, 1989; Landy & Mettee, 1969); 2. To demean others (Civikly, 1989; Zillman & Cantor, 1976); 19. To control others (Civikly, 1983, 1989; Goodchilds, 1959); and 22. To put others in their place (Byrne, 1956; Civikly, 1989)" (p. 168). Graham et al. (1992) created the Uses of Humor Index (UHI) to reflect the 24 functions they identified in the humor literature. Developing and validating the UHI, Graham et al. (1992) extracted three overarching functions of humor: positive affect, expressiveness, and negative affect. Positive affect defines the expression of affection and the use of humor to identify and connect with others. Expressiveness recognizes humor as a means of self-disclosure. Graham et al. (1992) concluded that "much disclosure takes the form of humorous comments because it is either difficult or socially unacceptable to disclose personal information in any other way" (p.175). The negative affect function encompasses the use of humor to demean and belittle others as a form of entertainment. Graham et al.'s functional taxonomy reflects the use of humor for both prosocial and antisocial purposes.

A second functional approach is Meyer's (2000) model of humorous communication, discussed in detail in chapter 2. Meyer delineated the functions of humor in terms of positive and negative outcomes, and organized the functions on a continuum ranging from the most unifying to the most dividing forms of humor. Two functions reside on the unifying end of the spectrum: identification and clarification. Identification defines humor that enhances mutual understanding and recognizes shared meaning between communicators. Clarification humor reveals a speaker's view on or belief about a norm or rule without criticizing or condemning the violator of the social norm. Both forms of humor underscore the connection between speaker and receiver, creating cohesion and strengthening interpersonal bonds. At the other end of the continuum are enforcement and differentiation, the divisive functions of humor. Enforcement humor classifies teasing as a means of disparaging the receiver for violating a social norm. Meyer (2000) defines differentiation as the most relationally dividing function of humor. The aim of this type of humor is clearly to distinguish the speaker from the receiver through the use of ridicule and mocking. Meyer's conceptualization sets humor functions on a single polarized array with prosocial humor positioned at one end and antisocial humor at the other.

A third modeling approach tackles styles of using humor. In developing and validating the Humor Styles Questionnaire (HSQ), Martin, Puhlik-Doris, Larsen, Gray, and Weir (2003) recognized the multifaceted nature of humor. The scholars identified "four dimensions relating to different uses or functions of humor in everyday life" (p. 51). These four dimensions characterize two broad forms of humor: adaptive humor and maladaptive humor. Adaptive humor refers to the positive expression of humor that can enhance relationships and increase feelings of well-being. Maladaptive humor is negative and "less benign and potentially even deleterious to well-being" (p. 51).

Martin et al. (2003) introduced a 2 X 2 psychological model, conceptualizing humor by integrating two central functions with two styles of humor. The model identified humor to "enhance the self" and humor to "enhance one's relationship with others" as the main functions that distinguish a person's intention for delivering humor. Self-enhancing humor acts as a form of protection against stress, adversity, insecurity, and tension. On the other hand, relationship-enhancing humor is delivered to strengthen interpersonal bonds, increase attractiveness, and minimize conflict (Martin et al., 2003). The model also characterizes humor as either benevolent and considerate to the self and others, or as "potentially detrimental or injurious either to the self or one's relationship with others" (p. 52). In combination, Martin et al.'s grid of functions and styles of humor plots four types of humor use: affiliative, self-enhancing, self-defeating, and aggressive.

Affiliative humor is demonstrated in unscripted joke telling and clever repartee that affirms the self and other and encourages an interpersonal connection. Second, self-enhancing humor attends to our intrapersonal needs by evoking a cheerful demeanor and "tendency to maintain a humorous outlook on life" (p. 71). Third, self-defeating humor positions the self as the locus of attack or target of disparaging humor. By serving as the "butt" of the joke or anecdote, one hopes to gain approval and acceptance from others. The fourth style is aggressive humor. Aggressive humor incorporates teasing, sarcasm, and ridicule to demean and degrade. The objective in using aggressive humor is to "say funny things that are likely to hurt and alienate others" (p. 54). Functional models deliver the conceptual tools to determine how uses of humor may connect to other constructs such as outcomes or effects. These models work well to address multiple dimensions of humorous communication. Although each is unique, these approaches and representative models cohere in recognizing that humor has both positive and negative dimensions.

Numerous researchers have examined the effects and outcomes of humor. Positive humor has been linked to beneficial outcomes that include bolstered psychological well-being (Martin, 2001); increased relationship satisfaction (Butzer & Kuiper, 2008; Ziv & Gadish, 1989); enhanced relational closeness (Alberts, Yoshimura, Rabby, & Loschiavo, 2005; Ziv, 1988); and reduced conflict in romantic relationships (Bippus, 2003; Campbell, Martin, & Ward, 2008). These outcomes endorse positive humor as a social lubricant that promotes both individual and relational health. In contrast, scholars who examine negative humor have identified such consequences as marital dissatisfaction (DeKoning & Weiss, 2002), conflict escalation (Bippus, 2003), strengthened ethnocentrism (Miczo & Welter, 2006), and lower job satisfaction (Avtgis & Taber, 2006). These latter outcomes reflect the divisive use of humor that disparages others and creates social isolation. The significant body of research examining the influences of humor accentuates the idea that humor can be employed for "positive purposes (i.e., to reduce tension and provide support) and for negative purposes (i.e., to create tension and attack and demean)" (Cann, Zapata, & Davis, 2009, p. 455).

The humor outcomes and effects research may employ functional or stylistic models that provide insight into the relational and contextual use of humor. Collectively, these research perspectives provide a global conceptualization of humor communication. That is, scholars must acknowledge generally the bright and the dark side of humor. Because the thrust of this chapter is the careful consideration of the divisive use of humor, the following sections articulate the Aggressive Communication Model (ACM) as it explains humor as aggressive communication. Before describing and explaining the ACM, a review of the concept of aggression is imperative.

AGGRESSION DEFINED

Among the variety of definitions of aggression used, early studies focused on physical aggression. Bandura (1978) referred to aggression as "behavior that results in personal injury and physical destruction" (p. 12). This suggests that aggressive behavior is determined by the outcome of the act. Bandura (1978) also speculated that attributed intention and responsibility influence perceptions of aggression. Similarly, Zillmann (1979) suggested aggressive behavior is defined as any attempt made to inflict physical pain on another. Felson (1978) presented yet another definition that identified aggression as an act in which a person attempts or threatens to harm another person regardless of the ultimate goal.

Other definitions create a broader perspective of aggression that transcends the physical component. Stronger, more useful conceptualizations of aggression define it as a multidimensional construct. Steinmetz (1977) defined aggression as "the intentional use of physical or verbal force to obtain one's own goal" (p. 19). Steinmetz (1977) argued that aggression is based on the intentionality of the act, the success or failure of the act, the instrumental or expressive use of the act, and the legitimacy or illegitimacy of the act. Steinmetz's conceptualization of aggression suggests that these factors of motivation, outcome, need, and perception all contribute to an outcome perceived as aggressive. These selected definitions of aggression relate to the uses and perceived functions of humor in that aggressive humor is engaged to elevate oneself and/or damage another by destructively employed social knowledge.

In conceiving his aggressive communication model, Infante (1987a) defined aggression as embedded within the context of interpersonal communication. He suggested that interpersonal communication demonstrates aggression "if it applies force physically and/or symbolically in order, minimally, to dominate and perhaps damage or, maximally, to defeat and perhaps destroy the locus of attack" that can include the other person's "body, material possessions, self-concept, positions on topics of communication, or behavior" (p. 158).

Infante's (1987a) definition is a most compelling explanation of aggression for several reasons. First, this definition focuses on communication as the observable behavior. Second, in this definition, aggression comprises both verbal and physical behavior. Third, this definition embraces positive and negative expressions of aggression via a wide range of behaviors.

AGGRESSIVE COMMUNICATION MODEL

How humor communicates aggression can be explained best through the lens of the Aggressive Communication Model (ACM). The ACM provides a framework to fully flesh out the nuances of humor used aggressively. The intrinsic rationale is that numerous messages constitute verbal aggression, and humor is one of those message types. A brief overview of the ACM will be explicated next in order then to extrapolate its utility in capturing humor as aggressive communication.

Infante (1987a) conceptualized the ACM within a personality framework. Central to Infante's (1987a) model is the trait model of personality. Infante (1987a) designed the model around four central aggressive personality traits: (a) verbal aggression; (b) argumentativeness; (c) hostility; and (d) assertiveness. The latter two traits, hostility and assertiveness, are located as general communication traits. On the other hand, verbal aggression and argumentativeness represent more specific communication predispositions. The model, as designed, conceptualizes argumentativeness as a subset of assertiveness, and verbal aggression as a subset of hostility.

The foundation of the ACM is rooted in a personality trait approach. In this way, traits are organized according to constructive (argumentativeness) or destructive (verbal aggressiveness) communication. Furthermore, as it has been used, the personality trait approach is conducive to an interactionist perspective (Infante, 1987b). The interactionist perspective of the personality trait approach suggests that the behavior or outcome represents the interaction between the individual and situation specific variables (Infante, 1987b). The interactionist perspective explains behavior by examining the influence of the environment on the expression of traits (Magnusson, 1990; Magnusson & Endler, 1977). Hall and Sereno (2010) posit that "negative humor use depends largely on context. … Negative put-down jokes are particularly audience and context sensitive" (pp. 355–356). To more fully grasp the nuances and outcomes of negative humor, they speculated that it is necessary to consider the perspectives or co-orientation of both interactants.

Infante (1987a) distinguished between the four traits of the model by identifying them as either constructive or destructive forms of communication. Aggressive behavior is classified as constructive if it encourages interpersonal communication satisfaction and increases the value of the dyadic relationship (Infante, 1987a). Aggressive behavior constitutes destructive communication when it leads to relationship dissatisfaction and at least one partner having negative opinions about him or herself and the relationship as a whole (Infante, 1987a). Finally, in addition to postulating the four personality trait components of the aggressive communication model, Infante (1987a) proposed two aggressive communication outcomes: (a) communication satisfaction and (b) relationship satisfaction. These outcomes serve as the criteria for assessing the constructive or destructive nature of the aggression traits. Aggressive communication outcomes are elucidated in a later section.

CONSTRUCTIVE DIMENSIONS: ASSERTIVENESS AND ARGUMENTATIVENESS

Assertiveness

Assertiveness characterizes a constructive form of aggressive communication (Infante, 1987a). Infante (1987a) defined assertiveness as a "person's general tendency to be interpersonally dominant, ascendant, and forceful" (p. 165). Other researchers have defined assertiveness as the ability to express emotions appropriately (Wolpe, 1973), to defend personal rights (Lange & Jakubowski, 1976), and act in one's own best interests without anxiety (Alberti & Emmons, 1986). These definitions are consistent with identifying assertiveness as a positive form of communication.

Aggression can be seen both in assertiveness and in hostility. Although assertiveness differs distinctly from hostility, both may be conveyed by the use of aggressive symbols (Infante, 1987a). It is social context that allows one to interpret an aggressive message as humorous rather than hostile (Gutman & Priest, 1969). "Ritual insults between old friends are not taken as insults" (p. 60). To clarify assertiveness as aggressive, yet constructive, consider the following example: An individual responds by "flipping the bird" to a friend who remarks sarcastically, "Nice hairdo" just after the individual arose from a nap with their hair protruding everywhere. Such a gesture generally is considered to be a hostile attack. However, if the interactants have an established relationship or long history that allows for a rude attack to be interpreted as assertive positive joking, then the gesture more likely will be considered as constructive teasing humor. The difference between the two centers on the intent behind the behavior. The main tenet of verbally aggressive behavior is that it is used to attack and damage the receiver's self-concept. Assertive behavior, however, uses symbols aggressively to improve the communication for both the individuals involved (Patterson, Littman, & Bricker, 1967).

Argumentativeness

Argumentative communication represents a second constructive form of aggression (Infante, 1987a; Infante & Rancer, 1996). In the aggressive communication model, argumentativeness is conceived as a subset of assertive communication. Argumentativeness is conceptualized as the predisposition to defend and refute controversial issues apart from the other person's self-concept (Infante & Rancer, 1982). Atkinson's (1964) theory of achievement motivation serves as a foundation for examining argumentativeness (Infante & Rancer, 1982).

The basic premise of Atkinson's (1964) theory revolves around a tendency to achieve success and avoid failure. The tendency to achieve success relies on two factors: (a) the incentives to achieve the task and (b) the perceived probability of success. The combination of these factors motivates a person to pursue the task and strive for success. People also have a propensity to avoid failure. This motivation is propelled by the fear of evaluation. When a person believes there will be some form of evaluation and a judgment will be made regarding their behavior, then their desire for success increases.

Building on this motivation perspective, Infante and Rancer (1982) conceptualized argumentativeness as "two competing tendencies: motivation to approach argumentative situations and motivation to avoid such situations" (p. 171). Similar to Atkinson's perspective, the probability of success or failure and the importance of success or failure influence the likelihood of engaging in argumentative communication (Infante & Rancer, 1982).

In defining argumentativeness as a constructive communication behavior, it is important to differentiate it from verbal aggression. The distinction between the two concepts centers on the locus of attack. As defined earlier, verbal aggression involves the attack of a person's self-concept. Argumentativeness, on the other hand, involves the attack of a person's opinions on controversial issues rather than his or her image (Infante & Rancer, 1982). Some research on ironic messages can illustrate and differentiate humor as verbal aggression vis-à-vis assertiveness.

Averbeck and Hample (2008) present findings from a study intended to illuminate nuanced conceptualization of the production of irony. They wished to go beyond the surface definition of irony as the "relatively transparent expression of a sentiment that is often the opposite of what one actually intends to communicate" (p. 396). To do so, they posit that one must account for not only understanding a message, but its intent as well. Furthermore, the sender and receiver must share key information "known to be factually incorrect" (p. 397). The ironic message produced typically approaches awkward conversation goals, while "simultaneously adhering to the necessities of social decorum" (p. 397).

The researchers investigated the strategic production of ironic messages, such as sarcasm as "a particularly nasty form of an ironic message" (p. 397). First, Averbeck and Hample connect these ironic messages—which generally have negative connotations and are potentially more hurtful than direct attacks—to trait verbal aggressiveness. The scholars indicated that a verbally aggressive person may endorse "the continued use of verbally aggressive messages" (p. 398). They reported results that supported their claim: "Using irony to condemn a behavior is an attempt to simultaneously be verbally aggressive (condemn behavior) and indirectly aggressive (dilute condemnation by deflecting target)" (p. 398). Averbeck and Hample extend their reasoning to a secondary motivation for "softening criticism through irony" (p. 399). Qualifying irony as indirect argument, Averbeck and Hample provided data that revealed a significant positive relationship between the endorsement of ironic messages and argumentativeness. Thus, verbally aggressive humor would be more direct. The humor employed by argumentative individuals, however, would likely be irony (such as sarcasm) in an attempt to protect the humorist and/or the relationship. In short, argumentative humor would be used to save face (cf., Ivanko, Pexman, & Olineck, 2004). It is out of some concern for outcomes for oneself and the other that individuals engage in verbally argumentative humor, as opposed to verbally aggressive humor.

DESTRUCTIVE DIMENSIONS: HOSTILITY AND VERBAL AGGRESSIVENESS

Hostility

Hostility characterizes a destructive form of aggressive communication (Infante, 1987a). Hostility is a personality quality that is demonstrated through aggressive behavior (Buss & Durkee, 1957; Steinmetz & Straus, 1974). Zillmann (1979) characterized hostility as an eagerness to interact aggressively. Costa and McCrae (1980) conceptualized hostility as one aspect of the neuroticism dimension, and defined it as a "generalized conceptualization of the affect of anger" (p. 93).

Similarly, Buss (1961, 1988) suggested that the presence of angry feelings can lead to the development of hostility. In developing the Hostility-Guilt Inventory, Buss and Durkee (1957) identified seven dimensions of hostility. Six of the dimensions of a hostile personality are related to destructive symbolic aggression (Infante, 1987a). The verbal hostility subset coincides directly with definitions of verbal aggression. Researchers (Averbeck & Hample, 2008; Yip & Martin, 2006) concur that it is likely that underlying hostile feelings drive the use of humor that is aggressive.

Verbal Aggressiveness

Verbal aggressiveness represents a second destructive form of communication (Infante, 1987a). Verbal aggression is defined as communication that attacks another's self-concept with the objective of inflicting psychological harm (Infante, 1987a; Infante, Trebing, Shepherd, & Seeds, 1984; Infante & Wigley, 1986). Although researchers have identified different types of aggressive verbal messages, they all share the same purpose: to harm or damage the target. Infante et al. (1984) labeled 10 communication behaviors as possible messages of verbal aggression: (a) character attacks, (b) competence attacks, (c) background attacks, (d) physical appearance attacks, (e) ridicule, (f) teasing, (g) threats, (h) swearing, (i) nonverbal emblems, and (j) maledictions. Infante, Riddle, Horvath, and Tumlin (1992) investigated the differences among message types. Results showed that high verbal aggressives demonstrated greater use of competence attacks, teasing, swearing, and nonverbal emblems than other message types.

In discussing their research findings about verbally aggressive messages, Infante et al (1992) suggested that high verbal aggressives' more frequent use of competence attacks, teasing, nonverbal emblems, and swearing may be a tactic "to express hostility in an indirect manner" (p. 123).

Further reflecting on the motivation underlying these message types, they speculated about the use of humor as verbal aggression. Both high and low verbal aggressives reported roughly similar frequencies of "verbally aggressive messages ... trying to be humorous" (p. 125). Although these percentages did not discriminate high from low aggression, Infante et al. (1992) suggested that the intention behind using humor aggressively could meaningfully distinguish between them.

> For high verbal aggressives, using humor may be a tactic for being mean to a disdained other, or it may be an "evasive" device which masks the use of personal attacks and avoids provoking physical violence. Recipients of aggressive messages in this form may perceive ambiguity in the seriousness of the message sender. For low verbal aggressives, on the other hand, humor may be a "softening" device which the message source uses to lessen the chance that critical comments will hurt the receiver. (p. 125)

Yip and Martin (2006) reported that some negative humor styles (aggressive teasing, use of sarcasm) were related indirectly to the social competencies of providing emotional support to others or managing conflict.

In essence, this body of research points to the perceived need for and problem of competing motives (and goals) for using humor to mask or soften aggression. Such a notion parallels Averbeck and Hample's (2008) work on using irony to deliver criticism in a less face-threatening manner than a literal criticism or insult. Teasing communication, the cousin of irony, can also help us to better understand humor as verbal aggression. Just as irony attempts to accommodate both hostility and politeness, teasing messages allow a source to straddle the fence between ridicule and jest.

DiCioccio (2010) defined teasing as "the purposeful selection and use of social knowledge in order to position the other as the focus of amusement or jocularity" (p. 342). This definition encompasses the complexity of teasing communication intended for both prosocial and antisocial purposes. Recognizing the dual function of teasing, DiCioccio (2010) asserted that teasing messages can be used affectionately and aggressively. Affectionate teasing expresses positive affect through playful joking while aggressive teasing inflicts psychological harm through harassment. Although these forms distinguish between message types, DiCioccio (2008) found that "both affectionate and aggressive teasing were related positively to verbal aggression" (p. 267). Her research suggests that regardless of the intentionality behind the use of teasing messages, they are perceived as inherently aggressive in nature. Reflecting on the use of teasing to demonstrate verbal aggression, Infante et al. (1992) suggest that:

> Teasing may be a vehicle for appearing humorous and thus not serious in attacking another person's self-concept. Perhaps by teasing through humor, high verbal aggressives attempt to keep the receiver guessing as to whether they mean, for example, to attack the receiver's competence. Another possible explanation is that through teasing the verbally aggressive person may simply want to be mean toward disdained others." (p. 12)

Both irony and teasing provide a clear window into aggressive humor. These insights reinforce Avtgis and Taber's (2006) claim that aggressive humor manifests trait verbal aggression. One may extrapolate from this skill deficiency or weakness that when hostility increases, the ability to manage conflict is reduced (Ivanko et al. 2004), and the potential for physical violence increases.

Infante and Wigley (1986) tested the relationship between hostility and verbal aggression to validate the Verbal Aggressiveness Scale. Infante and Wigley predicted that the Verbal Aggressiveness Scale and the Hostility-Guilt Inventory would be positively related and underscore the relationship between hostility and verbal aggression. Results showed that although the constructs are distinct, they are closely related. The relationship between hostility and verbal aggression is further supported in a study by Malamuth and Thornhill (1994). The goal of the study was to test the concept of "Hostile Masculinity" as a predictor of male dominance in same- and opposite-sex conversations. Results revealed that although hostile masculinity and dominance were not significantly related overall, when paired with female partners, there was support for the connection between hostility and verbal aggression. Ivanko et al. (2004) elaborated on the production, interpretation, and processing of verbal irony, i.e., sarcasm. Describing the results from their two studies, they observed clear gender differences in "the social impact of ironic speech" (p. 266). Replicating earlier research, Ivanko et al. found that women perceived ironic statements as less polite than did men. Furthermore, men were more likely to use sarcasm in most contexts than were women, except when women used a verbally ironic statement for self-criticism. Last, "a speaker's tendency to use sarcasm affects the way they [sic] interpret the speech of others" (p. 269). This research thus points to a connection between males' greater hostility and aggressiveness and more use of humor that is aggressive.

Finally, the Argumentative Skill Deficiency Model of Interspousal Violence (Infante, Chandler, & Rudd, 1989) connects verbal aggression and physical violence. A major premise of this model is that verbal aggression is most likely to escalate into physical violence among people predisposed to hostility. In addition, the model explains that people who demonstrate hostile dispositions are also identified by a lack of effective arguing skills (Infante et al., 1989). Averbeck and Hample (2008) lend credence to the model, stipulating that individuals lacking argumentative skills have limited repertoires. Aggressive individuals "tend to be less competent at ironic message production. The skill needed to focus the criticism on the behavior while accentuating the attitude (character) of the other person is on par with argumentative abilities. When this argumentative skill is lacking, there will be character attacks" (p. 408). These findings lend support to Infante's (1987a) aggressive communication model by underscoring the relationship between hostility and verbal aggression.

In addition to the four personality traits, the aggressive communication model proposes two aggressive communication outcomes: (a) communication satisfaction and (b) relationship satisfaction. These two communication outcomes reflect the influence of the constructive and destructive personality traits.

CONSTRUCTIVE AND DESTRUCTIVE COMMUNICATION OUTCOMES

Infante (1987a) identified two major communication outcomes of the aggressive communication model: communication satisfaction and relationship satisfaction. Both these outcomes represent central concepts in interpersonal research, and are useful measures for understanding how aggressive communication effects interpersonal relationships.

Communication Satisfaction

Hecht (1978b) suggested that communication satisfaction is the result of actual communication outcomes mirroring desired communication expectations. Hecht (1978a, 1978b) developed the concept of communication satisfaction based on the discriminant fulfillment approach. The discriminant fulfillment approach suggests that people draw connections between discriminant stimuli and response reinforcement. Hence, when the proper response to certain stimuli is reinforced, the result is communication satisfaction. Diverse literature has examined the effect of aggressive communication on communication satisfaction.

Research focusing on assertiveness and communication satisfaction has identified varying results. Zakahi (1985) investigated the relationship between assertiveness and communication satisfaction among stranger dyads. Findings revealed that other-reported assertiveness is significantly related to communication satisfaction.

Newton and Burgoon (1990) examined the effects of constructive and destructive communication on communication satisfaction of marital couples. The results showed that other-accusations such as criticizing or blaming were inversely related to the target's communication satisfaction. Onyekwere, Rubin, and Infante (1991) studied the relationship between argumentativeness and communication satisfaction. They predicted high argumentativeness would increase perceptions of credibility and satisfaction. Results indicated that when paired with high argumentatives in an argumentative situation, interactants reported higher communication satisfaction. Although communication satisfaction has not been examined outright in humor literature, scholars have attended somewhat implicitly to this construct, embedding it within the framework of relational satisfaction.

Relational Satisfaction

Relationship satisfaction reflects the emotional state of the relationship. The combination of positive and negative emotions influences the experience of the relationship (Rusbult, Drigotas, & Verette, 1994). The degree to which partners in the relationship feel their needs are being fulfilled determines perceptions of relationship satisfaction. Rusbult et al. (1994) suggested that positive interactions result in greater perceptions of relationship satisfaction.

Relationship satisfaction can be explained according to five aspects: (a) closeness, (b) communication, (c) conflict resolution, (d) cognitions, and (e) forgiveness (Worthington, 1991). Closeness is any type of behavior that is demonstrated by both partners and encourages intimacy. Communication is evaluated according to how appropriate it is. Conflict resolution defines a couple's ability to address and resolve relationship problems constructively. Cognitions reflect the perceptions and assumptions that partners hold for the other person. Finally, forgiveness concerns both partners' willingness to accept and forgive the other for faults and weaknesses.

The majority of literature examining aggression and relationship satisfaction centers on dating and marital relationships. Guerrero (1994) examined college dating and married dyads to investigate the link between relationship satisfaction and four types of aggressive communication: distributive-aggression, integrative-assertion, passive-aggression, and nonassertive-denial. Distributive-aggression is the direct expression of threatening anger. Integrative-assertion defines the assertive and empathetic expression of anger. Passive-aggression and nonassertive-denial are defined as indirect and threatening and indirect but nonthreatening, respectively. Findings showed that the only significant predictor of relationship satisfaction was integrative-assertion.

Aggressive humor has been found to relate negatively to relational satisfaction (Cann, Zapata, & Davis, 2011). Bippus (2003), in her examination of humor used in recalled conflict episodes, concluded that when receivers perceived aggressive source intentions in using humor, they also reported more negative relational outcomes. In developing the Relational Humor Inventory (RHI), DeKoning and Weiss (2002) looked at functions of humor to better understand marital relationships. Based on self- and partner assessments of humor use, they reported significant negative correlations between partner aggressive humor and marital satisfaction for both husbands and wives. In addition, husbands' aggressive humor use correlated negatively with their own marital satisfaction. Clearly, being on the receiving end of aggressive humor diminished the quality of the relationship for both partners.

Butzer and Kuiper (2008) corroborated and extended the findings of previous research about the link between aggressive humor use and marital satisfaction. Regardless of the context of the interaction, i.e., conflict or pleasure, greater use of aggressive humor correlated indirectly with relational satisfaction. The underlying premise seems to be that aggressive humor has a powerful influence on relational outcomes.

CONCLUSION

This chapter has expanded further the view that humor can be aggressive. There is no question that we experience both the affiliative and aggressive nature of humor in our routine interactions. These experiences are elucidated via exemplar contemporary models of humor, such as those of Graham et al. (1992), Meyer (2000), and Martin et al. (2003). Infante's Aggressive Communication Model is advanced as a useful mechanism to scrutinize humor as aggressive communication. The ACM provides a vital framework for conceptualizing aggressive messages as humor. This chapter delineates the ACM's four traits and its two outcomes, explicating its utility to enhance our understanding of humor as aggressive communication. Regardless of the specific model, the aggressive dimension of humor is articulated as central to our full grasp of humor.

References

Alberti, R. E., & Emmons, M. L. (1986). *Your perfect right: A guide to assertive living.* San Luis Obispo, CA: Impact.

Alberts, J. K., Yoshimura, C. G., Rabby, M., & Loschiavo, R. (2005). Mapping the topography of couples' daily conversations. *Journal of Social and Personal Relationships, 22,* 299–322.

Atkinson, J. W. (1964). *An introduction to motivation.* New York: D. Van Nostrand.

Averbeck, J. M., & Hemple, D. (2008). Ironic message production: How and why we produce ironic messages. *Communication Monographs, 75,* 396–410.

Avtgis, T. A., & Taber, K. R. (2006). 'I laughed so hard my side hurts, or is that an ulcer?' The influence of work humor on job stress, job satisfaction, and burnout among print media employees. *Communication Research Reports, 23,* 13–18.

Bandura, A. (1978). Social learning theory of aggression. *Journal of Communication, 28,* 12–27.

Baron, R. A. (1978a). Aggression-inhibiting influence of sexual humor. *Journal of Personality and Social Psychology, 36,* 189–197.

Baron, R. A. (1978b). The influence of hostile and nonhostile humor upon physical aggression. *Personality and Social Psychology Bulletin, 4,* 77–80.

Berkowitz, L. (1970). Aggressive humor as a stimulus to aggressive responses. *Journal of Personality and Social Psychology, 16,* 710–717.

Bippus, A. M. (2003). Humor motives, qualities, and reactions in recalled conflict episodes. *Western Journal of Communication, 67,* 413–426.

Buss, A. H. (1961). *The psychology of aggression.* New York: Wiley.

Buss, A. H. (1988). *Personality: Evolutionary heritage and human distinctiveness.* Hillsdale, NJ: Lawrence Erlbaum.

Buss, A. H., & Durkee, A. (1957). An inventory for assessing different kinds of hostility. *Journal of Consulting Psychology, 21,* 343–349.

Butzer, B., & Kuiper, N. A. (2008). Humor use in romantic relationships: The effects of relationship satisfaction and pleasant versus conflict situations. *Journal of Psychology: Interdisciplinary and Applied, 142*(3), 245–260.

Byrne, D. (1956). The relationship between humor and the expression of hostility. *Journal of Abnormal and Social Psychology, 53,* 84–89.

Campbell, L., Martin, R. A., & Ward, J. R. (2008). An observational study of humor use while resolving conflict in dating couples. *Personal Relationships, 15*(1), 41–55.

Cann, A., Zapata, C. L., & Davis, H. B. (2009). Positive and negative styles of humor in communication: Evidence for the importance of considering both styles. *Communication Quarterly, 57*(4), 452–468.

Cann, A., Zapata, C. L., & Davis, H. B. (2011). Humor style and relationship satisfaction in dating couples: Perceived versus self-reported humor styles as predictors of satisfaction. *Humor, 24*(1), 1–20.

Costa, P. T., & McCrae, R. R. (1980). Still stable after all these years: Personality as a key to some issues in adulthood and old age. In P. B. Bates & O. G. Brim (Eds.), *Life-span development and behavior* (Vol. 3, pp. 65–102). New York: Academic Press.

DeKoning, E., & Weiss, R. L. (2002). The relational humor inventory: Functions of humor in close relationships. *The American Journal of Family Therapy, 30,* 1–18.

DiCioccio, R. L. (2008). The development and validation of the teasing communication scale. *Human Communication, 11,* 255–272.

DiCioccio, R. L. (2010). The interactionist model of teasing communication. In T. A. Avtgis & A. S. Rancer (Eds.), *Arguments, aggression, and conflict* (pp. 340–355). New York: Routledge.

Felson, R. B. (1978). Aggression as impression management. *Social Psychology, 41,* 205–213.

Freud, S. (1960/1905). *Jokes and their relation to the unconscious.* (Ed. & trans. J. Strachey). New York: Norton.

Graham, E. E., Papa, M. J., & Brooks, G. P. (1992). Functions of humor in conversation: Conceptualization and measurement. *Western Journal of Communication, 56,* 161–183.

Guerrero, L. K. (1994). 'I'm so mad I could scream': The effects of anger expression on relational satisfaction and communication competence. *Southern Communication Journal, 59,* 125–141.

Gutman, J., & Priest, R. F. (1969). When is aggression funny? *Journal of Personality and Social psychology, 12,* 60–65.

Hall, J. A., & Sereno, K. (2010). Offensive jokes: How do they impact long-term relationships? *Humor, 23*(3), 351–373.

Hecht, M. L. (1978a). The conceptualization and measurement of interpersonal communication satisfaction. *Human Communication Research, 4,* 253–264.

Hecht, M. L. (1978b). Toward a conceptualization of communication satisfaction. *Quarterly Journal of Speech, 64,* 47–62.

Infante, D. A. (1987a). Aggressiveness. In J. C. McCroskey & J. A. Daly (Eds.), *Personality and interpersonal communication* (pp. 157–192). Newbury Park, CA: SAGE.

Infante, D. A. (1987b). Enhancing the prediction of response to a communication situation from communication traits. *Communication Quarterly, 35,* 308–316.

Infante, D. A., Chandler, T. A., & Rudd, J. E. (1989). Test of an argumentative skill deficiency model of interspousal violence. *Communication Monographs, 56,* 163–177.

Infante, D. A., & Rancer, A. S. (1982). A conceptualization and measure of argumentativeness. *Journal of Personality Assessment, 46,* 72–80.

Infante, D. A., & Rancer, A. S. (1996). Argumentativeness and verbal aggressiveness: A review of recent theory and research. *Communication Yearbook, 19,* 319–351.

Infante, D. A., Riddle, B. L., Horvath, C. L., & Tumlin, S. A. (1992). Verbal aggressiveness: Messages and reasons. *Communication Quarterly, 40,* 116–126.

Infante, D. A., Trebing, J. D., Shepherd, P. E., & Seeds, D. E. (1984). The relationship of argumentativeness to verbal aggression. *Southern Speech Communication Journal, 50,* 67–77.

Infante, D. A., & Wigley, C. J. (1986). Verbal aggressiveness: An interpersonal model and measure. *Communication Monographs, 53,* 61–69.

Ivanko, S. L., Pexman, P. M., & Olineck, K. M. (2004). How sarcastic are you?: Individual differences and verbal irony. *Journal of Language and Social Psychology, 23*(3), 244–271.

Lange, A. J., & Jakubowski, P. (1976). *Responsible assertive behavior: Cognitive/behavioral procedures for trainers.* Champaign, IL: Research Press.

Leak, G. K. (1974). Effects of hostility arousal and aggressive humor on catharsis and humor preference. *Journal of Personality and Social Psychology, 30,* 736–740.

Magnusson, D. (1990). Personality: Development from an interactional perspective. In L. A. Pervin (Ed.), *Handbook of personality: Theory and research* (pp. 193–222). New York: Guilford.

Magnusson, D., & Endler, N. S. (1977). Interactional psychology: Present status and future prospects. In D. Magnusson & N. S. Endler (Eds.), *Personality at the cross-roads: Current issues in interactional psychology* (pp. 1–17). Hillsdale, NJ: Lawrence Erlbaum.

Malamuth, N. M., & Thornhill, N. W. (1994). Hostile masculinity, sexual aggression, and gender-biased domineeringness in conversations. *Aggressive Behavior, 20,* 185–193.

Martin, R. A. (2001). Humor, laughter, and physical health: Methodological issues and research findings. *Psychological Bulletin, 127,* 504-519.

Martin, R. A., Puhlik-Doris, P., Larsen, G., Gray, J., & Weir, K. (2003). Individual differences in the uses of humor and their relation to psychological well-being: Development of the Humor Styles Questionnaire. *Journal of Research in Personality, 37,* 48–75.

Meyer, J. C. (2000). Humor as double-edged sword: Four functions of humor in communication. *Communication Theory, 10,* 310–331.

Miczo, N., & Welter, R. E. (2006). Aggressive and affiliative humor: Relationships to aspects of intercultural communication. *Journal of Intercultural Communication Research, 35,* 61–77.

Newton, D. A., & Burgoon, J. K. (1990). The use and consequences of verbal influence strategies during interpersonal disagreements. *Human Communication Research, 16,* 477–518.

Onyekwere, E. O., Rubin, R. B., & Infante, D. A. (1991). Interpersonal perception and communication satisfaction as a function of argumentativeness and ego-involvement. *Communication Quarterly, 39,* 35–47.

Patterson, G. R., Littman, R. A., & Bricker, W. (1967). Assertive behavior of aggression. *Monographs of the Society for Research in Child Development, 32,* 122–137.

Rusbult, C. E., Drigotas, S. M., & Verette, J. (1994). The investment model: An interdependence analysis of commitment process and relationship maintenance phenomena. In D. J. Canary & L. Staford (Eds.), *Communication and relational maintenance* (pp. 115–139). New York: Academic Press.

Steinmetz, S. K. (1977). *The cycle of violence: Assertive, aggressive, and abusive family interaction.* New York: Praeger.

Steinmetz, S. K., & Straus, M. A. (1974). *Violence in the family.* New York: Dodd, Mead & Company.

Wople, J. (1973). *The practice of behavior therapy.* New York: Pergamon Press.

Worthington, E. L. Jr. (1991). A primer on intake interviews with couples. *The American Journal of Family Therapy, 19,* 344-350.

Yip, J. A., & Martin, R. A. (2006). Sense of humor, emotional intelligence, and social competence. *Journal of Research in Personality, 40,* 1202–1206.

Zakahi, W. R. (1985). The relationship of assertiveness to communicative competence and communication satisfaction: A dyadic assessment. *Communication Research Reports, 2,* 36–40.

Zillmann, D. (1979). *Hostility and aggression.* Hillsdale, NJ: Lawrence Erlbaum.

Ziv, A. (1988). Humor's role in married life. *Humor, 1,* 223–229.

Ziv, A., & Gadish, O. (1989). Humor and marital satisfaction. *The Journal of Social Psychology, 129,* 759–768.

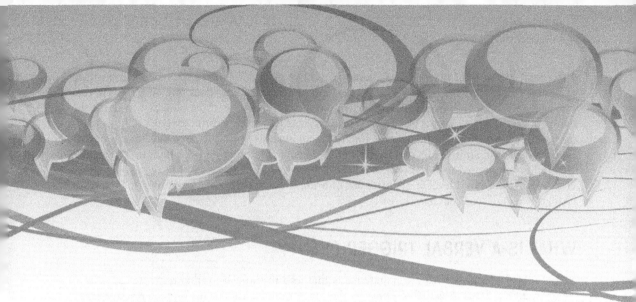

CHAPTER 7

HUMOR AS A VERBAL TRIGGER EVENT

Charles J. Wigley III
Canisius College

This chapter focuses on two primary questions and one secondary question. First, when does use of humor trigger verbal aggression by another person? Second, why does humor act as a verbal trigger event? To answer these two primary questions, the following topics are examined: (a) the nature of verbal trigger events (VTEs), (b) the broad structure of the primary types of humor, (c) the role of maladaptive humor as VTE (including an analysis of maladaptive humor as provocation), and (4) the limited role of affective and expressive humor as VTE (as indicated by consequentiality as opposed to intention). The fourth subpoint leads to a salient secondary question, viz., does the perceived level of offensiveness of humorous comments depend on permanency (or changeability) of receiver characteristics?

WHAT IS A VERBAL TRIGGER EVENT?

Verbal trigger events (VTEs) are "[s]tatements that lead to explosive verbal responses by others" (Wigley, 2006, 2010). A verbal response by the conversational interactant is called reactive verbal aggression (RVA). Regardless of the intention behind the VTE, VTEs consist of four primary components (Wigley, 2010, p. 388), viz., "1) it is comprised of one or more statements by an individual (I); 2) made to another person (O); 3) where the other person (O) reacts with verbal aggression; 4) but would not have so reacted without the initial statement or statements of the first individual (I)."

Verbal Trigger Events may take a variety of forms, appear in numerous contexts, involve myriad people, involve a multitude of topics, and be influenced by many conditions (both internal, e.g., communicative skill deficiencies, and external, e.g., type of relationships to the other communicators). It is important to note that VTEs may arise in situations where the trigger statement is a form of verbal aggression, but also when the trigger statement is innocuous and, essentially, made with an absence of malice.

Verbal Aggression Can Trigger Verbal Aggression

First, let's consider reciprocal verbal aggression. Previous research examining marital communication (Sabourin, Infante, & Rudd, 1993), for example, indicated that verbal aggression by one individual to another (i.e., the target of aggression) might lead to the reciprocal use of verbal aggression by the target. In such an instance, the statement by the first spouse serves as a VTE for the other spouse's reaction of verbal aggression. This example illustrates the concept of reciprocal aggression, i.e., aggression begets aggression. However, aggression does not always beget aggression. For example, other research in the marital domain by Infante (1989) found that when a spouse responded to marital partner with verbal aggression, husbands-victims-of-the-aggression were more likely than wives-victims-of-the-aggression to select an in-kind response (i.e., to opt for using reciprocal aggression). Thus, in the marital domain, whether a statement serves as VTE might depend on the biological sex of the person under attack. The research reported, *infra,* by Durbin in developing a taxonomy of VTEs examines this possible role of verbal aggression as a VTE more closely.

Innocuous Statements Can Trigger Verbal Aggression

Well-intended statements can, as well, trigger verbal aggression. Well-developed arguments using good evidence and reasoning presented by an individual (I) skilled in arguing to a less skillful other person (O) might be met with reactive verbal aggression because the less skillful person (O) has an argumentative skill deficiency (Infante, Trebing, Shepherd, & Seeds, 1984). Thus, an argumentative statement that may not constitute verbal aggression might trigger an explosive verbal reaction because of the situational factor that the responding person had Argumentative Skill Deficiency (ASD) (see Infante, Chandler, & Rudd, 1989). In this example, the well-intended statement of the first individual served as VTE for the aggressive response of the second individual (who had ASD).

Humor, Well Intended or Otherwise, Can Trigger Verbal Aggression

Argumentative statements (even when well intended) and verbally aggressive statements might serve as VTEs, but VTEs are not restricted to these presentational forms. Sometimes, a VTE might be composed of humor. Worth noting is the idea that using humor might result in an aggressive response when the humor is intended as aggression (e.g., ridicule) but, as well, when the humor is used with no aggressive intent (i.e., when it is well intended). To explore this possibility more fully, we need to identify, at the outset, the primary forms of humor.

WHAT ARE THE PRIMARY TYPES OF HUMOR?

In an excellent theoretical analysis of humor, Graham, Papa, and Brooks (1992) identified 24 categories from traditional research that suggested the primary functions of humor. A number of those categories might be considered forms of verbal aggression, most notably (Graham et al. 1992, pp. 167–168): "1. To transmit verbally aggressive messages (Berkowitz, 1970; Civikly, 1989; Landy & Mettee, 1969), ... 2. To demean others (Civikly, 1989; Zillmann & Cantor, 1976), ... 19. To control others (Civikly, 1983, 1989; Zillmann & Cantor, 1976), ... [and] 22. To put others in their place (Byrne, 1956; Civikly, 1989)." The researchers attempted to simplify this complex array of 24 functions and found three primary, overriding functions, viz., (a) positive affect, (b) expressiveness, and (c) negative affect. The authors explain (p. 169) negative affect as including "three antisocial uses of humor such as demeaning and belittling others, saying negative things, and putting others in their place." Positive affect is (p. 169) "making light of a situation, playful, and developing friendship items." Expressiveness (p. 169) refers to "reflecting self-disclosure and expression of feelings." When humor is used for any of these three functions (positive affect, expressiveness, negative affect), it might lead to RVA and, therefore, constitute a VTE. This chapter focuses on research on humor in any of its uses, whether for negative affect, expressiveness, or positive affect, as a Verbal Trigger Event.

Other researchers have developed a structure for understanding humor consonant with the Graham et al.'s explanation. Martin et al. (2003) describe humor as one of two styles, viz., adaptive versus maladaptive. Kuiper, Grimshaw, Leite, and Kirsh (2004) summarize adaptive humor as "tolerant and accepting of both self and others" and they say it can be considered self-enhancing or, alternatively, an affiliative behavior. Maladaptive humor is self-defeating or, alternatively, aggressive humor. Their description (2004) of aggressive humor is enlightening in conceptualizing humorous communication. "Here, individuals may use a variety of negative humor techniques, including teasing, ridicule, sarcasm, and disparagement to denigrate and put down others. Aggressive humor is displayed without regard for its potential negative impact on others, ultimately alienating those individuals and seriously impairing social and interpersonal relationships." Klein and Kuiper (2006) reiterate this explanation (pp. 385–386) and proceed to explain that bullying (in its direct form) can be physical (p. 389) "as well as verbal aggression involving name calling and ridiculing." Teasing, by definition, is a form of humor, as are ridicule, sarcasm, and name calling. These are forms of humor as negative affect and, on some occasions, some of these forms, such as teasing, can be used as positive affect (DiCioccio, 2010).

MALADAPTIVE HUMOR: NEGATIVE AFFECT HUMOR AS VTE

Why might a person respond to another person in an aggressive manner? It appears that three primary situational components that often lead to aggression are provocation, frustration, and self-focused attention (Wigley, 2010). Secondary to provocation, frustration, self-focused attention, but important in their degrees of influence, are argumentative skill deficiency, defensiveness, anger rumination, negative-urgency, and hypersensitivity (Wigley, 2010).

Negative affect is the most obvious trigger for RVA because negative affect serves as provocation and it is, often, defense arousing. Negative affect most clearly includes humor attempts that are intended as forms of aggression. Research by Infante (1987) found 10 primary forms of aggression, including character attacks, competence attacks, background attacks, physical appearance attacks, maledictions, *teasing, swearing, ridicule,* threats, and nonverbal emblems [emphasis added]. Other common forms of aggression include (Infante, 1995) blame, personality attacks, commands, global rejection, disconfirmation, negative comparison, sexual harassment, and attacking target's significant others. The response to the use of any of these 18 forms of verbal aggression is, often, reciprocated aggression. Thus, these 18 categories might be considered verbal trigger events.

Durbin (2008) was the first researcher to assess which of the common forms of verbal aggression are most likely to serve as a VTE. Durbin (2008) had respondents indicate the types of verbal messages that (pp. 58–62) "would cause you to respond in a verbally aggressive manner." After examining five categories of interactants, including bosses, family members, friends, significant other, and strangers, Durbin found that only character attacks and behavior criticism appeared in all five categories. This finding is salient because, as Durbin notes (p. 21), "choice of VTEs, and, also their relationship they hold with the recipient [have] a combined affect on the degree of hurt [that] they inflict upon the individual."

These findings suggest that any consideration of negative affect humor must address not only the verbal/nonverbal utterance, but the relationship between the conversationalists as well. Of particular interest is that neither teasing nor ridicule were identified by Durbin as being in the top five categories of method of attack by the initial communicant (for any of the five categories of interactant) that would lead to an aggressive response. Stated more succinctly, humor as aggression does not manifest itself in the top five methods of communicating by any of the five interactants in such a way that it serves to trigger a response of aggression. This does not mean that teasing and ridicule are not used, rather, they do not appear to be the primary triggers that usually result in RVA.

Aggressive humor may not be the most common verbal attack that leads to an aggressive response, but it might be, in fact, widespread and frequent in its use. Research by Romero, Alsua, Hinrichs, and Pearson (2007) addressed this issue. These authors examined four regions of the United States to determine whether there were significant differences among the regions in types of humor that were employed. The four regions were Alaska, Northwest Texas, Minnesota, and Southeast Texas. The authors measured, *inter alia*, aggressive humor using the Humor Styles Questionnaire (Martin et al., 2003). Results indicated (p. 195) that differences in means for aggressive humor scores in the four respective regions (27.03, 26.93, 28.43, and 27.76) failed to achieve significance when analysis of variance was used to compare the mean scores from the four regions. The mean scores (p. 195) for affiliative humor (44.93, 42.94, 45.87, and 40.54), as well as for self-enhancing humor (39.95, 38.81, 38.26, and 38.22), were, clearly, higher than the mean scores for aggressive humor. Statistically significant differences in the use of aggressive humor were found based on demographic characteristics including gender ($p < 0.01$), age ($p < 0.01$), and ethnicity ($p < 0.01$) with males using more aggressive humor than females and younger people using more aggressive humor than older people. It is not clear what the exact basis was for the authors' conclusion about ethnicity, but their sample included the following groups (p. 193), "Euro-American, Native American, Asian-American, Hispanic, African-American, [and] Other."

It is probably the case, based on the theoretical analysis of the humor construct by Graham et al. (1992) and that of Martin et al. (2003) and Kuiper et al. (2003) that some maladaptive humor serves as a form of aggression. Further, although empirical research by Durbin (2008) suggests that aggressive humor may not be the primary weapon of verbal attack and the research of Romero et al. (2007) supports the inference that aggressive humor may not be as common as affiliative and self-enhancing humor, research by Infante (1987, 1995) validates that aggressive humor, such as teasing, ridicule, and sarcasm, are among the most commonly employed weapons of verbal aggression. It is not clear, at this time, why the empirical evidence provides more support for the conclusion that attacks of a nonhumorous nature are more likely to serve as VTEs than negative humor.

Several plausible explanations might clarify the lack of empirical evidence that shows negative humorous attacks serve as VTEs. Two such explanations (which need empirical testing) include (a) direct, nonhumorous statements are stronger attacks, and (b) responding negatively to a humorous attack may seem to suggest that the target of the statement is thin skinned or unwilling to roll with the punches. Thus, the recipient chooses not to respond in a reactive manner.

ADAPTIVE HUMOR: POSITIVE AFFECT HUMOR AND EXPRESSIVE HUMOR AS VTE

While excellent attempts to measure humor have been with us for many years (see, e.g., Martin & Lefcourt, 1984), there is a paucity of research demonstrating that adaptive humor operates as VTE, so I hope the reader will afford me some latitude in suggesting some testable, but untested, hypotheses. The connection between adaptive humor and the VTE construct seems at least theoretically possible. A person attempting to use adaptive humor might not, ordinarily, associate it with provocation, frustration, self-focused attention, nor with argumentative skill deficiency, defensiveness, anger rumination, negative-urgency, and hypersensitivity, The receiver of the well-intended "humorous" message, however, might perceive the message as, for example, vulgar (or profane), sexist, racist, ethnic, or otherwise inappropriate and, therefore, as a message of provocation. The consequentiality of the statement to the receiver may be a more important consideration than the sender's intended purpose behind the humor attempt. Bippus explains (2003, p. 413, emphasis added) that in the case of conflict situations, for example, "Humor may not be well received by its target, *particularly* in conflicts, because recipients may see it as a personal attack (Zajdman, 1995) or an implication that the topic of the conversation does not warrant serious attention (Norrick, 1994)." Some well-intended humor attempts might be seen as personal attacks by the target, in part, because of noticeable and noted salient features of the recipient. This reasoning leads to an interesting question: Does the perceived level of offensiveness of humorous comments depend on permanency (or changeability) of receiver characteristics?

A distinction needs to be drawn between humorous messages that involve references to receiver characteristics that can be changed (by the receiver) without (relatively) considerable difficulty (idiographic characteristics) and references to receiver characteristics that cannot easily be changed by the receiver (ethnographic characteristics). Some characteristics of a receiver that can be relatively easy to change include, e.g., hairstyle, clothing, kemptness, and, arguably, body weight. Some characteristics of a receiver that are relatively difficult, if not impossible, to change include, e.g., biological sex, race, ethnicity, height, and religious affiliation. Whereas the easy categories involve idiographic characteristics, the "difficult" categories are largely ones involving membership in a class or group.

Keep in mind that this line of reasoning has not been empirically tested. It suggests, however, that well-intended, light-hearted kidding about idiographic characteristics, such as one's haircut (e.g., "When did your barber lose his eyesight?") or bodyweight (e.g., "Let's go, Chubby!"), might be less offensive and better received than similarly intended comments involving class characteristics (e.g., "You haoles all think alike!"). By way of explanation, I note that "Haole" (pronounced howlee) is a term in the Hawaiian language that generally, in modern times, connotes "foreigner" but, at times, has been used as a strong racial slur to describe Caucasian visitors to Hawaii. It seems reasonable to think that an individual might more easily dismiss humor directed at personal betterment (responding in a positive or neutral manner, "I need to get a new barber" or "I'd better lose some weight") than humor focused on things that cannot be changed (responding with aggression, "I'll never come to this stupid state of Hawaii again!"). While the sender of the message may not intend to arouse defensiveness, the receiver's need to protect the receiver's group identity from attack may trigger an aggressive response. Future research will focus on changeability of personal characteristics as a salient concern in developing more positive humorous messages.

CONCLUSION

As the situational determinants of verbal aggression continue to be studied, the role of humor as VTE will be more fully explicated. While current theory and research support the conclusion that maladaptive humor likely serves as VTE, future research will need to settle the question of how and why expressive and adaptive humor may operate to stimulate responses of an aggressive nature. One avenue that seems particularly worth studying involves the relationship between the "topic" of a message intended as humorous and the ability of an individual to see the message as intended (as opposed to seeing the message as maladaptive or aggressive). The target of an attempt at humor might more willingly "roll with the punches" when he or she believes that he or she can change in a way to escape victimization (as opposed to feeling helpless when the described characteristic is not under control of target). These research investigations should shed some light as to how humor might function more effectively in many of the contexts described in this book. When trying to manage one's interpersonal relations (a key factor in reducing aggression, see Wigley, 2008), the consequentiality of attempts at humor seem to be more important than the intentions underlying those attempts. One might say (to misquote a perditious old adage), when it comes to humor, the road to reactive verbal aggression is paved with good intentions.

References

Berkowitz, L. (1970). Aggressive humor as a stimulus to aggressive responses. *Journal of Personality and Social Psychology, 16,* 710–717.

Bippus, A. M. (2003). Humor motives, qualities, and reactions in recalled conflict episodes. *Western Journal of Communication, 67,* 413–426.

Byrne, D. (1956). The relationship between humor and the expression of hostility. *Journal of Abnormal and Social Psychology, 53,* 84–89.

Civikly, J. M. (1983, May). A comparison of male and female uses of humor types and humor functions. *Paper presented at the annual meeting of the International Communication Association Convention,* Dallas.

Civikly, J. M. (1989, November). Humor and teaching: The first years of teaching. *Paper presented at the annual meeting of the Speech Communication Association,* San Francisco.

DiCioccio, R. L. (2010). The interactionist model of teasing communication. In T. A. Avtgis & A. S. Rancer (Eds.), *Arguments, aggression, and conflict: New directions in theory and research* (pp. 340–355). New York: Routledge.

Durbin, J. M. (2008). *Toward the development of a taxonomy of verbal trigger events.* Unpublished Master's thesis. University of Akron. Akron, OH.

Graham, E. E., Papa, M. J., & Brooks, G. P. (1992). Functions of humor in conversation: Conceptualization and measurement. *Western Journal of Communication, 56,* 161–183.

Infante, D. A. (1987). Aggressiveness. In J. C. McCroskey & J. A. Daly (Eds.), *Personality and interpersonal communication* (pp. 157–192). Newbury Park, CA: SAGE.

Infante, D. A. (1989). Response to high argumentatives: Message and sex differences. *Southern Communication Journal, 54,* 159–170.

Infante, D. A. (1995). Teaching students to understand and control verbal aggression. *Communication Education, 44,* 51-63.

Infante, D. A., Chandler, T. A., & Rudd, J. E. (1989). Test of an argumentative skill deficiency model of interspousal violence. *Communication Monographs, 56,* 163–177.

Infante, D. A., Trebing, D. J., Shepherd, P. E., & Seeds, D. E. (1984). The relationship of argumentativeness to verbal aggression. *Southern Speech Communication Journal, 50,* 67–77.

Klein, D. N., & Kuiper, N. A. (2006). Humor styles, peer-relationships and bullying in middle childhood. *Humor: International Journal of Humor Research, 19,* 383–404.

Kuiper, N. A., Grimshaw, M., Leite, C., & Kirsh, G. (2004). Humor is not always the best medicine: Specific components of sense of humor and psychological well being. *Humor: International Journal of Humor Research, 17,* 135–168.

Landy, D., & Mettee, D. (1969). Evaluation of an aggressor as a function of exposure to cartoon humor. *Journal of Personality and Social Psychology, 12,* 66–71.

Martin, R. A., Puhlik-Doris, P., Larsen, G., Gray, J., & West, K. (2003). Individual differences in humor and their relation to psychological well-being: Development of the Humor Styles Questionnaire. *Journal of Research in Personality, 37,* 48–78.

Martin, R. A., & Lefcourt, H. M. (1984). Situational Humor Response Questionnaire: Quantitative measure of sense of humor. *Journal of Personality and Social Psychology, 47,* 145–155.

Norrick, N. (1994). *Conversational joking: Humor in everyday talk.* Bloomington, IN: Indiana University.

Romero, E. J., Alsua, C. J., Hinrichs, K. T., & Pearson, Y. R. (2007). Regional humor differences in the United States: Implications for management. *Humor: International Journal of Humor Research, 20,* 189–201.

Sabourin, T. C., Infante, D. A., & Rudd, J. E. (1993). Verbal aggression in marriages: A comparison of violent, distressed but nonviolent, and nondistressed couples. *Human Communication Research, 20,* 245–267.

Wigley, C. J., III. (2006). Verbal trigger events. In A. S. Rancer & T. A. Avtgis (Eds.), *Argumentative and aggressive communication: Theory, research, and application* (pp. 243–244). Thousand Oaks, CA: SAGE.

Wigley, C. J., III. (2008). Verbal aggression interventions: What should be done? *Communication Monographs, 75,* 339–350.

Wigley, C. J., III. (2010). Verbal trigger events—other catalysts and precursors of aggression. In T. A. Avtgis & A. S. Rancer (Eds.), *Arguments, aggression, and conflict: New directions in theory and research* (pp. 388–399). New York: Routledge.

Zajdman, A. (1995). Humorous face-threatening acts: Humor as strategy. *Journal of Pragmatics, 23,* 325–339.

Zillmann, D., & Cantor, J. (1976). A disposition theory of humour and mirth. In A. J. Chapman & H. C. Foot (Eds.), *Humour and laughter: Theory, research and applications* (pp. 93–115). New York: John Wiley & Sons.

PART TWO
HUMOR COMMUNICATION IN CONTEXT

Graduate Advisor-Advisee Communication and Use of Interpersonal Humor – *Narissra M. Punyanunt-Carter, Texas Tech University, & Jason S. Wrench, State University of New York at New Paltz*

Humor in Intercultural Interactions: Challenges and Pitfalls – *Nathan Miczo & Lisa A. Miczo, Western Illinois University*

Cross-Cultural Humor: A New Frontier for Intercultural Communication Research – *Yang Lin, Patricia S. Hill, University of Akron, & Sarah C. Bishop, University of Pittsburgh*

Disarmingly Funny: The Perils of Television's Political Comedy – *E. Johanna Hartelius, Northern Illinois University*

Wolfman Jay and the Writing Center Gang: Humor in Listserv Community Development – *Diana Calhoun Bell, University of Alabama, Huntsville*

CHAPTER 8

SEX, HUMOR, AND INTIMACY: AN EXAMINATION OF SEXUAL HUMOR USE IN CLOSE RELATIONSHIPS

Betty H. La France
Northern Illinois University

Jeffrey A. Hall
University of Kansas

"If a certain sexual position does not work the first time we try it, we will use humor to lighten the tension."

(Anonymous Respondent)

"We joke about the faces we make during sex. We like to try new positions, and when they don't turn out so well we make jokes about those. When the sex isn't the best we've ever had we make sarcastic remarks to one another."

(Anonymous Respondent)

"If something goes wrong or becomes awkward, we make it funny, rather than dwell on it. It makes it easier to move on and get back to sex."

(Anonymous Respondent)

The use of humor in close relationships has received considerable attention (e.g., Bippus, 2000; De Koning & Weiss, 2002; Hall, 2010; Hall & Sereno, 2010; Ziv, 1988; Ziv & Gadish, 1989). The humor couples use in their sexual relationship, however, has not received much scholarly attention. The dearth of research in this relational domain is particularly interesting given that research respondents readily acknowledge incorporating humor into their sexual relationships (Bell, Buerkel-Rothfuss, & Gore, 1987; Hopper, Knapp, & Scott, 1981; Ziv, 1988). Investigations examining humor in intimate relationships suggest that how people experience sexual humor and the relationship between sexual humor and sexual communication satisfaction is an important relationship to quantify, yet it is a relationship that has escaped scholarly inquiry. Therefore, the two main goals of this chapter are to (a) illuminate the correlates of sexual humor use within close relationships and (b) assess how sexual humor use is related to people's satisfaction with the sexual communication in their relationship. To accomplish these goals, a discussion regarding relevant research investigating humor use in interpersonal relationships is reviewed. This review is followed by a discussion of two perspectives that offer theoretical predictions for when individuals are likely to use sexual humor in their relationships. The first perspective is based on contributions scholars have made studying idiomatic communication—including sexual idioms—in close relationships (e.g., Hopper et al., 1981). The second framework, predicted outcome value theory (Sunnafrank, 1986, 1988), is useful for offering predictions regarding when dyadic members are likely to engage in sexual humor use. To begin, a discussion of extant research focusing on humor in close relationships is discussed.

THEORETICAL FRAMEWORK

Humor in Relationships

Given the relative paucity of empirical work investigating sexual humor, understanding how humor in general is used in close relationships is vital for anticipating how humor may function in individuals' sexual relationships. Hall and Sereno (2010) aptly declare that humor is "inherently shared" (p. 352). That is, in close relationships, the receiver or audience of such humor is one's relational partner. Empirical evidence has demonstrated that having a humorous relational partner is desirable (Gottman, Coan, Carrere, & Swanson, 1998; Wanzer, Booth-Butterfield, & Booth-Butterfield, 1996; Wildermuth, Vogl-Bauer, & Rivera, 2006), but having a relational partner with whom one shares a similar sense of humor is especially important (Hall & Sereno, 2010; Lauer, Lauer, & Kerr, 1990; Murstein & Brust, 1985; Priest & Thein, 2003).

Hall (Hall, 2010; Hall & Sereno, 2010) has profitably studied couple humor use by examining dyadic members' perceptions of their own use of humor and their partner's use of humor. Like other scholars who have recognized the potentiality of negative humor use (De Koning & Weiss, 2002; Graham, Papa, & Brooks, 1992; Martin, Puhlik-Doris, Larsen, Gray, & Weir, 2003; Meyer, 2000), Hall and Sereno (2010) studied how couples' positive and negative humor use influenced their perceptions of relational satisfaction and the importance of humor use within their relationship. They found that couples who perceived similarity in their negative humor use reported greater relational satisfaction than did couples who did not perceive symmetry in negative humor use. Furthermore, men's positive humor use was positively related to women's relational satisfaction, and women's positive humor use positively contributed to the importance women placed on the use of humor in their relationships. The strongest effect on men's perceived importance of humor use in their relationships was their own use of positive humor. These results offer compelling evidence to suggest that couples' humor use has important relational implications, including implications for the value individuals place on incorporating humor into their close relationships. Hall and Sereno's (2010) findings are also consistent with earlier work that revealed that humor—as expressions of positive affect—was positively related to both relational maintenance (Alberts, Yoshimura, Rabby, & Loschiavo, 2005; Bippus, 2000; Haas & Stafford, 2005) and relational stability (Gottman et al., 1998). Valued humor is a desirable relational commodity.

Scholars who have investigated humor typically approach the use of humor from a functional perspective. That is, their work often—explicitly or implicitly—posits that humor serves some sort of function or use within a relationship (Bippus, 2003; De Koning & Weiss, 2002; Graham et al., 1992; Hay, 2000; Martin et al., 2003; Meyer, 2000; Ziv, 1988). For example, Bippus (2000) found four categories of senses of humor that couples reported were part of their lives: active (e.g., pranks, poking fun, physical humor), receptive (e.g., laughing, being a good sport), bonding (e.g., references to bodily functions), and censured (e.g., inappropriate humor, sadistic humor, overbearing humor). One type of humor included under the bonding category was private references, which refers to a couple's use of humor to establish the importance of shared experiences. Another type of humor that constituted a bonding sense of humor was the use of pet names. Bippus' (2000) results indicate that couples perceived that the private language they created (e.g., pet names, private references) was a form of humor within their relationship—it was humorous for them to create and use such private codes.

Baxter (1992) investigated the intimate playfulness of same-sex friendships and opposite-sex romantic couples. She identified humor, in the form of teasing and private jokes, as a type of play dyadic members enact. She found that couples' private verbal codes (e.g., playful nicknames, jokes) were the most frequently reported type of play, and it was the type of play that rated highest in terms of intimacy. The use of such codes was also positively correlated with closeness for same-sex friendships. For opposite-sex couples, overall perceptions of playfulness (rather than specific types of play) were positively correlated with closeness. Verbal teasing, a form of humor, was the third most frequently reported type of play and also functioned to increase intimacy. People recognized that the humor they used in their close relationships was a form of adult play, play that was related to the intimacy they experienced in those relationships.

Alberts et al. (2005) investigated the mundane interactions of satisfied couples by tape recording daily interactions between members of several dyads. They found that couples used humor to maintain their relationships, and humor was used more frequently than positivity (e.g., expressions of affection) in daily conversations. In a more focused examination of how humor specifically functioned in conversation, Graham et al. (1992) found that humor use during conversations functioned to convey positive affect, negative affect, or to express information about one's feelings, beliefs, and attitudes. Their results demonstrated that using humor to create positive affect during conversations was positively related to various forms of interpersonal competence.

Lauer et al. (1990) reported that almost 75 percent of couples laugh together at least once a day. Similarly, Ziv (1988) found that 95 percent of husbands and wives reported that they or their spouse used humor, and 92 percent of individuals said that humor made significant contributions to their married life. Individuals' marital satisfaction was most impacted by their partner's humor (Ziv & Gadish, 1989). Ziv's (1988) investigation into married couples' daily humor use was one of the earliest explorations into how romantic couples report using humor within their relationships, and his results revealed that humor served five functions in marital relationships: aggressive, sexual (e.g., negotiating the tensions associated with the sexual episode), social (e.g., private jokes, private language), defensive, and intellectual. Unfortunately, few scholars since Ziv's (1988) identification of the sexual function of humor use within marital relationships have examined the specific benefits (and possible costs) sexual humor provides to dyadic members.

Aside from Ziv's (1988) sexual function of humor, sexual humor use in close relationships has not been examined frequently. Extant research that has examined sexual communication and humor use has done so by illuminating the private language or idioms that couples create. Although this approach conflates sexual communication and humor, it reveals that people generally perceive that their personal idioms—including private idioms related to sexual matters—are humorous (Baxter, 1992; Bippus, 2000; Ziv, 1988). Consequently, the idiomatic approach is useful for understanding how sexual idioms specifically function as a type of humor in close relationships. The literature that focuses on idiomatic communication is discussed next.

Idiomatic Communication

Using the relationships as cultures perspective (Oring, 1984), Hopper et al. (1981) offered a compelling seminal analysis of couples' personal idioms. They found that people's self-reported idiosyncratic language was classifiable into eight categories: nicknames, expressions of affection, labels for others, confrontations, requests/routines, teasing insults, sexual references/euphemisms, and sexual invitations. Hopper et al. (1981) defined sexual references/euphemisms as idioms that referred to genitals, breasts, sexual intercourse, sexual behavior, sexual techniques, etc. One example Hopper et al. (1981) offered from this category was the term wuzzer, which was used to refer to female genitalia (p. 26). Sexual invitations were idioms that initiated the sexual episode. Hopper et al. (1981) provided "let's go home and watch some television" as an example of a dyadic member's desire to engage in sexual intercourse with his/her partner (p. 26).

Baxter (1987) has also explicitly argued that relationships can be profitably studied using a cultural perspective. Implementing this framework, she found that individuals identified five unique types of relational symbols that represented certain aspects of their close relationships: behavioral actions (e.g., interaction routines, nicknames, affectionate terms), events (positive times during a relationship), objects (gifts or keepsakes), places (locations that hold significance), and artifacts (songs, films, books). Interviewees' most frequently identified relational symbol fell into Baxter's (1987) behavioral actions category. Perhaps most relevant for this chapter, the behavioral actions category included code words for sexual matters as well as nicknames and affectionate references. Baxter's (1987) results demonstrated that dyadic members used specialized verbal and nonverbal messages to relay sexually related information.

Bell and Healey (1992) found that the different types of personal idioms friends used were similar to the idioms couples used (Bell et al., 1987; Hopper et al., 1981). Bell and Healey (1992) argued that the use of idiomatic communication should parallel relationship development because personal idioms symbolize the intimacy relational partners feel toward one another. Indeed, their results revealed that perceptions of interpersonal solidarity were positively correlated with idiom use. Bell's work (Bell et al., 1987; Bell & Healey, 1992) provides strong evidence regarding the importance of sexual idioms within close relationships.

Part of a couple's language use is the idiosyncratic language partners develop within their sexual relationship. Relational partners typically perceive that their personal idioms are humorous (Bippus, 2000; Ziv, 1988). Humor use provides individuals with a means by which sensitive information can be conveyed in a way that minimizes threats to one's identity (Young & Bippus, 2001; Ziv & Gadish, 1990). Sexual humor can be used for the same reason. That is, sexual humor is one mechanism by which dyadic members are able to communicate their sexual desires, feelings, and attitudes about sexual matters without feeling as vulnerable as they would if humor were not used (Ziv, 1988). Research exploring idiosyncratic language use in close relationships provides the most specific information regarding how relational partners experience humorous sexual idioms. For example, Bell et al. (1987) demonstrated that the total number of idioms couples used was positively correlated with perceptions of loving, commitment, and closeness. Furthermore, the use of sexual references/euphemisms and sexual invitations were also positively related to love, commitment, and closeness.

Research regarding the relationship between intimacy and humorous idiomatic communication (Baxter, 1992; Bell & Healey, 1992; Bell et al., 1987) suggests that feelings of relational closeness should be related to sexual humor use. Recall that Graham et al. (1992) found that humor use during interactions functioned to convey positive affect and negative affect, and to express one's feelings and thoughts. This functional framework parsimoniously aids in the prediction of the ways in which sexual humor is anticipated to function within sexual relationships. Specifically, it is predicted that feelings of closeness and intimacy, or what Wheeless (1976) refers to as interpersonal solidarity, will be positively and significantly related to the use of positive sexual humor (H1) and expressive sexual humor (H2) but significantly and negatively related to negative sexual humor use (H3). Interpersonal solidarity, however, is not the only hypothesized influence of sexual humor use. It is also anticipated that dyadic members' forecasts about their future sexual relationship will also predict sexual humor use. Thus, predicted outcome value theory is discussed next.

Predicted Outcome Values

Consistent with the interdependence approach to relationships (Thibaut & Kelley, 1986), Sunnafrank's (1986, 1990) predicted outcome value theory posits that dyadic members' primary interactional goal is to maximize relational outcomes. According to Sunnafrank (1986, 1990), the extent to which individuals perceive that future exchanges with an interactional partner will be rewarding results in the formation of positive outcome values. When costs are associated with future interactions, negative outcome values are more likely. This parsimonious theory has substantial predictive power. For example, predicted outcome values have been positively related to amount of verbal communication, intimacy, nonverbal affiliation, liking, and similarity (Sunnafrank, 1988, 1990). Other scholars have found similar results. Strangers' predicted outcome values have been positively correlated with anticipated communication (Kennedy-Lightsey, Madlock, Horan, & Booth-Butterfield, 2008), and Houser, Horan, and Furler (2008) found that predicted outcomes were able to predict substantially speed daters' desire to go on a future date with someone with whom they had had a six-minute speed date. Consistent with predicted outcome value theory predictions, Houser et al. (2008) also found that predicted outcome values were positively correlated with interpersonal attraction, nonverbal immediacy, and homophily. Houser et al.'s (2008) results reveal that individuals who had made negative predicted outcome value judgments were significantly less likely to go on a future date than were individuals who made positive outcome value judgments.

Sunnafrank and Ramirez (2004) found that initial interactions between dyadic members firmly established their relational trajectory, and any subsequent interactions were unlikely to disturb this path. Specifically, dyadic members' predicted outcome values significantly predicted their partners' relational assessments, including amount of communication, long-term attraction, proximity, and relational development. This finding is consistent with other results assessing the importance of predicted outcome values. Peoples' relational forecasts have been associated with a variety of variables commitment and socialization (Madlock & Horan, 2009), instructor accessibility and mentoring abilities (Bippus, Kearney, Plax, & Brooks, 2003), amount of communication, information seeking, liking, and intimacy regarding a hypothetical gay/lesbian neighbor (Mottet, 2000), and the desire to live with a roommate (Marek, Wanzer, & Knapp, 2004).

Although predicted outcome value theory was formulated and has been applied in contexts in which interactants were strangers, it has recently been extended to predict communicative behavior in ongoing relationships. Ramirez, Sunnafrank, and Goei (2010) explored the impact of unexpected events that occurred within friendships and romantic relationships during an eight-week period. Their results revealed that predicted outcome values were positively correlated with liking, similarity, amount of communication, intimacy, and general information seeking. Furthermore, changes in predicted outcome values were positively associated with changes in these variables, except for intimacy.

The results of studies employing predicted outcome value theory provide compelling evidence that this theoretical perspective is useful for predicting a host of relational outcomes. Predicted outcome values seem particularly relevant for explaining the use of sexual humor in people's relationships. To the extent to which people perceive that their future sexual relationship with their partner will be beneficial, worthwhile, and positive will lead them to engage in sexual humor use. Specifically, it is hypothesized that predicted outcome values will be significantly and positively related to positive sexual humor use (H4) and expressive sexual humor use (H5), but significantly and negatively related to individuals' use of negative sexual humor (H6).

The arguments regarding idiomatic communication and predicted outcome values offered above reveal that two constructs are expected to predict an individual's use of sexual humor. Perceptions of interpersonal solidarity and predicted outcome values for one's future sexual relationship should contribute significantly to the prediction of sexual humor use, and the combination of both interpersonal solidarity and predicted outcome values should predict the use of sexual humor more than either construct alone. Thus, it is predicted that interpersonal solidarity and predicted outcome values will jointly and positively predict positive sexual humor use (H7) as well as expressive sexual humor use (H8). Interpersonal solidarity and predicted outcome values will jointly and negatively predict negative sexual humor use (H9). These predictions address the first goal of this chapter, which is to identify the correlates of sexual humor use in close relationships. The second goal of this chapter, the assessment of how sexual humor use is related to sexual communication satisfaction, must still be discussed. Thus, the extant literature investigating sexual communication satisfaction is presented next.

Sexual Communication Satisfaction

If, as was demonstrated above, the research on sexual communication and sexual humor use is scarce, then research examining sexual humor use and sexual communication satisfaction is practically nonexistent. This dearth of research is remarkable given the centrality of communication in sexual relationships. Although the importance of sexual communication in close relationships cannot be overstated (Cupach & Metts, 1991; Metts & Cupach, 1989; Metts & Spitzberg, 1996; Sprecher & Cate, 2004), the significance of being satisfied with the communication in one's intimate relationship is a more specific and desired relational state. Furthermore, how sexual humor use may contribute to dyadic members' sexual communication satisfaction is a worthwhile empirical question.

Wheeless, Wheeless, and Baus (1984) defined sexual communication satisfaction as "satisfaction with communication *about* sexual behavior with one's partner, and the satisfaction that sexual behavior itself communicates" (p. 221). They found that individuals who experienced sexual communication satisfaction did so as part of a highly developed relationship. Being satisfied with the sexual communication in one's relationship provides dyadic members with positive feelings toward the relationship as well as the sexual behavior that occurs within that relationship. For example, Cupach and Comstock (1990) found that married couples' sexual communication satisfaction was positively correlated with a host of positive relational attributes, such as sexual satisfaction, dyadic adjustment, dyadic consensus, affectional expressions, and dyadic satisfaction. Similarly, Brogan, Fiore, and Wrench (2010) found that sexual communication satisfaction was positively related to dyadic sexual communication and sexual satisfaction. Baus and Allen (1996) found that interpersonal solidarity combined with sexual communication satisfaction to predict relational satisfaction. The results from these studies demonstrate that sexual communication satisfaction positively contributed to dyadic members' relationships generally and to their sexual relationships specifically.

Byers and colleagues (Byers & Demmons, 1999; MacNeil & Byers, 2005) have examined the relationship between self-disclosure and sexual satisfaction in dating relationships. People's general predispositions to self-disclose and their specific sexual self-disclosures to their partners (i.e., what they liked/disliked to do sexually or what they liked/disliked about their partner's sexual behavior) were positively correlated with relationship satisfaction, sexual satisfaction, and sexual communication satisfaction (Byers & Demmons, 1999). Byers' work (Byers & Demmons, 1999; MacNeil & Byers, 2005) reveals that people's abilities to disclose their sexual likes and dislikes positively contributed to their relationship as well as to the sexual experiences they encountered within that relationship.

Extant work on sexual communication satisfaction reveals that experiencing a positive sexually communicative environment with one's relational partner was crucial for a host of relational outcomes. Consequently, dyadic members' happiness with the sexual exchanges within their relationships will be related to their desire to employ sexual humor. Therefore, it is predicted that sexual communication satisfaction will be positively related to positive sexual humor use (H10), expressive sexual humor use (H11), and negatively related to the use of negative sexual humor (H12).

METHOD

Participants

The sample consisted of 488 participants (42 percent men, 58 percent women). A majority of respondents identified themselves as Caucasian/White (82 percent), but individuals who identified as African-American/Black (11 percent), Hispanic (4 percent), Asian (2 percent), and other ethnicities (1 percent) also participated. The average research participant was 24 years old (SD = 7.87, $Mode$ = 21, Mdn = 22), single, and dating one person (52 percent), had been in two long-term relationships (M = 2.02, SD = 1.08), and had been in their current or most recent romantic relationship for approximately 2.5 years (M = 31.01 months, SD = 60.56 months, $Mode$ = 2 months, Mdn = 11.50 months). Participants reported having had several sexual partners (M = 7.63, SD = 7.50, $Mode$ = 1.00, Mdn = 5.00) and disclosed that, on average, they had sex with their current (or most recent) romantic partner about three times per week (M = 3.20, SD = 2.81). A majority of respondents were heterosexual (94 percent), although some participants self-identified as gay/lesbian (3 percent), bisexual (2 percent), and questioning (1 percent).

Instrumentation

As is recommended in the literature (Levine, 2005; Levine, Hullett, Turner, & Lapinski, 2006), all items measuring the main constructs were subjected to confirmatory factor analysis. Confirmatory factor analysis consists of internal consistency and parallelism tests (Hunter & Gerbing, 1982). These tests compare predicted errors with observed errors, which are generated using the product rule between inter-item correlations. Items were deleted from the measurement model if these analyses revealed large errors or if the inter-item correlations of alternate indicators were negative or approximated zero.1 Retained items were averaged to create each variable, and all items consisted of five-point Likert scales, where 1 indicated low levels of that construct and 5 indicated high levels of the construct.

Sexual humor use. All items assessing sexual humor use were prefaced with the following introductory clause: *During sexual interactions with my partner (or most recent partner).* Instructions preceding sexual humor use measures reminded participants that they were to respond to the statements considering their sexual interactions with their current or most recent romantic partner. Two types of sexual humor use were measured: overall attitudes toward sexual humor use and specific sexual humor use during sexual interactions.

First, an overall estimate of people's attitudes toward sexual humor use within their relationships was assessed using a scale specifically developed for this project. ***Attitudes about sexual humor use*** were measured using four items (e.g., Humor has been beneficial to our sexual relationship). Respondents reported that they held moderately favorable attitudes toward using sexual humor ($M = 3.49$, $SD = 0.83$, $\alpha = 0.80$).

Second, individuals' specific humor use during sexual interactions was measured using an adapted version of Graham et al.'s (1992) Functions of Humor in Conversations scale. This scale measures the use of positive humor, expressive humor, and negative humor. Participants responded to items considering their perceptions of their partner's sexual humor use and their own sexual humor use. ***Partner's positive sexual humor use*** was measured using two items (e.g., My partner is able to use humor to make light of an awkward sexual situation). Participants perceived that their partners engaged in positive sexual humor use ($M = 4.08$, $SD = 0.79$, $\alpha = 0.69$). ***Positive sexual humor use*** was also measured using two items (e.g., I am able to use humor to be playful). Respondents reported using positive sexual humor ($M = 3.98$, $SD = 0.79$, $\alpha = 0.82$). ***Partner's expressive sexual humor use*** was measured using four items (e.g., My partner is able to use humor to let me know his/her likes and dislikes). Respondents perceived that their partners used expressive sexual humor ($M = 3.70$, $SD = 0.82$, $\alpha = 0.83$). ***Expressive sexual humor*** use was also measured using four items (e.g., I am able to use humor to express my feelings). Participants reported using expressive sexual humor ($M = 3.60$, $SD = 0.82$, $\alpha = 0.84$). ***Partner's negative sexual humor*** use was assessed with three items (e.g., My partner is able to use humor to demean and belittle me). Participants perceived that their partner did not engage in negative sexual humor ($M = 1.85$, $SD = 0.96$, $\alpha = 0.91$). ***Negative sexual humor use*** was measured with three items (e.g., I am able to use humor to say negative things to my partner). Respondents did not generally engage in negative sexual humor ($M = 1.78$, $SD = 0.92$, $\alpha = 0.92$).

Interpersonal solidarity. Participants' perceptions of relational closeness or interpersonal solidarity were measured using nine items (e.g., We are very close to each other) from Wheeless' (1978) Interpersonal Solidarity Scale. Participants' interpersonal solidarity scores were high ($M = 4.02$, $SD = 0.69$, $\alpha = 0.88$).

Predicted outcome values. Predicted outcome values for participants' future sexual relationship with their partner were measured using four items (e.g., The future sexual relationship with my partner will be beneficial for me), which were adapted from Sunnafrank's (1988) predicted outcome value scale. Respondents were optimistic about their future sexual relationship ($M = 4.11$, $SD = 0.77$, $\alpha = 0.89$).

Sexual communication satisfaction. Perceptions of sexual communication satisfaction were measured using seven items from Wheeless et al.'s (1984) sexual communication satisfaction scale (e.g., I am pleased with the manner in which my partner and I communicate with each other after sex). Participants had moderately high levels of sexual communication satisfaction ($M = 3.88$, $SD = 0.70$, $\alpha = 0.86$).

Procedure

Data for this chapter were collected via survey. Undergraduate students enrolled in communication courses at a midsized Midwestern university earned credit for their own participation and for their friends' and family members' participation in this project. Participants were provided a link to the online questionnaire with instructions stating that they would be responding to items that referred to humor use in romantic relationships. They were also instructed that the online questionnaire contained items that addressed sexual humor use in those relationships. Participants responded to items that measured several relational constructs including the variables reported in this chapter, and they were also invited to leave open-ended comments regarding the use of sexual humor in their relationships. This project was approved by the university's Institutional Review Board.

RESULTS

Predicting Sexual Humor Use

Table 1 presents the correlations between study constructs. The first three hypotheses predicted that interpersonal solidarity would be positively related to positive sexual humor use (H1) and expressive sexual humor use (H2), but negatively related to negative sexual humor use (H3). The data were consistent with these predictions. Interpersonal solidarity was significantly and positively correlated with positive sexual humor use (respondents' sexual humor use and their perceptions of their partner's use of positive sexual humor) and expressive sexual humor use (respondents' own use and their perceptions of their partner's use). Individuals who experienced relational closeness reported engaging in sexual humor that demonstrated positive affect as well as expressed their beliefs and feelings about sexual encounters. As predicted, interpersonal solidarity was negatively correlated with negative sexual humor use for respondents as well as for respondents' perceptions of their partner's use of negative sexual humor (see Table 1). People who experienced relational intimacy refrained from using negative sexual humor, and they perceived that their relational partner also did not engage in negative sexual humor. Furthermore, the general measure of attitudes toward sexual humor use was also positively correlated with interpersonal solidarity.

Measure	1	2	3	4	5	6	7	8	9	10
1. SXHMR		0.55	0.59	0.57	0.60	0.04	0.03	0.20	0.27	0.24
2. PPH	0.41**		0.72	0.62	0.50	−0.15	−0.14	0.44	0.49	0.49
3. PH	0.48**	0.54**		0.52	0.75	−0.10	−0.08	0.39	0.34	0.33
4. PEH	0.46**	0.47**	0.43**		0.81	−0.01	−0.01	0.27	0.31	0.30
5. EH	0.49**	0.38**	0.63**	0.67**		0.05	0.07	0.27	0.23	0.19
6. PNH	0.03	−0.12*	−0.09	−0.01	0.04		0.76	−0.43	−0.34	−0.35
7. NH	0.03	−0.11*	−0.07	−0.01	0.06	0.69**		−0.38	−0.32	−0.34
8. IPSD	0.17**	0.34**	0.33**	0.23**	0.23**	−0.38**	−0.34**		0.66	0.62
9. POVS	0.23**	0.38**	0.29**	0.27**	0.20**	−0.31**	−0.29**	0.58**		0.75
10. SXCMSAT	0.20**	0.38**	0.28**	0.25**	0.16**	−0.31**	−0.30**	0.54**	0.65**	

Note: Correlations in the upper diagonal are corrected for attenuation due to error in measurement. SXHMR = attitudes toward sexual humor use; PPH = partner's positive sexual humor use; PH = positive sexual humor use; PEH = partner's expressive sexual humor use; EH = expressive sexual humor use; PNH = partner's negative sexual humor use; NH = negative sexual humor use; IPSD = interpersonal solidarity; POVS = predicted outcome values for the sexual relationship; SXCMSAT = sexual communication satisfaction.
$^*p < 0.05$
$^{**}p < 0.01$

It was also anticipated that predicted outcome values regarding one's sexual relationship would be positively correlated with positive sexual humor use (H4) and expressive sexual humor use (H5). The data were consistent with these hypotheses (see Table 1). Participants' predicted outcome values for their future sexual relationships were positively and significantly correlated with their own and their partner's use of positive sexual humor as well as their own and their partner's expressive sexual humor use. Predicted outcome values were also positively correlated with participants' overall attitudes toward sexual humor use. These data reveal that individuals who forecasted positive outcomes for their future sexual relationship felt comfortable using positive and expressive sexual humor and had partners who they perceived used positive and expressive sexual humor as well. Predicted outcome values for participants' future sexual relationship were expected to be negatively related to negative sexual humor use (H6). These data were also consistent with this hypothesis (see Table 1). Predicted outcome values were negatively correlated with respondents' use of negative sexual humor and their perceptions of their partner's negative sexual humor use. When participants anticipated that their future sexual relationship would be rewarding and satisfying, they tended not to engage in negative sexual humor use, and they thought their partner resisted from engaging in such negative sexual humor as well.

It was expected that interpersonal solidarity and predicted outcome values for participants' future sexual relationships would contribute to the prediction of participants' sexual humor use. Specifically, interpersonal solidarity and predicted outcome values were hypothesized to predict (positively) positive sexual humor use and expressive sexual humor use, and the combination of these variables would better predict positive sexual humor use (H7) and expressive sexual humor use (H8) than would either construct alone. The combination of interpersonal solidarity and predicted outcome values was also expected to predict (negatively) negative sexual humor use more so than either construct alone (H9). To test these hypotheses, a series of regression analyses were performed using the relevant type of sexual humor use as the criterion variable and interpersonal solidarity and predicted outcome values as the independent variables. The results of these analyses are presented in Table 2.

TABLE 2: REGRESSION ANALYSES FOR EACH TYPE OF SEXUAL HUMOR USE

Criterion	R	Predictors	B	95% CI	β	t	p
1. PPH	0.41	IPSD	0.21	[0.09, 0.34]	0.18	3.35	0.001
		POVS	0.28	[0.17, 0.39]	0.27	4.98	< 0.001
2. PH	0.35	IPSD	0.28	[0.15, 0.41]	0.24	4.30	< 0.001
		POVS	0.15	[0.04, 0.26]	0.15	2.59	0.01
3. PEH	0.29	IPSD	0.13	[−0.01, 0.26]	0.11	1.88	0.061
		POVS	0.22	[0.10, 0.34]	0.21	3.69	< 0.001
4. EH	0.25	IPSD	0.21	[0.07, 0.35]	0.17	3.00	0.003
		POVS	0.11	[−0.02, 0.23]	0.10	1.70	0.091
5. PNH	0.39	IPSD	−0.41	[−0.57, −0.26]	−0.30	−5.30	< 0.001
		POVS	−0.17	[−0.31, −0.04]	−0.14	−2.49	0.013
6. NH	0.35	IPSD	−0.34	[−0.49, −0.19]	−0.26	−4.53	< 0.001
		POVS	−0.16	[−0.29, −0.03]	−0.14	−2.40	0.017
7. SXHMR	0.23	IPSD	0.06	[−0.08, 0.20]	0.05	0.91	0.364
		POVS	0.21	[0.09, 0.33]	0.19	3.33	0.001

Note: PPH = partner's positive sexual humor use; PH = positive sexual humor use; PEH = partner's expressive sexual humor use; EH = expressive sexual humor use; PNH = partner's negative sexual humor use; NH = negative sexual humor use; IPSD = interpersonal solidarity; POVS = predicted outcome values for the sexual relationship; SXHMR = attitudes toward sexual humor use.

The results from the regression analyses reveal that these data were largely consistent with the predictions. Interpersonal solidarity and predicted outcome values significantly contributed to the prediction of positive sexual humor use (for respondents and their perceptions of their partner's use of positive sexual humor), and both constructs also predicted respondents' own negative sexual humor use and perceptions of their partner's negative sexual humor use, as well. Respondents' expressive sexual humor use was predicted by interpersonal solidarity; predicted outcome values for their future sexual relationships did not significantly contribute to this regression model.

Similarly, general attitudes toward sexual humor use were predicted entirely by respondents' predicted outcome values of their sexual relationships. Participants' perceptions of their partner's use of expressive sexual humor was predicted by predicted outcome values, but interpersonal solidarity did not significantly contribute to this regression model. Taken together, the results indicate that, overall, individuals use positive and expressive sexual humor within their close relationships (and avoid engaging in negative sexual humor) to the extent to which they feel relational intimacy and forecast positive outcomes for their future sexual relationship.

Predicting Sexual Communication Satisfaction

Sexual communication satisfaction was predicted to be positively related to positive sexual humor use (H10) and expressive sexual humor use (H11), but negatively related to negative sexual humor use (H12). The correlations in Table 1 reveal that the data were consistent with these predictions. Individuals who were happy and content with the sexual exchanges within their close relationships engaged in positive sexual humor use, expressive humor use, and refrained from engaging in negative sexual humor. They also perceived that their relational partners employed positive sexual humor and expressive sexual humor but avoided using negative sexual humor in their relationship. Furthermore, general attitudes toward sexual humor use were positively correlated with sexual communication satisfaction.

Additional Analyses

A series of one-sample t-tests were executed to determine the degree to which participants experienced sexual humor within their relationships. Using the scale midpoint (3) as the test value, these analyses revealed that participants' scores for positive sexual humor use, $t(446) = 26.11$, $p < 0.001$, expressive sexual humor use, $t(445) = 15.37$, $p < 0.001$, perceptions of their partner's use of expressive humor, $t(452) = 18.19$, $p < 0.001$, general attitudes toward sexual humor use, $t(446) = 12.58$, $p < 0.001$, sexual communication satisfaction levels, $t(445) = 26.79$, $p < 0.001$, and interpersonal solidarity, $t(467) = 32.22$, $p < 0.001$ were significantly above the scale midpoint. Respondents' use of negative sexual humor, $t(436) = -27.76$, $p < 0.001$, and their perceptions of their partner's negative sexual humor use, $t(438) = -25.14$, $p < 0.001$ fell significantly below the scale midpoint. Using 4 as the test value demonstrated that participants' predicted outcome values for their future sexual relationship, $t(426) = 3.06$, $p = 0.002$, and perceptions of their partner's use of positive humor, $t(454) = 2.06$, $p = 0.04$, were significantly above this scale value.

Paired samples t-tests were conducted on the positive, expressive, and negative sexual humor use measures to determine if participants' self-reported sexual humor use differed significantly from the sexual humor they perceived their partners used. Results demonstrated that respondents perceived that their partners used more positive sexual humor, $t(446) = 2.66$, $p < 0.001$, and expressive sexual humor, $t(444) = 3.12$, $p < 0.001$, than respondents used. There were no differences in perceptions of the use of negative sexual humor, $t(431) = 1.68$, $p = 0.094$.

Independent samples t-tests were performed to determine whether there were any sex differences regarding the constructs measured. Men and women did not differ with respect to general attitudes toward sexual humor use, $t(425) = 0.934$, $p = 0.351$ ($M_{women} = 3.45$, $SD = 0.83$, $M_{men} = 3.52$, $SD = 0.85$), positive sexual humor use, $t(363) = -1.96$, $p = 0.052$ ($M_{women} = 4.03$, $SD = 0.74$, $M_{men} = 3.88$, $SD = 0.82$), expressive sexual humor use, $t(421) = -1.02$, $p = 0.309$

(M_{women} = 3.63, SD = 0.78, M_{men} = 3.54, SD = 0.88), or respondents' perceptions of their partner's use of expressive sexual humor, $t(349)$ = −1.02, p = 0.296 (M_{women} = 3.73, SD = 0.76, M_{men} = 3.65, SD = 0.89). Men and women also did not differ significantly in the frequency with which they had sex, $t(311)$ = 1.77, p = 0.078 (M_{women} = 2.97 times per week, SD = 2.32, M_{men} = 3.48 times per week, SD = 3.32).

There were sex differences on the remaining variables. Women, more than men, thought their partners used positive sexual humor, $t(325)$ = −3.12, p = 0.002 (M_{women} = 4.17, SD = 0.70, M_{men} = 3.91, SD = 0.91), had higher levels of sexual communication satisfaction, $t(434)$ = −2.51, p = 0.012 (M_{women} = 3.95, SD = 0.69, M_{men} = 3.78, SD = 0.73), had higher levels of predicted outcome values for their future sexual relationship, $t(420)$ = −2.46, p = 0.014 (M_{women} = 4.19, SD = 0.75, M_{men} = 4.01, SD = 0.79), and experienced higher degrees of interpersonal solidarity, $t(438)$ = −2.60, p = 0.01 (M_{women} = 4.10, SD = 0.69, M_{men} = 3.93, SD = 0.68). Men, more than women, thought they used negative sexual humor, $t(325)$ = 4.35, p < 0.001 (M_{women} = 1.60, SD = 0.79, M_{men} = 2.00, SD = 1.01), perceived that their partners used negative sexual humor, $t(414)$ = 3.37, p = 0.001 (M_{women} = 1.71, SD = 0.88, M_{men} = 2.03, SD = 1.05), and had more sexual partners, $t(306)$ = 5.16, p < 0.001 (M_{women} = 6.00, SD = 5.95, M_{men} = 9.83, SD = 8.76).[2]

Inspection of the correlation matrix revealed the strong relationships between sexual communication satisfaction and interpersonal solidarity, and between sexual communication satisfaction and predicted outcome values for participants' future sexual relationships. Thus, a hierarchical regression analysis was performed using sexual communication satisfaction as the criterion variable. The six specific types of sexual humor use (respondents' use and their perceptions of their partner's use of positive sexual humor, expressive sexual humor, and negative sexual humor) were entered into the equation as the first block of predictors, and interpersonal solidarity and predicted outcome values were entered into the regression equation as the second block of predictors. The results of this analysis appear in Table 3. The addition of interpersonal solidarity and predicted outcome values significantly contributed to the prediction of sexual communication satisfaction. Indeed, after these relational variables were entered into the regression equation only respondents' perceptions of their partner's positive sexual humor use continued to contribute to sexual communication satisfaction scores. These results reveal that individuals were satisfied with the sexual communication in their relationships because they felt close with their partners, were able to make positive forecasts about their future sexual relationship, and perceived that their partners used positive sexual humor. The use of other types of sexual humor contributed to dyadic members' perceptions of sexual communication satisfaction through their influence on interpersonal solidarity and predicted outcome values for participants' future sexual relationship.

TABLE 3: REGRESSING SEXUAL COMMUNICATION SATISFACTION ON TYPES OF SEXUAL HUMOR USE, INTERPERSONAL SOLIDARITY, AND PREDICTED OUTCOME VALUES FOR SEXUAL RELATIONSHIPS

Criterion	R	R^2_{change}	Predictors	B	95% CI	β	t	p
1. SXCMSAT	0.49	0.24	PPH	0.22	[0.12, 0.31]	0.25	4.48	< 0.001
			PH	0.11	[−0.01, 0.21]	0.12	1.92	0.056
			PEH	0.12	[0.01, 0.22]	0.14	2.24	0.026
			EH	−0.07	[−0.19, 0.04]	−0.09	−1.25	0.213
			PNH	−0.12	[−0.21, −0.04]	−0.17	−2.81	0.005
			NH	−0.11	[−0.20, −0.02]	−0.14	−2.40	0.017
2. SXCMSAT	0.70	0.25	PPH	0.09	[0.01, 0.17]	0.10	2.22	0.027
			PH	0.04	[−0.05, 0.13]	0.05	0.95	0.344
			PEH	0.06	[−0.03, 0.15]	0.07	1.34	0.182
			EH	−0.07	[−0.17, 0.02]	−0.09	−1.52	0.130
			PNH	−0.02	[−0.10, 0.05]	−0.03	−0.65	0.515
			NH	−0.05	[−0.12, 0.03]	−0.06	−1.26	0.207
			IPSD	0.20	[0.11, 0.29]	0.20	4.26	< 0.001
			POVS	0.41	[0.33, 0.49]	0.46	10.02	< 0.001

Note: PPH = partner's positive sexual humor use; PH = positive sexual humor use; PEH = partner's expressive sexual humor use; EH = expressive sexual humor use; PNH = partner's negative sexual humor use; NH = negative sexual humor use; IPSD = interpersonal solidarity; POVS = predicted outcome values for the sexual relationship; SXCMSAT = sexual communication satisfaction.
$p < 0.01$

DISCUSSION

The importance of this chapter emanates from its accomplishment of two main goals. First, it contributes to a growing corpus of research investigating sexual communication in close relationships (Byers & Demmons, 1999; Cupach & Metts, 1991; La France, 2010a, 2010b; MacNeil & Byers, 2005; Metts & Cupach, 1989; Metts & Spitzberg, 1996; Sprecher & Cate, 2004; Wheeless et al., 1984) by identifying the correlates of sexual humor. Second, and perhaps more important, it is also one of the first empirical investigations that assessed the relationship between sexual humor use and sexual communication satisfaction. These findings provide crucial insights into how people experience sexual humor within their close relationships.

Sexual Humor Use

People actively engaged in constructive (i.e., positive and expressive sexual humor) sexual humor. They employed positive sexual humor as a form of play and to reduce the awkwardness that can occur during sexual interactions. In fact, this function of sexual humor received the highest ratings. The sexual episode is ripe with potential sources of anxiety. A position that did not work as planned, embarrassing bodily noises, unscripted verbal or nonverbal reactions to a partner, and unexpected collisions of body parts are examples of commonplace sexual experiences that can cause relational partners to become suddenly uneasy about a typically positive sexual encounter with their partner. The use of positive sexual humor allows for the negotiation of these challenges. Humor as a mechanism for reducing anxiety has been demonstrated elsewhere (Bippus, 2000; Ziv, 1988), and humor's general positive influence on close relationships has also been well established (Gottman et al., 1998; Lauer et al., 1990; Ziv & Gadish, 1989).

Sexual humor also functioned to allow for the revelation of people's sexual preferences, feelings, and attitudes. Participants reported that they used expressive sexual humor for this purpose—to engage in sexual self-disclosure to communicate their sexual desires to their partner as well as to come to know their partner's sexual desires. The use of expressive sexual humor reflects Altman and Taylor's (1973) recognition of the importance of self-disclosure in creating relational intimacy, and sexual self-disclosure substantially contributes to relational satisfaction and sexual satisfaction through its ability to increase relational partners' knowledge about each other's sexual needs (Byers & Demmons, 1999; La France, 2010a; MacNeil & Byers, 2005).

It is fortunate that participants did not report engaging in destructive or negative sexual humor because these data demonstrated that individuals who did use negative sexual humor likely experienced relational distance and expected unrewarding outcomes for their future sexual relationship. The use of negative sexual humor—humor that belittles one's partner or conveys unhelpful attitudes or feelings—is communication that detracts from the sexual episode. The sexual episode is replete with verbal and nonverbal cues that *may* lead to sex because some cues are less likely than other cues to achieve this goal (La France, 2010b). Communication exchanges that include negative sexual humor are unlikely to be used by satisfied relational partners who desire to engage in sex because those messages are hostile with respect to achieving that goal. Participants also perceived that their partners did not use negative sexual humor. Partners' perceived similarity regarding the frequency and importance of negative sexual humor use is important for predicting relational satisfaction (Hall & Sereno, 2010).

As predicted, two relational constructs independently and jointly contributed to participants' use of sexual humor within their close relationships. Feelings of interpersonal solidarity positively predicted all but two types of sexual humor use. Participants who reported feeling psychologically connected with their relational partners also reported engaging in positive sexual humor use and expressive sexual humor use, and resisted using negative sexual humor. These people also perceived that their partners used positive sexual humor and avoided using negative sexual humor. Private, sexual idioms provide couples with language that is idiosyncratic to their relationship. It functions to establish the couple as a couple, and the use of that language serves to increase perceptions of closeness and specialness. Idiomatic communication provides couples with a way to symbolize the intimacy they feel (Baxter, 1992; Bell et al., 1987; Bell & Healey, 1992; Hopper et al., 1981), and sexual humor represents an entirely idiosyncratic type of humorous language created and developed by relational partners.

The second relational construct—predicted outcome values for individuals' future sexual relationship—also significantly contributed to all but one type of sexual humor use. People who anticipated that their future sexual relationship would be rewarding, satisfying, and beneficial held generally positive attitudes toward the use of sexual humor, employed positive sexual humor, perceived that their partner engaged in positive sexual humor, and perceived that their partner engaged in expressive sexual humor. They tended not to use negative sexual humor and perceived that their partners also refrained from using negative sexual humor. The overall pattern in the data presented in this chapter revealed that interpersonal solidarity and predicted outcome values for future sexual relationship jointly predicted sexual humor use.

Sexual Communication Satisfaction

Given the importance of sexual communication satisfaction in close relationships (Baus & Allen, 1996; Brogan et al., 2010; Wheeless et al., 1984), it was instrumental to examine how sexual humor was related to sexual communication satisfaction. Results from the regression analyses demonstrated that respondents' perceptions of their partner's use of positive sexual humor, expressive sexual humor, and negative sexual humor as well as their own use of negative sexual humor contributed to the prediction of sexual communication satisfaction. Post hoc analyses revealed that perceptions of interpersonal solidarity and especially predicted outcome values for people's future sexual relationship also significantly predicted sexual communication satisfaction. Indeed, when these relational constructs were added into the regression model, participants' perceptions of their partner's positive sexual humor use were the sole direct predictors of sexual communication satisfaction. This finding supports a notable trend in research on humor in relationships; individuals' perceptions of their partners' humor use are more predictive of positive relational outcomes than individuals' self-reports of their own use of humor (Rust & Goldstein, 1989; Ziv & Gadish, 1989). Other types of sexual humor were related to interpersonal solidarity and predicted outcome values, and it is through this influence that sexual humor indirectly impacted sexual communication satisfaction.

CONCLUSION

The data presented in this chapter reveal that intimate couples engaged in sexual humor use. The use of constructive humor (i.e., positive sexual humor and expressive sexual humor) and the avoidance of destructive humor (i.e., negative sexual humor) resulted in greater levels of sexual communication satisfaction. These effects were both direct and indirect through the impact sexual humor use had on perceptions of interpersonal solidarity and predictions made about one's future sexual relationship.

Notes

1. Parallelism tests revealed that the errors generated for the items measuring positive sexual humor use and expressive sexual humor use (for respondents and for respondents' perceptions of their partner's sexual humor use) were larger than what would be expected given sampling error. This result was obtained because these types of humor use are consistent with a second-order unidimensional measurement model (Hunter & Gerbing, 1982). They were, however, retained in the measurement model for conceptual clarity and to test the hypotheses.

2. Given the observed sex differences for the types of sexual humor, interpersonal solidarity, and predicted outcome values for the future sexual relationship variables, the regression analyses testing the hypotheses were also performed entering sex into the regression equation. Entering sex into the regression equation functioned to change the size of the unstandardized regression coefficients such that the relative importance of one of the predictors (e.g., interpersonal solidarity) switched in favor of the second predictor (e.g., predicted outcome values). The resultant unstandardized regression coefficients, however, were not significantly different from each other. This conclusion is accurate except in one case: After controlling for the impact of sex, predicted outcome values for people's future sexual relationship significantly contributed to the prediction of general attitudes toward sexual humor use, $R = 0.23$, $\beta = 0.20$, B = 0.22, 95% CI [0.09, 0.34]. Interpersonal solidarity no longer impacted attitudes toward sexual humor use, $\beta = 0.06$, B = 0.07, 95% CI [−0.07, 0.21]. Sex did not contribute directly to the prediction of attitudes toward sexual humor, $R = 0.24$, $F_{change}(1, 416)$, $p = 0.113$, $\beta = −0.08$, B = −0.13, 95% CI [−0.29, 0.03]. Thus, the results from the regression analyses including sex as a predictor demonstrated that the reported sex differences do not change the overall conclusions reached after testing the hypotheses.

References

Alberts, J. K., Yoshimura, C. G., Rabby, M., & Loschiavo, R. (2005). Mapping the topography of couples' daily conversation. *Journal of Social and Personal Relationships, 22*, 299–322. doi:10.1177/0265407505050941

Altman, I., & Taylor, D. A. (1973). *Social penetration*. New York: Holt, Rinehart & Winston.

Baus, R. D., & Allen, J. L. (1996). Solidarity and sexual communication as selective filters: A report on intimate relationship development. *Communication Research Reports, 13*, 1–7.

Baxter, L. A. (1987). Symbols of relationship identity in relational cultures. *Journal of Social and Personal Relationships, 4*, 261–280. doi:10.1177/026540758700400302

Baxter, L. A. (1992). Forms and functions of intimate play in personal relationships. *Human Communication Research, 18*, 336–363. doi:10.1111/j.1468-2958.1992.tb00556.x

Bell, R. A., Buerkel-Rothfuss, N. L., & Gore, K. E. (1987). 'Did you bring the yarmulke for the Cabbage Patch Kid?': The idiomatic communication of young lovers. *Human Communication Research, 14*, 47–67. doi:10.1111/j.1468-2958.1987.tb00121.x

Bell, R. A., & Healey, J. G. (1992). Idiomatic communication and interpersonal solidarity in friends' relational cultures. *Human Communication Research, 18*, 307–335. doi:10.1111/j.1468-2958.1992.tb00555.x

Bippus, A. M. (2000). Making sense of humor in young romantic relationships: Understanding partners' perceptions. *Humor, 13*, 395–417. doi:0933-1719/00/0013-0395

Bippus, A. M. (2003). Humor motives, qualities, and reactions in recalled conflict episodes. *Western Journal of Communication, 67*, 413–426.

Bippus, A. M., Kearney, P., Plax, T. G., & Brooks, C. F. (2003). Teacher access and mentoring abilities: Predicting the outcome value of extra class communication. *Journal of Applied Communication Research, 31*, 260–275. doi:10.1080/0090988032000103476

Brogan, S. M., Fiore, A., & Wrench, J. S. (2010). Understanding the psychometric properties of the Sexual Communication Style scale. *Human Communication, 12,* 421–445.

Byers, E. S., & Demmons, S. (1999). Sexual satisfaction and sexual self-disclosure within dating relationships. *Journal of Sex Research, 36,* 180–189. doi:10.1080/00224499909551983

Cupach, W. R., & Comstock, J. (1990). Satisfaction with sexual communication in marriage: Links to sexual satisfaction and dyadic adjustment. *Journal of Social and Personal Relationships, 7,* 179–186. doi:10.1177/0265407590072002

Cupach, W. R., & Metts, S. (1991). Sexuality and communication in close relationships. In K. McKinney & S. Sprecher (Eds.), *Sexuality in close relationships* (pp. 93–110). Hillsdale, NJ: Erlbaum.

De Koning, E., & Weiss, R. L. (2002). The relational humor inventory: Functions of humor in close relationships. *American Journal of Family Therapy, 30,* 1–18. doi:10.1080/019261802753455615

Gottman, J. M., Coan, J., Carrere, S., & Swanson, C. (1998). Predicting marital happiness and stability from newlywed interactions. *Journal of Marriage and the Family, 60,* 5–22. doi:10.2307/353438

Graham, E. E., Papa, M. J., & Brooks, G. P. (1992). Functions of humor in conversation: Conceptualization and measurement. *Western Journal of Communication, 56,* 161–183.

Haas, S. M., & Stafford, L. (2005). Maintenance behaviors in same-sex and marital relationships: A matched sample comparison. *The Journal of Family Communication, 5,* 43–60. doi:10.1207/s15327698jfc0501_3

Hall, J. A. (2010). Is it something I said?: Sense of humor and partner embarrassment. *Journal of Social and Personal Relationships, 28,* 1–23. doi:10.1177/0265407510384422

Hall, J. A., & Sereno, K. (2010). Offensive jokes: How do they impact long-term relationships? *Humor, 23,* 351–373. doi:10.1515/HUMR.2010.016

Hay, J. (2000). Functions of humor in the conversations of men and women. *Journal of Pragmatics, 32,* 709–742. doi:10.1016/S0378-2166(99)00069-7

Hopper, R., Knapp, M. L., & Scott, L. (1981). Couples' personal idioms: Exploring intimate talk. *Journal of Communication, 31,* 23–33. doi:10.1111/j.1460-2466.1981.tb01201.x

Houser, M. L., Horan, S. M., & Furler, L. A. (2008). Dating in the fast lane: How communication predicts speed-dating success. *Journal of Social and Personal Relationships, 25,* 749–768. doi:10.1177/0265407508093787

Hunter, J. E., & Gerbing, D. (1982). Unidimensional measurement, second order factor analysis, and causal models. *Research in Organizational Behavior, 4,* 267–320.

Kennedy-Lightsey, C., Madlock, P., Horan, S. M., & Booth-Butterfield, M. (2008). Predicting future interactions: Predicted outcome value judgments, attraction, homophily, and immediacy. *Paper presented at the National Communication Association Annual Convention,* San Diego.

La France, B. H. (2010a). Predicting sexual satisfaction in interpersonal relationships. *Southern Communication Journal, 75,* 195–214. doi:10.1080/10417940902787939

La France, B. H. (2010b). What verbal and nonverbal communication cues lead to sex?: An analysis of the traditional sexual script. *Communication Quarterly, 58*, 297–318. doi:10.1080/01463373.2010.503161

Lauer, R. H., Lauer, J. C., & Kerr, S. T. (1990). The long-term marriage: Perceptions of stability and satisfaction. *International Journal of Aging and Human Development, 31*, 189–195.

Levine, T. R. (2005). Confirmatory factor analysis and scale validation in communication research. *Communication Research Reports, 22*, 335–338. doi:10.1080/00036810500317730

Levine, T. R., Hullett, C. R., Turner, M. M., & Lapinski, M. K. (2006). The desirability of using confirmatory factor analysis on published scales. *Communication Research Reports, 23*, 309–314. doi:10.1080/08824090600962698

MacNeil, S., & Byers, E. S. (2005). Dyadic assessment of sexual self-disclosure and sexual satisfaction in heterosexual dating couples. *Journal of Social and Personal Relationships, 22*, 169–181. doi:10.1177/0265407505050942

Madlock, P. E., & Horan, S. M. (2009). Predicted outcome value of organizational commitment. *Communication Research Reports, 26*, 40–49. doi:10.1080/08824090802637023

Marek, C. I., Wanzer, M. B., & Knapp, J. L. (2004). An exploratory investigation of the relationship between roommates' first impressions and subsequent communication patterns. *Communication Research Reports, 21*, 210–220.

Martin, R. A., Puhlik-Doris, P., Larsen, G., Gray, J., & Weir, K. (2003). Individual differences in uses of humor and their relation to psychological well-being: Development of the Humor Styles Questionnaire. *Journal of Research in Personality, 37*, 48–75. doi:10.1016/S0092-6566(02)00534-2

Metts, S., & Cupach, W. R. (1989). The role of communication in human sexuality. In K. McKinney & S. Sprecher (Eds.), *Human sexuality: The societal and interpersonal context* (pp. 139–161). Norwood, NJ: Ablex Publishing Corporation.

Metts, S., & Spitzberg, B. H. (1996). Sexual communication in interpersonal contexts: A script-based approach. In B. R. Burleson (Ed.), *Communication Yearbook 19* (pp. 49–91). Thousand Oaks, CA: SAGE.

Meyer, J. C. (2000). Humor as a double-edged sword: Four functions of humor in communication. *Communication Theory, 10*, 310–331. doi:10.1111/j.1468-2885.2000.tb00194.x

Mottet, T. P. (2000). The role of sexual orientation in predicting outcome value and anticipated communication behaviors. *Communication Quarterly, 48*, 223–239. doi:10.1080/01463370009385594

Murstein, B. I., & Brust, R. G. (1985). *Humor and interpersonal attraction. Journal of Personality Assessment, 49*, 637–640. doi:10.1207/s15327752jpa4906_12

Oring, E. (1984). Dyadic traditions. *Journal of Folklore Research, 21*, 19–28.

Priest, R. F., & Thein, M. T. (2003). Humor appreciation in marriage: Spousal similarity, assortative mating, and disaffection. *Humor, 16*, 63–78. doi:10.1515/humr.2003.005

Ramirez, A., Jr., Sunnafrank, M., & Goei, R. (2010). Predicted outcome value theory in ongoing relationships. *Communication Monographs, 77*, 27–50. doi:10.1080/03637750903514276

Rust, J., & Goldstein, J. (1989). Humor in marital adjustment. *Humor, 2*, 217–224.

Sprecher, S., & Cate, R. M. (2004). Sexual satisfaction and sexual expression as predictors of relationship satisfaction and stability. In J. H. Harvey, A. Wenzel, & S. Sprecher (Eds.), *The handbook of sexuality in close relationships* (pp. 235–256). Mahwah, NJ: Lawrence Erlbaum.

Sunnafrank, M. (1986). Predicted outcome value during initial interactions: A reformulation of uncertainty reduction theory. *Human Communication Research, 13*, 3–33. doi:10.1111/j.1468-2958.1986.tb00092.x

Sunnafrank, M. (1988). Predicted outcome value in initial conversations. *Communication Research Reports, 5*, 169–172. doi:10.1080/08824098809359819

Sunnafrank, M. (1990). Predicted outcome value and uncertainty reduction theories: A test of competing perspectives. *Human Communication Research, 17*, 76–103. doi:10.1111/j.1468-2958.1990.tb00227.x

Sunnafrank, M., & Ramirez, A., Jr. (2004). At first sight: Persistent relational effects of get-acquainted conversations. *Journal of Social and Personal Relationships, 21*, 361–379. doi:10.1177/0265407504042837

Thibaut, J. W., & Kelley, H. H. (1986). *The social psychology of groups.* New Brunswick, NJ: Transaction Books.

Wanzer, M. B., Booth-Butterfield, M., & Booth-Butterfield, S. (1996). Are funny people popular? An examination of humor orientation, loneliness, and social attraction. *Communication Quarterly, 44*, 42–52. doi:10.1080/01463379609369999

Wheeless, L. R. (1976). Self-disclosure and interpersonal solidarity: Measurement, validation, and relationships. *Human Communication Research, 3*, 47–61. doi:10.1111/j.1468-2958.1976.tb00503.x

Wheeless, L. R. (1978). A follow-up study of the relationships among trust, disclosure, and interpersonal solidarity. *Human Communication Research, 4*, 143–157. doi:10.1111/j.1468-2958.1978.tb00604.x

Wheeless, L. R., Wheeless, V. E., & Baus, R. (1984). Sexual communication, communication satisfaction, and solidarity in the developmental stages of intimate relationships. *The Western Journal of Speech Communication, 48*, 217–230.

Wildermuth, S. M., Vogl-Bauer, S., & Rivera, J. (2006). Practically perfect in every way: Communication strategies of ideal relational partners. *Communication Studies, 57*, 239–257. doi:10.1080/10510970600845891

Young, S. L., & Bippus, A. M. (2001). Does it make a difference if they hurt you in a funny way?: Humorously and non-humorously phrased hurtful messages in personal relationships. *Communication Quarterly, 49*, 35–52. doi:10.1080/01463370109385613

Ziv, A. (1988). Humor's role in married life. *Humor, 1*, 223–230. doi:10.1515/humr.1988.1.3.223

Ziv, A., & Gadish, O. (1989). Humor and marital satisfaction. *The Journal of Social Psychology, 129*, 759–768. doi:10.1080/00224545.1989.9712084

Ziv, A., & Gadish, O. (1990). The disinhibiting effects of humor: Aggressive and affective responses. *Humor, 3*, 247–257. doi:10.1515/humr.1990.3.3.247

CHAPTER 9

CHILDREN'S HUMOR: FOUNDATIONS OF LAUGHTER ACROSS THE LIFESPAN

Thomas J. Socha
Old Dominion University

Across the human lifespan, silly faces, funny noises, jokes, and other forms of humorous communication considered to be playful (Bateson, 1972) occur along with many forms of communication considered to be serious. Like its serious counterpart, humorous communication can affect many aspects of daily life: adults' health and wellness (Cousins, 1979), the quality of adults' relationships (Bippus, 2000, 2003; Young & Bippus, 2001), how college students learn (Bekelja Wanzer & Frymier Bainbridge, 1999; Bekelja Wanzer, Bainbridge Frymier, Wojtaszczyk, & Smith, 2006), and even how adults learn about politics from late-night TV comedy shows (Baek & Wojcieszak, 2009). In contrast to childhood, everyday adult life seems to be dominated by episodes of serious communication punctuated by moments of play and laughter as when viewing TV comedies, enjoying standup comedy acts, attending social gatherings to interact with friends who make us laugh, and more.

Humor, as a form of play, can also be considered positive communication (Socha & Pitts, 2012) because it prompts laughter, positive emotional states, and can serve numerous prosocial functions that can unite communicators (e. g., see Meyer, 2000). However, like all communication processes (serious and playful), humor also has a dark side when used as an instrument of intimidation and harm (Mills & Carwile, 2009; and see Socha & Kelly, 1994).

Given humorous communication's ubiquity and acknowledged importance as this volume attests, we would expect to find numerous research studies of humorous communication across the lifespan (childhood, adolescence, and adulthood) as well as considerable space devoted to humor in the communication field's college textbooks and classes. Unfortunately, this is far from the case.

Most communication instructors and students, for example, can recall the mention of humor in public speaking textbooks (as best approached with caution and practice, see Gruner, 1985) and the topic of comedy routinely appears in television and film textbooks and classes (e.g., Auter, 1990; Reincheld, 2006). However, it is difficult to recall the mention of humor in family, group, or interpersonal communication textbooks and classes. Why is this?

Somewhat akin to family communication textbooks and classes that overlook (or underrepresent) root topics like "love" (and its dark-side counterpart "hate"), most family, group, and relational communication textbooks and classes have forgotten that among our many serious communication moments in families, groups, and relationships are equally significant humorous moments of smiling and laughing. Further, since the field of communication focuses almost exclusively on adults' communication, it is also not surprising that children's communication, humorous or otherwise, with the exceptions of the work reviewed in this chapter, has also received little attention (see Socha & Yingling, 2010, for a recent overview of children's communication development).

The purpose of this chapter is twofold. First, to begin to connect the dots of humorous communication development across the lifespan, the chapter reviews what is known about humorous communication's development from its early roots in adult-infant play, through humorous message production and interpretation in childhood, up to the threshold of adult humor. And, second, echoing a much earlier call for a lifespan approach to the study of humor (McGhee, 1983), the chapter identifies some of the unanswered questions concerning children's humor and outlines the merits of a lifespan framing to study humorous communication as not only a conceptually useful way to organize humorous communication theory building and research, but also as an important means to spotlight humor's important place alongside our many serious human communication processes.

The chapter regards humorous communication as a form of communication play (Bateson, 1972; Socha & Kelly, 1994) and considers humor's many functions, forms, benefits, and pitfalls inside the communication worlds of children.

HUMOR IN INFANCY

It does not seem to have occurred to communication scholars that "humorous communication" can take place during infancy. In fact, this review is not aware of any studies published in the communication field's journals that specifically examine humorous communication during infancy. Why is this?

Conceptually, communication scholars' lack of attention to humor in infancy makes sense, if we limit our understanding of "humorous communication" to "linguistic humor" (that begins when language emerges at age 9–12 months). However, if humorous communication is conceived to encompass all forms of communication (verbal and nonverbal) that prompt "mirth-responses" (e.g., cackles, chortles, chuckles, giggles, guffaws, hoots, laughs, smiles, sniggers, snorts, titters, and so on), then conceptually, we must place the starting point of humorous communication development in infancy, and regard infants' mirth responses (smiles, laughter, etc.) during episodes of adult-infant play as our first "humorous messages," and first "humorous communication episodes," respectively. Even those who might counter-argue that adult-infant "tickle-giggle" episodes, for example, should not be classified as "humorous communication" would likely concede that (a) adult-infant play episodes prompting infants' smiling and laugh-like responses at least serve as primitive precursors of humorous communication's later development, (b) such episodes are important to study in their own right, and (c) make an interesting and conceptually rich place to begin a review of children's humorous communication development.

Smiling, Laughing, and Playing with Infants

Infants' smiles appear as early as age two months (Dickson, Walker, & Fogel, 1997). Infants smile while gazing at caregivers, when being tickled, and during mock rough-housing games (Dickson et al., 1997). Like adults, infants' smiles vary by: (a) type (e. g., Duchene smiles involve eye constriction, and non-Duchene, or duplay smiles—thought to indicate "genuine laugher"—add an open mouth, Messinger, Cassel, Acosta, Ambador, & Cohn, 2008), (b) intensity (from weak to strong, see Bolzani-Dinehart et al., 2005), and (c) duration. The type, intensity, duration, and patterns of infants' smiles can be reliably measured using sophisticated digital computer technologies (see Messinger et al., 2008).

During episodes of adult-infant play, adults attribute positive emotional experiences to smiling infants (Fogel, Nelson-Goens, Hsu, & Shapiro, 2000) and infants' smiles elicit smiles and positive verbal and nonverbal messages from adult caregivers (Messinger et al., 2008). Albeit primitive in form, and limited by infants' sound producing capacities, it is clear that episodes of adult-infant play eliciting infants' and adults' smiling and laugh-like-responses (e.g., see Kipper & Todt, 2003) contain what most humor scholars regard as typical, central defining elements of humorous episodes: a mirth-response to a stimulus that could include laughter itself (Provine, 1992).

Thus, if we regard adult-infant play episodes as a first and primary context where the foundations of humorous communication's development take root, what can studies of infants smiling/laughing during adult-infant play tell us about children's later social, emotional, and humorous communication development? Are there consistencies in mirth displays of infants and children?

Moore, Cohen, and Campbell (2001) exposed infants (age six months) to still-faced interaction with their mothers and later (at age 18 months) measured children's social development. Still-faced interaction is a commonly used procedure designed to elicit infants' emotional reactions. In the procedure, mothers convey a neutral expression (still face) to their infants for three minutes while researchers record infants' facial expressions. Moore et al. found that "infants who did not smile at all in the still-face interaction at [age] 6 months, compared with those who did, were rated by their mothers at [age]18 months as showing more externalizing behaviors, including opposition and aggression" (p. 711). In addition, Moore et al. investigated the role that displays of mothers' depressive symptoms had on infants' later social development. They found that "current maternal depression and infants' earlier affective responses to the still-face interaction made independent but comparable contributions to the prediction of mothers' ratings of internalizing and externalizing behaviors at [age] 18 months" (p. 713). Although the study's design was cross-sectional and correlational, its evidence suggests that infants' exposure to and reciprocation of adult's smiling (or lack of it) is likely to shape children's later mirth displays as well as potentially affect their emotional development.

Additional evidence that supports connections between infant' smiling and laughing and children's smiling/laughing and emotional development comes in a study of the continuity of infants' temperaments they move into early childhood (Komsi et al., 2006). Komsi et al. used Rothbart's theory of temperament (Rothbart & Bates, 1998) that defines temperament as "constitutionally based individual differences in reactivity and self-regulation … [where] infant temperament refers to early differences in motor activity (*activity level*), smile-proneness (*smiling and laughter*), soothability, attention span (*duration of orienting*), anger-proneness (*distress to limitations*), and fearful distress (*fear*)" (emphasis included, pp. 494–495). Komsi et al. studied 231 Finnish mother-infant pairs at an infants' average age of six months and later at the child's average age of 5.5 years. Relying on mothers' ratings of their infants, Komsi et al. found "*[s]miling and laughter* in infancy was associated significantly with smiling and laughter in middle childhood … [as well as] high levels of middle childhood approach/anticipation, soothability, low intensity pleasure, and perceptual sensitivity" (emphasis included, p. 500). Although Komsi et al. also used a cross-sectional and correlational study design, their data offer further evidence that displays of smiling and laughing (key aspects of humorous communication) are driven in part by biological underpinnings present in infancy that carry into childhood (and likely beyond).

The recent evidence of biology's role in infants' early mirth responses (to tickling, surprise silly face displays, and so on) is compelling, but we do not yet fully understand the later course of development of infants' early mirth reactions, or with the onset of language, if or how, infants' biologically driven mirth reactions connect into the development of a "sense of humor" (see McGhee, 1980, for an initial study) or orientation to humor (see Booth-Butterfield & Booth-Butterfield, 1991). Similar to temperament, human infants would seem to start with differing biological set points driving mirth reactions (e.g., infant's individual differences in giggling in response to tickling) and, since mirth is a component of temperament (assumed to be stable across the lifespan), individual mirth set points may not change much (if at all) across the lifespan (although I am not aware of a study of tickling-giggling across the lifespan that could help sort out the contribution of social learning). We do not yet fully understand if, or how, autonomic mirth reactions begin and develop, if or how they affect later humorous communication development, or even how infants' exposure to adult forms of humorous communication (beyond episodes of tickling-giggling) might later affect children's orientations to, and sense of, humor, or alter their developing abilities to interpret and produce humorous messages.

In sum, Komsi et al.'s (2006) work suggests that, on the one hand, there are biologically grounded, individual differences in infants' temperament with regard to mirth responses (smiling and laughing) that might form a kind of humor response set point that evidence shows continues at least into middle childhood. However, Moore et al. (2001) also suggest, on the other hand, that infants who are exposed to adults' smiling (or lack of it) might also later develop different mirth response patterns as well as different humorous communication abilities (including humor message production and interpretation skills development). While data do not yet exist that would allow us to definitively sort out the relative contributions of nature and nurture to humorous communication development, it seems clear that both nature and nurture are involved. That is, we may all begin life with a unique, genetically-inherited mirth response set point (that drives our mirth responses and mirth displays). Then, subsequent exposure to adults' mirth displays (smiling, giggling, laughing) during adult-infant play (or lack of it), may (or may not) affect our set point for mirth displays and responses. However, once we being to acquire language, and consistent with McGhee (1980), exposure to adults' mirth displays clearly would seem to affect the development of children's displays of mirth, their orientations to humorous communication, as well as their humorous message production and interpretation skills, although how this all connects to the continuing role of our genetically inherited mirth response set remains unclear.

Whether nature, nurture, or both, to build developmental theories of humorous communication, more research of infants' mirth responses as they play with their parents, family members, and caregivers in naturally occurring contexts is clearly warranted, as well as longitudinal studies that attempt to track infants' mirth displays (and levels of exposure to adults' displays) and begin to connect them to children's later humor orientations (e.g., see Booth-Butterfield & Booth-Butterfield, 1991), as well as their humorous message production and interpretation skills and abilities.

CHILDHOOD

When children's linguistic skills begin to emerge (about age 9 to 12 months), along with their advancing cognitive abilities, humor message production and humor interpretation (McGhee, 1971) horizons expand considerably. First, I review research of infants' smiling and laughter as they evolve into tools of social interaction. Next, I provide an overview of research about children's linguistic humor message production and interpretation including a rare study of preschool children's humorous communication in naturally occurring interactions. Finally, before turning attention to a lifespan framework for humor, I conclude the review with a line of research that examines adults using humor as they care for children in health care settings.

Smiling and Laughter

We know that adults attribute positive affective qualities to infants' smiling and laughter and respond to infants' displays of smiling and laughing as if they were overt mirth responses. As children begin to acquire language and develop social skills, mirth displays (smiling and laughing) also become tools of social interaction. In a classic study of children's humorous laughter, Chapman (1975) sought to determine the influence that children laughing in the presence of other children during a humorous event had on children's perceptions of humor—does laughing together make an event seem funnier? Children age 7 and 8 were placed in an experimental situation that manipulated the degree of social interaction and humor. Results showed that social interaction affects the experience of humor. On the theory that humor functions as a form of tension reduction, Chapman (1975, p. 46) concluded "sharing the social situation per se rather than sharing humor is important in the social facilitation of children's humorous laughter." Once children begin to acquire language, laughing and smiling are best understood as social enactments as well as mirth responses to stimuli. According to Chapman (1975):

> The primary and evolutionary function of laughter may be the alleviation of various forms of motivational arousal in a manner which is socially acceptable and physically harmless to others. Superimposed upon this function may be a number of others: For example, laughter may incidentally convey information, or it may sometimes be used as a means of gaining attention, but these are secondary functions. (p. 48)

Once we add language into the mix, the study of humor expands exponentially beyond adults' attributions of infants' emotional states, and infant's mirth stimulus-response sequences, to incorporate children's perceptions of humorous events, how children's mirth responses function communicatively (for both children and adults), how children strategically use humorous communication for many serious purposes (e.g., getting a parent to laugh at a mishap to avoid punishment), and much more.

As smiling and laughing become social interactional tools for children, studies show that cultural forces shape the development of smiling and laughing across the lifespan. Although not intended as a study of humorous communication, DeSantis, Mohan, and Steinhorst (2005), for example, examined thousands of published photographs of preschool children, adolescents, and adults in North America to ascertain continuities and discontinuities of male and female social smiling patterns (full, partial, or no smile). It is not surprising they found from preschoolers to adults, most everyone smiled in photographs. Boys and girls in preschool and grade school smiled similarly and there were no smiling differences between these age groups. However, they found that male adolescents displayed full smiles significantly less than female adolescents (who typically displayed full smiles when being photographed). The pattern of adolescent males displaying partial smiles and adolescent females displaying full smiles was found to continue into adulthood. Although infants were not included in the study, and its design is cross-sectional and post hoc, the data demonstrate that cultural social expectations are a contributing factor to explaining differences in displays of smiling. That is, their data show that in the U.S we expect that all children display positive affect in photos (full smiles), but later we have differing expectancies for adolescent/adult females (continue full smiling) and adolescent/adult males (decrease to a partial smile, possibly to look more serious). Yet, when photographed, everyone—children though senior citizens—is expected to smile when asked to say "cheese."

Studies of children's mirth responses have tended to focus on facial displays; however, Kipper and Todt (2003) examined the sound qualities of laughter. "In both non-human primates and humans, several acoustic parameters of a vocalization are used to encode and decode affective or emotional state: ... fundamental frequency, frequency shape, tonality, intensity, and tempo of a vocalization" (Kipper & Todt, 2003, p. 256).

In their study of adults' reactions to experimentally modified laughter, Kipper and Todt (2003) examined if adults' perceptions of laughter changed with different sound qualities of laughter and found:

> The serial organization of laughter is ... important in the recognition of laughter; in addition, the rhythmic structure ... may contain information that is used by listeners to evaluate the quality of laughter. Such information ... could relate, for example, to the disposition, underlying intentions, or the affective state of a laughing target. (p. 268)

That is, when adults hear laughter, they can attribute various kinds of meanings to its qualities, such as friendliness, genuineness, or perhaps mocking, and can replicate and strategically use social laughter (as in a mocking "ha-ha" laugh). Similarly for children, they begin to make connections between laughter sounds and meanings that can affect their degree of arousal in social contexts (Nwokah, Davies, Islam, Hsu, & Fogler, 1993). However, the development of the ability to strategically alter the production and interpretation of laughter sounds (for social purposes) is not the same for children with disabilities such as autism.

Hundenko, Stone, and Bachorowski (2009) found that 8–10-year-old children with autism "produced almost no 'unvoiced' laughter ... in striking contrast to the typically developing comparison participants, whose laughs were 37–48% unvoiced ... children with autism routinely produce fewer types of laughs than typically developing children because their laughter is more closely linked to their internal experience of positive affect" (p. 1398). Voiced laughter is thought to be a genuine reflection of an underlying emotional state, whereas unvoiced laughter (e.g., polite laugh) is not—thus when children with autism laugh, this study shows they mean it.

In sum, as children acquire symbolic language, it becomes possible to use smiling and laughter both as reflections of internal emotional states and instrumentally for a variety of purposes that, in general, have the potential to unite communicators (laughing with), or divide communicators (laughing at) (see Meyer, 2000). And, as children acquire language, they also try their hand at producing humorous messages and begin to build a personal sense of humor appreciation and orientation to humor (McGhee, 1980). While pre-linguistic infants' mirth responses are limited to their facial and sound production capacities, linguistic children have an incredible array of materials with which to "make fun."

Development of Linguistic Humor

Most research studies of children's linguistic humor development are conducted by means of laboratory experiments. In an early study representative of this kind of research, McGhee (1974) examined boys and girls in grades 1, 2, 4, and 6 to ascertain their abilities to differentiate a humorous response from a serious response to a prompt as well as their abilities to create humorous responses [e.g., children are presented an "absurdity riddle" such as "Why did the elephant lie across the road?" and then asked to identify which response is humorous and which is serious? (a) "To trip ants" (humorous) or (b) "because he wanted to rest" (serious), p. 553]. Children in first grade found it difficult to tell the difference between humorous and serious responses, but the as the children aged, so did their humor understanding. The study also found that when asked to develop funny answers to absurdity or wordplay riddle prompts, children across the grades found the task difficult, but that some (not all) children in grades 4 and 6 could generate funny responses. This led McGhee to conclude that humor message appreciation and humor message production are different processes that have different developmental arcs.

While laboratory studies of children's linguistic humor are common (see Semrud-Clikeman & Glass, 2010 for a recent review of normal and disabled children), studies of children's naturally occurring episodes of linguistic humorous communication are rare. One such study is Loizou (2007), who adopted the position that from birth infants are social and emotional beings, and since smiling and laughing are among our earliest social behaviors, it made sense to study children's humorous events in situ. Loizou observed two children, a boy age 18 months (Anthony) and a girl age 24 months (Katie), during 16 hours of free play over four months accompanied by interviews with caregivers.

Loizou (2007) refers to two theories (using her labels for each) that described the children's humor interactions: (a) theory of the absurd that refers to using incongruities—producing funny gestures/positions/sounds and (b) theory of empowerment that refers to creating and appreciating intended playful rule violations. During the observation period, Katie used a wide variety of incongruities in free play with objects and situations, and her caregivers reported that she was often "putting on a show" for them with her silliness and humorous messages. Although Anthony used incongruities, too, he relied more on violating caregivers' expectations as a means of conveying humorous messages. For example:

Anthony was at the table eating his lunch. When done, the caregiver gave him a sponge to clean up his space (a regular routine). Anthony held the sponge in his hand ... looked up ... smiled at her and put [the sponge] in his mouth. The caregiver commented on his action reminding him that the sponge is for cleaning. He would keep the sponge in his mouth and laugh even more as he listened to the caregiver (p. 201).

Loizou's (2007) theories (as displayed by these two children) are similar to two classic theories of humor: incongruity theory (see McGhee, 1979) that argues we create and appreciate humor in moments of release when an incongruity is understood and resolved, and superiority theory (see Gruner, 1997) that argues we create and appreciate humor from situations over which we experience a kind of triumph over another (e. g., laughing at a person who sidesteps a banana peel but falls into an open manhole—where the humor is derived from both surprise and feeling of superiority over another's misfortunes). A third classic humor theory—humor as a release of tension or nervous energy (Shurcliff, 1968) was not observed to be reflected in the children's behaviors.

Loizou (2007) concluded that children can rapidly fit into modes of what Ziv (1989) called "cognitive playfulness, the flexibility in changing frames of reference ... passing from reality to the imaginary, from seriousness to joking" (p. 108) as they played with each other and their caregivers. She also noticed that the caregivers played key roles in these children's enactments of humor either as an audience or as co-creators of humorous communication.

As children develop their language and cognitive abilities, so too do they advance their abilities to understand and appreciate humor as well as enact humor of increasing complexity. According to McGhee (1984), the development of children's humor appreciation (ages 2–7) can be described using a four-stage model: (Stage 1) pretend play with objects (emerges at age two years); (Stage 2) sound and wordplay—begins to learn to replace actions with words (ages three and four years); (Stage 3) situational play—can categorize objects and events and notices when things are not as they should be (age four to age five), and (Stage 4) riddles, puns, jokes, and more—develops the ability to restructure events and objects in novel and humorous ways (age seven years). Of course, children's early verbal humor development across these stages is heavily dependent on its contexts; that is, depending on exposure, some children will move rapidly toward increasing humor abstraction, if exposed to increasingly complex forms (Semrud-Clikeman & Glass, 2010). Also, it is clear that our ability to appreciate and tell what are linguistically recognized as jokes (e.g., knock-knock jokes) can emerge only after a basic level of linguistic mastery has been achieved at about age four (see McGhee, 1983). While most studies tend to stop at the threshold of middle childhood, we also still need to document humor appreciation's (as well as message production's) further development into adolescence, especially given the findings of Quatman, Sokolik, and Smith (2000) that having a sense of humor is among the top-rated aspects of popularity for young men and women.

Few studies exist of children's humorous message production across early, middle, and later childhood, as well as adolescence, particularly those that examine the development of humor content. One such study is Socha and Kelly (1994) who examined humorous messages produced by 208 children in grades prekindergarten (age 4) to eighth grade (age 14) in response to two vignettes: "Your teacher has had rough day in school. What would you say to your teacher to make him/her laugh?" (p. 243) and "Your best friend has had a rough day in school. What would you say to make him/her laugh?" (p. 243). Students were asked to produce as many messages as they could. Messages were audio recorded and later transcribed and content analyzed.

Socha and Kelly (1994) were interested in describing prosocial and antisocial content themes in the children's humorous messages, including identifying when antisocial themes emerged, the nature of these themes, as well as documenting any sex differences in the use of antisocial humor. The two vignettes were chosen to ascertain children's ability to adapt their humor to targets perceived to have different senses of humor (i.e., teachers preferring prosocial humor).

To both teachers and best friends, children in pre-K to third grade produced more prosocial humor (e.g., used language/logic incongruities) than children in grades four to eight (who used violations of decorum and politeness as they created antisocial forms of humor). Antisocial humor examples were found to begin in grade 4 (ages 9–10) and were created by boys for their best friends, but not for teachers (e.g., dirty jokes were not told to teachers, but were told to their best friends). However, a few boys did produce antisocial messages for a male teacher and seemed to feel comfortable creating a joking relationship with their teacher (Apte, 1985).

Socha and Kelly (1994) found their pattern of results mirrored what would be expected using Gilligan's (1982) theory of moral development insofar that girls produced prosocial humor themes consistent with the ethic of care, and boys' use of antisocial themes was targeted mostly at women and minorities consistent with an ethic of justice where everyone should be treated the same.

In sum, it is clear that if we are to begin to develop communication theories to explain humorous message production (as well as interpretation), we need more descriptive research of children's naturally occurring humorous messages as well as research that identifies significant predictors of children's humor message production abilities and their development from infancy into adolescence.

Applied Humor and Children

There is a line of research related to children's humor that examines how adults use humor as a means to reduce fear and anxieties of medical procedures. Fernandes and Arriaga (2010), in a study in Portugal, examined a sample of children ages 5–12 who were either accompanied by their parents, or accompanied by their parents and two clowns, for minor ambulatory surgery. The study measured differences in children's and parents' worries about the procedure as well as pre–post anxiety. Children's temperaments were also measured as a control. The clowns used age-appropriate routines that included magic, music, jokes, and games as well as clowning techniques. "The findings generally support our predictions: children in the clown group felt less worried about the hospitalization, the medical procedures, and the illness and its negative consequences; and also reported more positive emotional states (felt happier and calmer) than those in the comparison group in both operative phases" (p. 411).

Stuber et al. (2007) examined watching humorous videos (pre and post medical procedure) and helping children manage pain during medical procedures. The study found that although humorous video viewing did not decrease pain levels, children who viewed humorous videos did experience an increased tolerance for pain, thus confirming previous research of humorous communication as a positive distracter.

CONCLUSION

Infants smile, giggle, and laugh during play. Young children also smile, giggle, and laugh (in ways very similar to infants) as they react and interpret an expanding array of humorous messages (in ways consistent with their linguistic and cognitive developmental levels). Young children develop a sense of humor, an orientation to humor, as well as hone their humorous message production abilities, although differently for boys and girls. And, we know that adults use humor to ease children's pain and reduce their worries. However, it is clear that the research base supporting what is known about children's humor is limited and that we have many unanswered questions and more to learn. In the next, concluding section, I identify some of these questions and outline the utility of a lifespan-developmental approach to address them.

Toward a Lifespan Developmental Approach to Humorous Communication Nussbaum (2007, p. 4) outlined the following principles of a lifespan approach to communication theory and research:

1. The nature of communication is fundamentally developmental.

2. A complete understanding of human communication depends on multiple levels of knowledge that occur simultaneously.

3. Communicative change can be quantitative as well as qualitative.

4. Life span communication scholars can incorporate all current theories of communication into this perspective as long as the theories are testable, useful, and address change across time.

5. Unique methodologies are required to capture communication change across the life span.

Adopting these principles to inform a starting point for a lifespan approach to humorous communication involves: (a) developing thorough descriptions of humorous message interpretation and production processes in infancy, childhood, and adulthood, (b) describing qualitative and quantitative changes in humorous communication (message interpretation, message production, and uses of humor) across the stages of life, (c) examining the knowledge bases and factors that inform the development of creating successful (and managing unsuccessful) humorous communication messages, routines, and episodes, (d) examining the utility of classic theories of humor interpretation (e.g., incongruity, superiority, relief, and others) to explain humorous communication (message production, message interpretation, and uses of humor), and (e) continuing to develop new methods to examine the development of humorous communication in its many forms (including its appearance in new forms of humorous communication in digital media). Let me elaborate on each of these points.

First, the field of communication does not yet have an adequate descriptive understanding of the development of humorous communication within life's stages nor how humorous communication changes across life's stages. The studies included in the review are largely from outside of the field, many are dated experiments, and few examine naturally occurring humorous communication in everyday life. Descriptive studies are needed of humorous communication as it occurs in the lives of infants, children (early, middle, later childhood), adolescents, and adults as well as how it changes across life's stages. This work should attempt to identify potentially salient predictive factors that could later be tested.

Second, we need to better understand what explains differences in humorous message production abilities as well as message interpretation abilities. In the communication field's classic children's communication textbook, Wood (1976) outlined the elements of an instructional model of communication development intended to assist teachers as they helped children hone their communication skills. Her model included: (a) communication goals (the primary and secondary goals a communicator hopes to accomplish), (b) an understanding of critical communication situations (participants, setting, topics, tasks), (c) understanding the range of available communication strategies using words, syntax, semantics, voice, body, and space that support, (d) successful and unsuccessful messages and episodes (pp. 274–275). According to Wood, "[T]he primary goal is to increase the child's repertoire of communication strategies for critical communication situations

... [so that] children will participate in a greater variety of communication situations ... [and] feel confident that they can communicate appropriately" (p. 275).

Adapting Wood's (1976) model to explain humorous communication necessitates the communication field learning more, for example, about what motivates communicators to choose to use humorous communication and communication play, how humor and play are signaled, and how choices are made about humor's content, given the parameters of the critical communication situations faced by children. Socha and Kelly (1994), drawing on incongruity theory, argued that communicators draw on language, logic, and relational expectations that can be used to create myriad incongruities that can be used for humorous purposes, and that communication ethics may be one of many factors that can shape communicators' choices of humorous content. The ability to produce humorous messages is clearly an important communication tool that should be a part of the communication skills repertoire of all communicators, but right now we know little about the details of children's humorous communication instruction (formal and informal) and need to ask fundamental questions like: How do our most accomplished humorists learn their skills?

Third, pertaining to methodologies and theory development, today communication research studies of children face particularly stringent obstacles when they are reviewed by universities' Institutional Review Boards for the Protection of Human Subjects (IRBs). Although IRB regulations *do* make recruiting and including children in research studies more difficult than college sophomores, research about children outside of communication clearly has not come to a halt (although, it may seem children's human communication research has come to a halt, given Socha & Yingling's [2010] book is currently the only children's human communication volume in print in the communication field). Part of the problem facing communication researchers as they work with IRBs in proposing studies of children is the almost complete lack of graduate communication classes that would prepare communication researchers to employ the many methods typically used by those who study child development (surprisingly, the lack of preparation extends to graduate education in family communication, as most Ph.D. programs do not offer graduate courses in children's communication development nor require child development courses [Socha & Yingling, 2010]). A lack of training in children's communication research methods, coupled with a lack of theoretical understanding of child development and a lack of understanding of the rules and regulations created for children's protection are issues that must be addressed if we are to advance the study of children's communication, let alone our understanding of children's humorous communication.

Most all communication scholars and instructors will agree, superficially, that of course the study of children's humorous communication is important in its own right. However, it is quite another matter to convince the communication field's journal editors of the importance of publishing studies of kids' knock-knock jokes. With the exception of children and media, the communication field is currently ignoring children's human communication. Editors of communication journals routinely refer manuscripts that examine children's humorous communication to "child development journals" instead of publishing them for an audience of communication scholars. However, arguments in support of the importance of studying children's humorous communication clearly increase in persuasiveness when humorous communication is seen as an important lifespan-communication ability related to human health and wellness. For example, communication studies that examine relationships between humorous communication skills development and the development of skills of leadership, parenting, teaching, and more, place the study of children's humor in a central and pivotal position. With humorous communication's potential as a dark-side tool, as in the case of bullying, learning about and teaching children prosocial humorous communication would also seem to be an important remedy (or salve) for these kinds of societal ills.

This volume demonstrates that humorous communication holds an important place among the communication field's many serious communication pursuits and this chapter hopefully demonstrates that children are important humorous communicators, too.

References

Apte, M. L. (1985). *Humor and laughter*. Ithaca, NY: Cornell University Press.

Auter, P. J. (1990). Analysis of the ratings for television comedy programs 1950–1959: The end of "Berlesque." *Mass Communication Review, 17*, 23–32.

Bateson, G. A. (1972). Theory of play and fantasy. In G. A. Bateson (Ed.), *Steps to an ecology of mind* (pp. 150–166). New York: Ballantine.

Baek, Y. M., & Wojcieszak, M. E. (2009). Don't expect too much! Learning from late-night comedy and knowledge item difficulty. *Communication Research, 36*, 783–809.

Bekelja Wanzer, M., & Frymier Bainbridge, A. (1999). The relationship between student perceptions of instructor humor and students' reports of learning. *Communication Education, 48*, 48–62.

Bekelja Wanzer, M., Bainbridge Frymier, A., Wojtaszczyk, A. M., & Smith, T. (2006). Appropriate and inappropriate uses of humor by teachers. *Communication Education, 55*, 178–196.

Bippus, A. M. (2000). Humor usage in comforting episodes: Factors predicting outcomes. *Western Journal of Communication, 64*, 359–384.

Bippus, A. M. (2003). Humor motives, qualities, and reactions in recalled conflict episodes. *Western Journal of Communication, 67*, 413–426.

Bolzani-Dinehart, L., Messinger, D. S., Acosta, S., Cassel, T., Ambadar, Z., & Cohn, J. (2005). Adult perceptions of positive and negative infant emotional expressions. *Infancy, 8*, 279–303.

Booth-Butterfield, S., & Booth-Butterfield, M. (1991). Individual differences in the communication of humorous messages. *Southern Communication Journal, 56*, 205–218.

Chapman, A. J. (1975). Humorous laughter in children. *Journal of Personality and Social Psychology, 31*, 42–49.

Cousins, N. (1979). *Anatomy of an illness as perceived by a patient*. New York: W. W. Norton.

DeSantis, M., Mohan, P. J., & Steinhorst, D. K. (2005). Smiling in photographs: Childhood similarities between sexes become differences constant in adulthood. *Psychological Reports, 97*, 651–665.

Dickson, K. L., Walker, H., & Fogel, A. (1997). The relationship between smile-type and play-type during parent-infant play. *Developmental Psychology, 33*, 925–933.

Fernandes, S., & Arriaga, P. (2010). The effects of clown intervention on worries and emotional responses in children undergoing surgery. *Journal of Health Psychology, 15*, 405–415.

Fogel, A., Nelson-Goens, G. C., Hsu, H. C., & Shapiro, A. F. (2000). Do different infant smiles reflect different positive emotions? *Social Development, 9*, 497–520.

Gilligan, C. (1982). *In a different voice*. Cambridge, MA: Harvard University Press.

Gruner, C. R. (1985). Advice to the beginning speaker on using humor—what the research tells us. *Communication Education, 34*, 142–147.

Gruner, C. R. (1997). *The game of humor: A comprehensive theory of why we laugh*. New Brunswick, NJ: Transaction Publishers.

Hundenko, W. J., Stone, W., & Bachorowski, J. A. (2009). Laughter differs in children with autism: An acoustic analysis of laughs produced by children with and without the disorder. *Journal of Autism Development Disorders, 39*, 1392–1400.

Kipper, S., & Todt, D. (2003). The role of rhythm and pitch in the evaluation of human laughter. *Journal of Nonverbal Behavior, 27*, 255–272.

Komsi, N., Raikkonen, A., Pesonen, A-K., Heinonen, K., Keskivaara, P., Jarvenpaa et al. (2006). Continuity of temperament from infancy to middle childhood. *Infant Behavior and Development, 29*, 494–508.

Loizou, E. (2007). Humor as a means of regulating one's social self: Two infants with unique humorous personas. *Early Childhood Development and Care, 177*(2), 195–205.

McGhee, P. E. (1971). Cognitive development and children's comprehension of humor. *Child Development, 42*(1), 123–138.

McGhee, P. E. (1974). Development of children's abilities to create the joking relationship. *Child Development, 45*(2), 552–556.

McGhee, P. E. (Ed.). (1979). *Humor: Its origins and development*. San Francisco: W. H. Freeman.

McGhee, P. E. (1980). Development of the sense of humor in childhood: A longitudinal study. In P. E. McGhee & A. Chapman (Eds.), *Children's humor* (pp. 213–236). Chichester, UK and New York: John Wiley.

McGhee, P. E. (1983). Humor development: Toward a life span approach. In P. E. McGhee (Ed.), *Handbook of humor research: Basic issues* (Vol. 1, pp. 109–134). New York, NY: Springer-Verlag.

McGhee, P. E. (1984). Play, incongruity, and humor. In T. D. Yawkey & A. D. Pellegrini (Eds.), *Child's play: Developmental and applied* (pp. 219–236). Mahwah, NJ: Lawrence Erlbaum.

Messinger, D. S., Cassel, T. D., Acosta, S. I., Ambador, Z., & Cohn, J. F. (2008). Infant smiling dynamics and perceived positive emotions. *Journal of Nonverbal Behavior, 32*, 133–155.

Meyer, J. C. (2000). Humor as a double-edged sword: Four functions of humor in communications. *Communication Theory, 10*, 310–331.

Mills, C. B., & Carwile, A. M. (2009). The good, the bad, and the borderline: Separating teasing from bullying. *Communication Education, 58*, 276–301.

Moore, G. A., Cohen, J. F., & Campbell, S. B. (2001). Infant affective responses to mother's still face at 6 months differentially predict externalizing and internalizing behaviors at 18 months. *Developmental Psychology, 37*, 706–714.

Nussbaum, J. (2007). Lifespan communication and quality of life. *Journal of communication, 57*, 1–7.

Nwokah, E. E., Davies, P., Islam, A., Hsu, H. C, & Fogel, A. (1993). Vocal affect in the three year-olds: A quantitative acoustic analysis of child laughter. *Journal of the Acoustic Society of America, 94*, 3076–3090.

Provine, R. R. (1992). Contagious laughter: Laughter is a sufficient stimulus for laughs and smiles. *Bulletin of the Psychonomic Society, 30*, 1–4.

Quatman, T., Sokolik, E., & Smith, K. (2000). Adolescent perception of peer success: A gendered perspective over time. *Sex Roles, 43*(1/2), 61–84.

Reincheld, A. (2006). 'Saturday Night Live' and weekend update: The formative years of comedy news dissemination. *Journalism History, 3*, 190–197.

Rothbart, M. K., & Bates, J. (1998). Temperament. In W. Damon (Series Ed.) & N. Eisenberg (Vol. Ed.), *Handbook of child psychology: Vol 3. Social emotional and personality development* (5th ed., pp. 105–176). New York: Wiley.

Semrud-Clikeman, M., & Glass, K. (2010). The relation of humor and child development: Social, adaptive, and emotional aspects. *Journal of Child Neurology, 25*(10), 1248–1260.

Shurcliff, A. (1968). Judged humor, arousal, and relief theory. *Journal of Personality and Social Psychology, 8*, 360–363.

Socha, T. J., & Kelly, B. (1994). Children making "fun": Humorous communication, impression management, and moral development. *Child Study Journal, 24*, 237–252.

Socha, T. J., & Pitts, M. (Eds.). (2012). *The positive side of interpersonal communication.* New York: Peter Lang.

Socha, T. J., & Yingling, J. (2010). *Families communicating with children.* Cambridge, UK: Polity.

Stuber, M., Dunay Hilber, S., Libman Mintzer, L., Castaneda, M., Glover, D., & Zeltzer. L. (2007). Laughter, humor and pain perception in children: A pilot study. *Advance Access Publication 5*, 271–276. doi:10.1093/ecam/nem097 [Published by creativecommons.org/licenses/by-nc/2.0/uk/]

Wood, B. S. (1976). *Children and communication: Verbal and nonverbal language development.* Englewood Cliffs, NJ: Prentice Hall.

Young, S. L., & Bippus, A. M. (2001). Does it make a difference if they hurt you in a funny way? *Communication Quarterly, 49*, 35–52.

Ziv, A. (1989). Using humor to develop creative thinking. In P. E. McGhee (Ed.), *Humor and children's development: A guide to practical applications* (pp. 99–116). New York: Haworth Press.

CHAPTER 10

HUMOR IN FAMILIES: A CRUCIBLE OF HUMOR AND COMMUNICATION

Sandra M. Ketrow
University of Rhode Island

INTRODUCTION

Families provide our first, earliest, and ongoing engagement with humorous communication. Some scholars (Martin, Anderson, Burant, & Weber, 1997; Vogl-Bauer, 2003) claim that teasing, for example, is part of the daily fabric of family members' interactions. The family is a crucible[1] for human socialization regarding the use of humor in close relationships. Although many theories and functional analyses of humor exist, generally these perspectives have seen limited application to humor in families. This underscores the necessity to use functional models (cf., Graham, Papa, & Brooks, 1992; De Koning & Weiss, 2002) in extending the examination of humor employed in families.

This chapter takes an approach consonant with select family and small-group communication scholars (cf., Propp & Kreps, 1994; Socha, 1999, 2009; Socha & Yingling, 2010), who posited that small groups include families, and vice versa. Socha (1999, 2009) has maintained adamantly that family is the first "group." Even though families (usually) are naturally occurring and involuntary groups (Vangelisti, 1993), Bochner (1976) extended this condition by pointing out that families—like many other groups—are emergent rather than assembled. This is not to say that families and groups are the same. Rather, a case can be made to follow, analyze, or study group[2] processes as a way to inform the investigation of humor in families. Recognizing that family communication, including humor, shares commonly defining group characteristics like norms and standards presents an opportunity to explore family standards and the use of humor. Part of the rationale for this viewpoint is that literature targeting families and humor centrally is sparse, and tends to fall within the purview of family therapy or processes.

Lynch (2002) claimed that humor literature can be split into two levels of analysis—the individual and societal. However, an argument can be made to examine humorous communication at an intermediary level that intersects between the individual and society—the family. Socha (1999, 2009), Socha and Yingling (2010), and Vangelisti (1993) echo that the crucial point that distinguishes family from other group types is that it is a crucible in which "children acquire their initial (primitive) models of relational interaction as they communicate with adult caregivers" (Socha, 2009, p. 6). This chapter focuses on family humor from a communication perspective, examines the functions and standards that define family communication, presents findings of preliminary data from observational narratives of humorous communication employed in families, and finally, links family standards to the functions of humor.

THE FUNCTIONS OF FAMILY, FAMILY COMMUNICATION STANDARDS, AND THE FUNCTIONS OF HUMOR

Most people and social scientists would agree that the family is an essential social unit. Furthermore, in addition to sex/reproduction, intimacy, and emotional support, the family provides primary social functions that may be grouped into four broad categories: (1) family composition and membership (including individual identity), (2) economic support to meet family members' basic needs for, at minimum, shelter, food, and clothing, (3) protective family care across the life cycle, including safety, health, and general well-being, and (4) childrearing (Ooms, 1995, p. 21). Sociologist Talcott Parsons (Parsons & Bales, 1955) maintained that the main contemporary function for a family is the structuring of the personalities of young people and their stabilization as adults. The enactment of socialization is of interest for this chapter, because the socialization function includes the provision and shaping of life values and appropriate social behavior for all family members. Humor as a strategic mechanism serves a critical role in executing the construction, maintenance, and change for families.

This useful overarching view advances the notion that family communication patterns influence family members' perceptions of the world and their behaviors, specifically, the family's socialization of its members. This view also points to perceptions of social reality (Chaffee, McLeod, & Atkin, 1971; Meadowcroft, 1986; Saphir & Chaffee, 2002) as based in *socio-oriented* vs. *concept-oriented* family communication patterns. Socio-oriented communication patterns stress maximizing interpersonal relationships (in families). Concept-oriented family communication patterns stress more conceptual deviation and dissent, without worry that family social relationships will be harmed. This distinction provides a point of reference to differentiate positive from negative functions of humor.

In her study of a large sample of families with children, Meadowcroft (1986) reported that stages of cognitive development were related to shifts in family communication patterns. Her analyses revealed three overall patterns: (1) for families with children in grades 4–7, family interaction showed greater socio-oriented patterns; (2) for families with older children (grades (10–12), more concept-oriented family communication patterns were evident; and (3) family communication patterns were stable for families with adolescents (grades 7–10). These patterns, then, implicate age and cognitive maturity as factors that covary along the socio- and concept-oriented communication pattern continuum. Her inference regarding the dynamic, rather than stable, nature of longitudinal family communication patterns is valuable, supported by research findings and theory (Maccoby, 1992; Meadowcroft & Fitzpatrick, 1988; Saphir & Chafee, 2006) about the mutual influence of parents and children. The dynamic quality of the patterns provide insight into the uses of humorous communication in the family. These findings also support the modeling of Dixson (1985), Socha (1999), and Socha and Yingling (2010)—that children and parents (or caregivers) interact, and they mutually sculpt "each other's models of roles and rules in dynamic and ongoing ways" (Socha & Yingling, p. 95). One sculpting tool is humor. Humorous messages impact the speaker and the receiver regardless of whether that person is a parent, child, or sibling in a family. It is just as powerful for a child to joke or tease a parent about a funny mishap as it is for a parent to bestow an entertaining nickname on the child.

A related approach to assessing the place of humor in family communication is schema theory. Cognitive psychologists have labeled processes by which individuals perceive stimuli, events, or others, and organize this knowledge into patterns or categories as *schemata*. A schema contains not only recognized attributes of a given concept or stimulus, but also the relationships among these attributes. Types of schemata include organized knowledge about persons, self, roles, relationships, and events (e.g., episodes, scripts, frames). Loosely, a parallel in cognitive research may be drawn with respect to how people categorize objects (Moskowitz, 2005). Categorization is accomplished via the recognition of central tendencies, or prototypes. Knowledge about a category is composed of a typical or ideal instance—a prototype, balanced by a range of lesser exemplars.

Family members hold and enact relational prototypes, which extend to well-learned and probably automatic patterns of family communication (cf., Koerner & Fitzpatrick, 2002; Vangelisti, 1993). That is, what one believes is normative for a (family) relationship tends to influence one's spectrum of typical communication for that relationship. For example, if people believe that their family members are "inclusive, supportive and accepting, they may also believe that family communication has those characteristics" (Vangelisti, p. 47). The presence of certain patterns of normative control and support embedded in humorous messages and exchanged in families cannot be denied.

Ritchie and Fitzpatrick (1990) allow that "the family communication environment can be seen as one involving norms of control and supportive messages" (p. 525). Ritchie (1991) explained an apparent paradox—a positive relationship between socio-orientation and aggression vis-à-vis concept-orientation as negatively related with aggression. He stated, "[C]oncept-oriented children generalize their perceptions about their parents' approach to disagreement and conclude that differences are best handled by conversation, tact, and supportive communication rather than action" (p. 562). In a concept-oriented family, then, one would expect greater use of positive humor, and lower presence of negative or aggressive humor, such as sarcasm or teasing.

Caughlin (2003) posited that specific behaviors reflect overarching family communication standards. He generated both "real" and ideal family communication standards from respondent-developed examples, including: openness; maintaining structural stability; expressing affection; emotional/instrumental support; mindreading; politeness; discipline; regular, routine interaction; avoidance; and humor/sarcasm. DiCioccio and Ketrow (2009) inferred the utility of family standards as a way of interpreting messages. "From this perspective, family standards are subsumed under the broader construct of family schemata" (p. 168).

One emergent standard of Caughlin's 15 categories was humor/sarcasm, defined as a "family's tendency to joke, tease, or poke fun at each other" (p. 13). In the same article, Caughlin reported a second and third study in which 10 factors emerged and were replicated, leading to further category simplification. Humor/sarcasm continued as one of those 10 factors. He inferred from his results that family communication standards are related to schemata, albeit nonredundant. Importantly, he noted that variation in the average endorsement of humor/sarcasm suggests it "may be more idiosyncratic to individuals or families than standards like openness, which may reflect more general cultural values" (p. 34). However, in an examination of family argument processes, DiCioccio and Ketrow (2009) corroborated the notion that humor/sarcasm is an essential family communication standard (FCS).

Finally, Caughlin points to a result that an inverse relationship between topic avoidance and (family) satisfaction was diminished for those who favored a humor/sarcasm FCS. In a family in which individuals are low in endorsing openness, one might discover greater topic avoidance (or being less disturbed by it), and a concomitant belief in and use of more humor/sarcasm. Caughlin states that such a connection is consistent with Sillars' (1980) research, that "joking can be seen as a form of avoidance" (p. 36). Sillars, however, identified the use of joking as a type of indirect conflict strategy, omitting disclosure of actual negative emotions, and minimizing the seriousness of the problem. Sillars thus steered our attention to the use of humor as destructive. Taken together, Caughlin's and Sillars' implications parallel recent examinations of aggressive humor, such as irony (cf., Averbeck & Hample, 2008, who also identify sarcasm as a type of irony), teasing (cf., DiCioccio, 2010), ridicule and related forms of demeaning or disparaging, such as derision or put-downs (Infante, Riddle, Horvath, & Tumlin, 1992; Martin, Puhlik-Doris, Larsen, Grey, & Weir, 2003; Zillman, 1983), and extending these to occurrences within families (Wuerffel, 1986).

Employing such perspectives about humor in families allows one to predict that humor functions may be placed minimally within two relational dialectic tensions for humor: (1) *identification—differentiation* and (2) *control—resistance*. Lynch (2002) presents these two polar dimensions for humor functions. His model corresponds more or less to Meyer's (2000) effects-based functions of humor with regard to its two primary functions of unifying or dividing communicators. Lynch (2002) infers from a synthetic literature review of sociologically-oriented case studies to understand the function of humor in a social setting that "all social humor, particularly work humor, functions ultimately as control" (p. 424). Lynch also summarizes "communication humor research" by listing the "specific types of humor producing communicative functions (to tease, release boredom, gain attraction, persuade) in a smaller social context" (p. 431). Lynch's point that humor serves as a means for interactants to engage in relational (and environmental) negotiation is well taken. Lynch's model of humor in context shows the intersections of psychological, sociological, and communicative approaches to the study of humor in social situations. In general, family communication standards and family interaction serve to engage the social functions for family members. Specifically, Lynch's model acts as an archetype to analyze how the themes of humorous messages in family interaction embody the social functions and related communication standards of families.

The unique use of humor in families complicates its examination and conceptualization, yet validates a need for inductive or ethnographic investigation. Lynch's model is used to frame the analysis of a sample of humorous family messages. Based on a small sample of observations of humor in families, the author strives to resolve the following questions:

1. What themes of humor use emerge in bona fide families' interactions?
2. How does humor in families operate (e.g., in pro- or antisocial ways [adaptively or coercively; uniting or dividing])?

SOME FUNNY DATA

To illuminate the connection between family standards and the functions of humor discussed earlier in this chapter, a preliminary investigation identified the variety of behaviors and purposes associated with humorous communication used in families. The goal of this examination was to collect a broad range of humorous messages across different family configurations in the contextual setting of a common American holiday. To identify how humor is used in the family, actual interpretations of humorous messages and their functions from the viewpoint of those participating in the experience were obtained by using ethnographic observation.

The rationale for this approach was based on several premises. First, an inductive method is a useful mechanism to discover individual perceptions of humorous communication in families. It is a means of gathering authentic interactions and how they are perceived. Studying the family interacting in its own environment is consistent with continuing calls for studying natural (a.k.a. "bona fide") groups in context (Frey, 1994; Putnam, 1994; Putnam & Stohl, 1990) as well as in families (Petronio & Braithwaite, 1993), which necessitates the use of qualitative methods. An ideal way to garner messages and their impact is to collect interactants' "interpretations of their beliefs, values, and behaviors to construct reality from their point of view" (Frey, p. 562).

The observations reported here relied on purposive sampling. The sample for the study consisted of 29 observational narrative reports produced by 45 undergraduate students (sex = 22 females, 23 males; race/ethnicity = 44 Caucasian, 1 African-American). The initial group consisted of 55 upper-level undergraduate students in a communication research methods course who had been learning qualitative methodology and who had gained limited experience in ethnomethodology. From 30 narrative reports produced (several students worked in teams or pairs), all were selected for analysis as viable, although only 25 (these actually represented 39 observers' observation descriptions, impressions, and inferences) provided adequate detail to be acceptable for continuing examination following a first rough inclusion/exclusion. Because of the potential pervasiveness of humor especially during a family-centered holiday, this particular sample of 25 provided a reasonable data set to examine family communication and humor.

Students were given guidelines to conduct and report observations of their own family's use of humor. The guidelines consisted of four instructions: (1) Students were to observe their families on Thanksgiving Day during two different hours, and identify and catalogue humor that they noted. This setting was chosen because it provided a social opportunity that could potentially include nuclear, blended, and extended family members interacting over a period of time in a generally positively regarded family-oriented gathering; (2) Students were to describe participants who were interacting and their relationship(s) to one another; (3) Students were to articulate specifically how the humor was introduced (a brief back story) and the humorous act; and (4) Students were to provide their interpretation of why this act was performed and what they thought were the perceptions of and impact of the humor on their family and its members.

To fulfill these requirements prior to the actual observations, students practiced observing families interacting. Using video clips of family members interacting during holiday gatherings, students practiced identifying and describing behavior, rapid note-taking, and summarizing interpretations. This training aimed to help student researchers maximize their skills in recognizing and collecting observations of their families' interactions in real time (i.e., while engaged in their Thanksgiving celebrations and related activities). Five rounds of this training occurred until all student researchers achieved a minimum of 70 percent of intra- and inter-rater reliability in their data observations. The student researchers were to work primarily as observers in the field project, although they could interact with their family members if necessary. In their reports, the participant-observers attested that the interactions observed and reported met several standards for good data records, including: accuracy; contexted; thick descriptions; useful; and reflexive (Richards, 2005). Two details strengthened data validity. First, observers drew on their intimate social knowledge of other participants in the family group based on their roughly two decades of experience in their family's humorous communication. Second, observers recorded evidence that participants in the interaction perceived the episode or exchange as humorous as manifested in responses; e.g., "everyone laughed;" "When person X teased person Y, everyone responded with laughter." Third, 10 observers reported they used "member checking" (Richards, 2005) to further validate their descriptions and interpretations; either by discussing the project ex post facto with their families or providing their reports to family members whom they had observed for their concordance.

Data reduction consisted of these first notes and recorded transcriptions in the first stage. In the second stage of data reduction, the student participant-observers summarized their transcribed interactions, notes, and impressions as described above in the guidelines for the project. In their third stage of data reduction, the participant-observers submitted both written and oral reports that summarized the most central of their observations, notes, and perceptions.

Several limitations must be identified. First, novice researchers generated the data and summaries. Second, many summaries omit much thick description and/or contextual pieces that would allow better sense-making and interpretation. A third limitation is that family interactions were observed selectively, albeit for two requisite, separate, one-hour periods. Thus, participant-observers likely overlooked much information as well as many humor instances that occurred. Finally, and related to the last limitation, although observations occurred in a bona fide family context, observers did not record all interaction during the data collection periods. Full interaction records would have allowed tighter contextualization of the humorous communication, as well as revealing sheer frequencies or the weight of the humor.

How Are Bona Fide Families Funny?

This section details more intensive content analysis of the reports of bona fide families' interaction and humor. Again, from 30 narratives, 25 tenable humorous interaction reports were selected for content coding analysis. Relying on grounded theory (Glaser & Strauss, 1967), a researcher discovers that the data themselves suggest the categories that result from analysis. In a first pass of analysis, this author coded narrative reports according to descriptive topical similarities. Similarities emerged from scrutinizing language, context, locus of attack, and mode of delivery. From the narrative reports, six humor types categories emerged for using humor in these families:

1. Mocking someone out-group (nonfamily);

2. Mocking, teasing, using sarcasm, or denigrating (put-down) another family member, romantic partner of adult child, or close family friend (including telling funny story about other person);

3. Self-deprecating (usually to draw attention away from someone's own or another's embarrassment);

4. Joking or telling a funny story to alleviate relational tension, reinforce norm, control, or dominance;

5. Nonverbal acting to evoke laughter, amusement, or deflect attention;

6. Laughing at and commenting on humor in others' interaction, statements, behavior, or conflict (including someone else's physical humiliation).

Table 1 lists the six categories, the episode interactants and brief context for the example, and quotations from the particular selected family exchanges[3] determined by the student observers with coder agreement by the author to exemplify the category.

TABLE 1: CATEGORIES OF HUMOR TYPE FREQUENCIES WITH EXAMPLES

Category of Humor Type	Interactants	Example Interaction
1. Mocking out-group	A. Three brothers and others watching a ball game, reacting to poor penalty for game violation B. Grandmother to grandfather (her spouse) about granddaughter's new boyfriend who is tattooed, wild haired, and dresses like lead singer in a death metal band, comment meant to be just to him but overheard	A. Nonverbally imitating awful penalty for shot during a ball game B. "Are we sure he didn't bring any weapons?"
2. Mocking, teasing, sarcasm, denigrating (put-down) family member or friend (includes telling funny story about other)	A. Observer's uncle to observer's girlfriend who has gluten intolerance (with Irritable Bowel Syndrome [IBS]) B. Brother 1 about turkey size and Brother 2 (George)	A. "So have you and Arnold ever had a race to the bathroom together?" B. "That thing is almost as big as Georgie-Porgie." Followed by, "Let's send the leftovers to Ethopia."
3. Self-deprecating	A. Visiting foreign student from Italy to host's mother about her pasta (and anxiety about its quality)	A. "Martha, this is much different from my mother's, I love it, now I can go home and tell my mother I ate pasta, 'American' style."
4. Joking (verbal or nonverbal) or telling funny story to deflect attention or reinforce norm, control	A. Adolescent cousin walking back to his seat at dinner table with "whole plate of food" bumped into observer's father and dropped plate. Father commented. B. Younger cousins moved in front of older cousins at buffet; older ones physically moved them to back of line. Younger cousins commented.	A. "At least you didn't make me drop my plate too, then we really would have a problem." B. "Baby cousins eat first; we're hungrier!"

5. Nonverbal (physical) action(s	A. Three brothers playing NFL football video game B. Three siblings give knowing looks at one another during mother and partner saying they wanted to start their Thanksgiving dinner with their traditional drink toast, but wanted it to be a "joint toast."	A. One brother performing "goofy touchdown dance" after each scored goal. B. Sibs make smoking gestures to one another, laughing.
6. Laughing at or amused by interaction, behavior, etc.	A. Several family members listening to small Cuban grandmother cursing in Spanish B. Several family members watching and listening to observer's grandfather and mother arguing about seasoning turkey, screaming at one another; grandfather swearing in Italian, then denigrates daughter's cooking. Observer "chimed in that my grandfather had to be right since he's the best Italian cook in the family."	A. Laughing and commenting about her tendency to curse in Spanish as though they don't know what she's saying. B. Observer, sister, and cousins "found this extremely humorous because they both always seem to think that they're right, especially when it comes to cooking."

A second intermediary step was to ascertain the relative frequencies of humor type usage as reported, and as well informed in all cases/reports by the observers' intuited conclusions about the most used or most "important" category that occurred during their observation periods. One technique employed was to use a text search string in the database created from the reports that listed all descriptions in the observers' language, and observers' frequencies, using variant and standard spellings of terms. Frequencies were tallied for each humor usage term, and then summed for each of the six categories. These frequencies appear in Table 2.

TABLE 2: FREQUENCIES OF HUMOR TERM REPORTED IN OBSERVATION DESCRIPTIONS

Humor usage term	Frequency (descriptions + observer count)
Mocking (out-group)	16
Mocking (in-group; within family and/or friends)	8
Teasing	107
Joking	70
Telling (funny) story (sharing memory)	22
Telling (funny) story (teasing, put down)	14
Sarcasm	16
Denigrating/put down/poking fun/making fun of/ practical jokes	88
Self-deprecation	3
Nonverbal/physical action (to amuse)	6
Nonverbal action includes poking/touching (to tease or other aggressive use)	32

Closer scrutiny of the categories in Table 2, observers' notes, revealed inconsistencies in both nomenclature and how observers "counted" humor events, leading this author to conflate several humor terms. The goal was to collapse superficially different terms that carry the same connotation into broader term entities that captured underlying intent, explanations, and examples provided by student observers. Thus, *Denigrating* then enfolded the germane term categories of *Mocking (in-group)* and *Telling story (teasing, put down)*.

At this point, an unfortunate but significant snag was apprehended—additional limitation for these data. Most observers followed their training and coding practice, and used a fairly consistent definition of "humor" as well as understanding and tracking with a coding system for types of humor provided. However, in this stage of examination the author concluded there were mixed, inaccurate, faulty, careless, or hasty applications or understanding of this critical ethnography practice. For example, re-inspection of observer notes unearthed comments, such as "The most common to take place were the telling of jokes and laughing about them. Based on what I referred to 'jokes' as I would define 'jokes' as funny stories and sarcastic comments, not really just old-fashioned jokes." Not only were definitions of humor types fuzzy, but conflation of the types apparently occurred. For example, *Joking* as a category was further problematic since it seemed to include what Wuerffel defined as "putdowns," and others as disparagement humor (Sherman, 1975; Zillman, 1983). In his study of family humor and functioning, Wuerffel included in putdowns: "all forms of sarcasm, slurs, digs, barbs and satire. The 'butt' is either another person or oneself. Tricks and practical jokes would be included under putdowns-others" (p. 13). The fuzziness and conflation became more evident after reviewing reports for statements similar to the above representative comment. At a gross level, humor observed in this sample that fit a positive slant was 29.8 percent of the total humor events recorded. These types included mocking (out-group), joking, telling funny stories (memory sharing), and nonverbal or physical actions to amuse. Humor types that approximated putdowns or disparagement—negative in nature—were 70.2 percent of observed total incidents.

The author used analytical coding to identify what, if any, relationship these topical categories might have with functions of humor, family communication standards, and family functions. To achieve this objective, the author returned to the descriptions of and impressions about humor selected and reported, and the explanatory and interpretive notes of observers. She simplified the six categories further by inferring whether and how these aligned with functional models of humor.

The final derived functional typology aligned with Martin's (2007) three-category taxonomy of the psychological functions of humor: "(1) cognitive and social benefits of the positive emotion of mirth, (2) uses of humor for social communication and influence, and (3) tension relief and coping" (p. 15). He and other researchers maintain the crucial role humor plays in regulating the necessary close relationships required for survival by humans as social animals. Particularly salient are the "positive emotions" derived from merriment and "mutual laughter" for "identifying members of an in-group, … rewarding cooperative efforts, and enhancing interpersonal bonding and social cohesion" (p. 16). The "social play of humor" can be used pro- or antisocially as well—"to strengthen relationships, smooth over conflicts, and build cohesiveness"… or "…to ostracize, humiliate, or manipulate someone, or to build up one's own status at the expense of others" (pp. 18–19). Finally, employing humor in a social context to cope with adversity or other stressors allows people to relieve tension.

Martin's taxonomy presents a conundrum, however, in that some humorous behaviors and interactions may be multifunctional, particularly with regard to his third function of tension release/coping. To illustrate, consider that when an observer's father commented to her younger cousin after he tripped and dropped his full plate of food that it was good the cousin hadn't dropped his (the father's) plate. The comment served to relieve tension for the accident and the youngster's ensuing embarrassment, and to forgive the incident as well as reassure the child he was all right and enfold him in the family's membership. Another implication could be to take the comment as a warning about not violating the elder or the hierarchy. Many observers in this family study reinforced the multilevel attributions present, as well.

Everts (2003) explained this phenomenon by citing Lakoff and Tannen's (1984; Tannen 1984, p. 20; Lakoff and Tannen 1994, pp. 138) "concept of *pragmatic homonymy* to explain how a single linguistic or paralinguistic form can serve very different communicative functions and goals" (p. 372). As Everts notes, pragmatic homonymy prefigured Tannen's later thinking:

> 'the ambiguity and polysemy of conversational strategies' (1993, p. 165) … i.e., the idea that speakers and hearers will only rightly interpret each other's intentions to the extent that they share the same cultural background. This is as true of the culture of a family as it is of that of any other group. Evidence of this is the fact that humor is often not understood or appreciated by people outside the family who do not share the background and assumptions upon which the humor is predicated. (p. 372)

Everts coined a useful term for this unique family humor style developed over time—familylect.

These concepts parallel other central ideological streams in communication and sociolinguistics, including: (1) a message-oriented approach (senders and receivers share a coding system), (2) speech community (group of people with shared norms and expectations about the use of language and other communicative systems or media), and (3) Bormann's (cf., Bormann, 1985, 1996; Poole, 1999) symbolic convergence theory (which considers how groups "create a common consciousness with shared emotions, motives, and meanings that bind members into a coherent unit" [Poole, p. 46]). Martin's three functions, though, align more or less with De Koning and Weiss' (2002) functions of positive humor, negative humor, and instrumental humor (humor used "to avoid conflict, ease tension, or smooth over negative feelings" [p. 12]), but less well with Lynch's two dialectical tensions model.

Researchers have taken numerous novel approaches to investigating humor: theories; uses, purposes, or functions; types; orientations; outcomes; and correlations to such diverse concepts as personality, genetic predispositions, compliance, attraction, intimacy, and so on. Gonzales and Mierop (2004) produced a nicely conceived review of these areas, albeit not exhaustive. One clarification of their and other conceptualizations is the distinction between the uses of humor and the functions of humor. *Use* and *function* tend to be used interchangeably by many scholars, yet use suggests a source orientation, and function a receiver orientation. In other words, someone might use teasing as a gentle means of reminding the other(s) that there has been some boundary-rule-norm violation, but the "teasee" might discern the function as significant derision. Their research is useful, and one of a handful examining family humor. Gonzalez and Mierop (2004) adapted Booth-Butterfield and Booth-Butterfield's (1991) Humor Orientation Scale to measure how much humor was perceived to exist in "the family context" (p. 145). They discovered that levels of family satisfaction rose with increasing self-humor as well as perceived increasing family members' use of humor, although it was unclear whether humor types were positive or negative.

Limited inferences may be made for the present study that link the frequencies of valenced types with the models of humor functions, and hence, with family communication patterns. Negative vis-à-vis positive types of humor events were tallied roughly at a ratio of 2:1. Since no determination of family communication patterns nor other such indexes were used, the greater negativity could possibly indicate holiday "too much togetherness" tension, stress from producing a Thanksgiving Day meal, or even decreasing inhibition in adults due to drinking alcohol—a point made clearly in one-third of the observers' reports, or simply a function of the young adult ages of observers.

Observers, although uneven in their notes, generally noted when humor used was associated with positive or negative reactions, including hurt feelings, individuals leaving a room, or verbal or physical retaliation. The impressions of reactions to humor reported by observers counter the descriptive layer of humor behaviors, however. The observers evinced an ability to draw a boundary between their roles as participant-observer, and stated that laughter often accompanied or ensued humor events—more often "laughing with" rather than "laughing at." Additionally, in all but five reports, student observers made statements that reflected a sentiment of the generally positive role humor played in their families. One observer wrote, "I always knew that my family used humor as a way to show that we love and care for one another. Since the type of humor that we use is most often a form of mockery, it may be hard to see how my family actually appreciates each other. However, once I observed my family I realized that we use mockery and poking fun at one another because we love each other immensely." This student validated her perspective by retrospective processing with family members, who agreed with her inference. This astute insight echoed Everts' sociolinguistic analysis of one family (her own): "This family's style of humor, like many, consists of forms that are aggressive on the surface but serve to create involvement, solidarity, and even off-record intimacy, while socializing its users into the norms and standards of the family values of competence and strength" (2003, p. 370). Interestingly, the use of humor as noted frequently to reinforce hierarchy and family norms actually strengthens bonds and individual's group membership. The observations for this study generally reflected humor used to reinforce control, both in reestablishing hierarchy, but also enforcing or reminding family members to stay within normative behavior.

Even with limited empirical evidence to buttress this conclusion, this study's results challenge Wuerffel's (1986) findings in his study relating self-reported uses of humor with their measured family strengths. Wuerffel stated that stronger families reported using more humor; weaker families used less humor. Stronger families used humor "to maintain a positive outlook on life, for entertainment, to reduce tension, to express warmth, to put others at ease, to facilitate conversations, to lessen anxiety, and to help cope with difficult situations. Stronger families report negative effects when humor is used to put down other family members" (p. 117). Families with weaker family strengths used more putdowns of others than did stronger families; strong families used more positive types of humor (wit, jokes, family fun, and "other," but excluding putdowns of self or others) than did weaker families. Useful here is Zijderveld's (1983) caution that "Like all interactions, joking and jesting take place in social situations, and whether or not we can call them humorous depends on the definition of these situations by the parties to the joking and jesting" (p. 25). To reiterate an earlier point, DiCioccio and Ketrow (2009) substantiated humor/sarcasm as a family communication standard. This study bears out this result. Perhaps the contradiction with Wuerffel is due to his use of quantitative measures, and the richness of this study's qualitative information allows insight into how intimates in families use what Everts termed semiotic cues "to mark a humor frame," and offer recognition of and appreciation for family humor in a role to embody the essential functions of family.

Communication scholars lag behind other disciplines in investigating humor in family interactions. Future research could isolate and tighten foci on the links between humor and family communication standards or schema, particularly with regard to these as indexing better family functioning. Overall, despite conceptual distinctions weaknesses, methodological limitations, and a small purposive sample, the narrative categories and findings in this qualitative study scaffold better understanding of humorous communication in bona fide families.

I wish to acknowledge with much gratitude the good work, insights, and Thanksgiving holiday sacrifices of members of my Fall 2010 University of Rhode Island Communication Research Methods (COM382) sections (in alphabetical order) who graciously provided family humor observations data and reports: Michael Bartolemeo, Kwame Bediako, Katie Boutin, Keith Bruni, Rebecca Cable, Adam Chickman, Jessica Chindgren, Nicholas Coccio, Raymond Coia, Ashley Cordisco, Thomas Constantino, Andrew Corria, Christina DiGiovanni, Laura Egan, Joshua Einhorn, Nicole Fasullo, Nicholas Fiumefreddo, Morgan Flynn, Gregory Frasher, Andrew Kydd, Matthew Lenz, Franco Lo Presti, Olivia McDougall, Brendan Mitchell, Shannon Moran, Lauren Moody, Sarah Morrison, Alexa O'Rourke, Rory O'Neil, Matthew Osit, Kelsey Pennock, Lindsey Poole, Breana Quinn, Matthew Rhieu, Allison Schworn, Julie Showalter, Fallon Sjostedt, Casey Smith, Daniel Spitzfaden, Christopher Swanick, Kate Taito, Thomas Thornton, John Toner, Andrew Wallace, and Dana Yacyk.

Notes

1. Defining *crucible* in both senses—metaphorically, as a container that will hold substances that may be subjected to very high temperatures; and as "a situation of severe trial, or in which different elements interact, leading to the creation of something new." (Retrieved from oxforddictionaries.com/definition/crucible)

2. Locating group as a task-achieving collective residing within an organization.

3. Names of student researchers/observers and/or family members and friends have been changed to protect their privacy and confidentiality.

References

Averbeck, J. M., & Hample, D. (2008). Ironic message production: How and why we produce ironic messages. *Communication Monographs, 75*(4), 396–410. doi:10.1080/03637750802512389.

Bochner, A. P. (1976). Conceptual frontiers in the study of communication in families: An introduction to the literature. *Human Communication Research, 2*(4), 381-397.

Booth-Butterfield, S., & Booth-Butterfield, M. (1991). Individual differences in the communication of humorous messages. *Southern Communication Journal, 56*(3), 205-218.

Bormann, E. G. (1985). Symbolic Convergence Theory: A communication formulation. *Journal of Communication, 35*(4), 128–138.

Bormann, E. G. (1996). Symbolic convergence theory and communication in group decision making. In R. Y. Hirokawa & M. S. Poole (Eds.), *Communication and group decision making* (2nd ed, pp. 81–113). Beverly Hills, CA: SAGE.

Caughlin, J. P. (2003). Family communication standards: What counts as excellent family communication and how are such standards associated with family satisfaction? *Human Communication Research, 29*(1), 5–40.

Chaffee, S. H., McLeod, J. M., & Atkin, C. K. (1971). Parental influences on adolescent media use. *American Behavioral Scientist, 14*, 323–340.

De Koning, E., & Weiss, R. L. (2002). The Relational Humor Inventory: Functions of humor in close relationships. *The American Journal of Family Therapy, 30*, 1–18.

DiCioccio, R. L. (2010). The Interactionist Model of Teasing Communication. In A. S. Rancer & T. A. Avtgis (Eds.), *Arguments, aggression, and conflict: New directions in theory and research* (pp. 340–355). New York: Routledge.

DiCioccio, R. L., & Ketrow, S. M. (2009). Family communication, argument, and critical decision-making. In S. Jacobs (Ed.), *Concerning argument: Selected papers from the 15th Biennial Conference on Argumentation* (pp. 166–183). Washington, DC: National Communication Association.

Dixson, M. (1985). Models and perspectives of parent-child communication. In T. J. Socha & G. H. Stamp (Eds.), *Parents, children and communication: Frontiers of theory and research* (pp. 43–62). Hillsdale, NJ: Lawrence Erlbaum.

Everts, E. (2003). Identifying a particular humor style: A sociolinguistic discourse analysis. *Humor, 16*(4), 369–412. doi:0933-1719/03/0016-0369.

Frey, L. R. (1994). The naturalistic paradigm: Studying small groups in the postmodern era. *Small Group Research, 25*(4), 551-577.

Glaser, B. G., & Strauss, A. (1967). *The discovery of grounded theory: Strategies of qualitative research.* Chicago: Aldine.

Gonzales, S. M., & Mierop, J. (2004). Humor use and family satisfaction: A cross cultural approach. *Intercultural Communication Studies, 13*(1), 125–138. Retrieved from www.uri.edu/iaics/content/2004v13n1/index.php

*Graham, E. E., Papa, M. J., & Brooks, G. P. (1992). Functions of humor in conversation: Conceptualization and measurement. *Western Journal of Communication, 56*, 161–183.

Infante, D. A., Riddle, B. L., Horvath, C. L., & Tumlin, S. A. (1992). Verbal aggressiveness: Messages and reasons. *Communication Quarterly, 40*, 116–216.

Koerner, A. F., & Fitzpatrick, M. A. (2002). Toward a theory of family communication. *Communication Theory, 12*(1), 70–91.

Lynch, O. H. (2002). Humorous communication: Finding a place for humor in communication research. *Communication Theory, 12*(4), 423–445.

Maccoby, E. E. (1992). The role of parents in the socialization of children: An historical overview. *Developmental Psychology, 28*, 1006–1017.

Martin, M. M., Anderson, C. M., Burant, P. A., & Weber, K. (1997). Verbal aggression in sibling relationships. *Communication Quarterly, 45*, 304–317.

Martin, R. A. (2007). *The psychology of humor: An integrative approach.* Burlington, MA: Elsevier Academic Press.

Martin, R. A., Puhlik-Doris, P., Larsen, G., Gray, J., & Weir, K. (2003). Individual differences in uses of humor and their relation to psychological well-being: Development of the Humor Styles Questionnaire. *Journal of Research in Personality, 37*, 48–75. doi:10.1016/S0092-6566(02)00534-2

Meadowcroft, J. M. (1986). Family communication patterns and political development: The child's role. *Communication Research, 13*(4), 603–624.

Meadowcroft, J. M., & Fitzpatrick, M. A. (1988). Theories of family communication: Toward a merger of intersubjectivity and mutual influence processes. In R. P. Hawkins, J. W. Wiemann, & S. Pingree (Eds.), *Advancing communication science: Merging mass and interpersonal communication* (pp. 253–275). Beverly Hills, CA: SAGE.

Meyer, J. C. (2000). Humor as a double-edged sword: Four functions of humor in communication. *Communication Theory, 10*(3), 310–331.

Moskowitz, G. B. (2005). *Social cognition: Understanding self and others.* New York: The Guilford Press.

Ooms, T. (1995). Taking families seriously: Family impact analysis as an essential policy tool. *Paper presented at the Family Impact Seminar*, Washington, DC Retrieved from www.familyimpactseminars.org/pf_fis02suppreport.pdf

Parsons, T., & Bales, R. F. (1955). *Family, socialization and interaction process*. Glencoe, IL: Free Press.

Petronio, S., & Braithwaite, D. O. (1993). The contributions and challenges of family communication to the field of communication. *Journal of Applied Communication Research, 21*(1), 103–110.

Poole, M. S. (1999). Group communication theory. In L. R. Frey (Ed.), *The handbook of group communication theory and research* (pp. 37–70). Thousand Oaks, CA: SAGE Publications.

Propp, K. M., & Kreps, G. L. (1994). A rose by any other name: The vitality of group communication research. *Communication Studies, 45*(1), 7–16.

Putnam, L. L. (1994). Revitalizing small group communication: Lessons learned from a bona fide group perspective. *Communication Studies, 45*(1), 97-102.

Putnam, L. L., & Stohl, C. (1990). Bona fide groups: A reconceptualization of groups in context. *Communication Studies, 41*(3), 248-265.

Richards, L. (2005). *Handling qualitative data: A practical guide*. Thousand Oaks, CA: SAGE Publications.

Ritchie, L. D. (1991). Family communication patterns: An epistemic analysis and conceptual reinterpretation. *Communication Research, 18*(4), 548–565.

Ritchie, L. D., & Fitzpatrick, M. A. (1990). Family communication patterns: Measuring intrapersonal perceptions of interpersonal relationships. *Communication Research, 17*, 523–544.

Sherman, L. W. (1975). An ecological study of glee in small groups of preschool children. *Child Development, 46*(1), 53–61.

Sillars, A. L. (1980). Attributions and communication in roommate conflicts. *Communication Monographs, 47*(3), 180–200.

Socha, T. J. (1999). Communication in family units: Studying the first 'group.' In L. R. Frey (Ed.), *The handbook of group communication theory and research* (pp. 475–492). Thousand Oaks, CA: SAGE Publications.

Socha, T. J. (2009, November). Missing links between family and group communication: Children and communication development. *Paper presented at the 95th Annual Meeting of the National Communication Association*, Chicago.

Socha, T. J., & Yingling, J. (2010). *Families communicating with children*. Cambridge: Polity Press.

Vangelisti, A. L. (1993). Communication in the family: The influence of time, relational prototypes, and irrationality. *Communication Monographs, 60*, 42–54.

Vogl-Bauer, S. (2003). Aggressive expression within the family: Effects on processes and outcomes. In A. S. Rancer & T. A. Avtgis (Eds.), *Arguments, aggression, and conflict: New directions in theory and research* (pp. 318–339). New York: Routledge.

Wuerffel, J. L. (1986). *The relationship between humor and family strengths (putdowns, sarcasm, jokes, wit)*. Doctoral dissertation. ETD collection for University of Nebraska - Lincoln. Paper AAI8620825. Retrieved from Proquest: digitalcommons.unl.edu/dissertations/AAI8620825

Zijderveld, A. C. (1983). Humour: Playing with meanings. *Current Sociology, 31*(6), 6–25. doi:10.1177/001139283031003004

Zillman, D. (1983). Disparagement humor. In P. E. McGhee & J. H. Goldstein (Eds.), *Handbook of humor research: Basic issues* (Vol. 1, pp. 85–108). New York: Springer-Verlag.

CHAPTER 11

BUCKET HUMOR: THE SIGNIFICANT ROLE OF HUMOR WITHIN ORGANIZATIONAL CULTURE

Owen Hanley Lynch
Southern Methodist University

Jonny: "What do you study using humor?"

Owen: "I don't use humor, I study organizational culture by paying attention to the jokes and humor that members use at work."

Jonny: "Doesn't that kill the joke?"

Owen: "Yes ... But it reveals the culture!"

2010 conversation between Jonny Elbow, a stand-up comedian, and myself

Recently there has been an explosion of interest in the communicative role of humor at work (Holmes & Marra, 2006; Holmes & Stubbe, 2003; Martin, 2004; Mullany, 2004; Lynch 2002, 2007, 2009a, 2010; Tracy, Myers, & Scott, 2006; Westwood & Rhodes, 2007). Using a broad brush, these studies focus on how humor facilitates the formation and maintenance of organizational culture and its members' identities at work.

Why this focus on humor? First, because humor is a pervasive and meaningful aspect of organizational life; second, humor is fundamentally a communicative activity (Lynch, 2002) and as such "offers rich potential for understanding everyday experiences in organizational life" (Martin, 2004, p. 151). Humor is used at work to form and maintain group cohesion and group boundaries (Meyer, 1997), manage emotional stress (Shuler & Sypher, 2000), make the monotony of work bearable (Roy, 1958), maintain gendered identities, and manufacture consent (Collinson, 1988). Humor is used by managers to control employees indirectly and politely (Holmes & Marra, 2002a), and it is used by employees as a basis for social and professional control (Lynch, 2009a), and to actively resist management (Lynch, 2009a, 2010). Humor is also used to make sense of workplace paradox and ambiguity (Hatch & Sanford, 1993; Tracy et. al., 2006), to construct new shared meanings out of this ambiguity (Lynch, 2002, 2007), and to negotiate paradoxes of hierarchical power, structure, agency, and gendered identity (Martin, 2004). In short, humor is found in almost every workplace and clearly it does much more than make work life bearable. It is an essential way in which we form and negotiate our priorities, roles, and identities at work.

This chapter starts with how organizational and discourse scholars operationalize workplace humor, specifically how the operational definition guides the research method, process, and more important, what is recognized and is not recognized as humor. This is followed by a brief overview of the organizational humor research with an emphasis on humor's social and functional role at work. An in-depth case study is also provided of humor's use in an organizational crisis and labor negotiation.

OPERATIONAL DEFINITION OF HUMOR FOR WORKPLACE RESEARCH

Humor is complex, varied, and context specific. We know it when we see it or hear it, but we often "had to be there" to appreciate or fully understand it. When deciding what is or is not humor, researchers of conversational humor tend to play it safe (Hay, 2001). Observational researchers operationalize and identify "humor" in one of three ways: by sender's intention (Pizzini, 1991; Winick, 1976), by the audience's verbal (laughter) or nonverbal (smile) response (Martin, 2004), or by both the intention and response (Holmes & Hay, 1997; Holmes, 2000). Holmes has a widely used (Mullany, 2004; Holmes & Marra 2002a, 2002b, 2006; Marra, 2007) operational definition for humor that states any "utterances which are intended by the speaker(s) to be amusing and perceived to be amusing by at least some participants" (2000, p. 163).

This seemingly catchall operational definition is not without limitations, because it requires the researcher to determine if the humor message was intended to be funny by the sender, and to determine if the message was received and interpreted as funny. Lynch (2002) advocates an expanded operational definition of workplace humor as any "discourse or action that was found to be funny by the member of the work group" (Lynch 2002, p. 423). This definition has also been accepted (Bussiere, 2009; Chappel & Ziebland, 2004; Foxworth, 2008; Merolla, 2006; Ojha & Holms, 2010; Tracy et al., 2006) as it places focus on the interpretation of the receiver rather than the intentions of the sender. Lynch argues (2002, 2007) more than just observing feedback (laughter or smile) is needed to recognize humor at work for three reasons: (1) Things found funny by the members of a work group are *not* necessarily intended to be funny by the object/sender of the humor, (2) It is likely the things found funny by members of a work group may not be identifiable by an outsider, researcher, and/or manager. Sometimes organizational members may be stone-faced when they find something funny, but later when not under observation of management may laugh till their sides hurt, (3) What amuses one in-group in a specific workplace with specific tensions may not be amusing to another. It may even be considered disgusting or hostile by those outsiders of the group, including researchers, who are unfamiliar with the occupation setting (see Tracy et al., 2006 for an extended discussion on this last point). However, there is a catch with Lynch's definition. It requires at least participant observation by the researcher within the context and social process of the group being studied.

SOCIAL ROLE OF HUMOR AT WORK

Humor as Bonding and Biting

Workplace humor functions to strengthen workplace collegiality (Clouse & Spurgeon, 1995; Ehrenberg, 1995) and team fidelity (Meyer, 1997; Vinton, 1989). It helps facilitate relationship initiation as well as reduce tensions (Duncan & Fiesal, 1989). It can defuse anger (Consalvo, 1989; Coser, 1960) as well as soften criticism (Holmes, 2000; Martin, 2004; Morreall, 1991). However, Boxer and Cortes-Conde (1996) argue humor can also "bite"—be used to tease and hurt. Holmes and Marra argue that subtle quips and overt jocular abuse humor are used by workers to point out flaws or distance others at work (2002a). In friendship groups at work, humor can be both bonding and cruel, particularly in blue-collar work environments (Collinson, 1988; Roy, 1958). Humor "draws people together on the basis of their shared understandings, gives us a common form of expression, breaks down social barriers (but of course can also erect them), creates friendships and creates targets" (Hopfl, 2007, p. 44). This inclusion (bonding) and exclusion (distancing) role of relational humor at work engenders in-group and out-group conflicts. Coser (1959) argued the greater the "in-group cohesion" the greater the "out-group conflict." At work these in- and out-group boundaries are (re)produced by excluding individuals (or groups) who do not have the stock of the in-group's references, skills, language, and sense-making process (Tracy et al., 2006; Weick, 1979, 1995, 2001).

Humor as Expression of Identification

Professional and organizational identity is not constructed in isolation but in relation to organizational processes, structures, and (most important, from a relational perspective) the group we interact with and see ourselves part of in our everyday work (Dutton & Dukerich, 1991; Lynch, 2009a). Tracey et al.'s study of correctional officers, 911 call-takers, and firefighters is an example of how humor is used in an organization's identification processes. This study focuses on how these workers use humor to react to and manage their personal identity in response to their stressful work. They argue humor is used to elect meanings that affirm one's sense of self, as well as demonstrate how this humor conforms and constrains the group's identity and sense-making process at work. "Employees can rely on humor to subtly clarify and select a meaning that affirms one's sense of self. Humor provides a memorable and fun vehicle through which employees learn, select, confirm, challenge and transform identity" (Tracy et al., 2006, p. 301). In contrast, Lynch (2009a, 2010) provides examples of how humor is used in the process of organizing work itself to retain, protect, and reify the values and agency of workers within their actual work process. Humor is revealed to be more than a coping device in order to do your job; it is a means through which the workers actually make sense of and perform their organizing role.

USING HUMOR AT WORK

Functional Use of Humor

The functional use of humor is the "tactical use of humor to increase managerial and organizational effectiveness" (Lynch, 2010, p. 143). Duncan et al. recognized, that "humor may serve as a potentially important tool for organizational development" (Duncan et al., 1990, p. 275). This emerging focus on the tactical use of humor has gained an increased academic and business interest in recent years. Popular instructional books detail how humor can be used by managers to increase profit, increase worker compliance, and reduce stress (Kushner, 1990; Gibson, 1994; Paulson, 1989; Ross, 1989, 1992). Humor is therefore held as an important component of a successful business culture (Deal & Kennedy, 2000; Dwyer, 1991).

Warning! Just because humor can be used to improve organizational culture and processes does not mean it can easily be deployed or always have the intended effect. Collinson (2002) warns that humor is a double-edged sword, and attempts to manage humor may actually suppress humor, and attempts to control humor may lead to resurgence of undesired (unproductive) forms of workplace humor. This aspect of humor is termed *duality of humor*, when humor is assumed to have one function or support one meaning it always simultaneously supports (on some level) the opposite (see Lynch, 2002; Marra, 2007; Meyer, 2000).

Managerial Use of Humor at Work

Humor has been linked with effective transformative and transactional leadership alike (Avolio, Howell, & Sosik, 1999; Crawford, 1994; Holmes & Marra, 2006), and leaders who use humor find innovative solutions to problems (Dixon, 1980). Managers and those of hierarchical status can use humor effectively to gain compliance without emphasis on the power differentials (Holmes, 2000; Mullany, 2004). This managerial use of humor to reduce the sting of authoritative intent has been well documented in humor studies of workplaces (Duncan et al., 1990; Holmes, 2000; Holmes & Marra, 2002a; Mullany, 2004). While Martin (2004) reveals that humor's use has a wider significance for women managers, they use humor daily to reduce distance but also negotiate the paradoxes and pitfalls of being both a woman and a middle manager in gendered organizations.

Employee Use of Humor at Work

The most documented form of employee humor in case studies is humor used safely to criticize a higher member or an organizational process. Radcliffe-Brown (1952) argued that subordinate humor functioned as sanctioned disrespect. Subordinate humor resists the hierarchy, but it does not change the hierarchical power structure. Humor as "sanctioned disrespect" is found in many workplace studies (Boland & Hoffman, 1986; Bradney, 1958; Collinson, 1988, 1992, 1994; Coser, 1959, 1960; Davis, 1988; Holdaway, 1988; Levine, 1976; Linstead, 1985; Mulkay, 1988; Powell, 1988; Roy, 1958; Sykes, 1966). These organizational case studies supported Radcliffe-Brown's assertions that humor as resistance does not change the authoritative system. This humor may poke fun and even temporally resolve (allow us to make sense of and live with) organizational incongruity and paradox (Hatch & Sanford, 1993; Martin, 2004), but it does not seem to subvert or have a transformative effect on the target of the joke. With incongruity and/or relief as its basis without removing the cause for the tension itself, the brief respite gained from resistance humor is akin to blowing off steam or as *safety valve resistance* (Lynch, 2002). The recent work of Holmes and Marra (2002a, 2002b, 2006) and Marra (2007) can be used to emphasize this trend. Holmes and Marra, using recordings of workplace meetings, demonstrated that employees in these situations use down-up humor frequently to challenge the status quo on three levels: the individual—to take down a superior member of a group, the organizational—challenge the values of the larger organization, and the societal—to challenge the values of broader society (2002a).

Lynch (2009a, 2009b) argues there are two underdeveloped areas of organizational humor research: (1) how employees use humor to control each other—*concertive control humor* and (2) the use of humor by employees as a subversive act to resist managerial control or change organizational process—*resistance humor*. Concertive control asserts that workers develop the means for their own control as self-managed teams. Their communicative norms become the basis for rules that replace the centralized and hierarchical system of control (Barker, 1993, 1999). Concertive control humor occurs when in-group members use humor discourse to ensure all members of an organizational activity conform to the members' standards and norms. Perhaps nothing reflects the duality of humor more than the difference between humor used purposefully to conform to the standards and to dominate discourses and roles of the organizational culture, and humor used to purposefully and actively resist managerial discourse and roles. Lynch (2009a, 2010) provides case study examples of how humor is an effective medium for preserving in-group and self-identity by resisting external control of the labor process.

This chapter ends with a case study where employees use resistance humor to not only express grievance but resist managerial discourse that was dominating the ongoing organization's benefits negotiations. In a broader sense this case study demonstrates how discursive meanings are articulated and contested at work as well as how individuals create and display parts of their organizational identities through humor performances.

HUMOR CASE STUDY: NEGOTIATING CULTURAL VALUES

Description and Methodology

Arthur Asa Berger, one of the forefathers of popular culture studies, argued that it is observing others' humor that allows us to understand and see different perspectives (Berger, 1995). He argues that the goal of understanding humor in ethnography is to reach and understand the way of life for a group and then write this way of life up (Berger, 1989). To accomplish this, ethnographers must be fully embedded and affected by the processes of the group. Hatch (2002) argued that to understand dynamic organizational culture requires in-depth, prolonged ethnographic study. Clearly, to understand in-group humor and an organizational culture requires putting your time in. This case study comes from a three-year ethnography of "The Prep," a private middle school in the southern United States (close to 5,000 hours in field). This study was full-immersion ethnography where I worked as a fulltime teacher. The nature of the work (not physical and not in constant observation of other members) allowed for full-member participation and the jotting down of notes, key phrases, and words as head-notes for later writing up as field notes. Throughout the entire process many (in the hundreds) ethnographic interviews (Spradley, 1979; Lindlof, 1995) were conducted and reconstructed as quickly as possible (typically at the end of the school day) into field notes. Twice a week, or after significant events, field notes based on the head-notes and ethnographic interviews were written up as journal entries. Within the middle school every teacher and administrator taught at least one class that met daily for 50 minutes. The middle school had four administrators, an administrative assistant (who also taught a class), and 22 teachers.

The Prep, founded over 50 years ago, has a mix of boarding and day students. It sits on a 400-acre site in an affluent suburb of a southwestern town. The Prep is considered a premier academic school for its geographical region and is well regarded nationally. The Prep is a private school with a motto designed around developing the entire student body spiritually, academically, and athletically. The academics are highly regarded with students, and this is seen through the placement of The Prep's students in elite universities around the nation.

A large part of this academic environment stems from the close relationship between teachers and students. The classrooms are small with an average student-to-teacher ratio of six to one. Teachers are informally expected to be involved in extracurricular activities with students outside the classroom. Every teacher is also an advisor to a small group of students. Thirty percent of teachers live on campus but all are involved in the boarding community. The school started as a boarding school and culture was heavily influenced by this founding mission to be a school and a community for personal and academic growth of the student. The teachers are never *off duty*, several working from 7 a.m. to 9 p.m. It was a boarding school; the boundaries among work, home, family, community, teacher, and parent were blurred.

Context for the humor episode: The Prep was in fiscal crisis due to the gross mismanagement of funds, generous compensation packages for the old headmaster, and an ambitious expansion of campus buildings. As a result, the chief financial officer (CFO) and the headmaster were asked to resign. Though the faculty were not the cause of the fiscal crisis, it was widely expected that much of the fiscal crisis would be addressed through cuts in faculty compensation and/or benefits. A new headmaster was hired and one of his first actions was to hire a new CFO and establish a "benefits review committee": I found myself placed on this committee as a faculty representative, and here is the rest of the story ...

Case Episode: Drop in the Bucket

It started like any faculty meeting except more so. No one was absent. Every administrator, teacher, and staff member was cramped into the music recital room, shaped like a Greek amphitheater. The energy in the room was overwhelmingly tense. Instead of the loud, amiable chatter that usually preceded a faculty meeting, people filed in quietly. Billy leaned over to me and said, "It is as if they are coming to a funeral." The observational joke didn't need a punch line, "Perhaps they were."

The board of the school was already seated before the meeting. They sat in the front row facing the newly formed "benefits review committee." The chair of this committee was George, the newly hired CFO, who had started the week before. George sat at a small desk flanked on both sides: to his left sat the committee's three board representatives, to his right sat three faculty members: myself as the faculty representative; Billy, dean of faculty; and Brenden, head of the upper school. George started by introducing himself to the faculty as their new CFO. He joked that he could not imagine a worse way to start a new job by chairing this "informative town-hall meeting" on the school's fiscal crisis. Even though the crowd was hostile to the message and fearful of the pending cuts they laughed, recognizing and emphasizing his difficult position. It was a good start, which was followed by a sober half-hour presentation that outlined the past administration's mismanagement of funds, the current crisis, and suggestions/strategies to ensure the school's future solvency. To remain viable the school would need to conform to "best practices of peer institutions" as well as consider the following options: (a) selling some of the school's land (an option that contradicted the school's founding charter), (b) a fund-raising campaign focused on debt reduction, and (c) a cut in the "generous" staff benefits package.

Immediately after the presentation, Tim, the head of the board of trustees (and a nonvoting member of the benefits committee), got up from the front row and addressed the room. He efficiently outlined the problem with the first two options: Unfortunately the selling of land is not a solution right now as the alumni would be angered by this action and this anger could jeopardize the success of any fundraising campaign. But perhaps the biggest problem is that no one wants to give money to pay for past mismanagement and fiscal irresponsibility! Especially without clear evidence of the new administration's attempts to right the ship.

Tim was then interrupted by Chris, a well-respected faculty member, "Let me guess, this brings us to the third option." This statement was supported not by outright laughter or wry smiles, but a strange almost involuntary huffing and nodding from the crowd—a fine example of organizational gallows humor made by and for the condemned (Lewis, 1987).

The teachers, as academics, proved to be a terrible audience for George's frank and business jargon–filled presentation. They attacked the presentation's use of language and basis for evidence. Several of the teachers stood up and emphasized the irony of using the phrase as "*best* practice" to justify reneging on promised and time-honored benefits. Others attacked the concept of "*peer* institution," asking questions such as how can the committee compare this school, "the premier institution in the region" (phrase taken from the marketing literature), to other schools in the region. The last argument from the faculty centered on the concept of "community" and in particular on the CFO's suggestion that a necessary step was to cut the free tuition benefit for faculty and staff dependents. One of the teachers asked a board member, "How dare you expect me to create a community for your children when mine are not welcome?" To which the board member replied, "We have to cut somewhere. How fair is it to keep the tuition benefit when many of the teachers do not have children?" Frank, a usually silent teacher, stood up and declared passionately, "Hang on, I don't have kids, or dependents as you call them, but I don't want to teach, work, or live in a community that does not welcome the kids of my colleagues." Frank's comments drew wide support. It was closely followed by a direct question from Jane (another teacher), "George, in the big scheme of things, how much money would be saved by cutting the tuition benefit as many of the staff and teachers kids would receive financial aid?" George replied, "In the big scheme of things, it is only a drop in the bucket." This was met with audible gasps from the audience. The din that followed the "bucket comment" became heated. Faculty yelled at the indignity of cutting the tuition benefits, one teacher yelled, "Are you going to destroy this community over the price of one of your Lexus'?" Several of the faculty clapped as a sign of support. Attempting to regain control of the meeting, Tim stood up and thanked the teachers for their passion and suggested this was a "good place to stop the meeting." He then framed the cuts discussed today as "only ideas." Teachers stormed out, united in their cause and fired up in their solidified indignation.

The mocking phrases such as "best practices" and "peer institution" may have functioned to humorously unite the faculty but it also united George and the three voting board members on the committee (all the votes necessary for a 4 to 7 majority) in opposition to the faculty. The faculty had two legitimate concerns: (a) Which institutions should be used as a benchmark? and (b) What should our top concern be: upholding the current organizational standards or the larger industry standard? However, the public mocking of the business language itself caused the majority of the committee to frame the faculty as unreasonable and ignorant of business practices. The board basically felt comfortable dismissing the faculty input: "If they cannot accept the standard business practice, how can they have any reasonable input in this budgetary process?" I tried, as the faculty representative, to argue that it was not being measured to a standard that upset the faculty but rather the standard the committee was using to measure that was at question. This fell on deaf ears and the board, along with their representatives on the committee, was determined to dismiss the concerns and input of the faculty. The plan was to meet in a week and "go ahead and get this over with."

The next week the faculty joked about the meeting and especially about the "Lexus comment." The jokes functioned as *safety valve humor*. It released the tension building from the pending cuts but did nothing to address the cause for the tension itself. Many jokes seemed to make hay out of the budget crisis as the teachers attempted to make sense of the situation. A sense-making term that emerged was "freebies." The first time I heard the word being used was in connection to a false and exaggerated joke of George going down to the school's daycare (subsidized on-campus daycare for the staff's children) to "count the future freebies." This story jokingly made its rounds and one dean of the middle school (who had two young children) started signing her internal emails on the topic of the budget cuts as "freebie breeder."

There were several in-group bonding incidents with gallows humor but no joke became as symbolically significant as the picture of the bucket. The day after the faculty meeting, a photocopy picture of a bucket was put in every teacher's mailbox. The identity of the author/copier was a mystery, but a great topic of discussion itself. The picture was clearly referencing the "drop in the bucket" comment by George. It became a rally symbol as the photocopy was posted on George's and the new headmaster's doors. It was posted in clever places all over the school, on the wall of the faculty lounge, on the door of the stall in the men's bathroom next to George's office. It was even somehow placed with the agenda papers of the headmaster's division-head meeting that week. I personally observed a teacher who, finding the bucket picture in his box, laughed and then as he walked past the new headmaster's car put it under the wiper like a ticket. The bucket could not be avoided and it made every faculty member laugh.

The subsequent budget committee meeting was not as cut-and-dried as the board assumed it would be. The headmaster attended as a nonvoting member. Tim and George grew clearly frustrated when I referenced the "drop in the bucket" comment as a committee problem. Tim declared the flyers as "unfair" and "a misrepresentation issue." However, we, myself, and other faculty members on the committee highlighted an issue to the committee: that if the tuition benefits were cut, the headmaster would have to explain to the penny why "the drop" was necessary. This brought the discussion to focus not on "best practices" as a basis for making budget decisions but on the size, effect, and rationale behind the benefit cuts themselves. George had come prepared and provided budget projections with and without the tuition benefit cuts. It revealed that only one current faculty student would not qualify for need-based aid (part of our budget anyway). However, there were six children of current faculty who, if the faculty members remained employed for the next 15 years, would also not qualify. George added that "this was a drop in the bucket" but if we want to keep the benefit we needed to find a way to increase revenue or protect ourselves from the expense of future dependents and from new hires with dependents.

Billy, dean of the faculty, asked frankly, "If it is a drop in the bucket, why do this?" This was answered by Tim and another board member who said that certain big donors have expressed their reluctance to give money to a school in the next campaign because they think it is unfair that teachers who can afford the tuition get a "free ride." Brenden (faculty member and head of upper school) argued that this was not a good enough reason for these "draconian cuts." Tim and the same board member argued they were not "draconian but necessary." I asked, "Necessary or expedient?" Tim said, "Fine. Politically expedient. But we have to do something!" The headmaster, a good man who had inherited a mess, looked at me and asked, "What is the difference, Owen?" It was an opening, and I answered, "We have to decide which symbolically means more: a 'drop in the bucket' or a 'free ride.'" I relied on the fact that as an ordained minister the headmaster would understand the importance of symbols. I argued that if it were only an expedient and symbolic cut to satisfy big donors, perhaps we could give them what they want without reneging on promised benefits to current teachers and staff. It was quickly agreed on and voted on; tuition benefits would be cut for future hires, but existing staff and faculty would be grandfathered in. It was a compromise and, like all compromises, it was bittersweet.

As we left the room, I asked the headmaster, "Did you mean to give me the opening with the What is the difference question?" He paused, looked directly in my eye, and replied, "Perhaps," and smiled.

CONCLUSION

This case study illustrates that humor used during the faculty meeting, the subsequent sense-making process of the teachers, and finally the use of the "bucket" joke to influence the committee was not trivial but central to the organization's process and final compromise. It is interesting to note that a majority of jokes and humorous messages, including the "bucket" humor and picture reported in this case study, would not be considered humor using Holmes' (2000) definition for workplace humor. The significance of the sense-making process and bucket joke would have been overlooked. This is why this chapter argues that Lynch's operational definition of humor is advantageous for research interested in understanding the role humor has in forming and maintaining organizational culture. It is my hope that reading this case study made you laugh, yet simultaneously feel uncomfortable and somewhat empathetic toward all the agents (George, the board, the committee, the new headmaster, teachers, and the staff). This reflects the duality and complexity of situated humor. It is also my hope, that communication scholars keep and develop further the interest in humor's role at work.

References

Avolio, B., Howell, J., & Sosik, J. (1999). A funny thing happened on the way to the bottom line: Humor as moderator of leadership style effects. *Academy of Management Journal* *42*(2), 219–227.

Barker, J. (1993). Tightening the iron cage: Concertive control in self-managing teams. *Administrative Science Quarterly, 38,* 408–437.

Barker, J. (1999). *The discipline of teamwork: Participation and concertive control.* Thousand Oaks, CA: SAGE.

Berger, A. (1989). Getting serious about humor. *Journal of Communication, 26*(3), 20–22.

Berger, A. (1995). *Blind men and elephants.* New Brunswick, NJ: Transaction Publishers.

Boland, R., & Hoffman, R. (1986). Humor in a machine shop: An interpretation of symbolic action. In P. Frost, V. Mitchell, & W. Nord (Eds.), *Organization reality: Reports from the firing line* (pp. 371–376). Glenview, IL: Scott, Foresman.

Boxer, D., & Cortes-Conde, F. (1995). From bonding to biting: Conversational joking and identity display. *Journal of Pragmatics, 27,* 275–294.

Bradney, P. (1958). Quasi-familial relationships in industry. *Human Relationship, 11,* 179–187.

Bussiere, A. (2009). The effects of humor on the processing of word of mouth. *Advances in Consumer Research, 36*, 400–404.

Chappel, A., & Ziebland, S. (2004). The role of humor for men with testicular cancer. *Qualitative Health Research, 14*, 1123–1139.

Clouse, W., & Spurgeon, K. (1995). Corporate analysis of humor. *Psychology: A Journal of Human Behavior, 32*(3), 1–24.

Collinson, D. (1988). Engineering humor: Masculinity, joking and conflict in shop floor relations. *Organization Studies, 9*(2), 181–199.

Collinson, D. (1992). *Managing the shopfloor: Subjectivity, masculinity and workplace culture.* Berlin: Walter De Gruyter.

Collinson, D. (1994). Strategies of resistance: Power, knowledge, and subjectivity in the workplace. In J. Jermier, D. Knights, & W. Nord (Eds.), *Power and resistance in organizations* (pp. 22–68). London: Routledge.

Collinson, D. (2002). Managing humor. *Journal of Management Studies, 39*(3), 269–288.

Consalvo, C. (1989). Humor in management: No laughing matter. *Humor: International Journal of Humor Research, 2*, 285–297.

Coser, R. (1959). Some social function of laughter: A study of humor in hospital settings. *Human Relations, 12*, 171–182.

Coser, R. (1960). Laughter among colleagues: A study of social functions of humor among the staff of a mental hospital. *Psychiatry, 23*, 81–95.

Crawford, C. (1994). Theory and implications regarding the utilization of strategic humor by leaders. *The Journal of Leadership Studies, 1*, 53–68.

Davis, C. (1988). Stupidity and rationality: Jokes from the iron cage. In C. Powell & G. Paton (Eds.), *Humor in society: Resistance and control* (pp. 1–32). New York: St. Martin's Press.

Deal, T., & Kennedy, A. (2000). *The new corporate cultures.* London: Texere.

Dixon, N. (1980). A cognitive alternative to stress? In I. Sarasons & C. Speilberger (Eds.), *Stress and anxiety* (pp. 281–289). Washington, DC: Hemisphere.

Duncan, J., & Fiesal, J. (1989). No laughing matter: Patterns of humor in the workplace. *Organization Dynamics, 17*(4), 18–30.

Duncan, J., Smeltzer, L., & Leap, T. (1990). Humor and work: Applications of joking behavior to management. *Journal of Management, 16*(2), 255–278.

Dutton, J., & Dukerich, J. (1991). Keeping an eye on the mirror: Image identity in organizational adaptation. *The Academy of Management Journal, 34*(3), 517–554.

Dwyer, T. (1991). Humor power and change in the organization. *Human Relations, 44*(1), 1–13.

Ehrenberg, T. (1995). Female difference in creation of humor relating to work. *Humor: International Journal of Humor Research, 8*(4), 349–362.

Foxworth, T. (2008). *Using racial humor at work: Promoting positive discussions on race.* Unpublished Master's thesis. Oregon State University, Corvallis.

Gibson, D. (1994). Humor consulting: Laughs for power and profit in organizations. *Humor: International Journal of Humor Research, 7*(4), 403–428.

Hatch, M. (2002). The dynamics of organizational identity. *Human Relations, 55*(8), 989–1018.

Hatch, M., & Sanford, E. (1993). Spontaneous humor as an indicator of paradox and ambiguity in organizations. *Organization Studies, 14*(4), 505–526.

Hay, J. (2001). The pragmatics of humor support. *Humor: International Journal of Humor Research, 14*(1), 55–82.

Holdaway, S. (1988). Blue joke: Humour in police work. In C. Powell & G. Paton (Eds.), *Humor in society: Resistance and control* (pp. 106–122). New York: St Martin's Press.

Holmes, J. (2000). Politeness, power and provocation: How humor functions in the workplace. *Discourse Studies, 2*(2), 159–185.

Holmes, J., & Hay, J. (1997). Humor as an ethnic boundary marker in New Zealand interaction. *Journal of Intercultural Studies, 18*(20), 127–152.

Holmes, J., & Marra, M. (2002a). Over the edge? Subversive humour between colleagues and friends. *Humor: International Journal of Humor Research, 15*(1), 65–87.

Holmes, J., & Marra, M. (2002b). Having a laugh at work: How humor contributes to workplace culture. *Journal of Pragmatics, 34*, 1683–1710.

Holmes, J., & Marra, M. (2006). Humor and leadership style. *Humor: International Journal of Humor Research, 19*(2), 119–138.

Holmes, J., & Stubbe, M. (2003). *Power and politeness in the workplace: A sociolingusitic analysis of talk at work.* London: Pearson.

Hopfl, H. (2007). Humor and violation. In R. Westwood & C. Rhodes (Eds.), *Humour, work and organization.* London: Routledge.

Kushner, M. (1990). *The light touch: How to use humour for business success.* New York: Simon and Schuster.

Levine, J. (1976). The feminine routine. *Journal of Communication, 26*, 173–175.

Lewis, P. (1987). Joke and anti-joke: Three Jews and a blindfold. *Journal of Popular Culture, 21*(1), 63–73.

Linstead, S. (1985). Jokers wild: The importance of humor and the maintenance of organizational culture. *The Sociological Review, 33*(4), 741–767.

Lindlof, T. (1995). *Qualitative communication research methods.* Thousand Oaks, CA: SAGE.

Lynch, O. (2002). Humorous communication: Finding a place for humor in communication research. *Communication Theory, 12*(4), 423–446.

Lynch, O. (2007). *Humorous organizing: Revealing the organization as a social process.* Saarbruken, Germany: VDM Verlag Dr. Muller.

Lynch, O. (2009a). Kitchen antics: The importance of humor and maintaining professionalism at work. *Journal of Applied Communication Research, 37*, 444–464.

Lynch, O. (2009b). Humorous communication. In S. W. Littlejohn & K. A. Foss (Eds.), *The encyclopedia of communication theory* (pp. 480–485). Thousand Oaks, CA: SAGE.

Lynch, O. (2010). Kitchen talk: Cooking with humor: In-group humor as social organization. *Humor: International Journal of Humor Research, 23*, 127–160.

Marra, M. (2007). Humour in workplace meeting: Challenging hierarchies. In R. Westwood & C. Rhodes (Eds.), *Humour, work and organization* (pp. 139–158). London: Routledge.

Martin, D. (2004). Humor in middle management: Women negotiating the paradoxes of organizational life. *Journal of Applied Communication, 32*(2), 147–170.

Merolla, A. (2006). Decoding ability and humor production. *Communication Quarterly, 54*(2), 175–200.

Meyer, J. (1997). Humor in members' narratives: Uniting and dividing at work. *Western Journal of Communication, 61*(2), 188–208.

Meyer, J. (2000). Humor as a double-edged sword: Four functions of humor in communication. *Communication Theory, 10*, 310–331.

Morreall, J. (1991). Humor and work. *Humor: International Journal of Humor Research 4*(4), 359–373.

Mullany, L. (2004). Gender, politeness and institutional power role: Humor as a tactic to gain compliance in the workplace business meetings. *Multilingua, 23*, 13–37.

Mulkay, M. (1988). *On humor: Its nature and its place in modern society.* Oxford: Blackwell.

Ojha, A., & Holmes, T. (2010). Don't tease me, I'm working. *Qualitative Reports, 15*(2), 279–300.

Paulson, T. (1989). *Making humor work: Take your job seriously and yourself lightly.* Los Altos, CA: Crisp Publications.

Pizzini, A. (1991). Communication hierarchies in humour: Gender differences in the obstetrical/gynecological setting. *Discourse & Society, 2*(4), 477–488.

Powell, C. (1988). A phenomenological analysis of humor in society. In C. Powell & G. Paton (Eds.), *Humor in society: Resistance and control* (pp. 85–105). New York: St. Martin's Press.

Radcliffe-Brown, A. (1952). *Structure and function in primitive society.* New York: Free Press.

Ross, B. (1989). *Laugh, lead and profit: Building productive workplaces with humor.* San Deigo: Arrowhead.

Ross, B. (1992). *That's a good one! Corporate leadership with humor.* San Marcos, CA: Avant Books.

Roy, D. (1958). Banana time: Job satisfaction and informal interaction. *Human Organization, 18*, 158–168.

Shuler, S., & Sypher, B. (2000). Seeking emotional labor. *Management Communication Quarterly, 14*, 50–89.

Spradley, J. (1979). *The ethnographic interviewer.* New York: Holt, Rinehard & Winston.

Sykes, A. (1966). Joking relationships in an industrial setting. *American Anthropologist, 68*(1), 189–193.

Tracy, S., Myers, K., & Scott, C. (2006). Cracking jokes and crafting selves: Sensemaking and identity management among human service workers. *Communication Monographs, 73*(3), 283–308.

Vinton, K. (1989). Humor in the workplace: It's more than telling jokes. *Small Groups Behavior, 20*(2), 151–166.

Weick, K. (1979). *Social psychology of organizing* (2nd ed.). New York: McGraw-Hill.

Weick, K. (1995). *Sensemaking organizations.* Thousand Oaks, CA: SAGE.

Weick, K. (2001). *Making sense of the organization.* Malden, MA: Blackwell Business.

Westwood, R., & Rhodes, C. (2007). *Humour, work and organization.* London: Routledge.

Winick, C. (1976). The social context of humor. *Journal of Communication, 26*(3), 28–42.

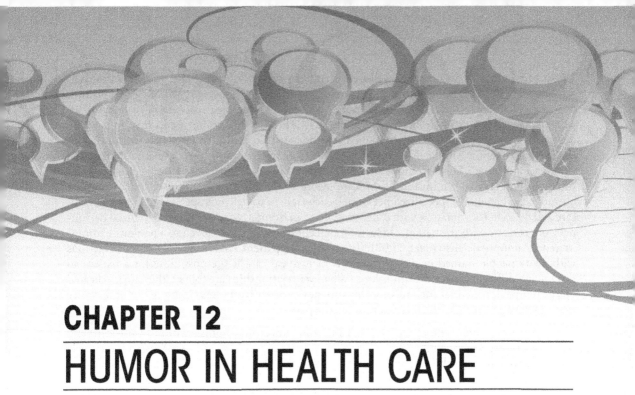

CHAPTER 12
HUMOR IN HEALTH CARE

Theodore A. Avtgis
Ashland University

The impact of humor on a person's well-being has been well documented and presented throughout this text. Whether it be within the context of intimate relationships, platonic relationships, or with acquaintances, the appeal of humor and humorous messages is ubiquitous not only in western culture, but throughout the world. However, there are few contexts and situations where the use of humor serves as many functions as it does within health care. Humor within health care has the potential, unlike other contexts such as romantic relationships or relationships in the workplace, to serve a host of unique functions. These functions emerge as a result of the unique situations and structure found in health care. More specifically, the health care system is a vast bureaucracy that entails specialized personnel, each trained to deliver a specialized form of health care and do so in coordination with other specialized personnel. Many of these specialized personnel work directly with the patient. In fact, 80 percent of medical care given to a patient is administered by nonphysicians (Kizer, 2002). The result of a patient having such diverse interactions with many people trained in different aspects of medical care is the possibility for a patient to form many different types of relationships. Whatever relationships are forged, they are predicated on the unique feature that such relationships are not necessarily of one's choosing but of necessity that can have life-and-death consequences for the patient.

This chapter presents some of the research findings concerning humor within health care and serves as an introduction and overview of the many foci of humor and humor research currently underway within the health care system. Throughout this chapter, numerous studies indicate that humor and humor use can be beneficial for both the physical and psychological health of a person as well as serve as a means to transcend the health care hierarchy; a hierarchy that often isolates and disenfranchises patients and hospital personnel alike.

HUMAN SURVIVAL AND HUMOR

Humor has been and will continue to be an important part of human existence that serves survival functions (Darwin, 1872). These survival functions include enhanced abilities to form groups, keep a group close knit (i.e., cohesive), and promote group harmony. It has long been known that there is "strength in numbers." What is assumed in this saying is that the survival of any one group member depends on the survival of the group as a whole. Humor is a tool for a person to become part of a group, remain part of a group, and contribute meaningfully to the survival of the group. For example, have you ever been part of a group where the tensions between two members were so great that it seemed as if a verbal or physical altercation were inevitable? Perhaps at this point, you or some other group member used a well-timed joke or humorous saying that diffused the situation and moved the group toward greater harmony. Such group harmony is believed to result in a greater chance of survivability for each individual within the group.

Based on these survival functions, can we assume that people who use humor actually live longer than those who do not? A fascinating study by Freidman et al. (1993), using data from the 1929 Terman Life Cycle Study, found that of the 1,178 people tracked throughout their lifetimes (beginning in 1929), the degree to which a person displayed a sense of humor and optimism (which together they termed "cheerfulness" and was assessed by the subjects' parents and teachers at the time) by age 12 had significantly greater mortality rates throughout the ensuing decades than those who did not display such humor and optimism. This contradictory evidence leaves us to wonder how such a result could be obtained. Before we fully indict humor and optimism as culprits leading to an early death, Freidman et al. concluded that such humorous and optimistic people may be either less concerned about their health or down-play any significant life-threatening symptoms. As an alternative to the Freidman et al. conclusion, it is conceivable that people who are humorous and optimistic are more social in nature and have more friends. As such, these social people may find themselves engaging in more risky behavior than the less humorous and optimistic people. For example, research indicates that people tend to engage in more risky decision-making behavior when in the presence of a group as opposed to the decisions one would make when alone. This phenomenon is known as *risky shift* (Pruitt, 1971; Stoner, 1968). As it currently stands, there is no compelling evidence (as demanded by the scientific method) that laughter and humor contribute to or detract from longevity. However, there is an abundance of anecdotal evidence (i.e., evidence based on personal stories and experiences as opposed to science) indicating that those years in which a person does live a life full of laughter and optimism tends to be a life better lived than those who do not.

During the Middle Ages, humor was thought of as a type of energy reflective of a person's health and disposition (Wooten, 1993). Early biologic studies have indicated that humor and laughter produce a sense of well-being and euphoria that are vital for biologic survival (McDougall, 1963). Whether it is a unique physiologic difference or one that is psychological in nature is still to be debated. Although it is beyond the scope of this chapter, currently, cognitive neuroscientists are actively researching humor and a person's reaction to humorous stimuli in an attempt to explain the "reward centers of the brain" that are activated by humor (see the Polack chapter in this volume) and why this unique form of communication is so valued and actively sought by human beings.

In addition to the belief that humor and humor use have survival functions, many believe humor and humor use are indicators of a person's current health and well-being. Whether it is known as witticism or pleasantry, such behaviors were considered outward signs of a person's vitality and personality. More specifically, scholars and medical practitioners of the Renaissance believed there were four types of humor representing different states of the individual, and each was associated with different bodily fluids. For example, *sanguine humor* was cheerful in nature and associated with the blood. *Choleric humor* was considered an angry humor associated with bile. *Phlegmatic humor* was thought to be apathetic in nature and associated with mucous. The final type, *melancholy humor*, was considered a depressing humor associated with black bile. Of these types of humor, only the sanguine was associated with cheerfulness and lightheartedness (Moody, 1978). As this indicates, humor has a long history in human development.

Humor and a person's physical and psychological well-being were assumed to be inextricably linked to one another. In the 1300s, surgeon Henri de Mondville was quoted as saying, "Let the surgeon to take care to regulate the whole regimen of the patient's life for joy and happiness, allowing his relatives special friends to cheer him, and by having someone tell him jokes" (Walsh, 1911, p. 270). This quote clearly indicates that the link between health and humor has been assumed and advocated for centuries. The same type of approach as that of de Mondville can be seen in the words of Dr. Vera Robinson (1991) who advocates that health care personnel should be willing to "open up yourself to humor, looking for absurdities of life and becoming more playful and less serious about life, is a broad perspective from which we might increase the use of humor in healthcare" (p. 185).

The American public became aware of the power of humor in medicine partly through the 1998 film *Patch Adams*, which was based on the life and times of a physician named Hunter Campbell.

In 1971, Campbell and some colleagues founded the *Gesundheit Institute*, which focused on the complementary and alternative effects of humor on pathology (i.e., disease). Recall from the Polack chapter (in this volume) that complementary medicine is used in conjunction with evidenced-based medicine (i.e., traditional medical science) whereas alternative medicine is used as a replacement of evidenced-based medicine. More recently, there have been several popular books written on the positivity of humor in health care including *Love, Medicine, and Miracles: Lessons Learned About Self-Healing from a Surgeon's Experience with Exceptional Patients* (1986) by surgeon Dr. Bernie Segal and *Quantum Healing: Exploring the Frontiers of Mind/Body* (1989) by Dr. Deepak Chopra. Again we see how the presence of humor, regardless of how it is conceptualized, has been a factor in medicine and medical science for centuries.

PRACTICE OF HUMOR BY HEALTH CARE PROFESSIONALS

Given the discussion thus far, we can conclude that humor can be considered a desired but not a necessary quality of successful health practitioners as well as a communication quality that contributes to both psychological and physical well-being to both patient and provider. However, given that humor has been defined as something that is contextually, culturally, and personality-bound, the development of this quality can be difficult. According to Hampes (2001), "both humor and empathetic concerns are associated with people who have emotional intelligence and use humor to interact effectively with other individuals" (p. 241). To negotiate the almost limitless factors associated with appropriate humor use, it takes a person who is both communicatively competent and cognitively flexible to encode humorous messages effectively. In other words, a person who successfully uses humor must be able to think fast, create humorous messages, and deliver those messages in creative and timely ways. Such humor use can be used to comfort a sick or distressed person and make it easier to establish trust. This "other-orientation" regarding the use of humor is believed to be evolved not for the effect it has on the person using it but for the effect it has on others (Provine, 2000). Some of the most effective health care professionals who successfully use humor with patients do so after years of honing their communication skills within the context of the patient-provider relationship. Such experience includes the ability to determine what is and is not an appropriate use of humor (see, for example, Wanzer & Wojtaszczyk, 2008).

There are numerous studies that show the many benefits that result from health care professionals engaging in humor with their patients. For example, the greater degree to which a physician engages in humor is related to a reduction in patient anxiety and stress, overall positive impression of the health care provider, and greater levels of patient satisfaction (Francis, Monahan, & Berger, 1999; Richman, 1995; Sala, Krupat, & Roter, 2002; Squier, 1996). Physicians who used humor were also found to have fewer liability claims than physicians who did not engage in humor with their patients (Levinson, Roter, Mullooly, Dull, & Frankel, 1997). This is not to say that physician humor use is always positive, but it is to say that when delivered effectively, humor serves many psychosocial benefits for the patient. Even though research indicates the positive outcomes associated with physician humor use, from a patient's perspective, humor is mostly associated with nurses as opposed to physicians (McCabe, 2004). Part of this perception may be due to the fact that nurses are expected to provide more psychological support to the patient, which is relayed via communication, whereas the physician is generally seen as a task-focused person who is treating illness with the nurse treating the psychological needs of the patient.

Health care practitioners who engage in humorous communication may or may not be doing so for the benefit of the patient. In fact, recent research has revealed how important humor use is in coping with stress and burnout in the workplace. Such workplace stress is not unique to health care workers but is more prevalent than it is in most other professions (Avtgis & Taber, 2006; Grugulis, 2002; Romero & Cruthirds, 2006; Rizzo, Wanzer, & Booth-Butterfield, 1999; Wender, 1996; Yarwood, 1995). Wanzer and colleagues conducted a study to identify the situations in which nurses use humor as a stress reliever or situational diffusing technique (Wanzer, Booth-Butterfield, & Booth-Butterfield, 2005). The results revealed that nurses reported using humor in the following situations: (a) to cope with the death of a patient or whose health is rapidly declining, (b) to diffuse an aggressive or uncooperative patient, (c) as a means to maintain positive relationships with colleagues, (d) as a cathartic response to a stressful day, (e) as a means to reduce anxiety that is regularly experienced by both patients and the patient's family members, (f) as a way to cope with the administrative tasks associated with patient care, and (g) as a way to address mistakes made throughout the day.

THERAPEUTIC HUMOR

Using humor to heal, as evidenced in the Polack chapter in this volume, is something that has not been supported scientifically, yet continues to be espoused as an attribute of the effective health care practitioner. In other words, although there has been no scientific proof as to the benefits of humor on physical illness (Angell, 1985), there remains a great deal of evidence as to the psychological benefits that can be realized by both the health care practitioner and patient alike. There is debate, however, that the lack of such conclusive evidence linking humor and healing is due to flawed research design, not to an actual disconnect between humor and health benefit. Health humor advocates believe that good science and carefully constructed experiments should yield valuable and conclusive results about humor and its influence on health. According to Dr. Rod Martin (2001),

> Much of the research to date, using experimental laboratory procedures with exposure to comedy video tapes, has either implicitly or explicitly focused on the hypothesis that health benefits result from physiologic changes accompanying laughter [the behavior] as a result of humor, however, the research fails to monitor the actual occurrence of laughter, or to examine the relationships between duration, frequency, or intensity of laughter and the physiologic outcome. Thus it may be that genuine physiologic effects of particular types or degrees of laughter have gone largely undetected in the research due to sloppy methodological procedures, resulting in the weak and inconsistent pattern of results with which we are now faced. (p. 515)

Therapeutic humor is a unique form of humor use that entails mindfulness, empathy, and compassion (Berger, Coulehan, & Belling, 2004). According to Polack and Avtgis (2011), *mindfulness* refers to the process of being aware of your behavior and basing your behavior on a specific situation as opposed to simply enacting a generic script used for a variety of situations. *Empathy* reflects the ability to show others that you have an understanding of how someone else is feeling or identifying with their emotional experience. *Compassion* refers to the general feeling of sadness and understanding for another person's circumstances.

Therapeutic medicine, the context in which therapeutic humor is used, is reflective of any intervention that promotes health and wellness by stimulating the discovery, appreciation, or expression of the incongruity/absurdity of life and life situations (Sultanoff, 2010). This incongruity/absurdity is constant in the health care realm where uncertainty and uncontrollability are common experiences for the patient (Polack & Avtgis, 2011). For example, a healthy and physically fit person who has never smoked a cigarette in their entire life is suddenly diagnosed with lung cancer. The absurdity of such a situation may be expressed in humorous irony as irony is often expressed through humorous communication. Such expressions, such as humorous irony, serve as a sense-making device of an otherwise inexplicable event.

Humor, Affect, and Cognition

In the early 20th century, little was known about the "black box" or the psychological processes of humor, much less any other phenomena that occurred within a person's mind. Almost all of the psychological perspectives of humor were based on the psychoanalytic theories of Sigmund Freud (1928). The Freudian theory of humor assumes that humans developed the capacity for humor to protect the ego from being distressed or free from suffering from a painful reality. Consider the following questions: Have you ever laughed at yourself and your past behavior? Could this same behavior be easily interpreted as rude, callous, or hurtful to another person? Did you choose to reflect on this past behavior in a humorous way to protect your self-esteem? Such a humorous interpretation of past behavior serves as a way to buffer the ego from the pain of having to cope with the reality of behaviors that can be seen as otherwise psychologically punishing. Although much of psychoanalytic theory has been discredited in terms of its limited capacity to explain the complexities and processes of the experience of humor (and many other phenomena for that matter), such conceptualizations have given rise to other theoretical approaches that can be used effectively in the therapeutic environment (Goldstein & McGhee, 1972). One such approach would be that of the Berlyne's (1969) theory of arousal and cognitive factors. This theory argues that humor is not only a present stimulus but a dynamic combination of the recollection of past experiences, the reality of the present, and the anticipation of the future. These humor experiences, however conceptualized, are believed to be key factors in the maintenance of both psychological and physical health in the face of the stressors that people encounter on a daily basis (Lefcourt & Martin, 1986). Given this, humor use, which is often viewed as being episodic or within the immediate situation, may likely be due to a person's past, present, and future expectations of both the sender and the receiver.

One would think that the therapeutic function of humor would be a topic replete with research and theory. However, the fact of the matter is that the paucity of research on humor and laughter in the therapeutic realm is largely due to the fact that since its inception, the field of psychology has primarily focused on the study of negative emotional states and pathologies. It was only relatively recently that researchers have focused on positive emotional states, which would include humor (Burgdorf & Panksepp, 2006). The rise of positive psychology and positive communication as legitimate disciplines attests to this rather recent shift in theoretical focus. An example of this positive focus on humor theory development include Frederickson's (1998) broaden-and-build theory of positive emotion as well as Gervais and Wilson's (2005) nonserious social incongruity approach.

Many scholars believe that the timely and effective use of humor can facilitate communication, promote bonding, and enhance patient satisfaction (Francis et al., 1999). Of course, as is presented later in this chapter, humor use depends on many factors surrounding the patient, the provider, and the illness. Generally speaking, taking into consideration the frustration experienced by many patients regarding the bureaucratic health care system, a caregiver's strategic use of humorous messages can circumvent such frustration and create a satisfying experience for the patient. This is especially important at a time when reimbursements from Medicare and Medicaid are partly based on the quality of the patient's experience. The quality of this experience is partly based on the perception of the patient. In fact, the interpersonal skills of the health care practitioner (including humor use) are becoming increasingly emphasized as a key factor that influences a patient's experience, that many organizations are requiring training for all members to receive certification. Perhaps the most obvious example of such requirements would be those put forth by the Accreditation Council for Graduate Medical Education (ACGME). The ACGME mandates all medical students demonstrate interpersonal competency in order to graduate. Such mandates attest to the significant impact of prosocial forms of communication on patient satisfaction. This is not to say that humorous communication, specifically, is a criteria for graduation, but it is to highlight the fact that all communication skills that are supportive and comforting in nature are to be developed and employed in the everyday practice of medicine. Humor can be and is an important aspect of this communicative skill set.

CONTEXTUAL CONSTRAINTS OF HUMOR USE

Given that humor and humor use are bound by a myriad of factors, including a person's personality, the relationship between the two interactants, the situation in which the humorous communication occurs, and the cultural background of the interactants, it is not a skill that is easily taught. In fact, the types of medicine practiced greatly dictate the types and styles of humor that are permissible or deemed appropriate. For example, humor and its many forms vary given the types of medical situations that can arise. From the providers' perspective, the types of humor used by a proctologist during a routine check-up may vary greatly from the humor used by an oncologist who is just about to follow up with a patient who has a malignant tumor. Another example of humor use regulated by type of medicine practiced would be that of emergency medicine. In this case, it is suggested that humor should be avoided and replaced by more sober and empathetic behaviors, such as holding a patient's hand, listening to the patient's story, etc. (Berger et al., 2004). Given that the types of medicine vary so greatly (e.g., family medicine versus palliative medicine), the perceptions of appropriate humorous communication also vary to an equal degree.

Although humor can provide an effective bridge for the disclosure of sensitive or vulnerable information, there is also a potential for destructive outcomes that all health care practitioners should be made aware of. According to Polack and Avtgis (2011), humor is counterproductive when it accentuates the distance between the patient and the provider or in some way serves to belittle the patient or their illness. Such a situation is easily realized with the use of humor at an inappropriate time or in an inappropriate way. An example of this is illustrated in the 1991 movie *The Doctor*. This film depicts a talented surgeon who shows little compassion or empathy toward his patients until he himself becomes a patient (suffering from throat cancer) who is treated in the same way, that is, treated without compassion or empathy. As a result of this inhumane treatment, a dramatic change occurs both in his perspective about people and the value of each and every human life. In one particular exchange, before he experiences his dramatic change in perspective, the doctor is conducting a follow-up exam on a female patient who has recently undergone a double mastectomy. Part of this follow-up exam was to remove the surgical staples used to close the incision site. The patient asked the doctor: "Doctor, my husband, he's a good man, and he …, I think he's a little nervous … will the scar always be so …?" To this question, which is asked from a psychological state of uncertainty, fear, and vulnerability on the part of the patient, the doctor replies: "Tell your husband you look like a playboy centerfold … you have the staple marks to prove it!" Such a lack of compassion and empathy in terms of this "joke" can have devastating consequences for the patient. The woman, in this case, was shocked and mortified at this callous response. Humor used solely for the exclusive enjoyment of the sender is almost invariably harmful to the receiver. Such comments that are encoded and sent show little to no consideration of the patient's feelings, perspective, or experience of illness.

As the world becomes smaller due to technological advancement and health care becoming a global commodity, the need to account for cultural variations on behalf of both the patient and provider is necessary in the contemporary practice of health care. Cultural variation can refer to age, sex, socioeconomic status, education level, ethnicity, religious beliefs, national origin, and beliefs about health care and health care personnel, among others. For example, there are important differences between the way African-American and Asian patients perceive health care, the health care practitioner, and the health care system as a whole. More specifically, African-Americans report a general distrust of the health care system based on past inequities in terms of access to quality health care (Dula, 1994; Murry, 1992) whereas Asians report great respect for the health care practitioners, communicating with deference and non-assertiveness when interacting with a health care provider (Cumura, 1992). Given this simple distinction, the same type of humor that may seem innocent and good-natured also can take the form of an aggressive act or an utterance that leads to the patient doubting the practitioner's medical expertise.

Given that there are so many contextual variables affecting the use of humor, should a health care practitioner even attempt to engage in humorous communication? On the one hand, humor serves to humanize the patient, reduce anxiety and uncertainty, as well as serve a sense-making function. On the other hand, humor use can have a significantly negative impact on the patient and the patient-provider relationship. Berger et al. (2004) offer several guidelines for humor use that can be applied across situations:

1. Be conservative in selecting both content of humor and the manner in which it is delivered. It may serve as a wedge between you and the power-disadvantaged patient.

2. The least risky type of humor is gentle self-deprecating humor that is externally focused. For example, discussing how difficult it was for you to park due to the snow that has accumulated and the effect of the snow on your diving ability, etc.

3. Avoid any facetious or flippant humor. Patients generally expect health care providers to be respectful and optimistic in their outlook. Such flippancy can come across as negative and mean spirited. This was illustrated earlier in the example used from the movie *The Doctor*.

4 Any humor used by the provider should be grounded in an accurate understanding of the patient's values, limits, predispositions, and receptivity to such communication (i.e., a general empathetic consideration of the patient and a mindfulness of the patient as an individual human being).

5 If the patient initiates humor, respond in kind (e.g., similar topic or an extension of their humorous message) with constructive humor.

6 Should the patient engage in destructive humor (e.g., You are late! What—were you out playing golf again?), it is appropriate to confront the patient in an effort to diffuse the aggressive form of humor and discuss the exact issue leading to the displaced hostility (e.g., waiting too long, not receiving enough information about their illness, not reacting well to uncertainty/anxiety, etc.).

In general, there is a dialectical tension that exists with humor use in medical care. According to Robinson (1991), "illness is a serious business, it is not a laughing matter" (p. XIV), yet when one is constantly dealing with "stress, illness, naked bodies, blood, guts, excrement, trauma, and death" (p. XIV), the humor is generally dark, sexual, and/or aggressive in nature. This indicates that humor, in terms of health care personnel, serves as a sense-making and coping function for psychological well-being. Dark humor or humor that could be seen as inappropriate, aggressive, distasteful, etc., can serve as a bonding or identification vehicle. Further, it may serve as a way to distinguish in-group membership for people who experience stressful or uncommon life events. Health care professionals are constantly faced with life and death, patients of all psychological and physical attributes, as well as a bureaucratic system that often impedes the ability to deliver quality health care (Robinson, 1991). In light of this unique set of circumstances, this "special" type of humor often emerges. Dark humor is also common in other professions, such as law enforcement and the military.

PATIENT HUMOR USE

Most humor research in health care has focused primarily on the health care practitioner with little to no focus on the patient's use of humor and the impact it has on the health care encounter. Within the health care system, there are behavioral expectations assumed on the part of both the practitioner and the patient. These "unwritten rules" include a level of respect and courtesy from both parties. However, as anyone who has worked in emergency medicine can attest to, many times the patient is under the influence of alcohol, drugs, psychologically imbalanced, or is simply a hostile person by nature. Humor, like any other form of communication, can be used for both constructive and destructive ends. Aggressive humor on the part of the patient can adversely influence the health care practitioner's ability to focus and provide effective care for the patient, which unnecessarily puts the patient at risk. Such events are so common that several states have passed laws prohibiting patients from using aggressive communication toward their caregivers, treating aggressive communication attacks similar to acts of physical aggression (Polack & Avtgis, 2011). That is, as a felony.

A patient is, by the nature of the health care system, put into a one-down power position. The patient enters a system with a clear hierarchy, a foreign language spoken only by those with specialized training, and a lack of understanding as to treatment options and the risks associated with such treatments. Such a power differential in medicine is known as the authority gradient, which reflects a system where the surgeon/physician is at the top and the patient at the bottom (Polack & Avtgis, 2011). Humor has the potential to serve as a means of empowerment that humanizes the patient in the eyes of the practitioner (Francis et al., 1999). When humor is used successfully, both parties (i.e., the sender and the receiver of the humorous message) share a synchrony that is relationally bound. It is in this moment of synchrony that the humanization of the other person occurs. This, in turn, decreases the authority gradient to a relationship that is based on mutuality or shared power (Polack & Avtgis, 2011). Patient behavior in general, and humor in particular, remains a relatively unexplored area of research that has the potential to contribute greatly to our understanding of humor in health care.

HUMOR AND HEALTH EDUCATION

Although the evidence concerning the effectiveness of humor in persuasion is mixed, in that some studies indicate effectiveness while others reveal no real advantage to humor use, humor continues to be used in health care education. The function of humor in many health messages is not necessarily to make light or poke fun at the health topic. Instead, the function is often to frame the message in ways that do not make discussing or addressing the subject so taboo, distasteful, or generally something that should be avoided. For example, a recent radio campaign advocates that people seek immediate treatment when experiencing symptoms of stroke. This radio commercial contains a humorous sequence of a stand-up comedian telling a story of a phone conversation with his uncle who is reporting stroke symptoms (e.g., slurred speech, dizziness, numbness, etc.). The audience is laughing as the story is being told of the phone conversation with the concluding voice-over message being, *"Stroke is no laughing matter; time saved is brain saved."*

In the case of socially sensitive or taboo practices or disorders (e.g., condom use and erectile dysfunction), humor is often used as an esteem protection for the person who has to address the issue or introduce the topic. The interjection of a clever joke or comment can open the door for more meaningful conversation. For example, starting a conversation with a teenager about illegal drug use may be well served using a humorous approach to overcome the awkwardness of the topic. On the other hand, how can humor be used to make mundane and uninteresting topics interesting and fun? One such example can be seen in an organization called *Healthworks*. Healthworks is based in South Bend, Indiana and was started in 2000. The organization's mission is to educate children about health and to make learning healthy ways of living fun. More specifically, Healthworks' purpose statement is to "infectiously contaminate kids of all ages, everywhere, to learn, have fun, and make great life choices. Let the epidemic begin!" (www.healthworkskids. org). The curricula range in topics from being responsible for your body to personal hygiene. In fact, when discussing personal hygiene with children, the interactive lessons involve things such as "boogers" and "poop." The kids respond well to such "gross humor" because such matters are framed as something that is indeed funny and fun and easy to identify with as opposed to something that is framed as lectured information that mandates a set of hygienic behaviors. Humor, when used in this way, is as a nonthreatening and easily accessible (i.e., cognitively pleasing and simple) message device that has shown incredible results. This success has resulted in the opening of another Healthworks Kinds Museum in Mississippi. This organization serves as the model for how effective humor-based framing of health messages can be.

CONCLUSION

Humor within health care is a dynamic and diverse phenomenon. As been evidenced throughout this chapter, humor pervades all aspects of health care. That is, from the healers, the healing, and the healed, humor is a device for making sense of perhaps one of the most uncertain and anxiety-producing experiences of the human condition; sickness and death. Moving forward, the investigation of humor effectiveness in the healing process must progress from the anecdotal and psychological to the scientific and physiological. By doing so, researchers have the potential to provide the needed science that conclusively informs the debate as to whether humor is a factor in medical healing. Whatever the outcome of such research, it is undeniable that humor has been something that has been written about, theorized about, and celebrated by human beings for centuries. The capacity for humor remains a unique human quality and, as such, we need to continue to investigate exactly what it is that humor does for the human condition.

References

Angell, M. (1985). Disease as reflection of the Psyche. *New England Journal of Medicine, 312,* 373–375.

Avtgis, T. A., & Taber, K. R. (2006). 'I laughed so hard my side hurts, or is that an ulcer?' The influence of work humor on job stress, job satisfaction, and burnout among print media employees. *Communication Research Reports, 23,* 13–18.

Berger, J. P., Coulehan, J., & Belling, C. (2004). Humor in the physician-patient encounter. *Archives of Internal Medicine, 164,* 825–830.

Berlyne, D. E. (1969). Laughter, humor, and play. *Handbook of Social Psychology, 3,* 795–813.

Burgdorf, J., & Panksepp, J. (2006). The neurobiology of positive emotions. *Neuroscience Biobehavioral Review, 30,* 173–187.

Chopra, D. (1989). *Quantum healing: Exploring the frontiers of mind/body.* New York: Bantam Books.

Cumura, R. (1992). Conflict and harmony in Japanese medicine: A challenge to traditional culture in neonatal care. In E. Pellagrino, P. Mazzarella, & P. Corsi (Eds.), *Transcultural dimensions of medical ethics* (pp. 145–153). Frederick, MD: University Publishing Group.

Darwin, C. (1872). *The expressions of emotions in man and animals.* London: John Murray.

Dula, A. (1994). African-Americans' suspicion of the health care system is justified: What do we do about it? *Cambridge Quarterly Health Care Ethics, 3,* 347–357.

Francis, L., Monahan, K., & Berger, C. (1999). A laughing matter? The use of humor in medical interactions. *Motti's Emotion, 23,* 155–174.

Frederickson, B. L. (1998). What good are positive emotions. *Review of General Psychology, 2,* 300–319.

Freud, S. (1928). Humor. *The International Journal of Psychoanalysis, 9,* 1–6.

Friedman, H. S., Tucker, J. S., Tomlinson-Keasey, C., Schwartz, J. E., Wingard, D. L., & Criqui, M. H. (1993). Does childhood personality predict longevity? *Journal of Personality and Social Psychology, 65,* 176–185.

Gervais, M., & Wilson, D. S. (2005). The evolution and functions of laughter and humor. A synthetic approach. *Quarterly Review of Biology, 80,* 395–430.

Goldstein, J. H., & McGhee, T. E. (1972). *The psychology of humor: Theoretical perspectives and empirical issues.* New York: Academic Press.

Grugulis, I. (2002). Nothing serious? Candidates' use of humor in management training. *Human Relations, 55,* 387–406.

Hampes, W. P. (2001). Relation between humor and empathetic concern. *Psychological Reports, 88,* 241–244.

Kizer, K. W. (2002). Patient centered care: Essential but probably not sufficient. *Quality and Safety in Healthcare, 11,* 117–118.

Lefcourt, H. M., & Martin, R. A. (1986). *Humor and life stress: Antidote to adversity.* New York: Springer-Verlag.

Levinson, W., Roter, D. L., Mullooly, J. P., Dull, V. T., & Frankel, R. M. (1997). Physician-patient communication: The relationship with malpractice claims among primary care physicians and surgeons. *Journal of the American Medical Association, 277,* 553–559.

Martin, R. A. (2001). Humor, laughter, and physical health: Methodological issues and research findings. *Psychological Bulletin, 127,* 504–519.

McCabe, C. (2004). Nurse-patient communication: An exploration of patients' experiences. *Journal of Clinical Nursing, 13,* 41–49.

McDougall, W. (1963). *An instinct of laughter: An introduction of social psychology.* New York: University Paperbacks.

Moody, R. (1978). *Laugh after laugh.* Jacksonville, FL: Head Waters Press.

Murry, R. F. (1992). Minority perspectives in biomedical ethics (pp. 35–42). Frederick, MD: University Publishing Group.

Polack, E. P., & Avtgis, T. A. (2011). *Medical communication: Defining the discipline.* Dubuque, IA: Kendall Hunt.

Provine, R. R. (2000). *Laughter: A scientific investigation.* New York: Viking Penguin.

Pruitt, D. (1971). Choice shifts in group discussion: An introductory review. *Journal of Personality and Social Psychology, 20,* 339–360.

Richman, J. (1995). The lifesaving function of humor with the depressed and suicidal elderly. *Gerontologist, 35,* 271–273.

Rizzo, B. J., Wanzer, M. B., & Booth-Butterfield, M. (1999). Individual differences in managers' use of humor: Subordinate perceptions of managers' humor. *Communication Research Reports, 16,* 360–369.

Robinson, V. M. (1991). *Humor and the health professions, the therapeutic use of humor in health care* (2nd ed.). Thorofare, NJ: Slack.

Romero, E. J., & Cruthirds, K. W. (2006). The use of humor in the workplace. *Academy of Management Perspectives, 20*, 58–69.

Sala, F., Krupat, E., & Roter, D. (2002). Satisfaction and the use of humor by physicians and patients. *Psychology and Health, 17*, 269–280.

Segal, B. (1986). *Love, medicine, and healing: Lessons learned about self-healing from a surgeon's experience with exceptional patients.* New York: Harper Collins

Squier, H. A. (1996). Humor in the doctor-patient relationship. *Family Systems Medicine, 13*, 101–107.

Stoner, J. A. F. (1968). A comparison of individual and group decisions involving risk. *Unpublished Master's thesis.* Cambridge, MA: MIT.

Sultanoff, S. M. (2010). *Humor matters.* Retrieved from www.humormatters.com

Walsh, J. J. (1911). *Old-time makers of medicine.* New York: Fordham University Press.

Wanzer, M. B., Booth-Butterfield, M., & Booth-Butterfield, S. (2005). If we didn't use humor, we'd cry: Humorous coping communication in healthcare settings. *Journal of Health Communication, 10*, 105–125.

Wanzer, M. B., & Wojtaszczyk, A. (2008). The benefits and drawbacks of using humor in healthcare settings. In E. P. Polack, V. P. Richmond, & J. C. McCroskey (Eds.), *Applied communication for health professionals* (pp. 227–248). Dubuque, IA: Kendall Hunt.

Wender, R. C. (1996). Humor in medicine. *Primary Care, 23*, 141–154.

Wooten, P. (1993). Laughter as therapy for patient and caregiver. In J. Hodgkin, G. Connors, & C. Bell (Eds.), *Pulmonary rehabilitation* (pp. 422–434). Philadelphia: Lippencott.

Yarwood, D. L. (1995). Humor and administration: A serious inquiry into official organizational communication. *Public Administration Review, 55*, 81–90.

CHAPTER 13

HUMOR AND LAUGHTER AS MEDICINE: PHYSIOLOGIC IMPACTS AND EFFECTS

E. Phillips Polack, MD
West Virginia University

For the most part, humor has been viewed as a social phenomenon that has its primary focus on human relationships. Most research takes the form of investigating the impact that humor and the communication of humor have on a variety of social situations, relational contexts, as well as the production of humorous messages. This chapter is a diversion from this traditional approach in that it has an inward focus on humor. That is, it looks at how humor and its close relative, laughter, affect the physiologic processes of the human body. Therefore, this chapter discusses some of the origins of humor and laughter in medicine as well as explains the psychobiological processes that underlie this complex form of human communication.

A pivotal article written in 1976 in the *New England Journal of Medicine* and a 1979 text entitled *Anatomy of an Illness as Perceived by the Patient: Reflections on Healing and Recovery* are attributed with stimulating a new field of research in modern medicine. The author, Norman Cousins stimulated research in the field of holistic medicine (i.e., holistic concepts in health care consider all parts of the human being, which includes the physical, mental, and social conditions of the patient), which quickly evolved into the modern medical movements known as *complementary* and *alternative* medicine. According to Bennet and Lengacher (2006), complementary medicine is any support method used to complement an evidenced-based treatment [scientific medicine] as established by the scientific method. These complementary therapies are not intended to substitute for mainstream treatment nor are they a sole cure for a disease. They are to be used in conjunction with mainstream treatment as they are believed to control symptoms and improve the well-being and quality of life. Alternative medicine, on the other hand, is anything that is not considered mainstream or anything that is not proven by the scientific method.

The reason that humor and laughter are not considered scientifically based therapies is due to the fact that there is not enough evidence as to their treatment effectiveness on disease as measured by the scientific method. In fact, in a metanalysis (i.e., a study of existing studies) investigating the curative effects of humor on disease, Martin (2001) concluded that there was little evidence as to the unique positive effects of humor and laughter on the health-related variable. One can easily conclude, based on this finding, that humor and laughter do not have important health outcomes in terms of medical care. On the contrary, Martin (2001) argued that the "genuine physiologic effects or particular types or degree of laughter have gone deeply undetected in research due to sloppy methodologic procedures, resulting in weak and inconsistent pattern of results with which we are now faced" (p. 515). It should be noted that the effects of humor were assessed through evidence-based criteria (Sackett, 1997), which, consistent with the scientific method, hold that assessment of any evidence-based practice must be assessed with the following three criteria, and that sloppy research design can easily jeopardize the assessment.

1. *Efficiency.* This criterion assesses the degree to which the variable under study (e.g., humor and laughter) actually has some effect on the outcome.

2. *Effectiveness.* This criterion assesses the degree to which the variable under study (e.g., humor and laughter) has the intended effect.

3. *Clinical Utility.* This criterion assesses the degree to which the variable under study (e.g., humor and laughter) can have the intended effect across a wide range of contexts (diseases, people, etc.).

There are two basic problems with scientifically evidencing humor and laughter in medicine. First, there is too little research being conducted on the subject and that which has been conducted has generally utilized poor methodological design. In fact, regardless of the discipline, be it geriatrics (treatment of the old), oncology (treatment of tumors and cancers), critical care, psychiatry (mental illness), rheumatology (arthritis), terminal or general patient care, true experimental methodologies have not been employed in validating the therapeutic efficiency of laughter (Rosner, 2002).

In one of the first and most comprehensive approaches to provide scientific evidence that humor and laughter are effective therapeutic tools in health care, Robinson (1991) published the text *Humor and the Health Professions: The Therapeutic Use of Humor in Health Care*. In this book, Robinson forwarded her theory that humor was a cognitive experience as well as a physical or psychological experience. This whole process refers to a witticism or humor that generates mirth or positive affect and, as a result, laughter may or may not result. This work was partly based on the work of Fry (1963), indicating that humor requires spontaneity and an element of surprise. Such spontaneity and surprise are person specific, meaning that what is interpreted as humorous to one person may not be so to another person.

The remainder of this chapter is divided into three main sections concerning the *anatomic* (i.e., how does the brain function in humorous situations), *physiologic* (i.e., the various elements of humor as an alternative therapy), and *pathological* (i.e., diseases or states where laughter is an element of the illness).

ANATOMY OF HUMOR AND LAUGHTER

The human brain is one of the most sophisticated communication systems in the world. It contains approximately 100 billion neurons (i.e., nerve cells) resulting in 100 trillion interconnections (Gazzaniga, Ivy, & Mangun, 2008). To understand the anatomical complexity of humor and laughter, we must understand the basic elements of the brain. According to Medina (2008), the brain has evolved in three distinct phases. The first phase is known as the *lizard brain* phase, which consists of the brain stem that controls such things as how the heart beats, breathing, motor coordination, and some rudimentary emotional functions. The second phase is known as the *mammalian brain* phase, which consists of the mid brain that sits on top of the lizard brain and is responsible for behaviors such as fighting, feeding, fleeing, and reproductive behaviors. Such behaviors are considered more "animal" in nature. It is within the mid brain that we find the control for generating ludic, or playful behavior. Most people are familiar with the other name for the mid brain which is the *limbic system* (Maclean, 1949). Figure 1 illustrates the Five Systems of the Limbic System.

FIGURE 1 FIVE SYSTEMS OF THE LIMBIC SYSTEM

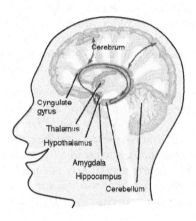

Although there are thousands of languages and dialects, everyone "speaks" laughter and smiles in virtually the same way. Human babies tend to smile after being given a bottle at about five weeks of age. At approximately four months of age, they will begin to laugh, and at 18 months, smile on average of once every six minutes. By four years of age, this rate of smiling will increase to once every 1⅓ minutes. The rate of smiling will increase as the child grows older (Stearns, 1972). Interestingly, children who are born blind or deaf still retain the ability to laugh, which indicates that even when a child has neither seen nor heard laughter, laughter is something that is hard wired within human beings as opposed to something that is learned.

The expression of laughter seems to depend on two independent neural pathways. The first is the "involuntary" or "emotionally driven" system comprised of the amygdala, thalamus/hypothalamus (i.e., the limbic system of the mid brain). The second system is the "voluntary system," which is part of the human or cortical brain that sits atop the mid brain (see Figure 1). Thus, laughter and its requisite triggers (e.g., humorous messages) are a function of both the more primal and modern aspects of the human brain.

It has been hypothesized that both humor and laughter have evolved as survival mechanisms. In fact, Charles Darwin (1872) argued that laughter, as a function of happiness, is a social expression necessary for group cohesion. Group cohesion and harmony serve as advantages to the probability of survival of any social group.

The universality of emotions associated with humor and laughter have been identified via the detection of nonverbal behavioral cues. More specifically, Ekman and Friesen (1975) developed the *Facial Action Coding System* (FACS), which consists of the six universal emotions of sadness, anger, disgust, fright, surprise, and happiness. Through this coding scheme, Ekman (1997) was able to identify 16 distinguishable types of smiles that can represent a variety of situations, such as smiling to express humor, to show scorn, to mock, to be socially appropriate, and the fake smile

(Ruch & Ekman, 2001). The interpretation of the act of smiling is difficult, especially when considering that there are close to 50 muscles in the face and approximately 22 of those are involved in the act of smiling.

Smiling is the behavioral response to a variety of emotional experiences, especially when considering both humorous communication and laughter. Ekman, Davidson, and Friesen (1990) distinguished between a fake smile and what is described as the *Duchenne display* (in honor of French neurologist G. B. Duchenne who was one of the first people to scientifically investigate facial expressions in the mid 19th century). The Duchenne display or genuine smile reflects that when a person displays a true smile in response to humor, the corners of the mouth will upturn with the lips going backward and upward. Further, the eyes will become narrow and there will be wrinkling at the side of the eyes. On the contrary, when someone only smiles in the mouth, without using the eyes, this is considered a "fake" smile. Figure 2 displays both the Duchenne and fake smiles.

FIGURE 2 DISPLAYS OF THE DUCHENNE AND FAKE SMILES

Smile Example

Genuine Smile   False Smile

Within the last two decades, the development of imaging technologies has made investigating the brain and its various functions possible. Moran, Wig, Adams, Janata, and Kelley (2004) determined that there is a "humor center" or "laugh center" of the brain. They found that the mid brain limbic system most likely mediates emotional expression from the cerebellum or the emotional generator located in the brain stem through the mid brain structures of the hypothalamus (i.e., the section of the brain that regulates the symptomatic manifestation of emotions, notably in its mid portion) and the amygdala (i.e., the almond shaped structure at the base of the brain, which is noted for the "fight or flight response," also involved in friendship, love, and affection). Figure 1 shows the structures in the brain's limbic system.

After traveling this path in the mammalian mid (emotional) brain, the humorous impulse then travels to the human (cortical) brain, which consists of both the frontal and temporal lobes (see Figure 3).

FIGURE 3 REGIONS OF THE HUMAN BRAIN

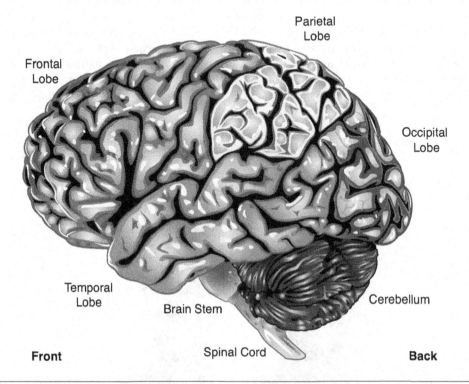

© MedusArt 2012. Under license from Shutterstock, Inc.

Laughter, or the response to humor, is an element unique to human beings. Although it has been documented that primates communicate and use a rudimentary form of language, humans have the unique ability to maintain a sustained breath when communicating such as when we sing, say words, or laugh out loud. In other words, throughout a single expiratory cycle a person can say *ha, ha, ha, ha, ha, ha* whereas a primate is only able to make a single sound for every exhalation (i.e., inspiration *ha*—expiration *ha*). Figure 4 illustrates the difference in laughter production between humans and primates.

Such a limitation on sound production makes it impossible for primates to create words due to their inflexible nervous system, which makes it impossible to make multiple sound utterances (e.g., the types of sound utterances required to articulate words or laughter; Provine, 2000).

FIGURE 4 LAUGHTER PRODUCTION DIFFERENCES BETWEEN HUMANS AND PRIMATES

PHYSIOLOGY OF HUMOR AND LAUGHTER

This portion of the chapter focuses on the treatment of humor and laughter as something that can be responsible for changes in our physical being as well as a regulator of several physiologic processes. According to Martin (2001), when we look at humor as medicine, there are four potential areas for theoretical exploration. The first area reflects the idea that *laughter might produce a physiologic change in various systems of the body.* Second, *humor as well as laughter might affect health indirectly by inducing positive emotional states.* Third, *humor could benefit health indirectly by moderating stress.* Finally, *humor may indirectly affect health as increasing one's likeability, thus garnering social support.* These four areas of exploration were developed in response to Martin's (2001) review of 41 published articles investigating the relationship between humor, laughter, and various aspects of health, including immunity, pain tolerance, blood pressure, longevity, and illness symptoms.

Immunity

Most of the studies investigating the impact of humor and laughter on immunity have been done through the assessment of Saliva (SIgA), which is found to be related to the body's defense against colds (e.g., upper respiratory infections). All the studies reviewed by Martin (2001) and later by Bennett and Lengacher (2006) were found to lack adequate control (i.e., weak experimental design). For example, were the alterations in SIgA level a result of observing laughter, amusement, or positive emotion, or some other physiological process? By having poorly controlled experiments, such determination is impossible. As a result of this problem throughout the studies, some of the findings indicated that humor and laughter indeed strengthen the immune system, with others indicating no effect. Therefore, there is a need for more research using better experimental design to definitely say whether there is or is not a connection between benefits to the immune system and humor or laughter.

Pain Tolerance

Studies that investigate the effects of humor and laughter on pain tolerance (i.e., analgesic effects) also suffer from a lack of experimental control. There have been findings indicating that there are indeed analgesic effects associated with both positive and negative emotional arousal. However, there is some evidence as to the relaxing properties associated with laughing (Paskin, 1932), which provides some insight into the impact that laughter and humor may have on pain reduction.

Blood Pressure

The effects and implications of blood pressure on health and disease are well documented. What is less known is the correlation between humor and blood pressure levels. Lefcourt, Davidson, Prkachin, and Mills (1997) conducted a study that revealed an association between a person's sense of humor score and systolic blood pressure. More specifically, females showed a negative correlation (i.e., the higher the sense of humor, the lower the systolic blood pressure, systolic blood pressure—if your blood pressure is 120/80 the systolic number is the 120 figure). The opposite finding was true for males. Males who were high in sense of humor also had increased levels of systolic blood pressure. How can such a finding be explained? The authors of this study believe that the answer can be found in the ways in which men and women express humor. Specifically, women tend to be more self-deprecating and adaptive in their use of humor, which can result in a more beneficial physiologic effect. Males, on the other hand, tend to engage in more aggressive humor where power and wit are constant factors in the use of humor. Such a use of humor is stressful on the nervous system.

Longevity

Factors that contribute to a long and productive life have commanded an abundance of attention from communication scholars. Humor and laughter have long been associated with a "good" and "prosperous" life and, therefore, are likely contributors to longevity. Freidman et al. (1993) examined data from the Terman Life Cycle Study, which tracked 1,178 males and females throughout their lifecycles starting in 1929. The assessment of the person's sense of humor and optimism was performed at age 12 by the participant's parents and teachers. Sense of humor and optimism were seen as the measures for what was termed "cheerfulness." The results of the finding indicated that those who were rated as being higher in cheerfulness at age 12 had significantly higher mortality rates throughout the ensuing decades. How can such a finding be true in light of what we currently know about being optimistic and cheerful? This, like many of the other studies, was not well controlled, meaning there were many other factors that contribute to a person's mortality. However, Freidman et al. (1993) concluded that those people who are optimistic may be either less concerned about their health or down-play any life-threatening symptoms. This explanation is at best speculative. There is no compelling evidence indicating that humor and laughter contribute to people living longer. On the other hand there is abundant anecdotal evidence (i.e., evidence based on personal stories and experiences as opposed to science) indicating that people who live their lives filled with humor and laughter enjoy life more fully.

Illness Symptoms

The concept that humor and laughter can be used as medicine has led researchers to look at possible medicinal effects of such behavior. Paskin (1932) argued that laughter is good exercise. This claim comes from the idea that the act of laughter incorporates several muscle groups, specifically, the use of the diaphragm and intercostal muscles that are also used in respiration. Laughing episodes often result in postlaughter relaxation states of up to 45 minutes. Think about your own past when you and a friend experience intense laughter fits. There is a feeling of relaxation and euphoria that remains after the laughing behavior subsides. Similar to the other research programs on laughter and humor, there is some evidence that humor and laughter assist (are complementary) in the healing of illness when added to traditional, evidence-based medicine. However, there is no conclusive evidence as to whether humor and laughter can be used as a therapy by themselves. In other words, the use of humor and laughter is not and cannot be a replacement for evidence-based medical therapy. Research continues on the complex role that humor plays in actual scientifically-based medical benefits and, until such evidence emerges, the debate will continue.

PATHOLOGICAL ISSUES OF HUMOR AND LAUGHTER

One of the more ignored aspects of both humor and laughter research in the medical field involves how such behavior is manifested in a variety of pathological disorders. When we speak of pathology, we are referring to disease. *Pathological laughter* is defined as anything from laughing at a politically incorrect joke or laughter that is a manifestation of a genetic disease. This section explores a few disease states manifested by pathologic laughter.

There is a form of epilepsy known as gelastic seizures. These seizures are associated with bizarre motor activity associated with inappropriate laughter. Such seizures are believed to affect the areas of the brain that seem to be responsible for the affective responses to humor, including the hypothalamus as well as the frontal and temporal lobes (Wild, Rodden, Grodd, & Ruck, 2003). Recall that such areas of the brain serve as important areas associated with any humorous response to a stimulus.

Another disease process that may be related to inappropriate laughter is that of poor brain circulation or a *stroke* (cerebrovascular accident). In such instances, the patient experiences uncontrollable laughter, which can be associated with paralysis of one side of the body or perhaps an inability to speak. This inability to speak is known as *aphasia* (Poeck, 1969).

Dementia and its various forms have been associated with inappropriate laughter behavior. One progressive form of dementia that affects people of younger age (between 40 and 60 years old) is a pathological condition known as *Pick's disease*. This disorder accounts for about 5 percent of all dementia cases and affects the temporal and frontal lobes of the brain (Wang, Zhu, Feng, & Wang, 2006; see Figure 3). Such patients have a tendency for inappropriate laughter within the context of social situations. Of greater significance is the epidemic of older age dementia known as *Alzheimer's disease*, generally diagnosed in people aged 65 or older. It has been projected that by the year 2050, 1 in 85 people (globally) will be affected. It is estimated that 14 percent of Alzheimer patients will have fits of crying, laughing, or a mixture of both (Provine, 2000).

In addition to dementia-related disease, there are several genetic syndromes that manifest laughter. *Rhett's syndrome* is a sex-specific disease that affects only young females and is believed to be within the autism spectrum of disorders. Eighty-three percent of these girls demonstrate a strange "solitary form" of laughter suggestive of spiritual possession (Provine, 2000). *Williams' disorder*, which can be considered somewhat the opposite of Rhett's in that unlike Rhett's syndrome where the patients tend to be aloof and lack basic social skills, Williams' patients tend to be charming, socially skilled, emotionally sensitive, and have great friendship-forming skills. Humor and laughter use in these patients is generally appropriate and well timed. However, they have difficulty performing basic cognitive tasks such as spelling words or doing basic mathematical calculations. *Wilson's disease* is a disorder of copper metabolism, which results in the patient having involuntary fits of laughter and being emotionally volatile. Taken as a whole, humor and laughter do manifest themselves within genetic disorders such as Rhett's, Williams', and Wilson's diseases, but such disorders are uncommon when compared with a more common genetic disorder known as Tourette's (Van de Wetering, & Heutink, 1993). Most people believe that Tourette's is a syndrome whereby the person uses inappropriate obscene words (known as *coprolalia*). Although a common assumption, such occurrences are relatively rare. More common in this population is a tic disorder, which can occur in as high as 10 children per every 1,000 live births. The patients tend to laugh normally but also be inclined to expressing an inappropriate laughter-like utterances such as an explosive "ha." Researchers have determined that such explosive laughter episodes are more characteristic of a tic than that of someone displaying an expression of humor (Shapiro, 2002).

CONCLUSION

The impact of humor and laughter in the human experience goes well beyond that of something used as a social performance. In fact, humor and laughter have profound impacts on our physical experience, as well. This chapter presented the anatomical, physiological, and pathological aspects of humor and laughter, and how such conceptualizations and research can assist scholars in better understanding the entire phenomena of humor and laughter. Researchers from both the natural as well as the social sciences need to collaborate in order to provide more satisfying and meaningful results as to how we can harness the energy and positive feelings that come from humor use and laughter expression into effective therapy and its resulting physiologic impact. Further investigation into the various pathologies of which laughter is either a symptom or manifestation may reveal new diagnostic protocols where assessment of humor use and laughter displays may be measured and used in diagnosis.

References

Bennett, M. P., & Lengacher, C. A. (2006). Humor and laughter may influence health II: Complementary and alternative medicine. *Evidence-Based Complementary and Alternative Medicine, 3*, 187–190.

Cousins, N. (1976). Anatomy of an illness. *New England Journal of Medicine, 295*, 1458–1463.

Cousins, N. (1979). *Anatomy of an illness as perceived by the patient: Reflections on health and recovery.* New York: Norton.

Darwin, C. (1872). *The expressions of emotion in man and animals.* London: John Murray Publisher.

Ekman, P. (1997). What we have learned by measuring facial behavior. In P. Ekman & E. L. Rosenberg (Eds.), *What the face reveals* (pp. 469–485). New York: Oxford University Press.

Ekman, P., Davidson, R. J., & Friesen, W. V. (1990). The Duchenne smile: Emotional expression and brain physiology: II. *Journal of Personality and Social Psychology, 58*, 342–353.

Ekman, P., & Friesen, W. (1975). *Unmasking the face: A guide to recognizing emotion from facial expression.* Englewood Cliffs, NJ: Prentice Hall.

Freidman, H. S., Tucker, J. S., Tomlinson-Keasey, C., Schwartz, J. E., Wingard, D. L., & Criquima, H. (1993). Does childhood personality predict longevity? *Journal of Personality and Social Psychology, 65*, 176–185.

Fry, W. F. (1963). *Sweet madness: A study of humor.* Palo Alto, CA: Pacific Books.

Gazzaniga, M., Ivy, R. B., & Magnum, G. R. (2008). *Cognitive neuroscience: The biology of the mind* (3rd ed.). New York: W. W. Norton and Company.

Lefcourt, H. M., Davidson, K., Prkachin, K. M., & Mills, D. E. (1997). Humor as a stress moderator in the prediction of blood pressure obtained during five stressful tasks. *Journal of Research and Personality, 31*, 523–542.

Maclean, P. D. (1949). Psychosomatic disease and the 'visceral brain': Recent developments bearing on the papez theory of emotion. *Psychosomatic Medicine, 11*(6), 338–353.

Martin, R. A. (2001). Humor, laughter, and physical health: Methodologic issues and research findings. *Psychological Bulletin, 127*, 504–519.

Medina, J. (2008). *Brain rules.* Seattle: Pear Press.

Moran, J. M., Wig, G. S., Adams, R. B., Janata, P., & Kelley, W. M. (2004). Neural correlates of humor detection and appreciation. *NeuroImage, 21*, 1055–1060.

Paskin, D. J. (1932). Effects of laughter on muscle tone. *Archives of Neurology and Psychiatry, 28*, 623–628.

Poeck, K. (1969). Pathophysiology and emotional disorders associated with brain damage. In P. J. Vinken & G. W. Bruyn (Eds.), *Handbook of clinical neurology* (Vol. 3, pp. 343–367). Amsterdam: Elsevier.

Provine, R. R. (2000). *Laughter: A scientific investigation.* New York: Viking Penguin.

Robinson, V. M. (1991). *Humor and the health professions: The therapeutic use of humor in health care* (2nd ed.). Thorofare, NJ: Slack.

Rosner, F. (2002). Therapeutic efficiency of laughter in medicine. *Cancer Investigation, 20*, 434–436.

Ruch, W., & Ekman, P. (2001). The expressive pattern of laughter. In A. W. Kaszniak (Ed.), *Emotion qualia and consciousness* (pp. 426–443). Hackensack, NJ: World Scientific Publishers.

Sackett, B. L. (1997). Evidence-based medicine. *Seminars in Perinatology, 21*, 3–5.

Shapiro, N. A. (2002). 'Dude, you don't have tourettes:' Tourette's syndrome, beyond the tics. *Pediatric Nursing, 28*, 243–246.

Stearns F. R. (1972). Laughing physiology, pathophysiology, psychology, pathopsychology and development. Springfield, IL: Charles C. Thomas.

Van de Wetering, B. J., & Heutink, P. H. (1993). The genetics of Gilles de la Tourette Syndrome: A review. *Journal of Laboratory and Clinical Medicine, 121*, 638–645.

Wang, L. N., Zhu, M. W., Feng, Y. K., & Wang, J. H. (2006). Pick's disease with Pick bodies combined with progressive supranuclear palsy without tuft-shaped astrocytes: A clinical, neuroradiologic and pathologic study of autopsy cases. *Neuropathology, 26*, 222–230.

Wild, B., Rodden, F. A., Grodd, W., & Ruck, W. (2003). Neural correlates of laughter in humor. *Brain, 126*, 2121–2138.

CHAPTER 14

THE INFLUENCE OF TEACHER HUMOR ON STUDENT LEARNING

Ann Bainbridge Frymier
Miami University

Marian L. Houser
Texas State University–San Marcos

"Don't smile before Christmas!" has been passed down through teaching generations for many years. Teachers have been told students needed to be handled with a strict hand to ensure classroom control, and one of the ways to do this was to maintain a stoic appearance and a stern presentational style. More recently, however, teachers and instructional scholars have come to understand the value of humor in the classroom. This view reflects contemporary research in myriad contexts that suggests humor and laughter promote physiological and psychological well-being (Bennett & Lengacher, 2006; Martin, 2001; Wanzer, Sparks, & Frymier, 2009), reduce job stress (Avtgis & Taber, 2006), enhance coping (Wanzer, Booth-Butterfield, & Booth-Butterfield, 2005; Wanzer et al., 2009), and improve a host of relationships such as those in the workplace (Martin, 2004; Rizzo, Wanzer, & Booth-Butterfield, 1999; Wanzer et al., 2005), friendships (Wanzer, Booth-Butterfield, & Booth-Butterfield, 1996), family (Afifi, Joseph, & Aldeis, 2008; Aune & Wong, 2002), and between teachers and students (Wanzer & Frymier, 1999).

It should not be surprising, therefore, to discover research suggesting the effectiveness and benefits of humor in the classroom. With student learning as the primary outcome focus, this chapter examines humor in the instructional context. The various types of humor used by teachers are discussed, followed by a discussion of the research linking humor and learning. The chapter concludes by presenting the instructional humor processing theory and implications for future research.

HUMOR IN THE CLASSROOM

Humor has been measured and described in a variety of ways, with none adequately capturing how humor occurs between teachers and students. Ziv (1979) depicted humor in the classroom as a method of getting students to pay attention—certainly a noble and worthwhile use for it. Although this purpose certainly makes sense, it does not incorporate the reciprocal process between teacher and student, nor does it reflect the value of the teacher-student relationship (Frymier & Houser, 2000). Research has suggested that much can be gained from teachers and students developing an interpersonal relationship within the classroom—specifically students are motivated and learn more. One way to do this would be for teachers to incorporate humor in their teaching repertoires. Booth-Butterfield and Booth-Butterfield (1991) define humorous behavior as (a) intentional and goal-directed, (b) integrating verbal and nonverbal elements of humor, and (c) eliciting a positive response from the receiver. Therefore, humorous instructors consciously aim to get students laughing, chuckling, and expressing other unplanned positive emotional responses. Early research by Bryant, Comisky, Crane, and Zillman (1980) reflected this definition, reporting that the most successful classroom humor was spontaneous.

Three theories have been used consistently to understand teacher humor and to explain students' reactions to humor in the classroom. This trilogy includes arousal relief or relief theory (Berlyne, 1969), incongruity theory (Berlyne, 1960), and disparagement or superiority theory (Wolff, Smith, & Murray, 1934). Proponents of arousal relief or relief theory argue that individuals experience humor and laughter in response to some stressful or difficult event or situation (Berlyne, 1972; Morreall, 1983). Working from this theory, humorous reactions result primarily from the cathartic release of pent-up emotions or tensions. Thus, when an instructor tells a humorous joke or story at the beginning of a lecture, students may laugh and subsequently release pent-up anxiety or stress. As a result, students may experience greater confidence and motivation leading to greater overall classroom learning.

According to incongruity theory, humorous reactions result from exposure to stimuli that are unexpected, shocking, or surprising (Berger, 1976; Berlyne, 1960; McGhee, 1979). A basic premise behind this theory is that people enter communication situations with a set of specific expectations and when something happens unexpectedly, it is often perceived as funny. Both Frymier and Weser (2001) and Vallade and Frymier (2011) have found that students expect relatively low levels of humor from their instructors. Therefore, when instructors attempt to use humor in the classroom, it may positively violate students' expectations and result in a positive evaluation of the teacher and/or the content. Even unintentional humor such as tripping or misspeaking may result in humor because of the unexpected nature of the behaviors. The online educational context is no different. Studies have reported that students expect so little when it comes to teacher humor in this environment that simple puns or word-play online creates student appreciation for both course and teacher (LoSchiavo & Shatz, 2005).

The third theory in the triad is disparagement or superiority theory (Feinberg, 1978; Gruner, 1978, 1997). This theory is based on the premise that people laugh at other's shortcomings, failings, or inadequacies (Wolff et al., 1934). Humor is enhanced by disparaging disliked others (Zillman, 1983), which is a common element in racist and sexist jokes. An underlying assumption of disparagement theory is that we make ourselves feel better by making fun of others. When instructors tease students about their classroom behavior, make fun of administrators, student groups, or others, instructors may make themselves feel better about their own abilities and shortcomings. Unfortunately, students do not typically appreciate teachers making fun of them, but self-disparaging comments are often perceived more positively (Frymier, Wanzer, & Wojtaszczyk, 2008). Self-disparaging humor can be especially effective to reduce the vast status differential that frequently exists between teacher and student (Korobkin, 1988).

Types of Humor

Bryant, Comisky, and Zillman (1979) and Bryant et al. (1980) developed a list of humor types that was one of the first major classification schemes developed in an attempt to define teacher humor. Bryant et al. (1980) reported that instructors presented multiple types of humor, with much of it off-topic and intended to cultivate student affect for learning in the course. Affective learning has been repeatedly linked with cognitive learning (Christophel, 1990; Rodriguez, Plax, & Kearney, 1996). Therefore, it makes sense that teachers' use of humor unrelated to course content can still be successful in the classroom. Bryant et al. (1979) ultimately reported that on average, teachers used humor 3.34 times during a 50-minute class period. The humor generally fell within six categories: jokes, puns, riddles, funny stories, funny comments, and other/miscellaneous. On the flip-side, Downs, Javidi, and Nussbaum (1988) reported their observations of instructor humor to be primarily focused on the course content. Though frequently aimed at "playing off" the teacher, students, and others not in the class, the focus remained on class material. Their categorization reflected the verbal coding scheme developed by Nussbaum, Comadena, and Holladay (1985) and intended to quantify instructor humor. Ultimately, Downs et al. (1988) reported that teacher humor appeared to gradually decrease over the course of the semester (beginning with 7.4 instances per class), and award-winning teachers consistently used moderate amounts, most often preferred by students. Excessive humor was deemed inappropriate (13.33 instances per class), with more effective instructors being able to better gauge the proper amount of humor. This appears to reflect the value in teachers knowing their students, being able to gauge their appreciation of classroom humor, and ultimately developing relationships with them.

To better understand the role of humor behaviors in perceptions of immediacy, Gorham and Christophel (1990) identified and described the types of humor used by teachers. They asked college students to record the humorous behavior of a teacher during five separate class sessions. The data coding resulted in 13 types of humor typically utilized in the classroom:

Brief, tendentious comments directed at

1. an individual student
2. the class as a whole
3. the university, department, or state
4. national or world events, or personalities, or popular culture
5. topic, subject, or class procedures
6. self (self-deprecating)

Personal anecdote or story

7. related to the subject/topic
8. not related to the subject/topic

General anecdote or story

9. related to the subject/topic
10. not related to the subject/topic
11. Joke
12. Physical or vocal comedy
13. Other

Gorham and Christophel concluded that the frequency of humor behaviors was related to perceptions of immediacy, but that humor had only a small relationship with learning outcomes. Additionally, Gorham and Christophel (1990) concluded that self-deprecating and tendentious humor had a negative impact on the general assessment of humor frequency. Therefore, it appears that students in Gorham and Christophel's study recognized self-deprecating and tendentious comments as humor, but did not necessarily perceive them as funny.

Neuliep (1991) examined high school teachers' use of humor and their perceptions of the types of humor identified by Gorham and Christophel (1990). Neuliep (1991) identified 20 types of humor used by high school teachers. In addition to the goal of surveying teachers, Neuliep also moved the context to the high school classroom in an effort to uncover more specificity in the categories/descriptions of humor in the classroom. The results revealed high school teachers generally use the same forms of humor as college instructors, but do so less frequently. In addition Neulip examined teachers' reasons for using humor in the classroom; identifying the following top 10 reasons.

1. Puts students at ease, relaxes them, or loosens them up

2. Attention-getting device

3. Shows teacher is human

4. Helps keep class semi-formal

5. Makes learning more fun

5a. Serves as tension releaser

6. Maintains student interest

7. Helps illustrate a point

8. Establishes rapport with students

9. Helps students remember a point

10. Change of pace/breaks up routine

By the early 1990's, the cumulative research clearly indicated that teachers frequently used a variety of humor behaviors while teaching and the research was fairly consistent in describing the types of humor used by teachers. While these descriptions of humor types were helpful in understanding *what* teachers actually did, they were not helpful in understanding *how* students responded to the humor.

Appropriate and Inappropriate Humor

In previous attempts to describe and categorize teacher humor, the appropriateness of humor was frequently recognized as important. Both students and teachers reported humorous stories and comments as good or bad, helpful or hurtful, useful or not, and so forth. However, little attention was given to systematically differentiating appropriate from inappropriate humor. Though not intended as an investigation aimed at developing a classification of appropriate humor, Torok, McMorris, and Lin (2004) used Bryant et al.'s (1979) humor types as a framework and examined both teachers' and their students' perceptions of each humor type. The forms of humor most highly recommended by students were: funny stories, funny comments, professional humor, jokes, and sarcasm. Torok et al. (2004) initially predicted that sarcasm would be perceived as inappropriate and would not be recommended, but this was not the case. The least recommended humor behaviors were those with sexual overtones, ethnic references, and aggressive/hostile humor, which was consistent with Torok et al.'s expectations. Torok et al. (2004) reported that when surveyed, 74 percent of students felt positive regarding the constructive use of humor by professors. In addition, when asked if the use of such humor assisted in learning concepts, 40 percent of respondents indicated that humor "often" facilitated learning and 40 percent reported that humor "always" aided in learning (Torok et al., 2004).

In 2006, Wanzer, Frymier, Wojtaszczyk, and Smith formalized our understanding of forms of humor that are considered appropriate or inappropriate. Students were asked to list examples of the appropriate and inappropriate instructor humor they had experienced. Using constant comparative methods, four major categories of appropriate and four major categories of inappropriate humor were identified.

Appropriate	Inappropriate
Related humor	Offensive humor
Unrelated humor	Disparaging student humor
Self-disparaging humor	Disparaging other humor
Unplanned humor	Self-disparaging humor

The four broad categories subsumed several subcategories that served to further explain and elaborate the major categories. Wanzer et al. (2006) noted overlap in appropriate and inappropriate humor, particularly with regard to both unrelated and self-disparaging humor. To help clarify these initial inductive findings, Frymier et al. (2008) conducted a follow-up study aimed at understanding why students perceived humor as either appropriate or inappropriate. In an effort to explain this, they put forth three explanations that were theoretically and conceptually framed. These explanations were based on the following: (1) Incongruity Resolution and Disposition Theories—humor is considered inappropriate if a) it is not recognized and resolved, and b) when it makes fun of others that students' like or perceive as similar; (2) Receiver personality traits/characteristics—perceptions of appropriateness are related to students' humor orientation, verbal aggressiveness, and communication competence; and (3) Teacher traits/characteristics—perceptions of appropriateness are related to teachers' exhibited levels of humor orientation, verbal aggressiveness, and nonverbal immediacy. Frymier et al. (2008) concluded that all three explanations were at least partially valid. First, consistent with disposition theory, students consistently viewed disparaging humor as inappropriate. Second, students high in verbal aggression and humor orientation generally perceived disparaging humor as more appropriate than students low in verbal aggressiveness and humor orientation. Third, teachers' levels of verbal aggressiveness, humor orientation, and nonverbal immediacy were related, with some forms of humor being perceived as more appropriate by students. Frymier et al. concluded that perceptions of appropriateness are influenced by social norms, student communication predispositions, and teacher communication predispositions.

THE HUMOR-LEARNING RELATIONSHIP

A number of studies have found a positive relationship between teachers' use of humor and student learning (Chapman & Crompton, 1978; Curran, 1972; Davies & Apter, 1980; Gorham & Christophel, 1990; Hauck & Thomas, 1972; Wakshlag, Day, & Zillmann, 1981; Weinberg, 1974; Ziv, 1979, 1988). While several studies provided support for the humor-learning relationship, others have not. There are a number of reasons why early studies using college students did not find a positive relationship between use of humor and learning (Gruner, 1967, 1976; Kennedy, 1972; Kilpela, 1961; Taylor, 1964; Youngman, 1966). One explanation for the failure to show support for the humor-learning effect was the length of these studies (Ziv, 1988). Several studies had brief exposures to humor, which may have been too brief to affect retention. For several studies, the duration of the experiment was 10 minutes or less (Kilpela, 1961; Taylor, 1964; Youngman, 1966). Additionally, Ziv (1988) noted that most of these studies were conducted in artificial experimental settings that did not resemble true academic situations that would not take into account the social norms, student communication predispositions, and teacher communication predispositions that Frymier et al. (2008) reported to influence humor perceptions.

Gorham and Christophel (1990) have also commented on the experimental procedures used to test the humor-learning relationship. They noted that a majority of the studies used similar procedures. Participants were tested for recall following lectures in which humor was introduced in the experimental condition and omitted in the control (Gorham & Christophel, 1990). From a communication perspective, it is difficult to generalize findings among the studies for two primary reasons. First, different types of humor (cartoons versus stories and jokes) and placement of humor (humor placed at key points of the lecture versus humor throughout the presentation) may elicit differential rates of retention. Second, researchers used different stimulus materials. Researchers used audiotapes (Kilpela, 1961; Taylor, 1964; Youngman, 1966), lectures (Weinberg, 1974, written speeches and tasks (Hauck & Thomas; 1972; Markiewicz, 1972), and video clips (Wakshlag et al. 1981) of humorous messages. Again, it is difficult to compare these studies' results when the manipulation of humor is vastly inconsistent. Differences in results may be a function of humor type and the way the humorous stimuli were presented.

Rather than manipulate some form of humor, Wanzer and Frymier (1999) examined humor orientation in the classroom. Humor orientation is a personality predisposition to create and use humor in a variety of situations (Booth-Butterfield & Booth-Butterfield, 1991). In this study, students self-reported their own humor orientation as well as perceptions of their teachers' humor orientation (HO). Frymier and Wanzer found that students high in HO reported learning the most when paired with a high HO teacher. Students low in HO also learned more with a high HO teacher; however they reported learning more with a low HO teacher than did the high HO students. This was the first study to provide evidence that the interpretation of humor in the classroom is influenced by an interaction of teacher and student characteristics.

One theoretical explanation for the humor-learning relationship is based on the attention-gaining and holding power of humor (Ziv, 1979). This theoretical explanation was also advanced by Kelley and Gorham (1988) to explain the immediacy-learning relationship. The attention-gaining explanation hypothesizes that teacher behavior (e.g., humor) gains students' attention, which is related to memory, which in turn is related to cognitive learning (Kelley & Gorham, 1988). The attention-gaining model advanced by Ziv (1979) and Kelley and Gorham (1988) has been the primary theoretical explanation for the humor-learning relationship in the college classroom. However, this model has not been fully tested or supported (Frymier, 1994). This model also does not address appropriate versus inappropriate humor and students' differing responses to humor in the classroom. In an attempt to address these issues, Wanzer, Frymier, and Irwin (2010) advanced the first theory of how humor functions in instructional settings.

Avtgis, T. A., & Taber, K. R. (2006). 'I laughed so hard my side hurts, or is that an ulcer?' The influence of work humor on job stress, job satisfaction, and burnout among print media employees. *Communication Research Reports, 23*, 13–18. doi:10.1080/17464090500535814HTH

Bennett, M. P., & Lengacher, C. (2006). Humor and laughter may influence health: II. Complementary therapies and humor in a clinical population. *eCAM, 3*(2), 187–190. doi:10.1093/ecam/nel014

Berger, A. A. (1976). Anatomy of the joke. *Journal of Communication, 26*, 113–115.

Berlyne, D. E. (1960). *Conflict, arousal, and curiosity*. New York: McGraw-Hill.

Berlyne, D. E. (1969). Arousal, reward and learning. *Annals of the New York Academy of Science, 159*, 1059–1070.

Berlyne, D. E. (1972). Affective aspects of aesthetic communication. In T. Alloway, L. Krames, & P. Pliner (Eds.), *Communication and affect: A comparative approach* (pp. 97–118). New York: Academic.

Booth-Butterfield, S., & Booth-Butterfield, M. (1991). The communication of humor in everyday life. *Southern Communication Journal, 56*, 205–218.

Bryant, J., Comisky, P., & Zillmann, D. (1979). Teachers' humor in the classroom. *Communication Education, 28*, 110–118.

Bryant, J., Comisky, P., Crane, J. S., & Zillmann, D. (1980). Relationship between college teachers' use of humor in the classroom and students' evaluations of their teachers. *Journal of Educational Psychology, 72*, 511–519.

Chapman, A. J., & Crompton, P. (1978). Humorous presentations of material and presentations of humorous material: A review of the humor and memory literature and two experimental studies. In M. M. Grunneberg & P. E. Morris (Eds.), *Practical aspects of memory* (pp. 84–92). London: Academic Press.

Christophel, D. M. (1990). The relationships among teacher immediacy behaviors, student motivation, and learning. *Communication Education, 39*, 323–340.

Curran, F. W. (1972). *A developmental study of cartoon humor and its use in facilitating learning*. Unpublished Doctoral dissertation. Catholic University of America, Washington, DC.

Davies, A. P., & Apter, M. J. (1980). Humor and its effect on learning in children. In P. E. McGhee & A. J. Chapman (Eds.), *Children's humor* (pp. 237–254). New York: Wiley.

Downs, V. C., Javidi, M., & Nussbaum, J. F. (1988). An analysis of teachers' verbal communication within the college classroom: Use of humor, self-disclosure, and narratives. *Communication Education, 37*, 127–141.

Feinberg, L. (1978). *The secret of humor*. Amsterdam: Rodopi.

Frymier, A. B. (1994). A model of immediacy in the classroom. *Communication Quarterly, 42*, 133–143.

Frymier, A. B., & Houser, M. L. (2000). The teacher-student relationship as an interpersonal relationship. *Communication Education, 49*, 207–219.

Frymier, A. B., Wanzer, M. B., & Wojtaszczyk, A. (2008). Assessing students' perceptions of inappropriate and appropriate teacher humor. *Communication Education, 57*, 266–288.

Frymier, A. B., & Weser, B. (2001). The role of student predispositions on student expectations for instructor communication behavior. *Communication Education, 50*, 314–326.

Gorham, J., & Christophel, D. M. (1990). The relationship of teachers' use of humor in the classroom to immediacy and student learning. *Communication Education, 39*, 46–62.

Gruner, C. R. (1967). Effects of humor on speaker ethos and audience information gain. *Journal of Communication, 17*, 228–233.

Gruner, C. R. (1976). Wit and humor in mass communication. In A. J. Chapman & H. C. Foot (Eds.), *Humor and laughter: Theory, research, and applications* (pp. 287–312). London: Wiley.

Gruner, C. R. (1978). *Understanding laughter: The working of wit and humor*. Chicago: Nelson-Hall.

Gruner, C. R. (1997). *The game of humor*. New Brunswick, NJ: Transaction Books.

Hauck, W. E., & Thomas, J. W. (1972). The relationship of humor to intelligence, creativity, and intentional and incidental learning. *Journal of Experimental Education, 40*, 52–55.

Kelley, D. H., & Gorham, J. (1988). Effects of immediacy on recall of information. *Communication Education, 37*, 198–207.

Kennedy, A. J. (1972). *An experimental study of the effects of humorous message content upon ethos and persuasiveness*. Unpublished Doctoral dissertation. University of Michigan, Ann Arbor.

Kilpela, D. E. (1961). *An experimental study of the effect of humor on persuasion*. Unpublished Master's thesis. Wayne State University, Detroit.

Korobkin, D. (1988). Humor in the classroom: Considerations and strategies. *College Teaching, 36*, 154–158.

LoSchiavo, F. M., & Shatz, M. A. (2005). Enhancing online instruction with humor. *Teaching of Psychology, 32*, 247–250.

Markiewicz, D. (1972). *The effects of humor on persuasion*. Unpublished Doctoral dissertation. Ohio State University, Columbus.

Martin, D. (2004). Humor in middle management: Women negotiating the paradoxes of organizational life. *Journal of Applied Communication Research, 32*, 147–170.

Martin, R. (2001). Humor, laughter, and physical health: Methodological issues and research findings. *Psychological Bulletin, 127*, 504–519.

McGhee, P. E. (1979). *Humor: Its origin and development*. San Francisco: W. H. Freeman.

Morreall, J. (1983). *Taking laughter seriously*. Albany: State University of New York.

Neuliep, J. W. (1991). An examination of the content of high school teachers' humor in the classroom and the development of an inductively derived taxonomy of classroom humor. *Communication Education, 40*, 343–355.

Nussbaum, J. F., Comadena, M. E., & Holladay, S. J. (1985, May). Verbal and nonverbal behavior of highly effective teachers. *Paper presented at the annual convention of the International Communication Association*, Honolulu.

Petty, R. E., & Cacioppo, J. T. (1986). *Communication and persuasion: Central and peripheral routes to attitude change.* New York: Springer-Verlag.

Rizzo, B., Wanzer, M. B., & Booth-Butterfield, M. (1999). Individual differences in managers' use of humor: Subordinate perceptions of managers' humor orientation, effectiveness, and humor behaviors. *Communication Research Reports, 16,* 370–376.

Rodrıguez, J. I., Plax, T. G., & Kearney, P. (1996). Clarifying the relationship between teacher nonverbal immediacy and student cognitive learning: Affective learning as the central causal mediator. *Communication Education, 45,* 293–305.

Taylor, P. M. (1964). The effectiveness of humor in informative speeches. *Central States Speech Journal, 5,* 295–296.

Torok, S. E., McMorris, R. F., & Lin, W. (2004). Is humor an appreciated teaching tool? Perceptions of professors' teaching styles and use of humor. *College Teaching, 52,* 14–20.

Vallade, J. I, & Frymier, A. B. (2011, April). Expectancy violation in the classroom. *Paper presented at the Eastern Communication Association Annual Convention*, Washington, DC.

Wakshlag, J. J., Day, K. D., & Zillmann, D. (1981). Selective exposure to educational television programs as a function of differently placed humorous inserts. *Journal of Educational Psychology, 73,* 27–32.

Wanzer, M. B., Booth-Butterfield, M., & Booth-Butterfield, S. (1996). Are funny people popular? An examination of humor orientation, loneliness, and social attraction. *Communication Quarterly, 44,* 42–52.

Wanzer, M., Booth-Butterfield, M., & Booth-Butterfield, S. (2005). 'If we didn't use humor, we'd cry': Humorous coping communication in healthcare settings. *Journal of Health Communication, 10,* 105–125.

Wanzer, M. B., & Frymier, A. B. (1999). The relationship between student perceptions of instructor humor and students' reports of learning. *Communication Education, 48,* 48–62.

Wanzer, M. B., Frymier, A. B., & Irwin, J. (2010). An explanation of the relationship between instructor humor and student learning: Instructional humor processing theory. *Communication Education, 59,* 1–18. doi:10.1080/03634520903367238

Wanzer, M. B., Frymier, A. B., Wojtaszczyk, A., & Smith, T. (2006). Appropriate and inappropriate uses of humor by teachers. *Communication Education, 55,* 178–196.

Wanzer, M. B., Sparks, L., & Frymier, A. B. (2009). *Health Communication, 24,* 128–136, doi:10.1080/10410230802676482

Weinberg, M. D. (1974). The interactional effect of humor and anxiety on academic performance. *Dissertation Abstracts International, 35*(1-B), 492–493.

Wolff, H. A., Smith, C. E., & Murray, H. A. (1934). The psychology of humor. *The Journal of Abnormal and Social Psychology, 28*(4), 341–365.

Youngman, R. C. (1966). *An experimental investigation of the effect of germane humor versus nongermane humor in an informative communication.* Unpublished Master's thesis. Ohio University, Athens.

Zillman, D. (1983). Disparagement humor. In P. E. McGhee & J. H. Goldstein (Eds.), *Handbook of humor research* (pp. 85–107). New York: Springer-Verlag.

Ziv, A. (1979). *L'humor en education: Approche psychologique.* Paris: Editions Social Françaises.

Ziv, A. (1988). Teaching and learning with humor: Experiment and replication. *Journal of Experimental Education, 57,* 5–15.

CHAPTER 15

GRADUATE ADVISOR-ADVISEE COMMUNICATION AND USE OF INTERPERSONAL HUMOR

Narissra Maria Punyanunt-Carter
Texas Tech University

Jason S. Wrench
State University of New York at New Paltz

Over the years, there has been an interest regarding academic advising at the undergraduate level (Barnes, Williams, & Archer, 2010). Research analyzing academic advising has focused on satisfaction (Lowe & Toney, 2000), retention (Cuseo, 2007), and the advisor role (Petress, 1996). Research looking at graduate advisors has been somewhat limited (Barnes et al., 2010). Nettles and Millett (2006) have shown that graduate students who have better advisors will have better experiences than those students who have poor advisor relationships.

Barnes and Austin (2009) noted that graduate programs in the United States are superior to other programs in the world. Advising for graduate students is extremely important because of the effects and results that it has for the advisee (Minor, 2003). Graduate advisors play a significant role in their advisee's lives because the advisor plays a huge role as the primary contact (Tinto, 1993). The advisor is the main connection to the department and/or discipline for that student. In turn, the advisor affects the advisee's experience in school, their postgraduate opportunities, their involvement in research projects and publications, and their ability to become part of the academic community (Barnes & Austin, 2009).

Research on graduate advising is not a new research trend. Barnes and Austin (2009) found that several studies have been conducted on advising. Mainly, these studies have examined undergraduate students looking at retention and satisfaction. Yet, there has been more interest in looking at the advising relationship in graduate programs (Nettles & Millett, 2006).

In this chapter we examine the importance of humor in the graduate advisor-advisee communicative relationship. To help us further our goals, we examine the nature of advisor-advisee relationships, explain the role of humor in post-graduate instructional communication, and lastly discuss our research that has specifically examined the role between humor and effective graduate advisor-advisee relationships

ADVISOR-ADVISEE RELATIONSHIPS

Advisors play many roles in graduate programs. Barnes and Austin (2009) believed that advisors are seen as role models, advocates, socializers, and sources of information. Ahern and Manthunga (2004) felt that doctoral advisors were oftentimes viewed as "clutch starts" for their stalled advisees. In other words, these advisors need to know when their students are stalled due to emotional, social, or intellectual issues, and then offer proper advisement to get the student progressing further in the program.

Oftentimes, the word "advisor" and "mentor" are used interchangeably. Johnson and Huwe (2003) noted that the advisor-advisee relationship is sometimes referred to as the mentor-mentee relationship. Nevertheless, Nettles and Millett (2006) described the advisor as the person who approves and discusses coursework issues, whereas the mentor is more involved with the relationship with the student. Moreover, Hawley (1993) stated that mentors assist in helping their students through the entire process of the program rather than only offering guidance for a degree plan.

It has been shown that graduate advising falls into four categories: advising influences, practices, outcomes, and selection (Barnes & Austin, 2009). The first area looks at the advising influences or what variables affect how advisors advise. The factors could include the advisee's needs, the personality of the advisor, and the area of expertise. Another influence could be how the advisor was advised in their graduate education. Moreover, the advisor's teaching philosophies and ethics will affect how the advisor interacts with their advisee. Lovitts (2004) found that there were six variables that affected students' satisfaction or dissatisfaction with their advisor: intellectual-professional development, interest in students, professionalism, personality, advising style, and accessibility. Lovitts discovered that students were more satisfied with their relationship if they also were satisfied with each of the dimensions.

The second area looks at advising practices. For instance, some advisors work at universities where research is more important than teaching. Hence, advising may not be rewarded or perceived in the same light as another advisor. Barnes and Austin (2009) determined five roles of the advisor for their advisee: (1) to assist in their success, (2) to advance their researching skills, (3) to cultivate their professional abilities, (4) to discern their passion, and (5) to offer guidance in their program. Hence, each advisor may view their role differently and practice advising differently. Holland (1998) found there were different types of advisor-advisee relationships: formal academic advising, academic guidance, quasi-apprenticeship, academic mentoring, and career mentoring.

The third area of graduate advising deals with outcomes. Various disciplines see the interactions between advisor and advisee differently. Some programs encourage more interactions and communication between advisors and their advisees. For instance, Golde (2005) noted that advisees in the hard sciences have more interactions with their advisors because their fields are more collaborative in regard to publishing and research than the social sciences. Also, Ferrer de Valero (2001) discovered that advisees who had closer relationships with their advisors were more likely to graduate and complete their degrees than the advisees who had distant relationships with their advisors. In addition, students who had better advisee-advisor relationships were more likely to collaborate and assist with research presentations and articles (Seagram, Gould, & Pyke, 1998). Lovitts (2001) noted that advisors have an impact on the advisee's understanding of the academic field and their roles in the discipline. O'Bara (1993) found that advisees were more likely to complete their program if they had more positive interactions with their advisor. Moreover, O'Bara found that the advisor's personality characteristics were an influential variable on the student completing their degree. Students who completed their degree tended to rate their advisors as more helpful, understanding, and approachable compared to students who did not complete their degree.

The fourth area is advisor selection. Barnes, Williams, and Archer (2010) noted that the advisor selection significantly impacts the advisor-advisee relationship. Fischer and Zigmond (1998) found that students want to be able to communicate with their advisors and desire mentoring that is compatible with their needs. It has been shown that the selection of advisor varies across the different disciplines (Zhao, Golde, & McCormick, 2007). Nevertheless, Lovitts (2006) noted that students who were able to pick their advisor based on common research interests and/or mutual respect had better relationships than students who were randomly assigned advisors. At the same time, Schlosseer, Knox, Moskovitz, and Hill (2003) found that graduate students were more satisfied with their education if they were able to select their own advisors than those students who are assigned advisors. Golde and Dore (2001) confirmed that there was "a strong association between the number of factors that a student considers when selecting an advisor and the student's satisfaction with that relationship" (p. 37).

Barnes and Austin (2009) summarized that many socio-psychological theories have been utilized to study the relationships between advisors and their graduate students. One theory that provides a good perspective for understanding the advisor's role is socialization theory. Coombs (1978) defined socialization as "the process of transforming a human being into a self who possesses a sense of identity and is endowed with appropriate attitudes, values, and ways of thinking, and with other personal yet social attributes" (p. 14). Socialization has also been described as "the process through which individuals gain the knowledge, skills, and values necessary for successful entry into a professional career requiring an advanced level of specialized knowledge and skills" (Weidman, Twale, & Stein, 2001, p. iii). Weidman et al.'s model of socialization emphasize four stages of socialization (anticipatory, formal, informal, and personal), three key elements (knowledge, acquisition, investment), and four elements to the socialization process (prospective students, professional communities, personal communities, and novice professional practitioners). Austin and McDaniels (2006) further elaborated on this area and felt that graduate students are socialized into the discipline into four areas. The first is conceptual understanding. The second is the faculty work. The third is interpersonal communication skills. The fourth is the professional behaviors and roles. This socialization process into the discipline is introduced to the student by the advisor. Although, Weidman et al. (2001) suggested that graduate students' socialization process into the discipline is affected by other factors such as family, cohorts, employers, and associations, the bulk of that responsibility comes for the advisor. Perhaps, the role of humor in the advisor-advisee relationship affects the socialization process, which in turn affects the outcomes of the advisee.

HUMOR IN POST-GRADUATE INSTRUCTIONAL COMMUNICATION

The effect of using humor during interpersonal relationships has been studied in a variety of contexts, all finding a positive effect on the relationship: interpersonal relationships (Booth-Butterfield & Booth-Butterfield, 1991), teacher-student relationships (Wanzer & Frymier, 1999), superior-subordinate relationships (Rizzo, Wanzer, & Booth-Butterfield, 1999), physician-patient (Wrench & Booth-Butterfield, 2003), coworkers (Wanzer, Booth-Butterfield, & Booth-Butterfield, 2005), and many others. One interpersonal relationship that has only initially been examined in the area of humor has been the graduate advisor-advisee relationship (Wrench & Punyanunt-Carter, 2008). In general, there is little research examining post-graduate instructional communication, and with the exception of the Wrench and Punyanunt (2004), Wrench and Punyanunt-Carter (2005, 2008), and Punayanunt-Carter & Wrench (2008) studies, very little research has examined graduate advisor-advisee instructional communication in general.

Unlike teacher-student relationships, the graduate advisor-advisee relationship contains functions of traditional classroom communication, interpersonal communication, and organizational communication (Wrench & Punyanunt, 2001). Ellis (1992) noted how graduate advisor-advisee relationships can impact advisees' success both in the classroom and professionally. Unfortunately, very little research has analyzed the advisor-advisee relationship, and most of the research has focused on undergraduates rather than graduate students (such as Althaus, 1997; Gorham & Millette, 1997; Scott & Rockwell, 1997).

HUMOR IN ADVISOR-ADVISEE RELATIONSHIPS

Thousands of years ago, in Homer's epic *The Odyssey*, the concept of a mentor was introduced. In *The Odyssey*, Homer describes how Ulysses pursues an adventure and selects his beloved friend, Mentor, to guide and supervise his son, Telemachus. In modern times, the word "mentor" has been used to describe a relationship where one individual with more experience and knowledge assists another individual who has less knowledge and experience (Richmond, Wrench, & Gorham, 2001).

In modern times, the concept of mentoring is often defined as a relationship between a more experienced individual (mentor) and a less experienced individual (protégé). The mentor usually helps their protégé in personal and professional development (Johnson & Nelson, 1999). For the protégé, mentoring can assist in her or his intellectual development, career expansion, and network with other individuals in the field (Wright & Wright, 1987). For the mentor, this relationship helps to increase intrinsic rewards (such as satisfaction and a sense of confidence) and extrinsic rewards (such as more productivity, power, and increased visibility) (Wright & Wright, 1987).

One rarely studied mentoring relationship is the mentoring relationship between graduate advisors and their graduate advisees (Hardy, 1994; Wrench & Punyanunt, 2004). Kram (1988) has noticed that graduate mentoring includes teaching, training, and socialization. Mentoring innately is a communication relationship where a senior person advises and encourages a junior person's professional and personal development (Hill, Bahniuk, & Dobos, 1989). To have a successful advisor-advisee relationship, both parties must communicate effectively (Hill et al., 1989). Kram (1988) further stated that mentoring tends to happen within strong interpersonal relationships in which both the mentor and protégé communicate effectively.

The advisor-advisee relationship is a crucial element in graduate education (Luna & Cullen, 1998). The effects of a great advisor on a graduate student's can be life altering. A great advisor can establish the ethics, determination, and skills to be both a great teacher and researcher. Moreover, Faghihi (1998) found that advisees' relationships with their graduate advisors were significantly related to the advisees' dissertation progress. Students who regarded their advisors more positively progressed faster in the dissertation process compared with those students who regarded their advisors negatively. In addition, Coran-Hillix, Gensheimer, Coran-Hillix, and Davidson (2000) found that graduate students who had favorable mentors in graduate school had more publications, more conference papers, more first-authored papers, and were more productive after graduate school when compared to those graduate students who did not have a mentor during her or his program. All in all, the graduate advisor can influence the advisee's perception of graduate school, learning, progress, and possibly future success. As the joke goes, the relationship between a graduate advisee and her or his advisor is more meaningful and lasts longer than most marriages.

In 2004, Wrench and Punyanunt initiated a new line of research to examine the communicative nature of graduate advisor-advisee relationships. In Advisor-Advisee One (AA-1), they found that the degree to which an advisee feels he or she is being mentored was positively related to advisee perceptions of her or his advisor's communication competence and perceived credibility. In addition, Wrench and Punyanunt found that advisor immediacy was positively related to advisee perceptions of advisor competence, caring/goodwill, trustworthiness, and communication competence. Lastly, the first study in this series reported that advisees perceive that they cognitively learn more and have more effective advisor-advisee relationships with more nonverbally immediate advisors.

Punyanunt-Carter and Wrench (2008) found a negative relationship between verbal aggression (tendency to attack an individual using putdowns and intelligence attacks instead of an individual's arguments) and advisee perceptions of affective learning and advisor credibility. The researchers also found a positive relationship between an advisee's perception of her or his advisor's humor assessment (see Chapter 5 in this book for a discussion of the Humor Assessment instrument) and advisee affective learning and perceptions of advisor source credibility.

Looking at humor specifically, Wrench and Punyanunt-Carter (2005) found there is a significant, positive relationship between humor and student affect. Wrench and Richmond (2000) discovered that there is a positive relationship between teacher humor assessment and student affect. Moreover, Wrench and Punyanunt-Carter noted that there was a slight relationship between humor and source credibility. Humor has an influence in the advisor-advisee relationship. However, the advisor's humor assessment does not impact the advisee's affect and perceptions of the advisor's credibility. Results from this study suggest that advisors who use humor in their advising relationships to increase perceptions of credibility will also lead to stronger mentoring relationships and increased advisee learning.

Punyanunt-Carter and Wrench (2005) also analyzed the relationship between advisee perceptions of advisor's use of verbal aggression and conflict styles management strategies on advisee perceptions of advisor credibility (competence, caring/goodwill, and trustworthiness). First, the study found that advisee perceptions of their advisor's credibility (competence, caring/goodwill, and trustworthiness) were positively related to advisee perceptions of advisor mentoring and an advisor's use of solution-oriented conflict management strategies. Second, advisee perceptions of advisor trustworthiness were positively related to advisee perceptions of advisor use of nonconfrontational conflict management strategies. Lastly, advisee perceptions of advisor competence were positively related to advisor use of control-oriented conflict management strategies.

Wrench and Punyanunt-Carter (2008) published an article specifically looking at the importance of humor in advisor-advisee graduate relationships in the *NACADA Journal*. NACADA (National Academic Advising Association) is the largest academic body devoted to both the practice and science of academic advising. While NACADA's focus is primarily on undergraduate advising, they do support and publish research on postgraduate advising as well. In this study, Wrench and Punyanunt-Carter found that a graduate advisee's perception of her or his graduate advisor's use of humor during their interactions correlated positively to a number of instructional communication variables: overall relationship satisfaction with one's advisor ($r = 0.51$, $p < 0.0005$), advisor's nonverbal immediacy ($r = 0.60$, $p < 0.0005$), perceptions of advisor's mentoring ($r = 0.49$, $p < 0.0005$), and advisor use of social support ($r = 0.48$, $p < 0.0005$). Once again, the power and benefits of humor within this unique interpersonal relationship are clear: Humor is a powerful and useful communicative skill that enhances the advisor/advisee relationship.

Overall, the results from all of these studies are in line with previous literature that has examined teacher-student relationships because it was suspected that the advisor-advisee relationship would be similar to the dynamics seen in previous immediacy studies that examined teachers and students in the traditional classroom setting (McCroskey & Richmond, 1992; Wanzer & Frymier,

1999). All and all, these studies suggest that how the advisor advises and the advisor's characteristics, such as humor and aggression, impact the relationship. To conclude, it is suggested that humor is a variable that can lead to stronger mentoring relationships.

CONCLUSION

As both researchers interested in advisor-advisee communicative interaction and in the academic study of humor as a communicative tool, we definitely believe our research examining advisor-advisee relationships further supports the positive benefits of humor in both interpersonal and instructional communication. However, both concepts are still under-researched by communication scholars, so there is ample opportunity for examining both concepts either separately or together in future research.

For advisor-advisee relationships, our published focus as researchers thus far has been on graduate advisor-advisee relationships, but there is little research in communication examining the importance of undergraduate advisor-advisee relationships. Graduate professors usually take on no more than a handful of advisees at any given time. Professors advising undergraduates, on the other hand, can have no undergraduate advisees or 20–50 advisees at any given time, depending on the college or university. As such, many professors have considerably higher quantities of undergraduate advisees, but are those advisees getting what they need out of those interpersonal interactions?

As for humor in advisor-advisee relationships, most of our examination of humor has predominantly examined the positive benefits of humor, which is based on self-report measures of advisee's perceptions of advisor's use of humor. Is the opposite also true? Are humorous advisees perceived as less serious, more frivolous, and ultimately, non-intellectually astute? Or are humorous advisees seen in a positive light by their academic advisors? Furthermore, we have not examined the impact that advisor or advisee humor has in the undergraduate advisor-advising relationship. Lastly, most of our research involving self-reports asks statements that lead to more positive perceptions of humor in the mind of the research participant. However, there are many people who think they are humorous, but the humor that is utilized is objectionable to some receivers. How does a "highly" humorous individual who depends on objectionable humor fare in these same research studies? Humor is often seen as a double-edged sword, but most of our humor communication research has on focused on one side of the blade.

Ultimately, there is still plenty ground to cover in understanding advisor-advisee relationships in general and how humor impacts these relationships. We hope this chapter has helped you understand the nature of advisor-advisee relationships, the role of humor in postgraduate instructional communication, and our research that has specifically examined the role between humor and effective graduate advisor-advisee relationships.

References

Ahern, K., & Manathunga, C. (2004). Clutch-starting stalled research students. *Innovative Higher Education, 28*(4), 237–254.

Althaus, S. L. (1997). Computer-mediated communication in the university classroom: An experiment with on-line discussions. *Communication Education, 46,* 158–174.

Austin, A. E., & McDaniels, M. (2006). Preparing the professoriate of the future: Graduate student socialization for faculty roles. *Higher Education: Handbook of Theory and Research, 21,* 397–456.

Barnes, B. J., & Austin, A. E. (2009). The role of doctoral advisors: A look at advising from the advisor's perspective. *Innovative Higher Education, 33,* 297–315.

Barnes, B. J., Williams, E. A., & Archer, S. A. (2010). Characteristics that matter most: Doctoral students' perceptions of positive and negative advisor attributes. *NACADA, 3,* 34–46.

Booth-Butterfield, M., & Booth-Butterfield, S. (1991). Individual differences in the communication of humorous messages. *Southern Communication Journal, 56,* 205-218

Coombs, R. H. (1978). *Mastering medicine.* New York: The Free Press.

Coran-Hillix, T., Genshiemer, L. K., Coran-Hillix, W. A., & Davidson, W. S. (1986). Students' views of mentors in psychology graduate training. *Teaching of Psychology, 13,* 123–128.

Cuseo, J. (2007). *Academic advisement and student retention: Empirical connections and systematic interventions.* NACADA Clearinghouse of Academic Advising. Retrieved from www.nacada.ksu.edu/clearinghouse/advisingissue/instrusive-freshman.html

Ellis, H. D. (1992). Graduate education in psychology: Past, present, and future. *American Psychologist, 47,* 570–576.

Faghihi, F. Y. (1998). A study of factors related to dissertation progress among doctoral candidates: Focus on student research self-efficacy as a result of their research training and experiences. *Dissertation Abstracts International Section A: Humanities & Social Sciences, 59*(5-A), 1456.

Ferrer de Valero, Y. (2001). Departmental factors affecting time-to-degree and completion rates of doctoral students at one land-grant research institution. *Journal of Higher Education, 72*(3), 341–367.

Fischer, B. A., & Zigmond, M. J. (1998). Survival skills for graduate school and beyond. In M. S. Anderson (Ed.), *The experience of being in graduate school: An exploration.* New Direction for Higher Education (No. 101, pp. 29–40). San Francisco: Jossey-Bass.

Golde, C. M. (2005). The role of the department and discipline in doctoral student attrition: Lessons from four departments. *Journal of Higher Education, 76*(6), 669–700.

Golde, C. M., & Dore, T. M. (2001). *At cross purposes: What the experiences of doctoral students reveal about doctoral education.* Retrieved from www.phd-survey.org

Gorham, J., & Millette, D. M. (1997). A comparative analysis of teacher and student perceptions of sources of motivation and demotivation in college classes. *Communication Education, 46,* 245–261.

Hardy, C. J. (1994). Nurturing our future through effective mentoring: Developing roots as well as wings. *Journal of Applied Sport Psychology, 6*, 196–204.

Hawley, P. (1993). *Being bright is not enough: The unwritten rules of doctoral studies.* Springfield, IL: Charles C. Thomas

Hill, S. K., Bahniuk, M. H., & Dobos, J. (1989). The impact of mentoring and collegial support on faculty success: An analysis of support behavior, information adequacy, and communication apprehension. *Communication Education, 38*, 15–33.

Holland, J. W. (1998). Mentoring and the faculty development of African-American doctoral students. In H. T. Frierson Jr. (Ed.), *Diversity in higher education* (Vol. 2, pp. 17–40). Stamford, CT: JAI Press.

Johnson, W. B., & Huwe, J. M. (2003). *Getting mentored in graduate school.* Washington, DC: American Psychological Association.

Johnson, B. W., & Nelson, N. (1999). Mentor-protégé relationships in graduate training: Some ethical concerns. *Ethics & Behavior, 9*, 1050–1084.

Kram, K. E. (1988). *Mentoring at work: Developmental relationships in organizational life.* New York: University Press of America.

Lovitts, B. E. (2001). *Leaving the ivory tower: The causes and consequences of departure from doctoral study.* Lanham, MD: Rowman & Littlefield.

Lovitts, B. E. (2004). Research on the structure and process of graduate education: Retaining students. In D. H. Wulff & A. E. Austin (Eds.), *Paths to the professoriate: Strategies for enriching the preparation of future faculty* (pp. 115–136). San Francisco: Jossey-Bass.

Lowe, A., & Toney, M. (2000). Academic advising: Views of the givers and takers. *Journal of College Student Retention, 2*, 93–108.

Luna, G., & Cullen, D. L. (1998). Do graduate students need mentoring? *College Student Journal, 32*, 322–330.

McCroskey, J. C., & Richmond, V. P. (1992). An instructional communication program for in-service teachers. *Communication Education, 41*, 216–223.

Minor, J. (2003). For better or worse: Improving advising relationships between faculty and graduate students. In A. L. Green & L. V. Scott (Eds.), *Journey to the Ph.D. How to navigate the process as African Americans* (pp. 239–253). Sterling, VA: Stylus Publishing.

Nettles, M. T., & Millett, C. M. (2006). *Three magic letters: Getting to Ph.D.* Baltimore: The Johns Hopkins University Press.

O'Bara, C. C. (1993). *Why some finish and why some don't: Factors affecting PhD completion.* Doctoral dissertation. Retrieved from The Claremont Graduate University, California. Dissertations & Theses: A&I database. (Publication No. AAT 9330356).

Petress, K. C. (1996). The multiple roles of an undergraduate's academic advisor. *Education, 117*, 91–95.

Punyanunt-Carter, N. M., & Wrench, J. S. (2005). Advisor-advisee communication three: Organizational communication variables in the graduate advisor-advisee relationships. *Paper presented at the National Communication Association's Convention*, Boston.

Punyanunt-Carter, N. M., & Wrench, J. (2008). Advisor-advisee three: Graduate students' perceptions of verbal aggression, credibility, and conflict styles in advising relationships. *Education, 12*, 579–587.

Richmond, V. P., Wrench, J. S., & Gorham, J. (2001). *Communication, affect, and learning in the classroom* (3rd Ed.). Acton, MA: Tapestry Press.

Rizzo, B., Wanzer, M. B., & Booth-Butterfield, M. (1999). Individual differences in managers' use of humor: Subordinate perceptions of managers' humor orientation, effectiveness, and humor behaviors. *Communication Research Reports, 16*, 370–376.

Schlosser, L. Z., Knox, S., Moskovitz, A. R., & Hill, C. E. (2003). A qualitative examination of graduate advising relationships: The advisee perspective. *Journal of Counseling Psychology, 50*(2), 178–188.

Scott, C. R., & Rockwell, S. C. (1997). The effect of communication, writing, and technology apprehension on likelihood to use new communication technologies. *Communication Education, 46*, 44–62.

Seagram, B., Gould, J., & Pyke, S. W. (1998). An investigation of gender and other variables on time to completion of doctoral degrees. *Research in Higher Education, 39*(3), 319–335.

Tinto, V. (1993). *Leaving college: Rethinking the causes and cures of student attrition* (2nd ed.). Chicago: The University of Chicago Press.

Wanzer, M., Booth-Butterfield, M., & Booth-Butterfield, S. (2005). 'If we didn't use humor, we'd cry': Humorous coping communication in healthcare settings. *Journal of Health Communication, 10*, 105–125.

Wanzer, M. B., & Frymier, A. B. (1999). The relationship between student perceptions of instructor humor and students' reports of learning. *Communication Education, 48*, 48–62.

Weidman, J. C., Twale, D. J., & Stein, E. L. (2001). *Socialization of graduate and professional students in higher education: A perilous passage?* San Francisco: Jossey-Bass.

Wrench, J. S., & Booth-Butterfield, M. (2003). Increasing patient satisfaction and compliance: An examination of physician humor orientation, compliance-gaining strategies, and perceived credibility. *Communication Quarterly, 51*, 482–503.

Wrench, J. S., & Punyanunt, N. M. (2001, November). Advisor-advisee communication one: An exploratory study examining interpersonal communication variables. *Paper presented at the National Communication Association's Convention*, Atlanta.

Wrench, J. S., & Punyanunt, N. M. (2004). Advisor-advisee communication: An exploratory study examining interpersonal communication variables in the graduate advisor-advisee relationship. *Communication Quarterly, 52*, 224–236.

Wrench, J. S., & Punyanunt-Carter, N. M. (2005). Advisor-advisee communication two: The influence of verbal aggression and humor assessment on advisee perceptions of advisor credibility and affective learning. *Communication Research Reports, 22*, 303–313.

Wrench, J. S., & Punyanunt-Carter, N. M. (2008). The influence of graduate advisor use of interpersonal humor on graduate students. *NACADA: Mentoring Journal*, 54–72.

Wrench, J. S., & Richmond, V. P. (2000, November). The relationships between teacher humor assessment and motivation, credibility, verbal aggression, affective learning, perceived learning, and learning loss. *Paper presented at the National Communication Association's Convention*, Seattle.

Wright, C. A., & Wright, S. D. (1987). The role of mentors in the career development of young professionals. *Family Relations, 36*, 204–208.

Zhao, C., Golde, C. M., & McCormick, A. C. (2007). More than just a signature: How advisor choice and advisor behavior affect student satisfaction. *Journal of Further and Higher Education, 31*(3), 263–281.

CHAPTER 16

HUMOR IN INTERCULTURAL INTERACTIONS: CHALLENGES AND PITFALLS

Nathan Miczo
Western Illinois University

Lisa A. Miczo
Western Illinois University

Teacher, academic, and humorist Leo Rosten wrote, "Humor is the affectionate communication of insight" (as cited in Eckhardt, 1992). While perspectives differ on humor's use for affiliative purposes, an analysis of humor in intercultural conversations demonstrates the intricacies of how this sharing of insight may succeed or fail. This chapter begins by defining culture as the foundation on which individuals orient to one another. This foundation functions as a shared framework of meanings by which interactants manipulate symbols to convey thoughts, feelings, and insights, including humor. In intercultural interactions the absence of such a shared framework poses challenges to communicators and it is this awareness that potentially influences perceptions of and responses to humor usage. The examination of humor in intercultural interactions has predominantly been studied from a conversation analytic perspective. This approach has generated ample descriptions of functions and forms of humor and for this chapter we have drawn on this body of work for our starting point. However, by definition, conversation analysis favors description over explanation and prediction. It is proffered that a deductive approach to humor in intercultural interactions allows for the application of general principles that may guide us in the understanding of why humor attempts in the intercultural context succeed or fail. The application of communication accommodation theory and expectancy violations theory leads to the conclusion that the nonnative speaker (NNS) should generally refrain from humor attempts. It is also argued that the cultural understanding and linguistic skill level of NNSs can unintentionally provide instances of humor that may function affiliatively while simultaneously marginalizing them. We begin with a decomposition of culture as shared understanding.

CONCEPTUALIZATION OF CULTURE

Culture involves schemas, or mental representations, that are widely shared and transmitted across generations. Spiro (1987) argues that culture consists of a cognitive system containing both descriptive and normative propositions about the world. Chesebro (1998) suggests a similar conception of culture as a social construction constituted through symbols. As a counterpoint to overly cognitivist approaches to culture, Geertz (1973) points out that, as a system of signs, culture is itself a framework of meanings. That is, to be shared and transmitted, culture must be enacted in speech and behavior. Yet, when people speak and act, they are doing things (e.g., performing speech acts, pursuing goals) that may be informed by cultural understandings to a greater or lesser degree. By this logic, culture consists of the most general and/or taken-for-granted meanings that can be attached to human activity. Culture in this sense is a distal variable; socialization and acculturation are the processes by which we learn how to interpret and talk about our thoughts and behaviors in ways that are understandable and acceptable to those around us. As cultural frameworks of meaning collide and intersect with each other, the boundaries separating one culture from another, and even the lines dividing one thing from another and marking it as cultural, become fuzzy. Language and national identity are convenient markers of culture though they can ever only be markers of culture and not culture itself. Thus, much of our review uses the terms "language" and "culture" interchangeably.

In their developmental framework, Miller and Steinberg (1975) distinguish three levels of information that communicators may draw on to try and understand the behavior of a partner. The cultural level consists of knowledge about the norms and values of the partner's culture. The sociological level involves knowledge about the receiver's membership in social groups. Groups and cultures differ from one another in some important respects. Groups typically contain fewer members than cultures. Members from a given culture may belong to several groups, while groups may consist of members from different cultures. Finally, groups often develop their own norms and values and these may differ or be more specific than the values of the broader culture. At the third level of analysis, the psychological level, communicators have unique and individuating information about the partner, which allows for maximal efficiency and effectiveness. Two implications follow from this framework. First, levels of information are not mutually exclusive. Rather, knowledge about another at the psychological level builds on a foundation of sociological and cultural-level information. Second, in making sense of the (interaction) environment, communicators will utilize whatever knowledge they have, or think they have, to orient themselves toward a partner.

Intercultural communication occurs when individuals from different cultures interact with one another. By definition, then, intercultural interaction makes salient the cultural level of knowledge. Ensuing difficulties can be highlighted by contrasting intercultural with intracultural interaction. Perhaps the most effortless interaction occurs between individuals who share the most demographic and communication characteristics (i.e., the same culture, language and dialect, educational background, peer group, and organizational affiliations). Their similarities allow them the ease of a "single discourse system" of shared communication practices and conventions (Norrick, 2007, p. 389). This shared knowledge of language and culture provides a foundation for mutual understanding that often masks assumptions and social constructions that interactants bring to conversation unless and until an awareness of differences in interpretation are activated. In many interactions, the degree of mutual understanding may be "good enough" to allow them to pursue goals without attending to discrepant interpretive frameworks. When, for whatever reason, those differences are activated, communicators then face decisions about how those differences will be negotiated (Bell, 2007a). This is clearly more complicated when individuals from different cultures interact in that they are negotiating meanings on still another level as they attempt to find mutual understanding among a collective pot of different cultural values (e.g., self-construal, high/low-context, power distance) (see Gudykunst & Matsumoto, 1996; Hofstede, 2001). This kind of communication has been referred to as interdiscourse communication (Scollon & Scollon, as cited in Norrick, 2007).

Successful negotiation of meaning is something that must be managed locally, however. Shea (1994) points out that, at the local conversational level, speakers must employ "creative flexibility" (p. 361) as they respond to one another. Cultural differences, then, become one more resource interactants may utilize to shape the course of the interaction. In particular, Shea proposes the dimensions of perspective (i.e., solidarity or congruity of perspectives) and production (i.e., power or symmetry of contribution) to analyze how native speakers (NSs) and NNSs negotiate alignments and contributions to discourse. One of his excerpts, for example, concerns an interaction between a Japanese woman (Kazuko) and two U.S. women, one of whom is a colleague of Kazuko's. Although the interaction seems friendly (i.e., displays congruity of perspectives), it is accomplished by an asymmetry of production in which the U.S. women interrupt Kazuko, finish her sentences, and overall give her little time to respond to their queries. The net result is that Kazuko's contribution is minimized, and therefore, her position as an outsider and NNS is reinforced. That Kazuko can make "meaningful" contributions is illustrated by an example where she and a friend collaborate in discussing the difficulties in being understood by others more generally. Shea's analysis directs our attention to the critical fact that intercultural interaction does not occur in a vacuum. Part of the context is the location of the interaction and that location typically privileges some cultural members' ways of speaking and interacting over others. Awareness of one's position as outsider can make the NNS reticent to speak and that reticence can be seized upon by NSs to discount or overlook the NNS's contributions. This is one reason why comfort and experience with intercultural interaction make a difference. One becomes aware of the adjustments that may need to be made and/or one works to ensure equality of contribution. Add to this the nature of humor, which relies on the cooperation and/or responsiveness of relational partners for its success, and one recognizes still another layer of complexity in intercultural interactions.

CONCEPTUALIZATION OF HUMOR

The human tendency to organize knowledge about the world into schemas and then use these knowledge structures to form expectations and make sense of our surroundings allows for humor insofar as the world does not always conform to our expectations. That is, humorous messages involve incongruities enacted or perceived through the lenses of play frames. As the conceptual meat of humor, incongruities can arise from many sources, both unintentional and intentional. We may perceive someone trip and fall where we expected him/her to walk upright, and we may laugh at the sudden violation of our expectations. Meyer (2000) provides several examples of unintentional humor, such as a sign that reads "The Low Self-Esteem Support Group will meet Thursday at 7:00. Please use the back door" (p. 315). Here, the incongruity turns on our understanding of the "back door" as an entrance used by lower-status persons and thus, contrary to the desires of someone trying to conquer low self-esteem. Intentional uses of humor exploit ambiguity, double meanings, and shifting frames of reference to produce effects (Chiaro, 1992). Jokes often involve a set-up (one meaning or frame of reference) and a punch line (a second meaning or frame that is somehow related to the first in a non-bona fide way). In conversational humor, joking is often interjected in the midst of serious, or bona fide communication and thus its interpretation depends on the frame to which it alludes. Attardo (2001) uses the term jab line to refer to the second part of a humor sequence, which creates the humor without necessarily bringing the conversation to a close.

The fact that conversational joking is often interjected into more serious forms of discourse suggests that interlocutors need ways to mark their humor. They accomplish this marking with the use of play frames, or contextualization cues that send the metamessage "this is play" and, therefore, not to be taken seriously. Play frames can be established in a variety of ways, including the use of joke forms (e.g., "Knock, knock"), joke-prefacing devices (e.g., "did you hear the one about …?"), marked speech, "deadpan" voice or facial expression, smiling and laughter, exaggerated facial expressions, mock aggression, repetition, and use of nicknames (Bell, 2007b; Lytra, 2007). Goffman (1974) points out that an actor who switches to a play frame obliges others to accept the statement as playful. When this is genuinely the case and the humor is intended to amuse recipients, we may refer to the humor as affiliative, serving to bring people together by creating bonds of solidarity in shared amusement. The obligation to accept humorous messages as "mere play," however, also allows communicators to strategically use humor to send messages intended to do more than amuse. Holmes and Marra (2006) provide an example of a workplace meeting where the team leader, Barry, has allowed a team member to take the blame for missing a point near the end of a report (p. 127). During the meeting, an employee, Eric, says: [smiling voice]:

"Barry sees those things too by the way notice that." After the group laughs, Barry responds: "I don't read them through [laughs]. I rely on you guys to read them." Notice that Eric's use of "smile voice" marks his own comment as an attempt at humor, even though it seems clear that a more serious relational message is being conveyed (i.e., the content of his statement is a criticism of his team leader). At one level, Barry's quick-witted comeback continues the joking frame while deflecting the criticism and reasserting his authority. This type of serious humor often overlaps with aggressive or disparagement humor; in these cases, the intention revolves around some kind of reproach, for example the enforcement of norms that have been violated or the denigration of someone based on a personal or group characteristic.

Many commentators have remarked on the social nature of humor. This sociality problematizes the definition provided above for its vacuum-like emphasis on the humorist. In other words, implicit in the definition given above is the sociality of humor. Jab lines have to be relevant to the ongoing flow of discourse and this requires a knowledge of co-actors' frames of reference and ongoing concerns. And the "obligation" to provide the preferred response to playful keying is not always taken up (Bell, 2009). Fine and De Soucey (2005) articulate the social nature of humor in their discussion of "joking cultures." They point out that humorous joking rarely occurs between strangers because strangers lack the background of shared references and experiences to joke about. Joking occurs not only between people who know one another, but who are also part of a shared network with its own idioculture. Such individuals have the right to joke with each other and get away with it precisely because their identities within the group are established. Thus, the norms of the group and the established identities of its members are part of the bona fide, serious frame of reference that is contrasted by the switch to a humorous mode of conversational joking. To be successful, therefore, humor must arise "organically" in response to a triggering event, be appropriate to the status system and moral boundaries of the group, and be linked to the ongoing goals or concerns of at least some group members. Humor becomes one means by which the group regulates its internal relations as well as its relations with the external environment, including contact with other groups. This regulation, however, may take the form of disparagement humor.

The regulatory function of disparagement humor has been noted by many theorists. Ferguson and Ford (2008) use social identity theory (SIT) (Tajfel & Turner, 1986) to examine why individuals use and/or enjoy disparagement humor. SIT proposes that individuals manage competing needs for two forms of identity support. Social identities are aspects of the self-concept derived from membership in social groups; personal identities are unique aspects of the self. We strive to maintain a positive sense of distinctiveness in both cases via social comparison processes. In interpersonal (or intragroup) settings, we often attempt to stand out and differentiate ourselves from other group members to establish a personal identity. In intergroup settings, we are likely to align ourselves with our group, downplaying internal differences and attempting to contrast our group positively with the rival group. According to the theory, when we cannot lay claim to a positive distinction from the rival group, we may instead look for some way to disparage the group, thereby elevating our status at their expense. Ferguson and Ford (2008) apply this logic to humor by proposing that an identity threat gives rise to disparagement humor, which leads to a perception of positive distinctiveness and subsequent amusement. In intercultural interaction, the otherness of "the stranger" can cause uncertainty and anxiety (Gudykunst, 1995). By definition, intercultural communication involves the salience of the cultural level of knowledge, and therefore highlights group identities. Foregrounding group identities can result in ethnocentrism, which has been linked to greater use of disparagement humor (Miczo & Welter, 2006).

Much of the work on humor in intercultural settings comes from sociolinguistic analyses examining conversations between NSs and NNSs. This research provides a rich corpus of material as well as insight into the microdynamics of interaction. However, the price of such rich description is a poverty of theoretical explanation and prediction. The paucity of theory-driven research in the area of humor usage in intercultural encounters suggests the need for a complementary deductive approach. In the next section, we have selectively chosen three approaches to illustrate how they can inform the reading of the conversation analytic literature. Communication accommodation theory was an obvious choice insofar as it was developed to examine how individuals with different speech patterns adjust to one another. Expectancy violations theory also seems especially apt, given its examination of expectancy violations and the definition of humor as incongruity. Finally, Davies' (1998) work on ethnic jokes, while not a theory per se, furnishes an interesting thesis that can be deductively extended into the realm of intercultural interaction.

COMMUNICATION ACCOMMODATION THEORY

Communication accommodation theory (CAT), in its original incarnation as speech accommodation theory, strove to explain communicators' choices to adjust (or not adjust) their individual dialects and words to accommodate a speaking partner (Giles & Powelsland, 1975). Since its inception, however, the theory has been prodigiously researched with its scope expanding to explain a broad range of adaptive behaviors that interactants may make in conversation in an effort to "reduce or magnify communicative differences between people" (Giles, 2008, p. 163). Specifically, CAT focuses on how the perceptions, choices, and behaviors of conversants affect their use of language, paralanguage, and other nonverbal behaviors as they relate to convergence, or accommodation, and divergence, or nonaccommodation, in interactions (Gallois, Giles, Jones, Cargile, & Ota, 1995).

Interlocutors are predicted to accommodate or modify their communication style to converge to their partners for affiliative reasons, as a response to a positively perceived level of power or status, to be more clearly understood, and to influence a partner. Conversely, CAT predicts maintenance or nonaccommodation (i.e., divergence) in communication style in those instances where there is a lack of affiliation, when there is the perception of comparatively low status or power, to emphasize individual or group differences and/or to demonstrate disrespect.

Recently, Giles, Willemyns, Gallois, and Anderson (2007) articulated four key principles of the theory for the purpose of framing communication practices as they apply to CAT. Principle one proffers that interlocutors

> will, up to an optimal level, increasingly accommodate the communicative patterns believed characteristic of their interactants the more they wish to: signal positive face and empathy; elicit the other's [sic] approval, respect, understanding, trust, compliance, and cooperation; develop a closer relationship; defuse a potentially volatile situation; or signal common social identities. (p. 147)

The second principle argues that receivers who attribute positive intent to perceived accommodation will experience increased self-esteem and satisfaction, as well as perceiving the speaker and the speaker's group more favorably. Principle three describes nonaccommodation, forwarding:

> Speakers will (other interactional motives notwithstanding) increasingly nonaccommodate (e.g., diverge from) the communicative patterns believed characteristic of their interactants, the more they wish to signal (or promote) relational dissatisfaction or disaffection with and disrespect for the others' traits, demeanor, actions, or social identities. (Giles et al., 2007, p. 148)

The final principle states that when nonaccommodation is attributed with harmful intent, receivers will react negatively to the speaker and/or perceive the speaker more negatively. The above motivations depicted for individuals' choices to converge or diverge seem especially relevant to humor attempts in intercultural interactions.

Humor is a useful communication tool in affinity-seeking and relational development and maintenance (Bell, 2006; Friedman, Friedman, & Amoo, 2002; Neumann, Hood, & Neumann, 2009). However, the implementation of humor in intercultural interaction poses its own hazards. Successful humor is negotiated between interaction partners. The acceptance of and/or collaboration in a humor attempt is really a privilege of sorts that is granted, supported, and shared by an interaction partner. Much like an audience's willingness to clap (let alone stand and clap) after a performance, participation in another's humor attempt (passive in the instance of laughter only, active when it involves making a contribution) is an honor bestowed on the creator/performer of the humor. And it is this dependence on one's interaction partner(s) that makes sharing humor a risk for anyone, with the risk even more evident in intercultural communication where the "right to joke" (Fine & De Soucey, 2005) may not be recognized.

Although humor is certainly universal, its framing, utilization, and the creation of humor itself differs across cultures (e.g., Cheng, 2003). Norrick (2007) acknowledges that cultural and linguistic differences themselves may be the topic of humor, yet interactants also face a challenge in trying to "convey humor across cultures and linguistic boundaries" (p. 391; see also Bell, 2006). Thus, the "[a]ccommodation [that] is central to interdiscourse communication as a set of procedures for avoiding misunderstanding" (Norrick, 2007, p. 390) is no less an issue than in the instance of humor attempts within intercultural interactions. In particular, the willingness of NSs to accommodate NNSs will be of chief impact on the success of humor attempts. Cheng notes, "Jocularity in conversation is sustained by means of participants engaged in making sufficiently regular, lucid, and playful responses to each other" (p. 290). However, NNSs may be recipients of nonaccommodation, as described by Bell (2006) in her discussion of transcripts of her informant Pum, a native of Thailand pursuing an M.B.A. in the U.S. Pum was sometimes treated as an outsider "through lack of uptake on her attempts at humor, a refusal to acknowledge any of her humor constructed around taboo topics, [and] direct attempts to socialize her into a certain type of humor" (p. 24). Whereas in other instances, when she was treated as an insider, "humor was marked by equal participation, which included playful banter and scaffolding of the participants' jokes" (p. 24). These examples aptly describe both attempts by relational partners to accommodate Pum in her efforts to be humorous or appreciate humor and instances where Pum received nonaccommodation, according to Bell because of her outsider status. While Bell's evaluation of the divergence experienced by Pum is clearly in line with the principle of nonaccommodation proposed by CAT, we do not know from this analysis what specific aspect of Pum or her behavior motivated the nonaccommodation, or for that matter the occurrences of accommodation. Nevertheless, it must be considered that the social identity of NNSs is perhaps one of the more potent factors affecting NSs' willingness to honor NNSs' humor attempts. Chiaro (1992) makes the case that humor produced by NNSs may simply be rejected by reasons of the speaker's outgroup status.

Likewise, issues of power should not be dismissed here. Burgoon and Dunbar (2006) remind us that matters of culture and social motives influence nonverbal displays of power and dominance. Pum was the recipient of nonverbal nonaccommodation behaviors seemingly aimed at stifling or rejecting her attempts to be affiliative with humor. Overaccommodation can also be utilized as a means of influencing power in relational dynamics, with the consequence of marginalizing a relational partner (Bell, 2006, 2007a; Giles, 2008). Pum experienced such responses in her interactions with NSs when they overemphasized what was intended to be humorous in circumstances where she did not experience (or express) amusement and when humor was made overly explicit to ensure she understood it (Bell, 2007a). While overaccommodation of this sort may occur in intracultural conversations where humor attempts are perceived to have failed, we must consider that in intercultural interactions where social identity is a salient cue, purposeful marginalization by overaccommodation may speak to displays of status or power.

EXPECTANCY VIOLATIONS THEORY

Expectancy violations theory (EVT), like CAT, began as a more narrowly focused theory, but has since expanded in its scope (Burgoon, 1978, 1983; Burgoon & Jones, 1976; Burgoon & Hale, 1988). In its initial form, EVT focused on proxemic violations and sought to predict interactants' responses to having their expectations violated. However, its utility has resulted in its application to departures from verbal communication expectations as well as other nonverbal communication behaviors. These expectancies encompass the behaviors individuals anticipate will be enacted in communication contexts, and are based on one's cultural and social knowledge (Burgoon & Walther, 1990). "These expectations, learned and reinforced within one's culture since birth, operate outside conscious awareness and produce habituated, automated behavior patterns" (Burgoon, Stern, & Dillman, 1995, pp. 94–95). Violations of expectations generate arousal, resulting in an attentional shift and need to make sense of the violation. Individuals are predicted to factor in consideration of the violation itself (its valence and magnitude) and the communicator who has committed the breach for his/her reward value in responding to the violation (White, 2008). When the enacted behavior is evaluated more favorably than the expected behavior, the result is a positive violation and subsequent favorable outcomes; on the other hand, if the enacted behavior is evaluated more negatively than what is expected, the result is a negative violation and unfavorable outcomes.

In applying EVT to intercultural communication, and the use of humor in intercultural interactions more explicitly, it becomes clear that the evaluative processing that EVT proposes would indeed be highly relevant. As nonnative interlocutors' appearance, dialect, accent, language competence, and other communication skills get processed as differences (categorizing them as not belonging to the NS's selfsame group or culture), NSs will become more conscious of group characteristic differences. NSs may presume that cultural differences and/or the NNS's lack of experience with the NS's culture will result in the NNS engaging in behavioral norms unfamiliar to the NS, making the NS uncertain as to what can be expected in terms of interaction behaviors. In this respect, definitive expectations on the part of the NS for the NNS would be difficult to ascertain as they would depend on the NS's knowledge of the other's cultural norms and the NS's assessment of his/her experience with and motivation to follow the norms of the NS's culture or his/her own culture. In the absence of this knowledge it is suggested that the NS is likely to default to evaluating the NNS's behavior by the NS's own cultural norms. However, in intercultural interaction, this is likely to activate a cultural level of group identity (aka SIT), thereby motivating the NS to distance him/herself from the NNS. Thus, differences in the way humor is constructed across cultures are likely to be seen as violations. The sum valence of these violations according to EVT would be a function of the NNS's reward value and the magnitude and valence of the violation.

One argument forwarded by researchers is that NSs may not expect or desire NNSs to imitate sociolinguistic norms, considering this a linguistic infringement, even offensive (e.g., Giles, 2008). Bell (2006) cites Eisterhold's (2005) study of NS and NNS teaching assistants (TAs) which found the humor of NNS TAs evaluated negatively, "actually caus[ing] disaffiliation" (p. 6). An example of a participant's negative comment toward an international TA from Eisterhold's study was, "Just get on with the lesson. We don't care about jokes and stuff ... I think he's nervous. Foreigners should just leave humor alone" (as cited in Bell, 2006, pp. 5–6). On one level, such a comment speaks to the TA's humor attempt as inept and reflects a general lack of patience or responsiveness to the instructor, which would appear to be more an issue of communicator reward value (low). However, on another level, the comment may reflect the student's frustration with trying to understand the lesson (perhaps having to work harder to do so because the TA's accent or delivery required the student to work harder to understand the material), and the TA's joke-telling is prolonging (and thereby emphasizing) his/her struggle. Taken in this context, the TA is compounding a negative role violation (i.e., instructors are supposed to be clear and easy to understand) by prolonging the student's discomfiture with what he/she perceives as poor attempts at humor. As a result, while in the instance of an NS TA, a failed attempt at humor might barely register with students (and is unlikely to factor into an overall evaluation of the TA as an instructor), for the NNS the interaction effect of a role violation and failed jokes may directly affect the student's evaluations of actual teaching effectiveness. This demonstrates how NNSs may become constrained as speakers by the identity constructed for them as outgroup members (see also Bell, 2006).

ETHNIC JOKES AND THE "STUPIDITY" OF OUTSIDERS

Although Davies (1998) has not examined intercultural interaction per se, his analysis of ethnic jokes has the potential to shed light on some specific ways that disparagement humor arises in those interactions. Davies (1998) contends that individuals tell "ethnic jokes" about groups that are similar to themselves but somehow not quite the same. The butts of a particular group's ethnic jokes tend to be marginal groups, reflecting a center-periphery division in terms of social status and/or political power. Typically, these jokes involve themes about the "stupidity" of the peripheral group. Rather than reflecting hatred and hostility, ethnic jokes reflect deep-seated anxieties about the self (e.g., Ojha's 2003 analysis of jokes between Asian Indians and Asian Indian Americans). Davies argues that in modern, industrial societies, specialization, and the division of labor have rendered intelligence and expertise critical to competence and effectiveness. Yet, the need to be competent, in particular with respect to technological advances, generates anxiety and doubt about one's ability to succeed. As Davies states, "By telling jokes about the stupidity of a group on the periphery of their society, people can place this despised and feared quality at a distance and gain a brief sense of reassurance that they and the members of their own group are not themselves stupid or irrational" (p. 64). It is important to note that joke-tellers may love, hate, or be indifferent to the group and/or any particular individual member of it who is the butt of the joke. In a study of recipient responses to ethnic jokes, Alberts and Drzewiecka (2008) found that recipients imputed two motives to tellers of ethnic jokes. The first was the nonmalicious or thoughtless use of an ethnic joke as a conversation starter, while the second was the malicious use of the joke as a put-down.

Davies' (1998) thesis presents an interesting perspective on the role of humor in intercultural communication. Technological competence is not the only form of skill that is necessary under the conditions of "high modernity" (Giddens, 1991). As Giddens argues, "In respect of control of the body and discourse, the actor must maintain constant vigilance in order to 'go on' in social life. The maintaining of habits and routines is a crucial bulwark against threatening anxieties, yet by that very token it is a tensionful phenomenon in and of itself" (p. 39). Increasingly, interpersonal competence is a necessary component of participation in the "global village" yet one's social identity, or face, is a fragile construction. A good deal of competence is discourse competence; that is, it is grounded in the taken-for-granted regulative and constitutive rules for discourse that are learned as part of one's socialization into one's culture. In intracultural interaction these competencies are taken for granted; the very taking for granted of these competencies does not guarantee success but it allows us to focus on the sociological and psychological level and often allows for "good enough" communication. One of the hallmarks of intercultural interaction is that we cannot take these rules for granted and thus we may become hypersensitive to them. Where languages differ, the NNS will especially struggle with these rules (cf., Kersten, 2009), and in some sense, that person's lack of knowledge of cultural rules renders him/her "stupid," someone from the periphery, with respect to NSs. Thus, we ought to expect some percentage of instances of humor and laughter in intercultural interaction to revolve around themes of the "stupidity" of the NNS (as a member of a peripheral group).

Cheng (2003) provides two examples of conversational joking between Hong Kong Chinese and native English speakers in Hong Kong that illustrate the thesis. In the first example, two males are talking about the city buses. At one point, it is "revealed that the NSE [native speaker of English] is confused about red-topped and green-topped minicab buses and also where in Hong Kong they are running (lines 1117–1118), which amuses the HKC [Hong Kong Chinese] who produces laughter (line 1121)" (p. 292). In the second example, a male NSE and a female HKC are discussing issues of humor, language, and culture. At one point, the NSE recounts an episode involving "a male Chinese colleague making fun of the NSE's rudimentary Chinese by deliberately substituting 'Chinese' with 'English' in 'oh it's nice to see that you can speak a little English' (line 685), which made the whole office break into fervent laughter" (p. 297). Whereas the first example involved a NS laughing at a NNS's lack of cultural knowledge, the second example involves a NS laughing at a NNS's lack of language mastery. Cheng's analysis of these excerpts focuses on the jocularity of the narratives, and how the speakers collaborate to mutually construct humor. And while there are examples within the longer excerpts that support that argument, it is also clear that some of the humor arises from cultural difference itself or turns on cultural understandings and background knowledge. In the same vein, Zamborlin (2007) provides examples from her experiences as a native Italian speaker living and working in Japan. Despite several years of residency and language lessons, there were still times when her lack of facility with the language produced "dissonances," or verbal behavior that violated the expectations of hearers because it failed to conform to "norms of linguistic etiquette" (p. 22). In virtually all of her examples, the response of her Japanese interlocutors to her inappropriate speech was laughter and/or smiling. Insofar as she was not intending to produce humor, it can be surmised that they were laughing at her lack of competence, or "stupidity." As these excerpts above illustrate, linguistic incompetence can produce a range of perlocutionary effects, from endearment to mockery. Although responses to NNS incompetence depend on the attitudes and evaluations of NSs, the overall effect is to reinforce the NNSs status as an outsider, serving a marginalizing function in intercultural encounters. Nevertheless it should be noted that while the end result may be the marginalization of the NNS, this may very well not have been the NS's intention and could even be something the individual feels bad about. Using the above example of linguistic incompetence, a NS may have some experience with interacting with NNSs and/or may approach such interactions with an understanding and compassionate attitude, yet a surprising linguistic construction could reflexively inspire laughter or amusement. In this instance, the response, though quickly bridled and perhaps even apologized for, has still emphasized the NNS's incompetence. NNSs themselves may be aware of linguistic mistakes and may use humor as a repair strategy (Kersten, 2009). Though the long-term effects of this strategy remain to be examined in the intercultural context, positive relationships between self-disparagement and negative mental health outcomes have been reported (e.g., Frewen, Brinker, Martin, & Dozois, 2008). What the theoretical applications and numerous examples from this review illustrate is that humor as a linguistic form in intercultural interactions is inherently risky and is more likely to produce negative outcomes for the NNS than positive ones.

CONCLUSIONS

This analysis of humor in the context of intercultural communication leads us, unfortunately, to take a cautionary stance regarding its use in mixed-culture encounters. The constraints imposed on NNSs by NSs would appear to put them in a double bind, with NSs experiencing negative violations (and rejecting humor attempts) both when NNSs follow their own or the NSs' cultural norms for humor use, and NSs experiencing positive violations (where NNSs are disparaged) when unintentional humor is aroused by an NNS's cultural or linguistic incompetence. NSs typically enjoy a linguistic power advantage in intercultural conversations and it is this advantage that places the onus on them to create a safe environment for humor by relaxing the various constraints that give rise to this double bind. Chiaro's (2009) study of humorous talk in bilingual married couples highlights the difficulties of this process. For these couples, jocularity was often restricted to the immediate family environment and even humor around in-laws could be problematic; some spouses "learned to live with" humor their partner enjoyed without particularly appreciating it themselves, and hurt feelings could still arise when a spouse used humor with other NSs that the NNS spouse could not understand. Despite these challenges, the couples in her study eventually developed their own forms of humor and language play, though it took time and was something that had to be managed on an ongoing basis. Likewise, it behooves us to persevere in our efforts to understand the dynamics of intercultural interactions as a means of improving their success and the success of the relationships they afford. In this age of increasing globalization, it seems clear that the incidence and pervasiveness of intercultural communication will only increase. Humor, as a universally used linguistic form, will be a relevant component of these exchanges.

References

Alberts, J. K., & Drzewiecka, J. A. (2008). Understanding the communication and relational dynamics of humor. In M. T. Motley (Ed.), *Studies in applied interpersonal communication* (pp. 229–244). Los Angeles: SAGE.

Attardo, S. (2001). *Humorous texts: A semantic and pragmatic analysis.* Berlin: Mouton de Gruyter.

Bell, N. D. (2006). Interactional adjustments in humorous intercultural communication. *Intercultural Pragmatics, 3,* 1–28. doi:10.1515/IP.2006.001

Bell, N. D. (2007a). How native and non-native English speakers adapt to humor in intercultural interaction. *Humor, 20,* 27–48. doi:10.1515/HUMOR.2007.002

Bell, N. D. (2007b). Humor comprehension: Lessons learned from cross-cultural communication. *Humor, 20,* 367–387. doi:10.1515/HUMOR.2007.018

Bell, N. D. (2009). Impolite responses to failed humor. In N. R. Norrick & D. Chiaro (Eds.), *Humor in interaction* (pp. 143–163). Amsterdam: John Benjamins Publishing Company.

Burgoon, J. K. (1978). A communication model of personal space violations: Explication and an initial test. *Human Communication Research, 4,* 129–142.

Burgoon, J. K. (1983). Nonverbal violations of expectations. In J. M. Wiemann & R. P. Harrison (Eds.), *Nonverbal interaction.* (pp. 11–77). Beverly Hills, CA: SAGE.

Burgoon, J. K., & Dunbar, N. E. (2006). Nonverbal expressions of dominance and power in human relationships. In V. Manusov & M. L. Patterson (Eds.), *The Sage handbook of nonverbal communication* (pp. 279–297). Thousand Oaks, CA: SAGE.

Burgoon, J. K., & Hale, J. L. (1988). Nonverbal expectancy violations: Model elaboration and application to immediacy behaviors. *Communication Monographs, 55,* 58–79.

Burgoon, J. K., & Jones, S. B. (1976). Toward a theory of personal space expectations and their violations. *Human Communication Research, 2,* 131–146.

Burgoon, J. K., Stern, L. A., & Dillman, L. (1995). *Interpersonal adaptation: Dyadic interaction patterns.* New York: Cambridge University Press.

Burgoon, J. K., & Walther, J. B. (1990). Nonverbal expectancies and the evaluative consequences of violations. *Human Communication Research, 17,* 232–265.

Cheng, W. (2003). Humor in intercultural conversations. *Semiotica, 146,* 287–306.

Chesebro, J. W. (1998). Distinguishing cultural systems: Change as a variable explaining and predicting cross-cultural communication. In D. V. Tanno & A. González (Eds.), *Communication and identity across cultures* (pp. 177–192). Thousand Oaks, CA: SAGE.

Chiaro, D. (1992). *The language of jokes: Analysing verbal play*. London: Routledge.

Chiaro, D. (2009). Cultural divide or unifying factor? Humorous talk in the interaction of bilingual, cross-cultural couples. In N. R. Norrick & D. Chiaro (Eds.), *Humor in interaction* (pp. 211–231). Amsterdam: John Benjamins Publishing Company.

Davies, C. (1998). *Jokes and their relation to society*. Berlin: Mouton de Gruyter.

Eckhardt, A. R. (1992). *Sitting in the earth and laughing: A handbook of humor*. New Brunswick, NJ: Transaction Pub.

Eisterhold, J. (2005). Rapport-building in the classroom: Barriers to successful NS-NNS communication? *Paper Presented at AILA 2005*, Madison, WI.

Ferguson, M. A., & Ford, T. E. (2008). Disparagement humor: A theoretical and empirical review of psychoanalytic, superiority, and social identity theories. *Humor, 21*, 283–312. doi:10.1515/HUMOR.2008.014

Fine, G. A., & De Soucey, M. (2005). Joking cultures: Humor themes as social regulation in group life. *Humor, 18*, 1–22.

Frewen, P. A., Brinker, J., Martin, R. A., & Dozois, D. J. A. (2008). Humor styles and personality-vulnerability to depression. *Humor, 21*, 179–195. doi:10.1515/HUMOR.2008.009

Friedman, H. H., Friedman, L. W., & Amoo, T. (2002). Using humor in the introductory statistics course. *Journal of Statistics Education, 10(3)* Retrieved from, www.amstat.org/publications/jse/v10n3/friedman.html

Gallois, C., Giles, H., Jones, E., Cargile, A. C., & Ota, H. (1995). Accommodating intercultural encounters. In R. Wiseman (Ed.), *Intercultural communication theory* (pp. 115–169). Thousand Oaks, CA: SAGE.

Geertz, C. (1973). *The interpretation of cultures*. New York: Basic Books.

Giddens, A. (1991). *Modernity and self-identity: Self and society in the late modern age*. Stanford, CA: Stanford University Press.

Giles, H. (2008). Communication accommodation theory. In L. A. Baxter & D. O. Braithwaite (Eds.), *Engaging theories in interpersonal communication: Multiple perspectives* (pp.161–173). Thousand Oaks, CA: SAGE.

Giles, H., & Powelsland, P. F. (1975). *Speech style and social evaluation*. London: Academic Press.

Giles, H., Willemyns, M., Gallois, C., & Anderson, M. C. (2007). Accommodating a new frontier: The context of law enforcement. In K. Fiedler (Ed.), *Social communication* (pp. 129–162). London: Psychology Press.

Goffman, E. (1974). *Frame analysis: An essay on the organization of experience*. Boston: Northeastern University Press.

Gudykunst, W. B. (1995). Anxiety/uncertainty management (AUM) theory: Current status. In R. L. Wiseman (Ed.), *Intercultural communication theory* (pp. 8–58). Thousand Oaks, CA: SAGE.

Gudykunst, W. B., & Matsumoto, Y. (1996). Cross-cultural variability of communication in personal relationships. In W. B. Gudykunst, S. Ting-Toomey, & T. Nishida (Eds.), *Communication in personal relationships across cultures* (pp. 19–56). Thousand Oaks, CA: SAGE.

Hofstede, G. H. (2001). *Culture's consequences: Comparing values, behaviors, institutions, and organizations across nations* (2nd ed.). Thousand Oaks, CA: SAGE.

Holmes, J., & Marra, M. (2006). Humor and leadership style. *Humor, 19*, 119–138. doi:10.1515/HUMOR.2006.006

Kersten, K. (2009). Humor and interlanguage in a bilingual elementary school setting. In N. R. Norrick & D. Chiaro (Eds.), *Humor in interaction* (pp. 187–210). Amsterdam: John Benjamins Publishing Company.

Lytra, V. (2007). Teasing in contact encounters: Frames, participant positions and responses. *Multilingua, 26*, 381–408. doi:10.1515/MULTI.2007.018

Meyer, J. C. (2000). Humor as a double-edged sword: Four functions of humor in communication. *Communication Theory, 10*, 310–331.

Miczo, N., & Welter, R. E. (2006). Aggressive and affiliative humor: Relationships to aspects of intercultural communication. *Journal of Intercultural Communication Research, 35*, 61–77. doi:10.1080/17475740600739305

Miller, G. R., & Steinberg, M. (1975). *Between people: A new analysis of interpersonal communication*. Chicago: Science Research Associates.

Neumann, D. L., Hood, M., & Neumann, M. M. (2009). Statistics? You must be joking: The application and evaluation of humor when teaching statistics. *Journal of Statistics Education, 17(2)*. Retrieved from www.amstat.org/publications/jse/v17n2/neumann.html

Norrick, N. R. (2007). Interdiscourse humor: Contrast, merging, accommodation. *Humor, 20*, 389–413. doi:10.1515/HUMOR.2007.019

Ojha, A. K. (2003). Humor: A distinctive way of speaking that can create cultural identity. *Journal of Intercultural Communication Research, 32*, 161–174.

Shea, D. P. (1994). Perspective and production: Structuring conversational participation across cultural borders. *Pragmatics, 4*, 357–389.

Spiro, M. E. (1987). Culture and human nature: Theoretical papers of Melford E. Spiro. In B. Kilborne & L. L. Langness (Eds.). *Culture and human nature*. Chicago: University of Chicago Press.

Tajfel, H., & Turner, J. C. (1986). The social identity theory of intergroup behavior. In S. Worche & W. G. Austin (Eds.), *Psychology of intergroup relations* (2nd ed., pp. 7–24). Chicago: Nelson-Hall.

White, C. H. (2008). Expectancy violations theory and interaction adaptation theory. In L. A. Baxter & D. O. Braithwaite (Eds.), *Engaging theories in interpersonal communication: Multiple perspectives* (pp. 189–202). Thousand Oaks, CA: SAGE.

Zamborlin, C. (2007). Going beyond pragmatic failures: Dissonance in intercultural communication. *Intercultural Pragmatics, 4*, 21–50. doi:10.1515/IP.2007.002

CHAPTER 17

CROSS-CULTURAL HUMOR: A NEW FRONTIER FOR INTERCULTURAL COMMUNICATION RESEARCH

Yang Lin
The University of Akron

Patricia S. Hill
The University of Akron

Sarah C. Bishop
University of Pittsburgh

Humor is a universal phenomenon, found in most human societies from ancient to modern day (Berger, 1987; Carrell, 2008; Davis, 1996; Martineau, 1972). While we may not all participate in or appreciate the same types of humor, humor exists in almost every aspect of individuals' private and social lives, and permeates a variety of social interactions (Berger, 1987; Ritchie, 2004). Researchers have explored this phenomenon from a range of disciplinary orientations rooted in such fields as philosophy, classics, literature, religious studies, rhetoric, psychology, anthropology, sociology, linguistics, communication, education, popular culture, health, and business. Using diverse research methodologies, scholars across these disciplines have recognized the influence of cultural similarities and differences as it manifests on the use of humor (e.g., Goldstein, 1977; Kuipers, 2008; Ruch, 2008). This chapter examines the relationship between culture and humor by reviewing the literature of cross-cultural humor research from the last two decades, and by exploring the potential for future study of humor from an intercultural communication perspective.

HUMOR AND HUMOR RESEARCH

Individuals employ many forms of humor within numerous contexts for a variety of purposes. The complexity of this phenomenon has not only fascinated ordinary individuals, but also intrigued great thinkers such as Aristotle, Hobbes, Bergson, and Freud. Likewise, many contemporary researchers have been attracted to the study of humor and made their own attempts to describe and explain the ways in which humor is both used and appreciated. While most agree that humor permeates nearly every aspect of human life, researchers differ widely in their approach to this somewhat intangible phenomenon.

Defining Humor

While some argue humor "can hardly be mistaken for anything else" (Berlyne, 1972, p. 44), others consider humor "elusive" (McGhee & Goldstein, 1983, p. v). Not surprisingly, there presently exists no single universally accepted definition of humor, but rather numerous definitions constructed by individuals throughout human history. For example, Carrell (2008) cited Aristotle's description of humor as "an imitation of men worse than the average" (p. 306); Hobbes believed "the passion of laughter is nothing else but sudden glory arising from some sudden conception of some eminency in ourselves, by comparison with the infirmity of others, or with our own formerly" (p. 307); and Bergson considered humor the result of "the trifling faults of our fellow-men that make us laugh" (p. 307). Freud (1905/1960) suggested that humor "is a means of releasing excessive 'psychic energy'" (cited in McGhee, 1983, p. 13).

Keith-Spiegel (1972) once noted that the number of definitions of humor seem to be as many as that of researchers of the phenomenon of humor. For instance, Apte (1985) viewed humor as "primarily the result of cultural perceptions, both individual and collective, of incongruity, exaggeration, distortion, and any unusual combinations of the cultural elements in external events" (p. 16). Davis (2008) suggested, "humor is any sudden episode of joy or elation associated with a new discovery that is self-rated as funny" (p. 547). Similarly, Martin (2007) regarded humor as:

anything that people say or do that is perceived as funny and tends to make others laugh, as well as the mental processes that go into both creating and perceiving such an amusing stimulus, and also the affective response involved in the enjoyment of it. (p. 5)

The many definitions of humor reflect its complexity as a subject of study as well as the development of the study throughout the course of human history.

Multi-Disciplinary Research of Humor

The lack of a universally accepted definition has never deterred researchers from studying humor (Carrell, 2008). In fact, in alignment with these theoretical traditions, scholars of various disciplines continue to conceptualize humor in varying ways, following diverse research traditions in their respective fields to define and study humor. For instance, humor has been considered a unique psychological phenomenon (Berlyne, 1972). Researchers in psychology believe research of the psychology of humor is "the study of humor and people" (Ruch, 2008, p. 17) and have been among those who contribute most to our understanding of humor. They investigate humor and its relation to cognition, motivation, and emotion. In psychology, a "sense of humor" has also been conceptualized as a personality trait to study individual differences of humor behavior (Ruch, 2008).

Anthropologists focus on "humor rooted in social relations and cultural understandings" (Oring, 2008, p. 184) and often discuss the relationship between humor and ethnicity, religion, language, and sexual inequality (Apte, 1985). Anthropologists make efforts to understand the function and meaning of humor in real-life situations where individuals or groups from different cultural backgrounds engage in social exchange, and their understanding of humor is largely based on their documentation, analysis, and interpretation of humor within such exchanges.

Sociologists examine the usage of humor in its relation to "the social, cultural and moral order of a society or a social group" (Kuipers, 2008, p. 361). Specifically, they study the function of humor in maintenance of social order, expressions of social conflict, and constructions of social meanings, relations, and social worlds. In the disciplines of arts, researchers consider humor a central feature of popular arts and entertainments, and text-analyze print popular literature, visual arts (e.g., cartoons), performances, and productions for mass media in attempts to illustrate the role of humor in society (Hempelmann & Samson, 2008; Mintz, 2008).

Communication researchers have made their share of contributions to humor research as well. They believe the use of humor can be viewed fundamentally as a communication phenomenon (Davis, 2008). From this perspective, they "focus on the qualities of a 'sense of humor' and what it brings to bear on the process of effective communication" (p. 545). Some researchers also consider humor a means of communication because humor exists within almost every form of human interaction (Martineau, 1972). A great number of studies analyzed the communication purposes of humor (e.g., Booth-Butterfield & Booth-Butterfield, 1991) and examined the functionality and applicability of humor in various contexts (e.g., Graham, Papa, & Brooks, 1992; Meyer, 2000).

In short, considering the broad array of disciplines that have advanced the study of humor, it is impossible to thoughtfully begin an examination of cross-cultural humor without first examining their contributions. Therefore, to lay the groundwork for future research and provide a foundation for approaching cross-cultural humor research from the perspective of intercultural communication, the authors of this chapter have included a review of existing cross-cultural humor research as found throughout these varying disciplines. The following section details our methodology for the literature review.

SCOPE OF THE REVIEW

Scope of Cross-Cultural Research

Traditionally, a cross-cultural approach to scholarly research of humor involves three types of cultural comparisons (Goldstein, 1977; Miller-Loessi & Parker, 2003). First, a comparison of characteristics is made explicitly between two or more cultures that are geographically distinct or between two or more nations. Second, a comparison of characteristics is made explicitly between two or more ethnic groups within a nation. Third, a comparison is made implicitly through a process in which the characteristics of a non-Western culture (where relatively few studies have been conducted) are discussed on the basis of the known characteristics of Western cultures in general or American culture in particular (where a great number of studies have been conducted). As "cross-cultural research," any article to be selected for this current review needs to be one of these three types.

Scope of Humor Research

Regarding humor research, it is possible for scholars around the world to publish their studies in a wide range of outlets and in many countries. Facing this reality, the authors of this chapter make no attempt to provide an exhaustive account of literature in cross-cultural humor research. Instead, the authors relied on a search through multiple widely used databases for academic purposes, such as *Academic Search Complete*, to identify published articles of cross-cultural humor research. *Academic Search Complete* provides the most comprehensive coverage of scholarly, multidisciplinary, full-text publications, and hosts more than 8,500 full-text periodicals, including more than 7,300 peer-reviewed journals (EBSCO Publishing Website: www.ebscohost.com/academic/academic-search-complete). In addition to full text, *Academic Search Complete* includes indexing and abstracts for more than 12,500 journals and a total of more than 13,200 publications including monographs, reports, conference proceedings, and other forms of publications.

It is evident through our search that the journal, *Humor: International Journal of Humor Research*, is the central outlet where a majority of the articles concerning humor research appear. This journal was first published in 1988 by Mouton de Gruyter in Berlin and New York. The articles published in this journal provide a credible representation of the recent history of humor research.

Selection of the Articles

Based on the above parameters, use of those articles with a cross-cultural approach from *Humor: International Journal of Humor Research* since 1988 served the authors well to accomplish the purpose of this chapter. For the sake of clarity and thoroughness, the authors also included a number of articles of cross-cultural humor research from other journals that were identified through our search in the databases. As a result, there were a total of 24 articles selected for review.

RESEARCH FOCI OF THE CROSS-CULTURAL HUMOR STUDIES

A primary goal of existing cross-cultural research of humor is to probe similarities and/or differences of various cultures with respect to humor (Goldstein, 1977). To accomplish this goal, researchers have narrowed in on some common facets of cross-cultural humor. Specifically, the research foci of the articles reviewed in this chapter can be summarized and grouped into four categories: style and content of humor, function of humor, appreciation of humor, and humor and personality traits. Some of the articles focused only on one such area, and some were concerned with two or more areas.

Style and Content of Humor

A good deal of recent humor research concerns the topic of humor styles and content. Because humor takes multiple forms, permeates countless contexts, and serves various functions, it is necessary to take a close look at what is actually contained in the humor itself. This is particularly relevant to intercultural interaction. Research suggests that understanding an individual's or culture's humor style can provide insight into both psychological aspects of humor as well as personality and character indicators (Chen & Martin, 2007; Kazarian & Martin, 2006). Humor is essentially a social phenomenon, yet it may say a lot about one's sense of self.

Chen and Martin (2007) studied humor styles, coping humor, and mental health among Chinese and Canadian university students. Exploring the potential universality of these constructs, they compared the structure and correlates of the Humor Styles Questionnaire (HSQ; Martin, Puhlik-Doris, Larsen, Gray, & Weir, 2003) and Coping Humor Scale (CHS; Martin & Lefcourt, 1984) in the Chinese context with those of Canadian samples. All instruments were translated into Chinese. The HSQ (Martin et al., 2003) used in this study, as well as several of the others reviewed, is a measure of four humor styles—two potentially beneficial (affiliative and self-enhancing) and two potentially detrimental (self-defeating and aggressive) humor styles. According to Martin et al. (2003), affiliative humor relates to the use of humor to enhance one's relationships with others, self-enhancing humor refers to using relatively benign humor to enhance self, aggressive humor refers to the use of humor to enhance self at the expense of others, and self-defeating humor is the use of humor at the expense of self.

In comparison to the Canadian respondents, Chinese participants reported significantly lower scores on the HSQ subscales and CHS, particularly on aggressive humor. The Canadian sample revealed that males reported more use of aggressive and self-defeating humor than did females. No significant gender differences were found on the four HSQ subscales in the Chinese sample. The authors suggested that "Canadian males who frequently joke and laugh in a friendly way with their friends also tend to engage in aggressive teasing and sarcasm" (p. 229). They suggested that Chinese tend use less aggressive humor to deal with life stress than Canadians. One explanation given was that while most "North American jokes are sexual and aggressive, Chinese jokes focus on social interaction, which, they argued, implies that North Americans endure and use more aggressive humor than do Chinese" (p. 229). No gender difference was found on coping humor in the Canadian samples; however, Chinese males had significantly higher scores on this scale than did females. In both the Chinese and Canadian samples, younger students reported more use of affliative and aggressive humor than did older students. The authors indicated that this difference could have correlated to the fact that the younger participants were full-time students and had more social interactions than do the older participants. The findings of this study support the theoretical structure and usefulness of the HSQ and CHS in the Chinese context and indicate some similarities and some differences in humor styles and coping humor between Chinese and Canadian samples. The authors suggested that these cultural differences of using humor "may be moderated by people's socioeconomic status, political atmosphere, social personality types, etc." (p. 230).

The same year that Chen and Martin (2007) examined international differences in humor styles, other researchers analyzed differences in humor styles between groups living in the same country. In an exploratory study, Romero, Alsua, Hinrichs, and Pearson (2007) investigated humor differences among four regions of the United States: Alaska, Northwest Texas, Minnesota, and Southwest Texas. Only U.S. citizens who were born and raised in the region sampled were included in the data set. Two humor measures were utilized in this study. The first measure was the previously described Humor Styles Questionnaire (Martin et al., 2003). The second measure employed was the Multidimensional Sense of Humor Scale (Thorson & Powell, 1993, as cited in Romero et al. 2007).

Results demonstrated that significant differences exist in humor across regions of the United States, particularly as they relate to affiliative and self-defeating humor, the creation and performance of humor, the use of humor in coping, and attitudes toward humor (Romero et al., 2007). Romero and associates (2007) found that, overall, U.S. men seem to use more humor than women, and U.S. youths use more humor than adults. Moreover, they found a potential correlation between level of education and humor styles. Those participants with master's degrees scored higher on self-enhancing and coping humor, while high school graduates scored highest on attitudes toward humor. Their findings reveal that diversity of ethnic and cultural backgrounds in the U.S. has an impact on how humor is used.

In another nationally oriented, style-focused study, Davies (1997) analyzed Canadian jokes about Newfoundlanders and found that these jokes often utilize materials specific to the life of Canadians and Newfoundlanders, and resemble those ethnic jokes shared in other nations. For example, traditionally, Newfoundlanders' way of life involves fish and fishing, and these Canadian jokes are often about Newfoundlander's stories related to fish and fishing and fish and eating.

With regard to its geographic location to the rest of Canada and its social, economic, and political influence on Canada as a whole, Newfoundland is sometimes considered peripheral and insignificant. These Canadian jokes, in their nature, are similar to a joke told by members of a dominant ethnic group about a marginalized ethnic group in any country. It is well known that many aspects of Canadian society have been influenced by British, French, and Americans. However, Davies' (1997) analysis showed that spoken Canadian jokes (in both English and French) often portray the Newfoundlanders as being dirty and stupid. This content characteristic has been found only in the ethnic stupidity jokes told in the United States, but not in those in Britain and France. This characteristic indicates that, in this respect, Canadians in general are closer to Americans than to Britain and France.

Kazarian and Martin (2006) extended research examining cultural differences and similarities in styles of humor and the role of humor styles in personality, health, and well-being among a sample of Armenians residing in Lebanon. Primarily, they looked at the structure and correlates of an Armenian translation of the Humor Styles Questionnaire (HSQ; Martin et al.; 2003); and, unlike previous studies, drew from a sizable and diverse sample of the general Armenian population living in Lebanon to make this assessment. A second aim of the study was to investigate the relationship of humor styles to appraisals of health psychological aspects of humor in this ethnic group as well as family adjustment. A third aim was to investigate the culture-related personality dimensions of individualism and collectivism.

Results illustrated that as in the original Canadian samples, Armenian-Lebanese participants obtained significantly lower scores on all four humor scales (for affiliative, self-enhancing, aggressive, and self-defeating humor) (Kazarian & Martin, 2006). The authors maintained that these differences suggested that Armenians in Lebanon were less likely to use all four styles of humor as compared to individuals of other cultures. Generally, males and females in this sample obtained significantly lower scores on all four humor scales. Although compared to females, males reported significantly more use of all four styles of humor, particularly aggressive and self-defeating humor. Correlations between each of the four HSQ scales and the ICS horizontal and vertical individualism and collectivism supported expectations. Higher scores on aggressive humor related to higher vertical individualism and lower horizontal and vertical collectivism. However, self-defeating humor was negatively correlated to vertical collectivism and affiliative humor was not correlated to horizontal collectivism. The authors noted that "those that place greater emphasis on the independence of individuals in social groups, and who expect inequality and competition among individuals, appear to use humor in more aggressive ways" (p. 419). Thus, Kazarian and Martin (2006) posited that aggressive humor in this cultural orientation might be one means of competing with others and striving to win at the expense of others. Further analyses indicated that aggressive humor was negatively related to both horizontal collectivism and vertical collectivism, indicating that those who place greater emphasis on the importance of the group rather than the individual are less likely to engage in sarcastic or disparaging forms of humor, which would tend to impair group cohesion.

Humor styles correlated differentially with perceived health, psychological well-being, and family adjustment, although they were unrelated to depression (Kazarian & Martin, 2006). Kazarian and Martin (2006) suggested that "individuals who maintain a humorous out-look during time of stress perceive themselves to be more physically healthy" (p. 416). Perceptions of life satisfaction, high energy, and positive moods were positively associated with a generally humorous outlook on life and a tendency to laugh and joke with others. Overall, the findings revealed a positive relationship between well-being and affiliative and self-enhancing humor; self-defeating humor styles and anxious attachment styles.

Though ethnic differences in humor styles are often highlighted, Nilsen (1997) found that humor of different ethnic groups sometimes shows remarkable similarities. For example, an analysis of Irish literature by Nilsen (1997) suggested that Irish humor and Jewish humor share many characteristics. For example, both Jewish humor and Irish humor includes much wordplay. Additionally, many Jewish and Irish individuals are "bilingual and/or bicultural, relating to both the Gaelic/Celtic and to the English language and culture" (p. 378). Also, Nilsen found both Jewish and Irish people use humorous literature to establish their cultural roots and identity. In addition, Nilsen mentioned that Irish humor is closely tied to Irish people's life and courting, drinking, and fighting are among the most important subjects involved in humor. At pubs, Irish people share humorous stories to develop a bond for close social groups.

Finally, Norrick (2007) offered a framework for understanding what he termed "interdiscourse humor" which characterizes contact between different discourse systems. This includes:

> participants with different first languages (dialects) or different levels of competence in the language(s) used in the interaction, members of different groups and cultures with different assumptions about appropriate speech events and ways of speaking as well as different (cultural) background knowledge across separate discourse systems. (pp. 389–390)

Informed by literature on dialects, language style, code switching, and theoretical frameworks on incongruity and speech accommodation, Norrick (2007) looked at the following inquiries: (1) How do we communicate forms of humor across cultures, languages, and styles? (2) What are the common features of accommodation and translation of humor among groups and languages? (3) How do we exploit differences between cultures and languages to create humor? His analysis showed that linguistic and cultural differences are exploited for humorous purposes in communication between different discourse systems. The findings revealed what the author called various types of "contrast" and "merging" strategies in cross-cultural humor. In contrast strategies, humorists highlight linguistic and cultural differences, stressing misunderstanding between languages. In merging strategies, humorists switch between languages to create humor and ratify group identity. Findings also suggested a range of accommodation practices for conveying humor across language and cultural boundaries, from various strategies for insuring uptake and understanding to outright explanation of background knowledge and translation between languages and cultures. Norrick (2007) posits that findings illustrate how accommodation works, but also "how it may fail, particularly when ways of speaking are not shared" (p. 411). He maintained that interdiscourse humor is worthy of continued investigation and that future research should also interrogate contrast and merging between different languages and varieties of discourse.

Through review of the previous six articles, one may begin to recognize the complexity of culturally compared humor interactions. As discussed in the following section, an individual may employ a certain style of humor not arbitrarily, but to accomplish a social purpose.

Function of Humor

In light of the varying content and style of cross-cultural humor, some researchers have examined the ability of certain types of humor, such as ethnic jokes, to serve certain functions in society. Specifically, several of the following articles suggested that humor is used to serve somewhat divisive functions. For example, there exists a common belief that dominant groups within a society generally use insulting, aggressive, and obscene ethnic jokes—defined by Schutz (1989) as humor directed at ethnic groups—to ridicule members of other cultures. As a result, these divisive jokes may aid in the marginalization of subordinate cultural groups. Other researchers, however, argued for a more optimistic view of the social function of humor.

Schutz (1989) believed most ethnic jokes are devised for intragroup communication (occurring within one group) and intergroup confrontation (between two or more groups). Though many of these jokes contain aggressive content, Schutz believed the jokes "[transform] the aggressiveness benignly and, thereby, [perform] a positive social function" (p. 171). On one hand, when used in a context of intragroup communication, these kinds of jokes can perform a function that helps decrease or defuse tensions between ethnic groups. On the other hand, when used in a context of intergroup communication, they are considered a means of "social assimilation" for individuals to learn the customs and values of different ethnic groups. Furthermore, Schutz (1989) identified another social function of ethnic jokes: They can be used by individuals of any ethnic group as a mechanism of self-defense or self-promotion.

Similarly, Salmons (1988) analyzed the humor stories in the German-American bilingual communities in Southern Indiana. Individuals of these immigrant communities had experienced many changes regarding the language environment in which they lived. On one hand, many of them (particularly those of younger ages) went through local public schools in which English had been the primary language since World War I and were exposed to local media (e.g., newspapers) published in English. On the other hand, they still spoke German in many settings such as family conversations and neighborhood interactions. Those humor stories "… are told in a language [i.e., German] (and a specific dialect) not (or no longer) used as a daily means of communication by the tellers" (p. 162). In terms of their contents, many of those humor stories are based largely on the perception of language and linguistic competence that, sometimes, reflect "self-derogatory linguistic image" (p. 169). Regarding their specific social functions, telling each other jokes in German helped the younger generation of the bilinguals demonstrate their "linguistic competence" and reaffirm their affiliation with a marginalized group and its fading traditions, and, thus, reinforce their ethnic/cultural identity. In this case, it is the jokes that provided an opportunity for those individuals to use the language of their heritage as a means of communication.

In addition to diffusing tension, demonstrating linguistic competence and reaffirming cultural identity, humor may simply function as a channel to relay important social information to members of a community. Some researchers, such as Epskamp (1993), have analyzed this purpose in detail. Epskamp (1993) found that, in several Asian countries, popular theater exists to serve average members of local communities, and classical types of drama often are performed in this kind of theater. In these dramas, it is common to have comic interludes where a clown appears. The clown uses jokes to make a living, and he is "…either in solo performances or as part of any type of theatrical art" (p. 271). The clown is always a male figure who is "… grossly unattractive: a heavy, big-bellied shape and large ears, nose, genitals, or bottom" (p. 276). However, with his jokes, the clown in popular theater performs unique functions for local communities. For example, the clown figures in popular theater in India are usually the most familiar and identifiable character in the different performing arts, and humor delivered by them often refers to everyday life in the communities. Through joking a clown may help connect "… the philosophical, timeless contents of the story and present-day societal developments in general" (p. 278). Because of this particular function of the clowns, the Information Ministry of India planned to use the clowns as its "principal mouthpiece" to spread information about ongoing social events. In Java and Bali of Indonesia, the clowns are considered "a translator of ideas" (p. 279), and, through their performance, they help the members of local communities (particularly in the rural areas) understand the new developments and programs in society. For instance, the clowns helped increase the locals' awareness of the importance of family planning through birth control. Based on his analysis, Epskamp contended that, although the mechanisms of humor may be universal, any function of a particular type of humor is meaningful only in a specific cultural context.

Just as humor functions within a social or interpersonal realm to achieve some social goals, it may also be employed within pedagogical contexts. The classroom is a multilayered context with overarching pedagogical objectives. Several of the articles reviewed recognized that teachers might incorporate humorous examples and exercises to acclimate students to the presence of humor in discourse and to demonstrate its patterns of usage (e.g., Schmitz, 2002; Bell, 2007a).

Although a review of pertinent literature from humor discourse and foreign language teaching reveals many positive effects of humor in the classroom, Schmitz (2002) reported that pedagogical humor is still underused, especially in the foreign language and translation classroom. Schmitz argued that classroom exposure to humor facilitates students' comprehension during real communicative language interactions, and hypothesized that humorous discourse, in the form of anecdotes, jokes or puns, should be introduced from the initial stage of language instruction and continued through the language program. Moreover, he asserted that the humorous material should be selected in a way to gear the linguistic competence of learners. Schmitz (2002) claimed that the organization of humorous discourse could be classified into three basic groups that serve as a pedagogical framework for teaching humor in both language and translation classrooms. First, universal or reality-based humor entails humor obtained mainly from the context and the general functioning of the world. Second, The Cultural Joke is based on cultural knowledge. To understand this type of joke, one must possess sufficient knowledge about the target. Third, particular language features of phonology, morphology or syntax of particular languages governs The Linguistic Joke or word-based humor.

Schmitz (2002) also suggested strategies for the presentation and teaching of humor at three levels for joke comprehension and making classrooms more enjoyable. Learners at the basic level were advised to start with universal jokes. He maintained that "the early introduction of humor makes it necessary to provide students as soon as possible with appropriate vocabulary ... the teacher may introduce 'quips', that is 'smart' answers or retorts to questions or statements" (p. 98). Humor at the intermediate level would then follow for students with a more expansive vocabulary and "more solid control of the syntax of the language" (p. 99). Finally, humor at the advanced level would be characterized by The Linguistic Joke and The Cultural Joke. He argued at this particular level, the use of humor in the form of jokes "can provide the 'incidental vocabulary in the classroom" (p. 102). He also noted that in the advanced level, puns are appropriate and provide linguistic as well as cultural information of the source language. Moreover, he maintained that at the advanced level, in addition to introducing cultural jokes, the instructor should have students critically reflect on the target culture. Schmitz asserted, "the ability to tell a joke, to be a good story teller, on the part of the learner permits the bonding of speaker and listener, of joke teller with joke receiver" (p. 106).

To the claim of the benefits of humorous material to teaching approaches in foreign language and translation classrooms, Schmitz (2002) argued that humor provides teachers and students with the opportunity for a "respite" from the formal class material. Moreover, he asserted that humor facilitates the engagement of creativity, noting, "humor material can add variety to the class, providing a change of pace and can contribute to reducing tension that many learners feel during the learning process" (p. 98).

Deneire (1995) concurred with the complementary relationship of humor and education, and agreed that the use of humor has not been successfully integrated into the teaching approaches, but argued against broad applications of humor at all levels of foreign language teaching in favor of a more specified determination of when and how instructors should integrate humor into the classroom. As previously seen in Schmitz's work, practically, humor can be employed either as a technique to bring new linguistic phenomena and cultural knowledge to the learner or as a means to illustrate and reinforce the linguistic and cultural knowledge already acquired by the learner. Deniere argued against the first approach and discussed the advantages of the latter approach within the framework of intercultural communication.

Deneire (1995) pointed out that, although the classroom is a part of the larger society in which we all live, society in general has different expectations for teachers and students in the classroom regarding their behaviors and activities. Such expectations also exist regarding what types of humor are (in)appropriate in the classroom. He believed that sexual jokes, ethnic jokes, and political jokes should not be considered classroom appropriate. For example, ethnic jokes are normally based on common beliefs about individuals of a particular ethnic group (sometimes a nation) about another group (a nation), and these beliefs most often show the feelings of superiority of one group (nation) over the other. These jokes may thus lead the learner into development of stereotypes and prejudices toward people of different ethnic groups (nations).

Expanding on Schmitz's (2002) and Deneire's (1995) discussion of the linguistic facets and challenges of humor in pedagogical contexts, Bell (2007) looked at the ways in which humor was negotiated in social interactions by three-second language (L2) speakers with native English speakers across a variety of contexts. Bell asserted that the use and understanding of humor in intercultural interaction is an aspect of sociolinguistic competence that might be "especially prone to misinterpretation … while the occurrence of humor is universal, what is considered funny, as well as when, where and whom and under what conditions a person may joke differs cross-culturally" (p. 28). Even advanced second language speakers are generally challenged in the construction and comprehension of verbal humor, because "humor often relies on social inappropriately using, for example, risqué topics or overt jabs at other people" (p. 28). Bell calls on the work of Adelsward and Oberg (1988 as cited in Bell, 2007), who looked at the functions of laughter and joking among non-native speakers. Findings from their study indicated that status came from both the speaker's interactional position and position of negotiation. Following Adelsward and Oberg, Bell's (2007) study interrogated how humor was constructed and interpreted in such a way as to avoid misunderstandings. Noting that humor can often carry an implicit negative message and be potentially dangerous to use, she argued that it poses a particular challenge for L2 (second language) speakers and can negatively impact intercultural interaction.

Bell's (2007) findings revealed that L2 stories illuminate two important aspects. First, awareness of humor "acts as an aid to communication" because both parties in the interaction utilize caution in their choice of "vocabulary, topics and interpretations" (p. 44). Secondly, with its important function of "marking in-group and out-group identities," humor can position L2 speakers as marginal conversational partners. Thus, these findings have clear implications for intercultural communication and merit further attention to comprehend how these differences continue to affect interaction.

In addition to the interpersonal and pedagogical functions previously discussed, the authors of this chapter also found attention given to the ability of humor to function within cross-cultural marketing schemes, with some limitation (Unger, 1996; Alden, Hoyer, & Lee, 1993).

In advertising, a humorous message is the one that is perceived to be funny and entertaining by the audience (Unger, 1996). Employing humor in advertising can help make an advertisement effective in persuading consumers. In his review of literature, Unger (1996) summarized that the past research suggested two models to explain the persuasive power of humor: the cognitive model and the affective model. In the cognitive model, it is believed that humor in an advertisement serves as a distraction that helps lower the mental guard of the audience against persuasion and prevent them from engaging in selective attention in their exposure to the advertisement. Also, such use of humor helps get the audience involved—humor arouses the audience's interest in the beginning, and the audience's interest is satisfied only when the humor is understood. In the affective model, it is believed that warmth and humor can work together to become an effective technique in advertisement. Warmth is "… positive, mild, volatile emotion involving physiological arousal and precipitated by experiencing directly or vicariously a love, family, or friendship relationship" (Aker, 1986, p. 366, as cited in Unger, 1996, p. 149). In advertisement, humor is often used to generate warmth, and warmth often includes humor. For example, the humor of children has become a cross-cultural appeal in international advertising.

Alden, Hoyer and Lee (1993) recognized humor as one of the most popular and effective techniques in recent American advertising, but found little existing evidence to support whether humorous advertisements maintain functionality when transferred to cultures other than the ones in which they were created. Hence, they wished to examine which characteristics of humorous television advertising could be effectively globally standardized, and which "should be adapted to match local expectations" (p. 64). The possibility of effective humor standardization across cultures raises the question of whether the cognitive processes involved in humor consumption are culturally situated, or exist universally.

To address this query, Alden, Hoyer, and Lee (1993) hypothesized that "most television advertising from diverse national markets in which humor is intended exhibits incongruent contrasts" (p. 67). Furthermore, the authors set out to identify different *types* of contrasts or incongruencies present in humorous advertisements in order to address which aspects of humor may function interculturally and the most effective approach(es) to the standardization process. To this end, three types of contrasts, adapted from linguist Victor Raskin (1985), were considered: (a) actual/not actual, (b) expected/unexpected, and (c) possible/impossible. Finally, Alden, Hoyer and Lee (1993) considered whether the intercultural communication concepts of individualism/collectivism and power distance could be employed to predict which kinds of humorous advertisements typically appear in dissimilar cultures. They expected to find that advertisements within collectivist cultures would feature more central characters than advertisements within individualist cultures, and that "relationships between central characters in which humor is intended are more often unequal in high power distance cultures and in low power distance cultures, in which these relationships are more often equal" (p. 68).

In order to test these assertions, Alden, Hoyer, and Lee (1993) chose advertisement samples from two sets of countries "that had similar characteristics within each set but differed between sets on several important dimensions" (p. 68). The first set consisted of advertisements retrieved from The United States and Germany (both considered Western, individualist and low-power distance), and the second set was taken from Korea and Thailand (both considered Asian, rapidly developing, collectivist and high-power distance).

Findings revealed support for the assertion of the presence of all three types of incongruent contrasts in a majority of humorous television ads from all four countries, with little country-to-country variation in type or amount of contrast (Alden, Hoyer, & Lee, 1993). Furthermore, Alden, Hoyer, and Lee (1993) found that a substantial number of ads from Korea and Thailand featured three or more characters, while the majority of ads from Germany and the United States featured only one or two characters, thus supporting their assertion that highly collectivist cultures feature more characters than highly individualist cultures. Finally, 63% of advertisements from Thailand and Korea featured unequal status between central characters, while 71% of advertisements from Germany and the United States featured equal status relationships, confirming the authors' predictions regarding the likelihood that high power-distance cultures would produce more advertisements featuring obvious power distance.

In light of their findings, Alden, Hoyer, and Lee (1993) concluded, "it appears that the basic cognitive structure approach underlying humorous appeals may not be 'culture-bound'" (p. 72). However, because of the significant differences in individualism/collectivism and high/low power distance revealed by the number and relationships of central characters within the humorous advertisements studied, the authors warn against the proposition that all humorous advertisements can be successfully standardized, and suggest instead that aspects of an advertisement's message "may continue to benefit from adaptation to the targeted national culture" (p. 74).

Appreciation of Humor

Research has interrogated which aspects are reflected in individual differences in the perception of humor. Typically, research in the area of psychology pays more attention to the mechanisms or the process of appreciating humor than to the elements of the humor that is appreciated (e.g. Carretero-Dios & Ruch, 2010 and Proyor, Rauch et. al. 2009). The following review gives mention to several articles that examined the variables involved in humor appreciation, as well as some suggestions for future analysis in this area.

In an effort to determine the extent to which humor styles, appreciation, and functions vary across cultures, Nevo, Nevo, and Siew Yin (2001) analyzed the humor responses of Singaporean students in order to compare their findings to similar studies examining humor responses in the United States and Israel. This study utilized both qualitative and quantitative measures, including the Situational Humor Response Questionnaire (SHRQ; Martin & Lefcourt, 1984), the Coping Humor Scale (CHS; Martin and Lefcourt, 1983), the Production and Appreciation Scale of Humor (PASH; Ziv, 1981), and two open ended questions, the first of which asked students to write down "a joke they found particularly funny," and the second of which asked participants to describe a person they "considered to possess an outstanding sense of humor" (p. 148-149).

Contrary to Nevo, Nevo, and Siew Yin's (2001) expectations, gender did not have any significant bearing on appreciation or production of humor overall, though both the Singapore study and a comparable study conducted in Israel reported a similar (but not statistically significant) trend of men scoring higher on production of humor and women on appreciation (Teshimovski-Ardity, 1991, as cited in Nevo, Nevo, & Siew Yin, 2001). Almost 53% of the Singaporean students provided an aggressive joke on the questionnaire, making aggressive jokes the most common of the five types. Though also popular within American reports of joking, aggressive humor was provided relatively more often by Singaporean students than American students. However, Singaporean students provided significantly fewer examples of sexual humor than did American students. Concerning joke targets, the authors found female Singaporean participants provided significantly more jokes featuring a male target. In response to the prompt asking for a description of an individual with an outstanding sense of humor, 76% of the responses described a male.

Nevo, Nevo and Siew Yin (2001) expressed support for belief in the universality of humor behavior as confirmed by their finding that "students in the three countries reported almost the same amounts of laughter, smiles, and joke telling in a variety of situations" (p. 153). They suggested that the significant differences in use of aggressive and sexual humor between Singaporeans and Americans reflect "the different cultural norms regarding public expression of sexual behavior and aggression in the two countries" (p. 153). Finally, they discussed the possibility that their unexpected findings regarding a lack of statistically significant gender differences may be attributed to an unintended sample of "non-traditional" women involved in this study as a result of the competitive admissions processes at the university where the study took place.

Ruch and Forabosco (1996) made an attempt to compare humor appreciation among individuals of Italy and Germany. The theoretical basis for their study is a two-mode model for humor apprehension developed by Ruch. This model consists of a response mode and a stimulus mode. Two components in humor appreciation, funniness and aversiveness, are in the response mode. Incongruity-resolution humor, nonsense humor, and sexual humor are three dimensions in the stimulus mode. Funniness deals with positive responses to humor, such as amusement, while aversivenss represents negative responses to humor, such as embarrassment. This two-mode model defines humor taxonomy. An analysis of an individual's "... response profile in this 2 x 3 ... model (p. 4)" helps assess his/her humor appreciation. Although this humor taxonomy was originally developed in two German-speaking countries (Germany and Austria), studies showed that it can be used in such countries as France (Ruch, Ott, Accoce, & Bariaud, 1991) and Italy (Ruch & Forabosco, 1996). In other words, the three humor categories, incongruity-resolution, nonsense, and sexual, are believed to be similar in the above countries. With this stability, it is possible to investigate the cultural/national differences in humor appreciation that is, which of the three humors is judged to be funnier or more/less aversive by individuals in different cultures/nations. For example, Ruch and Forabosco (1996) found that the Italian participants of their study showed more appreciation of sexual humor and less appreciation of nonsense humor than the German participants.

Several studies mentioned the effect of language comprehension or competence on humor appreciation. In one such study, Deneire (1995) asserted that communication competence is necessary for the foreign language learner to understand humor of a different culture. Two essential elements of communication competence are linguistic competence and cultural competence. Linguistic competence refers to the knowledge of rules for sentence structure and syntax, and cultural competence refers the knowledge of various aspects of culture such as values, beliefs, attitudes, artifacts, and social rules of language usage. Deneire suggested, to understand a joke of the target language/culture is very difficult, and, sometimes, may even be impossible for a beginner of foreign language because it is quite often that a simple joke may consist of a great amount of implicit cultural meanings. He argued that it is the interaction of the above two competences that helps the learner obtain an understanding of humor in an intercultural context. In other words, the foreign language learner needs to develop a certain level of both linguistic competence and cultural competence in the target language before he/she can appreciate any humor in an intercultural context.

Within his previously mentioned study examining the use of humor in advertising, Unger (1996) pointed out a few comprehension-related problems related to the use of humor in a global context. The first problem is humor's potential interference with the audience's comprehension of the content of an advertisement. Unger's review of literature identified the "detrimental effect" of humor found in the U.S. studies. This effect negatively influences the audience's ability to remember the content of ads, and, thus, their reception of the information of ads. However, Unger's review of another study suggested that British advertising executives do not necessarily agree with the above conclusion that humor impairs audience's understanding of and memory of the information in ads. The second problem is that audiences of various cultures may have different tastes in humor. In other words, what is considered funny in one culture may not be so in another culture. For example, Caucasians in America were found to pay more attention to humorous print ads for liquor than African Americans; the former is also more receptive to slapstick humor than the latter. In addition, humor is often language specific. Verbal humor (e.g., puns and "one-liners") is found to be very difficult to use in different cultural contexts. However, visual forms of humor (e.g., animation and visual juxtaposition) have been effectively used across cultures.

In the last and most recent appreciation-focused article reviewed, Carretero-Dios and Rauch (2010) posited that sensation seeking (SS) is able to predict both the structure and content of jokes and cartoons. They noted that, in existing literature, sensation seeking is assigned a unique role, as it was shown to be predictive of humor appreciation of both content and structure. They drew on the conceptualizations of SS by two researchers: (1) Zuckerman (1979, cited in Carretero-Dios & Rauch, 2010) who utilized the Sensation Seeking Scale (SSS) to assess four components of general sensation seeking; and (2) Arnett's (1994, cited in Carretero-Dios & Rauch, 2010) conceptualization using the Sensation Seeking (AISS) scale. Extending sampling not previously considered (German and Spanish), their findings revealed that Experience Seeking and Novelty were predictive of low appreciation of incongruity-resolution humor and high appreciation of nonsense humor. Disinhibition and Intensity were positively correlated with funniness of sexual, black, man-disparagement and woman-disparagement humor, and negatively with their aversiveness. When the structure variance from the content categories was removed, the correlations between appreciation of humor contents and sensation seeking increased. Carretero-Dios and Rauch (2010) maintained that these findings showed that studies of appreciation of content must separate structure and content both theoretically and empirically. Finally, older participants considered incongruity-resolution humor funnier and nonsense humor more aversive than the younger participants.

Carretero-Dios and Rauch's (2010) results support the proposed relationship between sensation seeking and appreciation of humor content and structure. They note that as in prior studies, the scale coefficients tended to be low and partly overshadowed by other effects, and that special indices were employed to verify the proposed relationship. They suggested that future studies need to interrogate the invariance of findings in the relationship between sensation seeking and humor structure and content, as well as the issue of why some of the correlations are low.

Humor and Personality Traits

A small but significant body of work seeks to identify the connection between personality (or cultural) traits and humor, especially in terms of the relationship between fear and participation in humor. For example, Saroglou and Scariot (2002) attempted to (a) cross-validate the Canadian-originated Humor Styles Questionnaire (HSQ; Martin et al. 2003, as cited in Saroglou & Scariot, 2002) within a new (Belgian) culture, (b) explicate the relationship between personality traits and humor styles, and (c) assess whether Belgian students' humor styles may impact their school performance. In order to examine the personality and educational correlates of humor styles, the authors administered the HSQ (Martin et al. 2003, as cited in Saroglou & Scariot, 2002), a description and questionnaire of attachment styles (Bartholomew and Horowitz, 1991, as cited in Saroglou and Scariot, 2002), the Need for Closure Scale (NFCS; Webster and Kruglanski, 1994, as cited in Saroglou and Scariot, 2002), and bipolar rating scales based on the Five-Factor Model of personality (Roskam, de Maere-Guadissart and Vandenplas-Holper, 2000, as cited in Saroglou and Scariot, 2002) to a sample of undergraduate Belgian students. In a second study, the authors administered the HSQ (Martin et al. 2003, as cited in Saroglou & Scariot, 2002), the Big Five Bipolar Scale (Roskam, de Maere-Guadissart and Vandenplas-Holper, 2000, as cited in Saroglou & Scariot, 2002), the Self Esteem Inventory (Coopersmith, 1981, as cited in Saroglou & Scariot, 2002), and the School Motivation Questionnaire (Forner, 1987, as cited in Saroglou & Scariot, 2002) to a sample of Belgian high school students.

The two studies revealed a positive correlation between social and self-enhancing humor styles and three personality traits: Extraversion, Agreeableness, and Openness. Hostile humor was also correlated positively with Extraversion (but negatively with Agreeableness), leading the authors to see Extraversion as a "major personality factor associated with almost all humour constructs" (p. 51). The finding that all styles of humor except for hostile humor were associated negatively with need for closure "seems to correspond to the theoretical assumption that humour, in general, is based on playfulness, transgression of rules and conventions, surprise, and play with meaning" (p. 51). Social and self-enhancing humor styles shared significant personality correlates and were both positively associated with Agreeableness, Openness, and self-esteem. Hostile humor seemed "to be characteristic of an extraverted person with high social self-esteem, but who is neither agreeable nor conscientious." And finally, self-defeating humor seemed "to clearly emerge from a problematic pattern of low self-esteem, insecurity in relationships, low Emotional Stability, and low Conscientiousness" (p. 52). Both hostile and self-defeating humor proved negatively related to school motivation, and the authors concluded the propensity to use certain humor styles had no impact on school performance.

Though Saroglou and Scariot's (2002) two studies worked to solidify previous speculation involving the relationship of personality traits to humor styles, they suggested that future research should address the possibility that these humor/personality links may be used to predict outcomes "related to health, education, and work" (p. 53).

In the first international study of its kind Proyer, et al. (2009) investigated the question of whether or not the fear of being laughed at (gelotophobia) could be studied reliably and in a valid way in cross-cultural research using the GELOPH—a 15-item self-report instrument in different regions of the world. They claimed that findings from German researchers support the existence of good and bad-natured laughter worldwide. In a review of relevant literature, the authors found that laughing at others is a "know phenomenon across all cultures and regions of the world" (p. 255). Their study had three specific aims: (a) to assess whether the GELOPH could provide reliable results cross-culturally (b) to provide evidence for the actual existence of gelotophobia worldwide (c) to rule out linguistic differences in the translation of the GELOPH as an explanation for international variation.

Proyer and his associates (2009) maintained that the analysis identified two dimensions: (a) insecure vs. intense avoidant-restrictive and (b) low vs. high suspicious tendencies towards the laughter of others that the authors believed were significant in the data. Thus, the study reveals that gelotophobia can be assessed reliably by means of a 15-item self-report instrument in cross-cultural research. They noted that a problem in the use of subjective measures is that there is empirical evidence that cultural dimensions (e.g. individualism and collectivism, uncertainty avoidance, etc.) are related to response styles such as acquiescence, and this should be interrogated in future studies.

Miczo and Welter (2006) examined the relationship between the usage of affiliative and aggressive types of humor and intercultural communication apprehension, ethnocentrism, emulation, and intercultural willingness to communicate. They speculated that an individual's usage and preferred type of humor even within seemingly tolerant environments may expose underlying cross-cultural communication insecurities.

To test the validity of their suspicions, Miczo and Welter (2006) utilized a security theory previously developed by Miczo (2006) that proposed, "humor production skills are rooted in underlying feelings of communication security (i.e. less communication anxiety, a greater approach orientation to interactions)" (as cited in Miczo & Welter, 2006, p. 62). In order to clarify the scope of their study, they first defined humor as "verbal and/or nonverbal messages that contain incongruous elements," excluded unintentional humor from the discussion, and posited that although humor is most often associated with play behavior, it may also operate within more serious, goal-oriented contexts as well (p. 62).

Miczo and Welter (2006) found support for their hypotheses that individuals reporting higher levels of ethnocentrism showed greater propensity for aggressive humor, a type of humor associated with "division, hierarchy, and control" (p. 64). Additionally, individuals reporting higher levels of intercultural communication apprehension reportedly use less affiliative humor, associated with "integration, equality, and inclusion" (p. 63). Though the authors expected to find a positive association between intercultural willingness to communicate and affiliative humor, as well as a negative association between intercultural willingness to communicate and aggressive humor, this hypothesis was not supported.

In a similar study, Hackman and Barthel-Hackman (1993) inspected the potential link between sense of humor, communication apprehension, and willingness to communicate within the United States and New Zealand. The authors cite previous research revealing the relationship between high communication apprehension and low willingness to communicate (e.g., Daly & Stafford, 1984, as cited in Hackman & Barthel-Hackman, 1993; Richmond and Roach, 1992, as cited in Hackman & Barthel-Hackman, 1993), and posit, "Humor may be used to diffuse apprehension in the short-term or as part of a long-term therapeutic process" (p. 283). In validation of the decision to compare New Zealand and the United States, Hackman & Barthel-Hackman reference Dutch sociologist Geert Hofstede's (1984, as cited in Hackman & Barthel-Hackman, 1993) continuum of individualism and collectivism, which ranks New Zealand as more individualistic than collectivist, yet still far less individualistic than the U.S. (which, according to Hofstede, hosts the most individualistic culture in the world).

The results of Hackman and Barthel-Hackman's (1993) study revealed that New Zealand students possessed a significantly higher degree of overall communication apprehension (though no significant difference within dyadic and group contexts) and were significantly less willing to communicate than U.S. students in all contexts tested (dyad, group, meeting, public speaking). U.S. students reported a significantly greater liking for humor and "saw themselves as more able to recognize humor in situations than did New Zealand students" (p. 286). Additionally, New Zealand students were less likely to use humor for coping with stress and reported significantly lower sensitivity to and appreciation for humor than the U.S. students. Within the U.S. sample, communication apprehension was negatively correlated with liking of humor, sensitivity to humor, and the ability to use humor as a method for coping with stress, and willingness to communicate was positively correlated with coping humor and sensitivity to humor. Interestingly, "the relationship was reversed for New Zealand students; there was a significant positive correlation between communication apprehension and the three humor variables (liking of humor, sensitivity to humor, and coping humor)" (p 286). The only exception to the otherwise significant distinctions existed within group and dyadic contexts, where New Zealanders' and American students' levels of communication apprehension were not significantly dissimilar.

Hackman and Barthel-Hackman (1993) suggested these findings were indicative of New Zealand's more collectivist culture, as well as of the New Zealand lifestyle, wherein "higher levels of communication apprehension and lower willingness to communicate may be related to the physical isolation and general lack of opportunity to communicate with people outside one's immediate social group" (p. 288). They found the lack of a statistically significant difference between communication apprehension within group and dyadic contexts as further proof of this supposition, noting that "these contexts are more collectivistic contexts than the public speaking or meeting contexts in which one individual usually controls interaction" (p. 288). Reiterating the exploratory nature of their study, Hackman and Barthel-Hackman (1993) concluded, "In an individualistic culture, the ability to recognize and use humor may serve to bolster confidence ... [and] [i]n a collectivistic culture, such abilities may generate inappropriate individual attention, leading to feelings of anxiety" (p. 289).

CROSS-CULTURAL HUMOR AND INTERCULTURAL COMMUNICATION RESEARCH

Our review of these 24 selected articles provides a glimpse of the research foci in cross-cultural humor studies in the last two decades. These research foci, to a certain extent, reflect a collective view of researchers regarding which factors are considered significant in the domain of cross-cultural humor, and they shed some light on our understanding of the multi-disciplinary research traditions in this subject area. There are two additional issues, however, that surfaced during our examination of existing cross-culture humor research. We believe that these issues are especially relevant to the interests of communication researchers and necessitate further discussion.

Issue One: Studying Humor, but not Cross-Cultural Humor

Communication researchers have created an impressive body of research on humor during the last thirty years (Davis, 2008), for example, in the educational context, Banas, Dunbar, Rodriguez, and Liu (2011), Frymier, Wanzer, and Wojtaszczyk (2008), Wanzer, Frymier, and Irwin (2010); in the interpersonal context, Bippus (2003, 2000), Cann, Zapata, and Davis (2009), Graham (1995), Young and Bippus (2001); in the organizational context, Rizzo, Wanzer, and Booth-Butterfield (1999), Martin and Gayle (1999); and in the context of health care, Wanzer, Booth-Butterfiled, and Booth-Butterfield (2005).

Clearly, communication researchers have engaged with the phenomenon of humor for a long time, and considerable work has been done across diverse contexts. We notice, however, though communication researchers are actively contributing to the discourse on humor, our search process identified only one article (i.e., Hackman and Barthel-Hackman, 1993) written by communication researchers in our review of cross cultural humor research. In other words, we find that while communication researchers have studied humor in a variety of contexts (e.g., interpersonal, organizational, educational, and health care), not much attention has been given to the cross-cultural context. In our view, this fact manifests an important issue concerning the general interests of communication researchers.

Issue Two: Studying Cross-Cultural Phenomena, but not Cross-Cultural Humor

The second issue is concerned with the specific interests of intercultural communication researchers. Studies with a focus on cross-cultural issues represent one of the fastest growing areas of communication research. Guided by three research perspectives: interpretive, critical, and social science, researchers have developed many theories of cross-cultural communication (Ting-Toomey, 2010). For example, as Ting-Toomey (2010) illustrated, speech code theory (Philipsen, Coutu, & Covarrubias, 2005) is linked to the interpretive perspective, cultural identity theory (Collier, 2005) and co-cultural theory (Orbe & Speller, 2005) are linked to the critical perspective, and conversational constraints theory (Kim, 2005), conflict face-negotiation theories (Ting-Toomey, 2005), communication accommodation theory (Gallois, Ogay, & Giles, 2005), and integrated communication theory of cross-cultural adaptation (Kim, 2001 & 2005) are linked to the social science perspective. Within these theoretical frameworks, researchers, particularly those of the communication discipline, have explored many aspects of cross-cultural interactions and produced a great number of studies, such as predispositions of verbal communication (e.g., Kim, 1999), effectiveness of intended human interaction (e.g., Chen & Starosta,1996), apology (e.g., Lee & Park, 2011), deception (e.g., Kim, Kam, Sharkey, & Singelis, 2008), conflict (e.g., Cai & Fink, 2002), speech pattern (e.g., Miller, 2002), and cultural identity (e.g., Jackson & Garner, 1998).

Again, through the aforementioned search process, we find, to our surprise, that intercultural communication researchers have contributed tremendously to the understanding of a variety of communication phenomena in cross-cultural contexts, but not much to that of this unique phenomenon, humor. That is, there is no shortage of intercultural communication studies, but there is clearly a void of such studies on humor.

Studying Cross-Cultural Humor from Communication Perspectives

We believe the above two issues both should be and can be resolved by the researchers in the field of intercultural communication. Our recommendation is simple: in light of the foundational understandings already provided by their discipline, intercultural communication researchers should take up the agenda of studying cross-cultural humor. We argue that a general communication perspective in conjunction with the three intercultural communication perspectives—interpretive, critical and social science—can help develop research topics and define research approaches to cross-cultural humor study. The following rationale will provide further justification for this claim.

One of the first contemporary models to describe human communication process consists of four basic elements: sender, message, channel, and receiver. As the knowledge of communication process increases over years, more complex models have been developed to include many other elements such as context, feedback, noise, and effect. These elements themselves and the relationships among them have become focal points of communication research. They are now considered essential elements of a general communication perspective toward the understanding of human interaction. Davis (2008) identified a list of elements that "... recognize the complexity and nuances of understanding ... humor from [this] communicative perspective" (pp. 549-550). These elements are, for example, sender, receiver, culture, environment, surroundings, situational characteristics, channel of communication, message, and context. Specifically, "situational characteristics" refer to the demographics of the senders and receivers and their state of life (e.g., preschool, grad school, etc.). "Message" refers to the form (e.g. verbal or nonverbal), purpose, content, and function of humor. "Context" refers to interpersonal, small group, organizational, and mass media settings. It also includes educational, intercultural, political, and religious settings. Based on the analysis of the earlier models of the communication process, it is clear that his list of elements that constitute a communication perspective to study humor essentially are: a) communicators (sender and audience/receiver) of humor, b) humor message (including the form, purpose, content, and function of humor), c) context where humor occurs, and d) medium through which humor is exchanged.

With this perspective, any act of humor communication consists of at least a few of these basic elements. We suggest that focusing on these elements in research may lead to an understanding of humor as a communication act. For example, our earlier review of cross-cultural research of humor shows that the majority of the articles focus on one or more of these four issues: style and content of humor, function of humor, appreciation of humor, and humor and personality traits. From the general communication perspective described above, those studies examined the issues related to two basic communication elements: communicators (individual appreciation of humor and personality traits), and message of humor (style, content, and function of humor). Aided with the three intercultural communication perspectives (interpretive, critical, and social science), these elements can be further analyzed within the framework of cross-cultural communication research.

We agree with Davis' (2008) assertion that "[h]umor can be used as the most vivid prototype for all manner of communication because of its great depth ... as well as its amazing breadth and persistence across cultures and contexts" (p. 563). Cross-cultural humor should occupy an important place in the field of intercultural communication research.

CONCLUSION

This chapter provides a review of the literature of cross-cultural humor research from the last two decades. The research foci of the past studies have been synthesized into four general categories: style and content of humor, function of humor, appreciation of humor, and humor and personality traits. In the process of the review, our attention was drawn to two emerging issues that pertain to the interests of intercultural communication researchers: (1) while many works have been published concerning humor, cross-cultural humor is seldom addressed; (2) much research has been dedicated to the key role that communication plays in cross-cultural communication in a variety of contexts, but cross-cultural humor is seldom considered from a communication perspective. Clearly, cross-cultural humor is a piece of unchartered territory in the field of intercultural communication research. We argue, a new frontier of intercultural communication research that will engender cross-cultural understanding has appeared on the horizon, awaiting researchers to explore and develop. In our changing world—with growing differences in cultural backgrounds, cultural experiences, ways of thinking, values, beliefs, norms of behaviors and customs, and many obstacles in understanding one another, now is a particularly opportunistic moment for scholarship to explore the issue of cross-cultural humor in more depth and breadth. We believe, guided by the general communication perspective and three intercultural communication perspectives, intercultural communication researchers are ready for these challenges now.

References

Alden, D. L., Hoyer, W. D. & Lee, C. (1993). Identifying global and culture-specific dimensions in humor in advertising: A multinational analysis. *Journal of Marketing, 57*(2), 64-75.

*Apte, M. L. (1985). *Humor and laughter: An anthropological approach*. Ithaca, NY: Cornell University Press.

Banas, J. A., Dunbar, N., Rodriguez, D., & Liu, S. J. (2011). A review of humor in educational settings: Four decades of research. *Communication Education, 60*, 115-144.

Bell, N. D. (2007). How native and non-native English speakers adapt to humor in intercultural interaction. *Humor–International Journal of Humor Research, 20*(1), 27-48.

*Berger, A. A. (1987). Humor: An introduction. *American Behavioral Scientist, 30*(1), 6-15.

*Berlyne, D. E. (1972). Humor and its kin. In J. H. Goldstein and P. E. McGhee (Eds.), *The psychology of humor: Theoretical perspectives and empirical issues*, (pp. 43-60). New York: Academic Press.

Bippus, A. M. (2003). Humor motives, qualities, and reactions in recalled conflict episodes. *Western Journal of Communication, 67*, 413-426.

Bippus, A. M. (2000). Humor usage in comforting episodes: Factors predicting outcomes. *Western Journal of Communication, 64*, 359-384.

*Booth-Butterfield. S. ,& Booth-Butterfield, M. (1991). Individual differences in the communication of humorous messages. *Southern Communication Journal, 56*, 205-218.

Cai, D. A., & Fink, E. L. (2002). Conflict style differences among individualists and collectivists. *Communication Monographs, 69*, 67-87.

Cann, A., Zapata, C. L., & Davis, H. B. (2009). Positive and negative styles of humor in communication: Evidence for the importance of considering both styles. *Communication Quarterly, 57*, 452-468.

*Carrell, A. (2008). Historical views of humor. In V. Raskin (Ed.), *The primer of humor research*, (pp. 303-332). New York: Mouton de Gruyter.

Carretero-Dios, H., & Ruch, W. (2010). Humor appreciation and sensation seeking: Invariance of findings across culture and assessment instrument? *Humor–International Journal of Humor Research. 23*(4), 427–445.

*Chen, G., & Martin, R. (2007). A comparison of humor styles, coping humor, and mental health between Chinese and Canadian university students. *Humor–International Journal of Humor Research, 20*(3), 215–234.

Chen, G. M., & Starosta, W. J. (1996). Intercultural communication competence: A synthesis. In B. R. Burleson (Ed.), *Communication Yearbook 19*, (pp. 353-383). Thousand Oaks, CA: Sage Publications.

Collier, M. J. (2005). Theorizing cultural identifications: Critical updates and continuing evolutions. In W. B. Gudykunst (Ed.), *Theorizing about intercultural communication*, (pp. 235-256). Thousand Oaks, CA: Sage.

*Davies, C. (1997). The Newfoundland joke: A Canadian phenomenon viewed in a comparative international perspective. *Humor–International Journal of Humor Research, 10*, 137-164.

*Davis, C. (1996). *Ethnic humor around the world: A comparative analysis*. Bloomington, IN: Indiana University Press.

*Davis, D. (2008). Communication and humor. In V. Raskin (Ed.), *The primer of humor research*, (pp. 543-569). New York: Mouton de Gruyter.

Deneire, M. (1995). Humor and foreign language teaching. *Humor–International Journal of Humor Research, 8*, 285-298.

Epskamp, K. P. (1993). The political exploitation of the clown figure in traditional and popular theater in Asia. *Humor–International Journal of Humor Research, 6*, 271-284.

Frymier, A. B., Wanzer, M. B., & Wojtaszczyk, A. M. (2008). Assessing students' perceptions of inappropriate and appropriate teach humor. *Communication Education, 57*, 266-288.

Gallois, C., Ogay, T., and Giles, H. (2005). Communication accommodation theory. In W. B.

Gudykunst (Ed.), *Theorizing about intercultural communication*, (pp. 121-148). Thousand Oaks, CA: Sage.

*Goldstein, J. H. (1977). Cross cultural research: Humour here and there. In A. J. Chapman and H. C. Foot (Eds.), *It's a funny thing, humour*, (pp.167-174). NY: Pergamon Press.

Graham, E. E. (1995). The involvement of sense of humor in the development of social relationships. *Communication Reports, 8*, 158-169.

*Graham, E. E., Papa, M. J., & Brooks, G. P. (1992). Functions of humor in conversation: Conceptualization and Measurement. *Western Journal of Communication, 56*, 161-183.

Hackman, M. Z. & Barthel-Hackman, T. A. (1993). Communication apprehension, willingness to communicate, and sense of humor: United States and New Zealand perspectives. *Communication Quarterly, 41*(3), 282-291.

*Hempelmann, C. F., & Samson, A. C. (2008). Cartoons: Drawn jokes? In V. Raskin (Ed.), *The primer of humor research*, (pp. 609-640). New York: Mouton de Gruyter.

Hofstede, G. (1984). Cultural dimensions in management and planning. *Asia Pacific Journal of Management*, 81-98.

Jackson, II, R. L., & Garner, T. (1998). Tracing the evolution of "race," "ethnicity," and "culture" in communication studies. *The Howard Journal of Communications, 9*, 41-55.

*Kazarian, S., & Martin, R. (2006). Humor styles, culture-related personality, well-being, and family adjustment among Armenians in Lebanon. *Humor–International Journal of Humor Research, 19*(4), 405-423.

*Keith-Spiegel, P. (1972). Early conceptions of humor: varieties and issues. In J. H. Goldstein & P. E. McGhee (Eds.), *The psychology of humor: Theoretical perspectives and empirical issues*, (pp. 3-39). New York: Academic Press.

Kim, M. S. (1999). Cross-cultural perspectives on motivations of verbal communication: Review, critique, and a theoretical framework. In M. E. Roloff (Ed.), *Communication Yearbook 22*, (pp.51-89). Thousand Oaks, CA: Sage Publications.

Kim, M. S. (2005). Culture-based conversational constraints theory: Individual- and culture-level analyses. In W. B. Gudykunst (Ed.), *Theorizing about intercultural communication*, (pp. 93-118). Thousand Oaks, CA: Sage.

Kim, M. S., Kam, K. Y., Sharkey, W. F., & Singelis, T. M. (2008). "Deception: Moral transgression or social necessity?": Cultural-relativity of deceptions of deceptive communication. Journal of International and Intercultural Communication, 1, 23-55.

Kim, Y. Y. (2005). Adapting to a new culture: An integrative communication theory. In W. B. Gudykunst (Ed.), Theorizing about intercultural communication, (pp. 375-400). Thousand Oaks, CA: Sage.

Kim, Y. Y. (2001). *Becoming intercultural: An integrative theory of communication and cross-cultural adaptation*. Thousand Oaks, CA: Sage Publications.

*Kuipers, G. (2008). The sociology of humor. In V. Raskin (Ed.), *The primer of humor research*, (pp. 361-398). New York: Mouton de Gruyter.

Lee, H. Y., & Park, H. S. (2011). Why Koreans are more likely to favor "apology", while Americans are more likely to favor "thank you." *Human Communication Research, 37*, 125-146.

Martin, R. A. (2007). *The psychology of humor: An integrative approach*. San Diego, CA: Elsevier Academic Press.

Martine, D. M., & Gayle, B. M. (1999). It isn't a matter of just being funny: Humor production by organizational leaders. *Communication Research Reports, 16*, 72-80.

Martin, R. A., & Lefcourt, H. M. (1984). Situational humor response questionnaire: Quantitative measure of sense of humor. *Journal of Personality and Social Psychology, 47*, 145-155.

*Martin, R. A., Puhlik-Doris, P., Larsen, G., Gray, J., & Weir, K. (2003). Individual differences in uses of humor and their relation to psychological well-being: Development of the Humor Styles Questionnaire. *Journal of Research in Personality, 37*, 48-75.

*Martineau, W. H. (1972). A model of the social functions of humor. In J. H. Goldstein and P. E. McGhee (Eds.), *The psychology of humor: Theoretical perspectives and empirical issues*, (pp. 100-125). New York: Academic Press.

McGhee, P. E. (1983). The role of arousal and hemispheric lateralization in humor. In P. E. McGhee & J. H. Goldstein (Eds.), *Handbook of humor research*, (pp. 13-37). New York: Springer-Verlag.

*McGhee, P. E. & Goldstein, J. H. (1983). Preface. In P. E. McGhee & J. H. Goldstein (Eds.), *Handbook of humor research*, (pp. v-viii). New York: Springer-Verlag.

*Meyer. J. C. (2000). Humor as a double-edged sword: Four functions of humor in communication. *Communication Theory, 10*, 310-331.

Miczo, N. & Welter, R. (2006). Aggressive and affiliative humor: Relationships to aspects of intercultural communication. *Journal of Intercultural Communication Research, 35*(1), 61-77.

Miller, A. N. (2002). An exploration of Kenyan public speaking patterns with implications for the American introductory public speaking course. *Communication Education, 51*, 168-182.

*Miller-Loessi, K., & Parker, J. N. (2003). Cross-cultural social psychology. In J. Delamater (Ed.), *Handbook of social psychology*, (pp. 529–553). New York: Academic/Plenum Publishers.

*Mintz, L. E. (2008). Humor and popular culture. In V. Raskin (Ed.), The primer of humor research, (pp. 280-302). New York: Mouton de Gruyter.

Nevo, O., Nevo, B., & Yin, J. L. S. (2001). Singaporean humor: A cross-cultural cross-gender comparison. *Journal of General Psychology, 128*(2), 143-156.

*Nilsen, D. L. F. (1997). The religion of humor in Irish literature. *Humor–International Journal of Humor Research, 10*, 377-394.

*Norrick, N. R. (2007). Interdiscourse humor: Contrast, merging, accommodation. *Humor–International Journal of Humor Research, 20*(4), 389–413.

Orbe, M. P., and Spellers, R. E. (2005). From the margins to the center: Utilizing co-cultural theory in diverse contexts. In W. B. Gudykunst (Ed.), *Theorizing about intercultural communication*, (pp. 173-192). Thousand Oaks, CA: Sage.

*Oring, E. (2008). Humor in anthropology and folklore. In V. Raskin (Ed.), *The primer of humor research*, (pp. 183-210). New York: Mouton de Gruyter.

Philipsen, G., Coutu, L. M., and Covarrubias, P. (2005). Speech codes theory: Restatement, revisions, and response to criticisms. In W. B. Gudykunst (Ed.), *Theorizing about intercultural communication*, (pp. 55-68). Thousand Oaks, CA: Sage.

{Proyer, R. Ruch, W, et al.} (2009). Breaking ground in cross-cultural research on the fear of being laughed at (gelotophobia): A multi-national study involving 73 countries. *Humor–International Journal of Humor Research, 22* (1-2), 253–279.

*Ritchie, G. (2004). *The linguistic analysis of jokes*. New York: Routledge.

Rizzo, B. J., Wanzer, M. B., & Booth-Butterfield, M. (1999). Individual differences in managers' use of humor: Subordinate perceptions of managers' humor. *Communication Research Reports, 16*, 360-369.

*Romero, E. J., Alsua, C., Hinrichs, K. T., & Pearson, T. R. (2007). Regional humor differences in the United States: Implications for management. *Humor – International Journal of Humor Research, 20*(2), 189–201.

*Ruch, W. (2008). Psychology of humor. In V. Raskin (Ed.), *The primer of humor research*, (pp.17-100). New York: Mouton de Gruyter.

Ruch, W., & Forabosco, G. (1996). A cross-cultural study of humor appreciation: Italy and Germany. *Humor–International Journal of Humor Research, 9*, 1-18.

Ruch, W., Ott, C., Accoce, J., & Bariaud, F. (1991). Cross-national comparison of humor categories France and Germany. *Humor–International Journal of Humor Research, 4*, 391-414.

Schmitz, J. R. (2002). Humor as a pedagogical tool in foreign language and translation courses. *Humor–International Journal of Humor Research, 15*(1), 89–113.*

*Schutz, C. E. (1989). The sociability of ethnic jokes. *Humor–International Journal of Humor Research, 2*, 165-177.

*Salmons, J. (1988). On the social function of some southern Indiana German-American dialect stories. *Humor–International Journal of Humor Research, 1*, 159-175.

Saroglou, V. & Scariot, C. (2002). Humor Styles Questionnaire: Personality and educational correlates in Belgian high school and college students. *European Journal of Personality, 1*(1), 43-54.

Ting-Toomey, S. (2010). Applying dimensional values in understanding intercultural communication. *Communication Monographs, 77*, 169-180.

Ting-Toomey, S. (2005). The matrix of face: An updated face-negotiation theory. In W. B. Gudykunst (Ed.), *Theorizing about intercultural communication*, (pp. 71-92). Thousand Oaks, CA: Sage.

Unger, L. S. (1996). The potential for using humor in global advertising. *Humor–International Journal of Humor Research, 9*, 143-168.

Wanzer, M., Booth-Butterfield, M., & Booth-Butterfield, S. (2005). "If we didn't use humor, we'd cry": Humorous coping communication in health care settings. *Journal of Health Communication, 10*, 105-125.

Wanzer, M. B., Frymier, A. B., & Irwin, J. (2010). An explanation of the relationship between instructor humor and student learning: Instructional humor processing theory. *Communication Education, 59*, 1-18.

Young, S. L., & Bippus, A. M. (2001). Does it make a difference in they hurt you in a funny way? Humorously and non-humorously phrased hurtful messages in personal relationships. *Communication Quarterly, 49*, 35-52.

CHAPTER 18

DISARMINGLY FUNNY: THE PERILS OF TELEVISION'S POLITICAL COMEDY

E. Johanna Hartelius
Northern Illinois University

On September 13, 2008 the season premier of *Saturday Night Live* opened with comediennes Tina Fey and Amy Poehler as Alaska Governor Sarah Palin and New York Senator Hillary Clinton. The sketch aired in the final months of election coverage, and introduced what would become Fey's most noted and celebrated *SNL* character. Greeting the audience of a "press conference," a smiling Fey-Palin recounts how excited she was to learn that she would be sharing the stage with Poehler-Clinton. The latter, visibly unhappy to share the spotlight with anyone, much less her nemesis, wryly remarks that she was told that she would be appearing alone. As the two women comment on their campaign experiences, Fey-Palin suggests that, regardless of politics, "women everywhere can agree that it is time for a woman to make it to the White House!" Poehler-Clinton's reaction is a brawling "Mine!" Pounding her fist on the podium: "It is supposed to be mine. ... I didn't want a woman to be president. I wanted to be president. ... And I don't want to hear you compare your road to the White House to my road to the White House. I scratched and clawed through mud and barbed wire. And you just glided in on a dogsled!" As the sketch ends, Fey-Palin reflects on the prospect of being "one heartbeat away from the presidency." She infers that, "Anyone can be president; all you have to do is want it." In response, Poehler-Clinton cackles, "You know, Sarah, looking back, if I could change one thing, ... I probably should have wanted it more!" She concludes, "I invite the media to grow a pair. And if you can't, I will lend you mine."

The prevalent impression of this sketch, for which the actresses and *Saturday Night Live* earned popular acclaim, is of Palin as a dimwitted dilettante and of Clinton as a power-hungry careerist. The sketch thus encapsulates the dominant representations that circulated in the 2008 election coverage regarding Sarah Palin and Hillary Clinton. Specifically, the brief depiction contains traces of the major criticisms launched against them as female political actors and candidates. It illustrates central themes of the negative construction of women in politics that comedy facilitates. More generally, the sketch is part of a public discourse that relies heavily on humor to disparage "Others" who seek power but often fail.

Theorists and critics from a variety of camps write enthusiastically about the social and political powers of humor and comedy. In his much-cited work on frames, Burke (1984a) proposes that a comic frame of motives allows one to (re)interpret oppressive or brutal circumstances in such a way as to enable action toward change (pp. 170–171). Carlson (1986), Christiansen and Hanson (1996), Powell (1995), and others concur; their analyses of the activism of Gandhi, ACT-UP, and the Association of Southern Women for the Prevention of Lynching support the argument that the positive orientation inherent in the comic frame enables identification and ethical relationships. Other scholars locate comedy's subversive force in Bakhtin's notion of the carnivalesque (Bakhtin, 1984, pp. 235–239, 259). Carnivale suspends the norms of everyday life, granting the public respite from familiar restrictions (Martin & Renegar, 2007, p. 302). It inverts conventional hierarchies and roles (Bakhtin, 1984, p. 197; see also Stallybrass & White, 1986); in carnivalesque playfulness, subjects "enter a liminal realm of freedom and in so doing create a space for critique that would otherwise not be possible in 'normal' society" (Bruner, 2005, p. 140). Still other critics explicate comedy's directly political significance (Brewer & Cao, 2006; Murphy, 1989; Mutz & Nir, 2010; Smith & Voth, 2002). Many survey more generally transgressive symbolism as cultural critique, a mechanism for altering pervasive attitudes and stereotypes (Cooper & Pease, 2002; Gilbert, 1997). Considered among the especially potent forms of such comedic interventions is parody (Hariman, 2008; Shugart, 2001). To wit, with a few exceptions (Carlson, 1988; Ford, Wentzel, & Lorion, 2000; Gring-Pemble & Solomon Watson, 2003), scholarly work on comedy and humor harbors great optimism regarding these rhetorical strategies' inherent possibilities.[1]

I propose that, amid the scholarly excitement regarding the democratizing potential of political humor, it is important not to lose sight of the weaknesses in this widely endorsed position or of comedy's potential dangers. This chapter advances the following claims: (1) Political comedy on television relies on aggressive humor and a stance of superiority; (2) this is pleasurable for the humorist to the extent that deriding another allows one to experience power over him/her; (3) this kind of humor, moreover, is based on sarcasm, a trope that characterizes a cynical orientation; and (4) a cynical orientation is antithetical to political change, since it is fundamentally grounded in apathy rather than engagement. In the remainder of the essay, I draw on Freud's and Hobbes' superiority theories of humor to analyze remarks made by late-night comedians about Sarah Palin and Hillary Clinton. I explicate the prevalent ways in which the two are received with comedic hostility, particularly in their roles as would-be authority figures. I discuss the mechanisms of this political humor, paying particular attention to the difficulty that targets of recurrently derisive humor have responding to comically-packaged criticism.

Two notes for clarification are warranted: First, the category of political humor on television could potentially include (a) variety shows like the *Late Show* with David Letterman, the *Tonight Show* with Jay Leno, and the *Late Night* show with Conan O'Brian, whose monologues and intermittent commentary draw heavily on political news; (b) mock-news (e.g., Stephen Colbert's *The Colbert Report* and Jon Stewart's *The Daily Show*);[2] this category also comprises especially political portions of comedy programs (e.g., *Saturday Night Live*'s recurring news segment "Weekend Update"); or (c) political content in television comedies that otherwise are not obviously about politics (e.g., when *The Simpsons* encourage Krusty the Clown, a recurring character, to run for election to Congress). This essay focuses on the first category with the assumption that its topics are the most explicitly political. The remaining two categories are further removed from genuine or "sincere" news and commentary, as both Stewart and Colbert are heavily invested in parody and satire. Further, the treatments of political topics are, in the first category, comparatively longer than the political fragments in the latter two. It should be noted, however, that similar issues arise in the latter categories regarding comedic television's construction and dissemination of political discourse.

Second, it is difficult as a critic to draw attention to the marginalizing or silencing effect of any rhetorical strategy, including humor. When it is most successful, the silencing of any group eventually leads not to the production of rhetorical artifacts but, indeed, to silence. Those who are targets of the kind of humor designed to intimidate and eliminate sometimes disappear from the public scene altogether, complicating a rhetorical analysis of them and the reason for their disappearance. Therefore, I examine two representatives of such a group in whose case the strategy has been less than effective. Palin and Clinton both have successful political careers. But even though comedic hostility has not "worked" on them—they are certainly not silent—the language of comedy that confronts them reflects the same suppressive techniques that have been effective in other instances. For this reason, careful analysis is warranted.

SUPERIORITY, HOSTILITY, AND SEX

An extensively theorized function of humor is the experience and assertion of superiority. By deriding others' shortcomings and follies, people celebrate that they do not suffer the same misfortune. This tradition of humor analysis is commonly traced to classical philosophers, including Plato,

Aristotle, Cicero, and Quintilian (Billig, 2005, pp. 37–56; Chapman & Foot, 1976, pp. 1–7). In their accounts, humor is conceived generally as a base and sometimes malicious mockery of the ridiculous and pitiable. They attest to the powerful response that rhetors may evoke using humor as a means of persuasion, but caution against its potential backlash. Noted superiority theorist Hobbes claims that humor separates people from certain undesirable characteristics with which they fear being associated. He proposes, "The passion of laughter is nothing else but sudden glory arising from sudden conception of some eminency in ourselves by comparison with the infirmity of others, or with our own formerly" (quoted in Berger, 1993, p. 2; see also Boskin & Dorinson, 1987, p. 98). Denigrating others is a critically comparative form of amusement that relies on an elevated sense of self-worth.

Superiority humor as a model and practice assumes or reflects hostility. It generates a relationship between the humorist, the message, and the target characterized by malice, aggression, derision, or disparagement (Raskin, 1985, p. 36). As Plato (1987) notes in the *Republic*, when indulged "in excess," humor is likely coupled with a violent impulse (§III388e). Freud (1960) likewise describes how tendentious jokes allow the individual to express a level of aggressiveness that she/he would likely disavow in concrete action (pp. 96–103). Similarly Singer (1969) argues that the innocuous character of humor allows a humorist to conceal destructive motives and express attitudes that normal inhibitions would likely prevent even in speech when the speech is sincere (pp. 104, 125).[3] Hostile humor thus supplants physical (or sexual) brutality. At the same time, a positive attitude and response to hostile humor may reflect an underlying disposition of hostility (Dworkin & Efran, 1969, p. 101). Those who prefer hostile humor as a way to engage a certain subject may harbor resentment toward this subject. Further, Freud (1960) argues, aggressive jokes may "turn the hearer, who was indifferent to begin with, into a co-hater or co-despiser" (p. 133). In other words, when comedy aligns hierarchically the comedian and the "butt of the joke," aggression is a dominant communication mode.

Sarah Palin

The 2008 presidential election gained much of its media energy from Governor Sarah Palin. And while she herself generously supplied network reporters with quotable sound bites, much of the attention came from late-night comedy. Long-time hosts David Letterman, Jay Leno, and Conan O'Brien thrived for months on the material that Palin's candidacy provided for their monologues and banter. In nightly ridicule, Palin's physical appearance, alleged ignorance, political inexperience, and misguided ambition were the subject of extensive and detailed commentary. Millions of viewers received noted media personalities' interpretation of a political candidate—in the complex and problematic rhetorical mode of humor.

One of the most prevalent tropes recurring in comedic criticism of Sarah Palin is femininity. Her gender is emphasized repeatedly as a way to characterize and dismiss her as a plausible political agent. David Letterman, vocally critical of Palin, compares her appearance to that of traditional female roles and caricatures:

> Do you like Sarah Palin? I like Sarah Palin. She looks like the dip sample lady at Safeway. She looks like the nurse who weighs you and makes you sit alone in your underwear for 20 minutes. She looks like the Olive Garden hostess who says "I'm

sorry, your table's not ready yet." She looks like the infomercial lady who said she made $60,000 a month flipping condos.[4]

I do, I kind of like that Sarah Palin. You know, she reminds me, she looks like the flight attendant who won't give you a second can of Pepsi. "No, you've had enough. We're landing." Looks like the waitress at the coffee shop who draws a little smiley face on your check. "Have a nice day."

Framed in this way, Palin is connotatively closer to a woman in the service industry than a vice president. Letterman's analogies relegate Palin to menial tasks typically performed by women, and diffuse the situation's inherent tension—that she might rise to a high political office. And while Letterman's audience may be comfortable resentfully accepting the flight attendant's power, the same could not be said for that of the vice president.

This feminizing of Palin serves not only to moderate her role-related power, but to trivialize her. Palin's physical attractiveness and alleged interest in fashion—a predictably feminine interest—is reported as a sign of her preoccupation with lesser things than government. Jay Leno notes,

Sarah Palin made three campaign stops today: Saks, Nieman Marcus and Bloomingdales.

It was disclosed that the Republican Party spent $150,000 on clothes and makeup for Sarah Palin to try and make her look better. Why? She looks fine, doesn't she? We're better off spending that money trying to make McCain look a little bit better. She looks great. Leave her alone. Do something for him.

The implication in the first excerpt is that, to Palin, upscale department stores compare in significance to the speaking commitments of a vice presidential candidate. The amount of money spent on Palin's wardrobe, a frequent topic in late-night comedy, suggests that her priorities are misaligned. In this criticism, Palin indulges in frivolities like shopping while the nation struggles with an economic crisis.

In close rhetorical association with the feminizing of Palin is the emphasis on her sexuality. Confesses David Letterman,

I'm feeling a little sheepish, ladies and gentlemen. I have a confession to make. Last night, I had my first naughty dream about a vice presidential candidate. And it wasn't Joe Biden.

Listen to this. I just got my 2009 Sarah Palin calendar. Yep. Wow. Exciting, sexy photos of Sarah Palin. In one of them, I think it's February, she is holding a soapy sponge, scrubbing a moose.

Jay Leno similarly sexualizes Palin's candidacy:

Hugh Hefner has asked Sarah Palin to pose naked for *Playboy*. Because right now, you know, she's busy posing as a vice-presidential candidate.

They began filming a porno movie this week called "Nalin' Palin." They've hired a woman who looks like Governor Palin to star in this porn movie. It's called "Nalin' Palin," and they expect a lot of guys to go see it. The porn movie nobody wants to see? "Ridin' Biden."

In these representations, Palin is evidently different from other candidates. Unlike the vice presidential candidate on the Democratic ticket, Joe Biden, she is sexually desirable. She is available to Leno's viewers and the electorate as a pornographic object. She is unlike the familiar notion of a political agent to the extent that she is a female, that is, sexual, body. As Raskin (1985) explains, "The political figure is not supposed to be thought of in sexual terms, and any attempt to present him or her as functioning in the capacity of a [potential] sexual partner is viewed as degrading and compromising … and disqualifies the politician from the job" (p. 224). The embodied discrepancy, moreover, between Palin and "the norm" is rhetorically associated with her political pretense. She poses as a candidate as one might pose for Hugh Hefner's camera. The simulated performance is, according to Leno, comparable.

Letterman's confession about naughty dreams and moose scrubbing is illustrative of a theme in his sexualizing comedy. When he discusses Palin's sexual appeal, he connects her femininity—symbolized by her beauty pageant past—to another frequently recurring trope in this critical discourse, namely, Palin's alleged ignorance. He states,

> But now we see some bitterness. We see some back biting, and Sarah Palin is saying that the reason they lost the election is the media. The media is to blame for losing. It's the media. Well, yeah, because it's their fault that she entered beauty contests instead of a library.

Echoing this inferential argument in which beauty contests and libraries represent mutually exclusive skill sets, Conan O'Brien comments on the *Playboy* matter: "Hugh Hefner has asked Sarah Palin to pose nude for *Playboy* magazine. Yeah, and Palin said she'd agree to pose for *Playboy* as long as there's no interview."

Letterman's and O'Brien's remarks taken together illustrate a particular media response to Palin, especially to her eventual decision to decline exclusive interviews. If the relationship between these media sources and Palin was hostile for most of the campaign, the quotations above demonstrate how this hostility grew when Palin condemned reporters for their coverage of her. The sexual humor has a retaliatory tone, mocking Palin's lack of the kind of formal education that might have served her well in, for example, interviews.

More generally, Palin's intelligence and education are fodder for much comedic criticism. For example, addressing the publication of her book *Going Rogue* (2009), Letterman, Leno, and O'Brien all joke about the number of books that Palin may or may not have read, and how her agonizing over every word will be matched by a similar agony among readers. In addition, the ignorance that these comics attribute to Palin is constructed as synonymous with, or indicative of, incompetence as a politician:

Leno: Sarah Palin was also asked if we might have to go to war with Russia, and she said, "Perhaps so." Isn't that like a magic eight ball kind of answer?

Leno: I'm not sure if Sarah Palin knows what to do about the economy either. Do you think she has any experience? She was asked today what to do in a bear market. And she said, "Well, you should shoot it, then skin it."

Letterman: Oh, but Sarah Palin, you know, was at the UN yesterday, and she was a big hit. She's over there meeting all of the world leaders. She's still learning who the world leaders are. Right now, she thinks that Warren Buffett is the head of Margaritaville.

O'Brien: Now, of course, everyone's still talking about Sarah Palin's interview with Katie Couric, where Palin was unable to answer a question about the Supreme Court. Yeah, apparently, Palin thought the Supreme Court was a regular court with extra cheese.

O'Brien: Earlier today, Governor Sarah Palin held a meeting with several leaders from other countries to showcase her foreign policy expertise. That's right, yeah. Experts say the meeting took 90 seconds.

Reflected in these excerpts, and articulated through humor, is the assumption that Sarah Palin is not only stupid, but professionally inept. The implication is that she has no place in, or experience with, government. Her decision making, for lack of a more informed heuristic, is likely to be guided by toy-like randomness. A stark contrast is established in the jokes between the serious business of national politics—represented by a bear market and the Supreme Court—and less serious, more popular things like hunting and pizza. Palin's foreign policy knowledge, O'Brien suggests, can be summarized in less than two minutes. She becomes, in this comedic portrayal, the ridiculous and pitiable person who orders extra cheese but is hopelessly unfit for the United Nations.

As several of the excerpts above indicate, constructing Palin as incompetent and inexperienced allows humorists to identify her as a Washington "outsider." In Palin's own campaign message, this trait was frequently proffered as an asset, positioning her as unspoiled by Capitol Hill corruption. Indeed, it created the "maverick" persona for which the McCain-Palin movement became famous. In late night comedy's characterization, however, outsider status is a liability. Palin is politically "out of the loop," which ultimately undermines her potential capacity to operate powerfully within "the loop."

O'Brien: Officials in Missouri have finally finished counting the presidential ballots, and they say that John McCain won that state. As a result, Sarah Palin now thinks she's the Vice President of Missouri.

Leno: Sarah Palin spoke out this week against the health care reform bill, saying, "Elections have consequences." Well, of course, elections have consequences. That's why right now, instead of being vice president of the United States, she's trying to get a reality show on the Animal Planet.[5]

O'Brien's comment criticizes Palin for not realizing what appears to be obvious to everyone else, specifically everyone involved in politics. Likewise in Leno's quip, she simply "doesn't get it." And as long as politics and government are thoroughly impenetrable for Palin, citizens would be foolish to support her. The humor that locates her outside of government maintains staunchly the moat between politics-as-usual and any unknown or suspect creatures, in this case Sarah Palin.

Hillary Clinton

As a noted member of the United States' political ensemble, and as the first former First Lady to run in a presidential primary, Hillary Clinton is perennially the subject of media commentary. As she lost the Democratic nomination to Barack Obama, and eventually assumed the cabinet office of Secretary of State, Clinton figured prominently in both traditional journalism and late-night comedy. And while the former's praise and blame are relatively transparent as such, the latter's criticism is veiled. To put it another way, the latter's disparagement of Clinton, as a function of humor, denies itself; it is a speech act that contains and relies on disavowing its own potency.

While the comedians discussed above criticize Palin for being inexperienced and unfamiliar with the inner workings of government, they deride Clinton for her lack of perspective. She, too, is accused of failing to recognize that she remains, despite her enduring efforts, a "wannabe." Clinton is, in these comic analyses, always on the outside looking in. The comedians claim,

> O'Brien: Hillary Clinton says she isn't dropping out because there are still six states that haven't had their Democratic primary. That's right. Barack Obama's favored in the states of Oregon, Montana, and South Dakota, and Hillary is favored in the state of denial.[6]

> O'Brien: Hillary Clinton is still campaigning hard. In a speech this weekend that she just gave, Hillary Clinton said that John McCain "couldn't be more out of touch." Yeah, then Hillary said, "Now, if you'll excuse me, I'm about to win the Democratic nomination."

> Leno: It's official. Hillary Clinton is running for president of the United States. She said on her website, "I'm in it to win." That may seem obvious, but for Democrats running for president, they have to keep reminding themselves.

The two excerpts from O'Brien bespeak Clinton's "state of denial," constructing her as a kind of make-believe candidate, competing not against a real opponent, but in an imaginary race. She refuses to realize her own defeat, even as it is a matter of voter records and polling. She becomes in this joke a double loser: she gets neither the primary victory nor the reality of her own downfall. Ironically, Clinton is vulnerable to precisely the charge that she advances regarding John McCain—she is out of touch. This disconnect between Clinton's campaign and the electorate's preference is further emphasized in the suggestion that she must confirm publicly her intention to win. For a typical candidate, this agenda is assumed. But Clinton is, as evidenced by Leno's remark, no typical candidate.

Similar to the representations of Palin, Clinton is comically sexualized. That is, discourses that characterize and critique her are sexual in content and topic. In comparison to Palin, however, the descriptions trace an object not of desire, but of repulsion:

O'Brien: Political experts are now saying that to win the presidency in 2008 a candidate has to get hot at the right time. After hearing this, Bill Clinton said, "Hillary's doomed."

O'Brien: According to a new survey, Hillary Clinton's popularity rating is down to its lowest point in over a year. When Bill Clinton heard this, he said, "If there's one thing Hillary can do, it's bring polls down."

Leno: Although Hillary Clinton set the mark by raising $26 million for her presidential campaign in the first quarter of 2007, Mitt Romney, the Republican, was right behind her with $23 million. That's something Hillary hasn't felt in 20 years: a man breathing down her neck.

Leno: In an interview over the weekend on Japanese television, Bill Clinton said Hillary would make a great president. Lousy intern, but great, great president.

To some degree, these remarks render Clinton a victim of comedy aimed at her husband, specifically his infidelity. She is caught in the crossfire of the by now well-rehearsed and familiar Bill Clinton adultery humor. Nevertheless, these are gibes at Hillary Clinton. She is, according to O'Brien, incapable of hotness, political or sexual, giving polls/poles a downward turn. This, of course, is an allusion to the 1990s incident with White House intern Monica Lewinsky, and thus sexual by implication. And while Clinton may be professionally strong, as in Leno's joke, she is sexually weak.

Jay Leno's interpretation above of campaign fundraising illustrates a recurring theme in comedic criticism of Clinton. Indeed, this theme resonates with a common trope in antifeminist humor writ large. Leno states that in 20 years Clinton has not felt "a man breathing down her neck." This double entendre, characterizing Clinton's sex life as sparse or infrequent, may conceivably refer to Bill Clinton's sexual inactivity with his wife. More plausibly, however, it implicates Hillary Clinton's sexual deficiency. She is constructed, in a rhetorical coupling with her publicity and professionalism, as asexual. Leno confirms this perception, commenting on the White House portraits: I'm surprised they did a portrait of Hillary. I thought maybe an ice sculpture would have been more appropriate.

In concurrence with a commonly circulated impression of feminism, Clinton is described as frigid. The expected inference of the ice sculpture and the Mitt Romney arguments taken together is that Clinton's frostiness can be "cured" by that which she has been 20 years wanting: a sexual encounter.

What renders Clinton inadequate or undesirable in the comedy that sexualizes her as a political agent can often be traced to the portrayal of her as masculine. As with the notion of frigidity, this is a predictably recurring commonplace in antifeminist discourse. O'Brien divests Clinton of a conventional marker of femininity by attacking her personal style and clothing:

Earlier today, President Barack Obama, Vice President Joe Biden and Secretary of State Hillary Clinton all appeared together at a press conference. They were all there. It's cool. There was an awkward moment when both men realized they were wearing the same suit as Hillary.

Clinton is here juxtaposed with male politicians, but the common denominator, rather than influence, skill, or experience, is attire. And while she may dress the part, her attributed masculinity is comically turned against her. As the men in the scenario are subtly feminized—one expects women rather than men to be concerned with the awkwardness of unplanned wardrobe coincidence—Clinton is masculinized and derisibly off-putting.[7]

The comedy characterizing Clinton as masculine repeatedly cites and builds on her supposed powers of emasculation. She undermines structures that guarantee maleness. In one of Letterman's jokes, for example, Clinton joins a cast of female characters in a familiar drama with President Obama as the male lead. Letterman states,

> Barack Obama is putting his team together to take over the administration. So far, he's got his mother-in-law, who is going to be living with him, and they are talking about Hillary for secretary of state. You have your mother-in-law and Hillary Clinton. Sounds like smooth sailing to me.

The focus here is the regrettable position of the man, surrounded by demanding women. Clinton is positioned as the counterpart in government to the mother-in-law in the family. She, in both versions, is opinionated, controlling, and ultimately a threat to the man's dominance in his home. The comic scenario, and the jokes available within, are well-established from television situation comedies. Hilarity ensues as Obama is trapped between a rock and a hard place, neither of which entails positive connotations for Clinton.

In less circumspect comedy, Clinton's political ascendance is narrated as a series of explicit castrations:

> Letterman: It's true, everybody is in the holiday spirit. Last night, Bill Clinton saw the *Nutcracker*. Not the ballet, Hillary.

> O'Brien: Today, Bill Clinton said, if it will help Hillary become secretary of state, he'd be willing to release his financial records. Yeah. Yeah, meanwhile, Hillary said, if it will help her get the job, she'll release Bill's testicles. They've been in the jar so long.

Calling Clinton a "nutcracker" *in jest* becomes *in effect* a public revelation not primarily of Bill Clinton's lack, but of Hillary Clinton's violence. The jokes are about, and on, her. Continued references in late-night comedy to Bill Clinton's sexual appetite, flirtatious persona, etc., preclude the notion that the symbols of his prowess are anywhere but in their rightful place. However, the humorous suggestion that Hillary Clinton's rise to power threatens the "nuts" of the males around her both reflects and evokes hostility.

Although not always associated with castration, a persistent criticism of Clinton is her aggressiveness. She is made fun of for being "angry," a conventionally undesirable trait for a woman. As Anderson (1999) argues, she is a "bitch." Letterman asks,

Did you hear what the Republicans have said about Hillary Clinton? They say she's too angry to be president. Hillary Clinton, Senator Hillary Clinton, too angry to be president. When she heard this, Hillary said, "Oh yeah? I'll rip your throats out, you bastards."

He continues,

How about that Hillary? She's all upset because they have been using her recorded message of her criticizing Barack Obama. The McCain campaign got a hold of this audio where Hillary is saying unflattering things about Barack Obama, and they're using them now. They call it one of those robocalls. Do you ever get some of those? Hillary is furious, because she wanted to make those calls herself.

In the first excerpt, following the recounting of Republicans' characterization of Clinton as "too angry," the punch line displaces any number of directions in which the "conversation" might go. What evidence suggests that Clinton is "angry," and what defines such anger? What would a genuine and realistic response to Republicans' argument be? Instead, Letterman's insertion of an imagined rebuttal from Clinton confirms the accusation. And therein comedy is achieved. In this rhetorical move, importantly, the explicated anger becomes a reality.

In the second joke, Clinton's anger or resentment is a function of her reluctance to admit defeat. Her aggressiveness is attributed to a(n overly) competitive nature. She is, in other words, ambitious. Humor related to Clinton's professional ambition is as persistent as, and often linked to, humor about her anger and masculinity:

Letterman: And did you hear what happened down in Washington, D.C. earlier today? Guards had to wrestle and apprehend an intruder who was trying to jump over the White House fence. Nice try, Hillary.

O'Brien: This is one of those sweet stories, a woman in Illinois has discovered that her Jeep Cherokee used to be owned by Barack Obama. Yeah. You can tell the Jeep is Obama's because Hillary Clinton keeps trying to get in the driver's seat.

Leno: Hillary Clinton said on Fox News there's no chance of her running for president again—this year.

Leno: We love Joe Biden. But he put his foot in his mouth the other day, again. When out on the campaign trail, he told a crowd of people that "Hillary Clinton might have been a better pick for vice president." To which Hillary said, "It's not too late!"

Letterman's comment implies that Clinton's desire for power cannot be fenced in, or out, as it were. O'Brien further suggests that, even when the power is not hers, Clinton attempts to usurp it. These impressions are developed further in Leno's jokes, describing Clinton's ambition as so intense that she cannot recognize the limits of her own popularity and potential. This, once again, resonates with the discussion above of Clinton's delusions.

At least two theories of comedy may account for the humor that late-night hosts generate from female ambition. It should be noted that, while less often than Clinton, Palin, too, is derided for the intensity of her political drive. The comic effect may be attributed to "perspective by incongruity" (Burke, 1984b, p. 90). By discursively situating women with symbols and in contexts that, for them, are nontraditional or unfamiliar, comedians surprise their audiences. Amusement arises from the experience of the unexpected. Women are not expected to run in a presidential campaign; beauty pageant contestants are not expected to attend a meeting at the United Nations; and vice-presidential candidates are not expected to announce that they can "see Russia from [their] house." Incongruity allows comedians to cope with the unfamiliar by interpreting it as funny.

On the other hand, the structure of this comedy may be more like imposed buffoonery. The actions of Palin and Clinton are depicted and perceived as comic by individuals who, for whatever reason, can either attain what Palin and Clinton seek with greater success, or chase it with greater subtlety. The professionally ambitious woman becomes a comic caricature—an exaggeration, an overzealous Trimalchio—when attention is drawn to the difference between her obsequious behavior and the less obvious scheming and consorting of male counterparts. At stake here is not whether male or female politicians are more ambitious or more subtle about it. Rather, the issue is the extent to which the latter are in effect blocked from pursuing this ambition with any subtlety by those whose interests are served by directing attention toward any such pursuits. The spotlight itself, in other words, makes overt careerism overt. This is the role that powerful comedians play as the wielders of critical spotlights.

IMPLICATIONS: REBELLION AND COMEDIC EVASION

Aggressive humor, the comedic and simultaneously hostile expression of superiority, contains the rhetorical potential to either control or rebel (Boskin & Dorinson, 1987, p. 99; Lynch, 2002, p. 426). The preceding section offers multiple examples of the ways in which humor constrains women's role in national politics. Emphasizing rebellion, Freud (1960) explains that comedy makes "criticism possible against persons in exalted positions who claim to exercise authority" (p. 105). This resonates powerfully with the scholarship reviewed in the early section of this essay, celebrating the subversive and/or democratizing potentials of humor. The hope, for instance, of Bakhtin's carnivalesque irreverence is that this mode of comedy enables critique of those in political, cultural, and economic power. The suspension of seriousness facilitates the articulation of impermissible arguments and perspectives.

Importantly, this comedic rebellion against authority can be functionally adapted to critique would-be authority figures, that is, those who either pursue positions of power or perform their distinctive features. In her analysis of Comedy Central's *The Man Show*, Johnson (2007) explains that the program's confrontational style, what Johnson characterizes as protest rhetoric, posits viewers as agitators against *imagined* female dominance. By incorporating the fantasy that women dominate politics or public culture into the show's narrative framework, the hosts can permissibly engage in, and allow viewers to participate in, a simulated rebellion. An analogous reading might be instructively applied to late-night comedians' interpretation and critique of Palin and Clinton. The latters' petition for positions of power, combined with their public performances of the power that they already posses, make them targets for revolt. This insurgence from Letterman,

Leno, O'Brien, and their cohort and audience is at once preemption and pretense; the comedy is a staged protest.

The critique implicit in superiority comedy generates pleasure for the humorist and the audience or confederates. As Aristotle (1991) explains, connecting laughter and the criticism of "one's neighbors" (§1371b27-29), the power we experience when appearing to be wise or appearing as a leader is pleasant. Freud's (1960) model of the comedic release of aggression confirms the significance of pleasure (pp. 195–199). He posits, "By making our enemy small, inferior, despicable or comic, we achieve in a roundabout way the *enjoyment* of overcoming him—to which the third person, who has made no efforts, bears witness by his laughter" (p. 103, emphasis added). Thus, while making fun of someone to his face may be fun or feel good, it is less fun, and considerably less rhetorical than making fun of someone before the network television audience. The former entails a private and pleasurable expressive exercise; the latter constitutes a powerful assertion of superiority, accessible to a third party.

The potency of comedy is partly a function of its nimble evasion of accountability. This shapes the abovementioned dynamic between the humorist, audience, and victim, and speaks to the rhetorical sophistication of humor. Put simply, when the victim of a comically framed accusation attempts to defend herself, the comedian may simply deflect this response with the suggestion that the victim failed to receive the remark in the spirit in which it was intended (Gilbert, 1997, pp. 97, 317). The victim either did not "get the joke" or did not understand that the comedian was "just joking." The familiar trope that women in general and feminists in particular lack a sense of humor creates a rhetorical context in which women have the choice of two evils: They can either accept being the target of sexist jokes or respond. If they choose the former, they resign themselves to various forms of verbal accosting. If they opt for the latter, they step into the strike zone for a different kind of joke, namely, that they have no sense of humor.

This capacity for deflection is inherent in one of late night comedy's staples, sarcasm. Sarcasm, as Kaufer and Neuwirth (1982) explain, is the "use of irony for the particular purpose of causing hurt" (p. 28; see also Kaufer, 1977). It elevates the comedian's opinion over his opponent's at the latter's expense. As a rhetorical practice, sarcasm is germane to Cynicism, an orientation in which social injury is relatively insignificant. The original Cynics exiled themselves from community and convention, rejecting norms as false and counterproductive.[8] From a Cynical point of view, therefore, ridiculing someone publically, or tarnishing their reputation is immaterial, since the very notion of social status is an illusion. What remains for Cynics is to savor immediate gratification and pleasure, including the pleasure that one might get from derisive comedy.

The significance in this context of sarcasm and, by extension, of Cynicism is that they are means and forms of detachment, not engagement. They are integral to a worldview in which the organizing principle—itself an oxymoron in the chaos advocated by true Cynics—is apathy. The Cynics encouraged followers to rid themselves entirely of desire; this, they insisted, would interrupt the hunt for progress that civilization mandates. Diogenes, one of history's most noted Cynics, proudly calls himself a "prophet of indifference" (Malherbe, 1977, p. 115). Desire and motivation, however, are prerequisites for the pursuit of social or political change (Cutler, 2005, p. 20). Thus, despite the scholarly and popular enthusiasm regarding late night hosts' witty political analyses, the civic potential of such comedy is limited. It reduces criticism of political actors from inquiry and advocacy to a form of aggressive mockery.

Televised political comedy is hostile, effective, and impervious. It asserts superiority at its victims' expense, generating pleasure for both comedians and audiences. It denigrates with a wink—"Just kidding!" When a response is proffered, comically inflected criticism disavows its own impact. This is at once the promise and danger of comedy. That a progressive, subversive rhetorical act, when executed within a comedic performance, is safe from retribution by implication means that comedic disparagement against non-authorities is likewise inaccessible for interrogation. And while Sarah Palin and Hillary Clinton have achieved considerable professional success, the resentment with which they have been met—explicitly by political opponents and implicitly by the funny guys of late night entertainment—is instructive. Analyzing it reveals comedy as a double-edged sword. Thus if most of us agree that it is a good thing when the disempowered can critique authority and be safe from penalty or retaliation, we could perhaps also agree that it is a dangerous thing when the disempowered can be critiqued without any means holding their critics accountable.

Notes

1. Ford, Wentzel, and Lorion (2000) as well as Gring-Pemble and Solomon Watson (2003) argue that humorous discourses sometimes invite audiences to accept as permissible the point of view that the humorist seeks to critique. Carlson (1988) examines the American women's movement's use of comedy as a rhetorical resource. Her discussion of its limitations, in contrast to my approach in this chapter, focuses on the women's use of the comic frame rather than the public's use of comedy to reject women's advocacy. My perspective is similar to that of Olbrys (2006), who notes that "while humor analysts, social critics, and an impressive number of theorists of the modern and postmodern have long celebrated laughter's emancipatory and subversive potential, significantly less attention has been paid to rituals that unsympathetically yoke liberating laughter and invite audiences to delight in that disciplinary act" (p. 241). Olbrys' analysis of comedian Chris Farley's carnivalesque performance explicates the liabilities of humor and the process by which an object is transformed into a victim of derision.

2. Remarkably, an entire body of research is emerging devoted solely to Stewart and Colbert. See for example Baym, 2005, 2007; Colletta, 2009; Fox, Koloen, and Sahin, 2007; Holbert, Lambe, Dudo, and Carlton, 2007; Morris, 2009; Warner, 2007.

3. It must be noted, however, that, while Singer's insights regarding inhibitions and humor are compelling, his research methodology and design are seriously politically problematic.

4. Unless otherwise noted, excerpts were retrieved from Joke Central, accessed October 23, 2010, www.mustsharejokes.com.

5. About.com, accessed October 16, 2010, politicalhumor.about.com/od/sarahpalin/a/palin-jokes.htm.

6. About.com, accessed October 16, 2010, politicalhumor.about.com/od/hillaryclinton/a/hillaryclinton.htm.

7. The simultaneous sexualization and masculinization of Clinton speak to the political and gendered functions of humor explicated by Palczewski (2005). Palczewski argues that, responding to the suffragettes' activism, comically framed criticisms of women who pursued public issues assumed two forms: women were either sexualized as indecorous, promiscuous, and "easy" or masculinized in clothing and behavior such as overalls and smoking. In Clinton's case, however, the pursuit of a public life and career receives comic reprimand on both terms. She is represented in sexual contexts, but ultimately rendered sexually unviable as a result of being "too masculine" (e.g., by being angry, ambitious, etc.).

8. The objective here is not to begin a discussion about Cynics or cynicism writ large. For a treatment of historical environments that are especially ripe for classical Cynicism drawing parallels to postmodernity, see Cutler (2005) and Sloterdijk (1987). Other scholars explore more specifically the nexus of cynicism, postmodernism, and contemporary politics (Bewes, 1997). Still others focus on cynical tendencies in American culture (Kanter & Mirvis, 1989).

References

Anderson, K. V. (1999). 'Rhymes with rich': 'Bitch' as a tool of Containment in contemporary American politics. *Rhetorical and Public Affairs, 2*, 599–623.

Aristotle. (1991). *On Rhetoric.* (G. A. Kennedy, Trans.). New York: Oxford University Press.

Bakhtin, M. (1984). *Rabelais and his world.* (H. Iswolsky, Trans.). Bloomington: Indiana University Press.

Baym, G. (2005). *The Daily Show:* Discursive integration and the reinvention of political journalism. *Political Communication, 22*, 259–276.

Baym, G. (2007). Representation and the politics of play: Stephen Colbert's *Better Know a District. Political Communication, 24*, 359–376.

Berger, A. (1993). *An anatomy of humor.* New Brunswick, NJ: Transaction.

Bewes, T. (1997). *Cynicism and postmodernity.* New York: Verso.

Billig, M. (2005). *Laughter and ridicule: Towards a social critique of humour.* London: SAGE Publications.

Boskin, J., & Dorinson, J. (1987). Ethnic humor: Subversion and survival. In A. Power Dudden (Ed.), *American humor* (pp. 97–117). New York: Oxford University Press.

Brewer, P. R., & Cao, X. (2006). Candidate appearance on soft news shows and public knowledge about primary campaigns. *Journal of Broadcasting and Electronic Media, 50*, 18–35.

Bruner, M. L. (2005). Carnivalesque protest and the humorless state. *Text and Performance Quarterly, 25*, 136–155.

Burke, K. (1984a). *Attitudes toward history* (3rd ed.). Berkeley: University of California Press.

Burke, K. (1984b). *Permanence and change.* Berkeley: University of California Press.

Carlson, A. C. (1986). Gandhi and the comic frame: 'Ad bellum purificandum.' *Quarterly Journal of Speech, 72*, 446–455.

Carlson, A. C. (1988). Limitations of the comic frame: Some witty American women of the nineteenth century. *Quarterly Journal of Speech, 74*, 310–322.

Chapman, T., & Foot, H. C. (1976). *Humour and laughter: Theory, research and applications.* London: John Wiley & Sons.

Christiansen, A. E., & Hanson, J. J. (1996). Comedy as cure for tragedy: ACT UP and the rhetoric of AIDS. *Quarterly Journal of Speech, 82*, 157–170.

Colletta, L. (2009). Political satire and postmodern irony in the age of Stephen Colbert and Jon Stewart. *Journal of Popular Culture, 42*, 856–874.

Cooper, B., & Pease, E. C. (2002). 'Don't want no short people 'Round Here': Confronting heterosexism's intolerance. *Western Journal of Communication, 66*, 300–318.

Cutler, I. (2005). *Cynicism from Diogenes to Dilbert.* Jefferson, NC: McFarland & Company.

Dworkin, E. S., & Efran, J. S. (1969). The angered: Their susceptibility to varieties of humor. In J. Levine (Ed.), *Motivation in humor* (pp. 96–102). New York: Atherton Press.

Ford, T. E., Wentzel, E. R., & Lorion, J. (2000). Effects of sexist humor on tolerance of sexist events. *Personality and Social Psychology Bulletin, 26*, 1094–1107.

Fox, J. R., Koloen, G., & Sahin, V. (2007). No joke: A comparison of substance in *The Daily Show* with Jon Stewart and broadcast network television coverage of the 2004 presidential election campaign. *Journal of Broadcasting and Electronic Media, 51*, 213–227.

Freud, S. (1960). *Jokes and their relation to the unconscious.* (J. Strachey, Trans.). New York: W. W. Norton and Company.

Gilbert, J. R. (1997). Performing marginality: Comedy, identity, and cultural critique. *Text and Performance Quarterly, 17*, 317–330.

Gring-Pemble, L., & Solomon Watson, M. (2003). The rhetorical limits of satire: An analysis of James Finn Garner's *Politically correct bedtime stories. Quarterly Journal of Speech, 89*, 132–153.

Hariman, R. (2008). Political parody and public culture. *Quarterly Journal of Speech, 94*, 247–272.

Holbert, R. L., Lambe, J. L., Dudo, A. D., & Carlton, K. A. (2007). Primacy effects of *The Daily Show* and national TV news viewing: Young viewers, political gratifications, and internal political self-efficacy. *Journal of Broadcasting and Electronic Media, 51*, 20–38.

Johnson, A. (2007). The subtleties of blatant sexism. *Communication and Critical/Cultural Studies, 4*, 166–183.

Kanter, D. L., & Mirvis, P. H. (1982). *The cynical Americans: Living and working in an age of discontent and disillusion.* San Francisco: Jossey-Bass.

Kaufer, D. S. (1977). Irony and rhetorical strategy. *Philosophy and Rhetoric, 10*, 90–110.

Kaufer, D. S., & Neuwirth, C. M. (1982). Foregrounding norms of ironic communication. *Quarterly Journal of Speech, 68*, 28–36.

Lynch, O. H. (2002). Humorous communication: Finding a place for humor in communication research. *Communication Theory, 12,* 423–445.

Malherbe, A. J. (1977). *The cynic epistles.* Atlanta: Scholars Press.

Martin, P., & Renegar, V. (2007). 'The man for his time': *The Big Lebowski* as carnivalesque social critique. *Communication Studies, 58,* 299–313.

Morris, J. S. (2009). *The Daily Show with Jon Stewart* and audience attitude change during the 2004 party conventions. *Political Behavior, 31,* 79–102.

Murphy, J. M. (1989). Comic strategies and the American covenant. *Communication Studies, 40,* 266–279.

Mutz, D. C., & Nir, L. (2010). Not necessarily the news: Does fictional television influence real-world policy preferences. *Mass Communication and Society, 13,* 195–217.

Olbrys, S. G. (2006). Disciplining the carnivalesque: Chris Farley's exotic dance. *Communication and Critical/Cultural Studies, 3,* 240–259.

Palczewski, C. (2005). The male madonna and the feminine Uncle Sam: Visual argument, icons, and ideographs in 1909 anti-woman suffrage postcards. *Quarterly Journal of Speech, 91,* 365–394.

Palin, S. (2009). *Going rogue: An American life.* New York: Harper Collins.

Plato (1987). *Republic.* (T. Griffin, Trans.). New York: Cambridge University Press.

Powell, K. A. (1995). The Association of Southern Women for the Prevention of Lynching: Strategies of a movement in the comic frame. *Communication Quarterly, 43,* 86–99.

Raskin, V. (1985). *Semantic mechanisms of humor.* Boston: D. Reidel Publishing Company.

Shugart, H. A. (2001). Parody as subversive performance: Denaturalizing gender and reconstituting desire in *Ellen. Text and Performance Quarterly, 21,* 95–113.

Singer, D. S. (1969). Aggression arousal, hostile humor, catharsis. In J. Levine (Ed.), *Motivation in humor* (pp. 103–127). New York: Atherton Press.

Sloterdijk, P. (1987). *Critiques of cynical reason.* Minneapolis: University of Minnesota Press.

Smith, C., & Voth, B. (2002). The role of humor in political argument: How 'strategery' and 'lockboxes' changed a political campaign. *Argumentation and Advocacy, 39,* 110–129.

Stallybrass, P., & White, A. (1986). *The politics and poetics of transgression.* Ithaca, NY: Cornell University Press.

Warner, J. (2007). Political culture jamming: The dissident humor of *The Daily Show with Jon Stewart. Popular Communication, 5,* 17–36.

CHAPTER 19

WOLFMAN JAY AND THE WRITING CENTER GANG: HUMOR IN LISTSERV COMMUNITY DEVELOPMENT

Diana Calhoun Bell
University of Alabama in Huntsville

As individuals become more immersed in online discourse, the rhetorical ways in which face-to-face humor emerges as an important part of the written lexicon remain an important facet of effective communication. Social media, listservs, blogs, email, and collaborative virtual environments all require sophisticated forms of communication; the rhetoric of humor and laughter is no small part of this written discourse (Hubler & Bell, 2003). Interestingly, in electronic spaces, linguistic forms of humor, joking, and laughter disconnect from verbal and nonverbal cues; instead, laughter, joking, and humor become increasingly more textual (Bell & Hubler, 2003), thus increasing the need to understand the rhetorical power of humor in these virtual environments. Williams, Caplan, and Xiong (2007) posited that "the diminished nonverbal cues in text-based computer-mediated communication (CMC) have given rise to a variety of theories seeking to explain how reduced relational cues may affect interpersonal interactions online" (p. 427).

Humor, as an important part of online discourse and online interpersonal interaction, is central to creating and sustaining both group and individual identities (Bell & Hubler, 2001, 2003) as well as creating and sustaining an inviting place to play and work within an educational work environment. Joking, humor, and laughter are inescapable functions of the culture of online discourse (Hubler & Bell, 2003), and the study in this chapter assesses the rhetorical functions of humor in the online narratives of computer-mediated communication (CMC) as demonstrated through a university student work-related asynchronous listserv. *Community* can be defined as a group of people who are "linked by social ties, share common values, and even are involved in a joint action" (Shen & Chiou, 2009, p. 394) in specific geographic or virtual settings. Online community formation occurs in two distinct phases (Bell & Hubler, 2001), and those phases shape the ethos of the overall group identity and emerging "strategic identities" (Talamo & Ligorio, 2001) of individuals within the group. An online strategic identity can be defined as an identity that is co-created and contextually situated (p. 114, 120). Specifically, this research had four particular findings, two findings in each of the two phases of community development. In the first phase of community formation, humor was used in two important ways:

1. humor was an important part of individual strategic identity formation;
2. humor helped establish important community identity boundaries.

In the second phase of community formation, humor is just as important, if not more so, as members of the online community use humor in distinctly different ways than during the initial phase. During this second phase, findings showed that humor was used to:

3. deliver instructions and information in palatable ways;
4. create a textual playground, a place distinctly separate from the rigors of the writing center educational and work environment.

HUMOR AND CONSTITUTIVE LANGUAGE

The first step in effectively negotiating linguistic humor in virtual spaces is to understand the power of textual language. Scholars in the fields of rhetoric, composition, and communication understand language to be constitutive rather than reflective. In other words, language is powerful because it can create reality, rather than merely reflect a reality that already exists. Positing that strategic identity is communicated through language practices, Berlin (1990) asserted that language helps "define the subject, the self, other subjects, the material world, and the relation of all these to each other [and is] is thus inscribed in language practices" (p. 429). Similarly, DeJoy (1994) explained that the foundation for this kind of constitutive rhetoric is the concept of language as a contextualized, or inextricably intertwined with subject, self, other, and material world. Bruffee (1986) explained, "[W]riting is primarily a social act. A writer's language originates with the community to which he or she belongs" (p. 784). Echoing Morkes, Kernal, and Nass (1999), Bruffee asserted, "[W]e use language primarily to join communities we do not yet belong to and to cement our membership in communities we already belong to" (p. 784). Once we move this theory of language as constitutive to the context of online environments, then we can come to understand how important language is in online communities. By connecting what humor theorists already recognize as a social dimension in joking (Hertzler, 1970; Holcomb, 1997; Mulkay, 1988; Robinson & Smith-Lovin, 2001) to contemporary interpretations of language as a constitutive force, this study analyzes the ways in which humor becomes an important constitutive linguistic strength within the online community.

Morkes, Kernal, and Nass (1999) presented possible effects of humor in task-oriented human-computer interaction: likability, cooperation, similarity, mirth response, joking and sociability, task time, and effort. As it relates to online social networking and group formation, the four most important effects are likability, cooperation, similarity, and joking and sociability factors. Humor, according to the authors via Wilson (1979), "fosters rapport and attraction between people" (p. 400). In other words, people who create laughter in social groups, whether online or face-to-face, become associated with positive experiences, and thus become more likable within that group. Similarly, humor, laughter, and joking foster greater cooperation among group members and can create cohesiveness (Duncan & Feisal, 1989). Part of creating cohesiveness among members through humor is by recognizing similarities among members of the group. Morkes, Kernal, and Nass (1999) explained, "[H]umor, by eliciting smiling and laughter, evokes explicit shared sentiment among its participants" (p. 400). Thus, through sharing a joke, laugh, or smile, group bonding occurs. The authors also argued that since people who effectively use humor are seen as more likable, others, especially those within a social group, respond to them positively.

PLAYFULNESS AND CREATIVITY

Csikszentmihalyi's (1990) flow theory helps explain the importance of playfulness in electronic discourse and online group formation. Csikszentmihalyi (1993) devised a theory of motivation with the basic precept proving that individuals are moved to actively participate when they reach an emotional state of, what he calls, flow, more commonly known as "getting in the flow," which occurs when individuals challenge themselves through enjoyable activities. Csikszentmihalyi (1990) explained,

> Enjoyment is characterized by forward movement: by a sense of novelty, of accomplishment ... After an enjoyable event we know that we have changed, that our self has grown: in some respect, we have become more complex as a result of it. (p. 46)

Thus, enjoyment is closely tied to the concept of flow because the state of flow creates the impetus for self-identification and fosters play. Csikszentmihalyi (1990) posited that enjoyment often occurs during play, "in games, sports and other leisure activities that are distinct from ordinary life" (p. 59).

Cundall (2007) talked more specifically about the relationship between humor and creative play. He explained that humor performs a significant role in the concept of creativity and underscores the way that groups will often facilitate humor. Cundall explained, "[H]umor can give insight into creativity and playfulness" (cf., O'Quin & Derks, 1994), especially within groups because of the shared sentiment and knowledge that the "getting" of a joke requires. He asserted that "the originality in some humor requires and needs a group setting to succeed" (p. 204). The playfulness inherent in sharing a joke creates, rather than reflects, group cohesiveness. Humor creates a playful context through which members of a group can demonstrate their creative use of language and shared sentiment.

METHODOLOGY AND RESEARCH DESIGN

The research model used in this chapter is a mixed method form of qualitative assessment: ethnography, case study, and linguistic analysis. Ethnography relies heavily on researcher observation and the interpretation of that observation. *Ethnography* is best defined as the study of a culture or social groups from the perspectives of its members (Agar, 1980; Fetterman, 1989). When ethnography is conducted thoroughly, it has the potential of cultural description that provides an exact and detailed portrait of the people under study. Gerring and McDermott (2007) explained that the *case study* "is a form of analysis where one or a few units are studied intensively" (p. 688) and is commonly used in social science research. Like ethnography, case study research is usually observational instead of experimental (George & Bennett, 2005; Gerring & McDermott, 2007). The benefit of case study research is that it allows the researcher to "explore, describe or explain the case of interest and enable holistic and meaningful, context-constituted knowledge and understandings about real life events" (Luck, Jackson, & Usher, 2006, p. 103). Mixed methodology is often found in qualitative, observational research to ensure triangulation—a form of content validity that reinforces the findings.

The particular mixed method study in this chapter can best be described as an ethnographic case study of humor using linguistic analysis that combines the generality of a broad observational component in conjunction with specific excerpts from the transcripts. The study analyzed transcripts of an online community that emerged through the exchange of 287 posts over a period of two consecutive 14-week semesters. The group comprised 14 student employees, called writing consultants, working in a writing center at a research institution in the southeastern region of the United States. The research focused on members of this online community as they used humor rhetorically to create and negotiate the online social group through a work-related listserv.

The goal was to study ways in which this particular community discursively utilized humor and online forms of laughing during the two distinct phases of community development (Bell & Hubler, 2001). The research produced two significant findings in each of the two phases of community formation. In the first phase, participants created their identities within the group and established important community boundaries; in the second phase, they softened the delivery of instructions or providing tertiary information and created a space for play and enjoyment.

HUMOR AND PHASE 1 OF COMMUNITY FORMATION

During the first phase of community development, occurring the first four weeks of the online group, humor performs an important role in establishing individual identities. During this seminal 4-week period of the 28-week online community, there were 48 total entries from all 14 participants. Of these 48 postings, 80 percent (N = 48/n = 10) used humor in some unequivocal way.

The first important way that humor was used during phase 1 of group formation was to establish self-identity within the group. Several members began using monikers, either to identify themselves or demarcate their postings. The use of monikers and nicknames is ubiquitous in virtual environments (Talamo & Ligorio, 2001) as members construct their online identities. For this study, in only the third overall listserv posting at the onset of the online community, Callie, a nontraditional student and returning consultant, began using a humorous moniker to identify her posts, calling them Callie-O-Grams. By so doing, she established a lighthearted manner through which others could interpret her contributions to the dialogue. Callie also used humor throughout her first Callie-O-Gram to the group by posting the following:

> One question I would post to all writing consultants is similar to the what comes first question … the chicken or the egg … or in the writing center concern … the content or the capitals and dotted I's (I had a consultation today that challenged my beliefs)
>
> And … since the client was bigger than me and since I am basically a coward I … (right or wrong) helped her dot the I's. Feedback?

In this, her first posting to the group, Callie created two important rhetorical moves using humor. First, she quickly began to establish group identity by alluding to writing theory that encourages practitioners to focus on content before grammar. Her first paragraph used a funny analogy to reinforce that collective wisdom. However, she also began effectively establishing her individual identity, first by demonstrating that she was willing to be a maverick and contest the theory when necessary, and second by joking about her small physical size and her lack of courage. Callie used humor to discursively situate herself within the group as someone who doesn't take herself too seriously. But, she also wanted to gauge the group's feelings about going maverick, textually wondering if she was appropriate in this case or not and unambiguously asking for feedback from the group. In this very important post, Callie created her own virtual identity and established that identity within the context of the specific online community. Callie's post was important because she initiated a thread that continued for a week and a half, with all subsequent posts implicitly or explicitly responding to the first Callie-O-Gram. In effect, Callie's post launches the online community. Yu and Young (2007) explained that

> group identity shapes the motivation behind voluntary engagement in cooperative behavior, which is linked to a person's desire to receive feedback from the group and to create, maintain, and enhance a favorable identify for the group. (p. 87)

A good example of one reply to the Callie-O-Gram in the thread came from Jay, a newly hired consultant. Similar to the rhetorical move of the Callie-O-Gram, Jay began identifying himself as Wolfman Jay to help those online identify him as different from another member in the group with the same name. Wolfman Jay built on Callie's call for feedback by responding to the thread that she started. Following up on Callie's first posting in which she alludes to being little, Wolfman Jay posts the following:

> Hey Callie,
>
> Maybe you should just call in backup. :) I'm sure your client couldn't be as big as me or Jake. lol Just kidding. And it's not that I'm afraid to talk on this, just haven't had any worthy input yet. Of course, this isn't really good input either but oh well :)
>
> Wolfman Jay

Wolfman Jay's first posts helped create his online persona within this online community. With his first post, less than two weeks into the life of the community, Wolfman Jay identified himself with this moniker and used humor to demonstrate his desire to become a member of the group.

The moniker "Wolfman" played on Jay's physical similarity to an imaginary "wolf man" because of his long, wavy hair and abundance of facial hair. Thus, Wolfman Jay took his face-to-face persona and extended that identity to the virtual environment. Since the members of this group did not regularly meet face-to-face with the exception of those who worked similar hours, Jay's moniker helped others recognize him both in the online and face-to-face environments. Wolfman Jay was "big" both literally and symbolically in this community.

Additionally in this post, Wolfman Jay apologized for not joining the dialogue earlier, signaling his novice status when saying that he didn't have anything yet to contribute. However, within 24 hours of Wolfman Jay's first post, three others in the online community reference, in their posts, his strategic identity as being "big" in opposition to Callie's being "little" and also reference his moniker, Wolfman Jay, thus, rhetorically inviting him into the group (Bell and Hubler, 2001). Beach and Doerr-Stevens (2009) asserted that this kind of authority is a function of "collectively responding to others' acts and voices … to engage in a dialogue that listens, speaks, and expects a response" (p. 463). Wolfman Jay began creating his authority and strategic identity within the group through his use of humor in his posts.

Although all Wolfman Jay's posts within the first phase of community development have to do with establishing himself as a viable member of the group by talking about his training and his knowledge of writing and learning theory, he sprinkled them with various levels of humor, demonstrating that he had learned that humor was a valued rhetorical skill in this online environment. For example, soon after his first post Wolfman Jay acknowledged and celebrated his inclusion and acceptance into the online group. Following up on another new consultant's posting that continued the "big" and "little" thread, Janie identified herself as a "wee little new person." Wolfman Jay quickly replied, "OK, I'm also just a 'wee little new person' too, but a big one at the same time." Here Wolfman Jay continued to establish his identity in physical ways in the online environment.

In contrast to being a "wee little new person" Wolfman Jay is a big man, well over six feet tall and 200 pounds. Although his physical description fit more with the moniker "Wolfman," Jay juxtaposed that physical description with his rhetorical position within the group as a "wee little new person." By adopting the stance of a "wee person," Jay demonstrated a tentative move to use humor to rhetorically align himself with another new member of the group (Bell & Hubler, 2001) and to acknowledge his novice standing. To reinforce that novice position, later in the post Wolfman Jay said, "I am growing up rapidly, aren't I? I even answered the phone today all by myself. Just ask Hailey, she does a great Southern mom impression." Here, Wolfman Jay not only realigned himself with Janie as a "wee little new person" by talking about growing up, but he pulled into his joke an important returning consultant by saying that Hailey had a Southern mom impression.

Clearly, within two weeks of this online group being formed, Wolfman Jay realized the importance of including humor in his posts in order to be welcomed into the group. Taking his cue from Callie, a returning consultant with established credibility within the group, Wolfman Jay used rhetorical savvy through humor to create his individual identity while also demonstrating his adherence to learning theory as practiced in the work environment.

An important part of this project included the foregrounding of language as a constitutive practice—emphasizing the creativity over the reflexivity of language, thereby (re)seeing language as having agency or the ability to create reality within an online social group rather than passively reflecting that group. Language, then, including and emphasizing humorous language and online forms of laughter, as seen through the early posts of Wolfman Jay, helped establish group and individual identity. This analysis showed that discursive practices of online humor can and does create strategic identities for its members.

Perhaps it is worth noting the final posting referring to the "wee little people," occurring four weeks after the first post to the listserv, is the point at which phase 1 of community building shifts. Hailey, a returning consultant and work supervisor in the face-to-face environment, posts the following:

> We of diminutive stature are small and easy to push, but isn't it Piglet who always steers Winnie the Pooh to the path of understanding? If it weren't packed in a box somewhere at my new house I'd quote from the Tao of Piglet. I'm finding the "new kids" are doing very well in handling the more intimidating circumstances, big and small.
>
> On another small note … press harder when filling out those big ole ROS forms!
>
> And in closing, I'll quote my fiancé: "It's the small ones you've go[t] to watch out for! They bite!" (interpret however you'd like ;)

In this pivotal post, Hailey demonstrated powerful rhetorical moves. First, she acknowledged acceptance into the community for all "wee little new people" by rhetorically aligning herself with them when she wrote "We of diminutive stature." She then authorized the power of being small in guiding others toward the "path of understanding." This post ended both the thread of "big" and "little" and thus symbolically ended the first phase of community building by hinting at the way the group's use of humor began shifting during the second phase.

HUMOR AND PHASE 2 OF COMMUNITY BUILDING

In her pivotal post, Hailey clearly demonstrated the first way that humor became important during the second phase of community. Continuing her play on the words "big" and "small," she delivered instructions to the group. Referring to the big ole ROS forms, she was directing the consultants to recognize the importance of making sure the in-house triplicate Record of Session (ROS) forms on which consultants took session notes were legible. Although Hailey had the responsibility of delivering this directive, she did it with humorous rhetorical flair. Throughout the life of this online community, humor emerged as an important part of making palatable directives and explanations.

Beginning with Hailey's posting at the end of the first phase of community development in which she used humor to direct the consultants to press harder on triplicate Record of Session (ROS) forms, the online community began creating humorous ways to deliver "housekeeping" responsibilities and other forms of information as well as to discuss important theoretical and practical issues in the teaching of writing.

This skill became increasingly important to the group dynamic. For example, Allie, after a couple of weeks without participating in the listerv, announced, "I have awakened and will sound my barbaric YOWP!" The broad point of Allie's post was to explain the reasons for focusing students' attention on global rather than surface feature revisions and to provide some ways to go about "coaching" students in this new direction. Taking a cue from Hailey, Allie understood that for the online community to read and acknowledge her post, she must follow the rhetorical act of utilizing humor to get and keep their attention. Morkes, Kernal, and Nass (1999) explained that "joking lubricates social relations and may improve performance by improving group cohesiveness" (p. 400). Thus, utilizing humor even in postings with serious content demonstrated a desire for collaboration and unity and solidified shared sentiment.

Further demonstrating the concept of shared sentiment, a new consultant, Jake, when posting about effectively organizing papers stated,

> I am STILL trying to cope with the harsh reality that I cannot tell developmental students to use the five paragraph thing. :(What is this world coming to? OK, I'm being a little dramatic.

Both Jake and Allie's posts had an overarching goal to discuss writing theory and practice, but, as members of this online community, they understood the importance of utilizing humor when relaying information to the rest of the group. Participants understood that the use of humor in their posts was a valued part of the discursive practices of the online community.

Jackie demonstrated another example of the way members used humor to communicate effectively. She posted the following:

> I know we've had our fair share of scary people (and before Halloween too!) this semester, but what I am wondering about is how many of us are dealing with borderline or slightly past the line frustrated. Lately I seem to be consistently consulting some who come in regularly. I think I'm getting old and easily irritated like my grandpa—whose favorite expression is "well what the hell did you do that for?"

Jackie continued by talking about how she helps these frustrated students revise while also working on their attitudes about writing. Dorman and Biddle (2006) explained that the role of humor in learning environments is advantageous in "sustaining emotion and cognitive engagement, as well as stimulating social presence" (p. 411). Jackie expressed some frustration at her work environment and the students with whom she worked. Couched in humor, this novice consultant was seeking responses that might help alleviate her frustration. Her goal was to effectively learn how to negotiate the work environment more productively. Hailey replied to Jackie by couching her advice in humor, saying,

> Sometimes they just want to talk ... but because of that I know about the situation in Kosova (and that the preferred spelling ends in 'a'), I found out about the possibility of the birth of a giant baby, keep tabs on Dr. R's crazy lectures, and learned an excellent recipe for mashed potatoes!

Hailey used humor to identify with Jackie and her frustration, while also humorously demonstrating the perks of listening to students talk about subjects other than writing. As a seasoned writing center consultant, Hailey helped Jackie see beyond the utilitarian work-related goal of helping students by explaining that it is often in those off-task spaces that teachable moments occur. Studies show that humor improves educational spaces by creating environments that are cheerful and that dissipate pressure, thereby promoting positive interaction among students and between students and their teachers (Dorman & Biddle, 2006). Interestingly, Hailey identified a teachable moment for Jackie, and emphasized the importance of listening and learning from students as a peer rather than taking a superior role; however, Hailey imparted this information with tact and humor. Cundall (2007) explained,

> In any joke or humorous situation, there is an invitation for the hearer to come close to [the speaker's] outlook or take on a situation. In sharing a joke, or recognizing together something as humorous, we reinforce our closeness, or sense of community. (p. 208)

Because of the public nature of the shared listserv, Hailey understood that her reply to Jackie resonated not just with Jackie, but echoed throughout the entire online community. Talamo and Ligorio (2001) explained that online environments that are supportive of collaborative work function effectively because they provide the opportunity for members to carry over learning opportunities, work tasks, and important topics at a distance. The topics that emerged as important ones in this online environment were those that began with some type of humor to initiate the conversational thread.

Finally and most meaningfully Hailey's pivotal post demonstrated a turning point in community development by initiating a way of using humor that was consistent throughout the rest of the life of this particular online community. Notice that Hailey used wordplay when she wrote about "intimidating circumstances, big and small," extending creative wording from a skill used in strategic identity formation and physical description to other related circumstances. The word play that Hailey began in that post caught on quickly within the group; for the remaining 24 weeks of the online community, wordplay was an important part of the group dynamic. Csikszentmihalyi (1990) explained, "If the only point of writing were to transmit information, it would become obsolete. But the point of writing is to create information, not to simply pass it along" (p. 131). Hailey began a trend of using language in creatively humorous ways.

A day later in a lengthy email, of which parts are excerpted here, Hailey began more candidly creating a virtual playground for writing consultant wordsmiths. Recognizing the group's obvious enjoyment of clever word usage, Hailey introduced the term syllipsis to the group from Word-A-Day (wordsmith.org). She explained that a syllipsis is a "construction in which a word governs two or more other words but agrees in number, gender, or case with only one, or has a different meaning when applied to each of the words." She expressed a theme for the group, challenging them to creatively use "words about words." Here, Hailey overtly invited the group into creative wordplay. The members quickly showed enthusiasm for the challenge. Amber used the example "The man lost his temper and his false teeth" for a syllipsis. Another consultant, Jake, posted, "I lost my keys and my mind," referring to her loosing her keys in the writing center the day before. Jackie joins in by saying, "He took my advice and my wallet." For this group, clever wordplay intellectually challenged them and provided a means to share an enjoyable activity.

Other forms of humor as play developed throughout the semester. Perhaps the one that the consultants had the most fun with was the "whispering consultant" thread. To provide context, Callie suffered a sore throat one day and couldn't speak above a whisper during her work hours in the writing center. This particular playful thread began when Jackie posted,

> After hearing Callie whisper to her clients yesterday I noticed that the instinct is for them to whisper back. Callie, I think you're on to something! We could all only speak in whispers. It would be a lot like a monastery or convent with relaxed vows of silence. WC could stand for Whispering Consultants.

To which Callie replied:

> I'm glad I afforded at least Jackie with a moment of amusement. I like the idea of whispering consultants. That might have positive implications for the long term. My voice is still on the fritz ... so for anyone wanting a demonstration in conducting silent consultations as in working as a mime or using italian hand speak, I'll be working tomorrow. My regulars are enjoying this ... I can't yell at them this week about their ideas.

Soon after this exchange, the listerv erupted with allusions to whispering, which eventually became part of the actual lexicon of the post. Yu and Young (2007) help explain this phenomenon by stating that these kinds of online communities are "dynamic and meaningful systems in which languages, actions, cultures, and norms fuse into a discursive process" (p. 87). The specific rhetorical move took place when Janie posted:

> Ok ... shhhh ... the whispering worked for c ... so I thought this would get your attention ... psst ... hey guys ... there's a meeting tomorrow ... Friday, 3–4ish ... its important ... there will be guests ... please be neat and clean ... we want to make a good impression ... mla workshop ... unlock the mystery that is documentation ...

Here, Janie symbolically and lexically represented the concept of whispering, merging text, and meaning making. Juxtaposed against online "yelling" being represented textually with all caps, Janie used all lower case to indicate her textual whisper. She then played off that whisper by signing off with her name in all caps with the explanation "SORRY, UNCONTROLLABLE URGE TO SHOUT!" This example of online play and creativity provided members with a "congenial means of interaction" (Dorman & Biddle, 2006, p. 413). Exchanging wordplay and jokes not only solidified group identity, but became a fun and pleasurable activity for the members. The witty banter used to mix work and play created the organizational culture of the group by providing an outlet through which socialization between group members could occur (Plester & Sayers, 2007). The members of the group used humor in creative ways that both reflected and constituted the group and individual strategic identities.

HUMOR AND THE ONLINE COMMUNITY

This study analyzed the way in which members of online communities demonstrated rhetorical savvy in their use of humor within the text of a listserv. Each new school year, as novice and returning writing center consultants converge on the campus and populate the listserv, a new online dynamic is created in which individuals must negotiate their identities as well as the collective identity of the group. As demonstrated in this study, this process of negotiation can happen early in the life of the community and establishes strategic identities for each member as well as defines the boundaries of the community. This study showed that as the community became more established and initial identity formation had occurred, the group continued using humor in interesting ways: by creating humorous ways to deliver important information about the group, individual work responsibilities, and learning/writing center theory and practice as well as by creating a textual playground in which members could work with words in a humorous and playful way. This study demonstrated that, of all rhetorical devices, the effective use of humor can be an integral part of building and sustaining online communities.

References

Agar, M. H. (1980). *The professional stranger: An informal introduction to ethnography.* New York: Academic.

Beach, R., & Doerr-Stevens, C. (2009). Learning argument practices through online role-play: Toward a rhetoric of significance and transformation. *Journal of Adolescent & Adult Literacy, 52*(6), 460–468.

Bell, D. C., & Hubler, M. T. (2001). The virtual writing center: Developing ethos through mailing list discourse. *The Writing Center Journal, 21,* 57–77.

Bell, D. C., & Hubler, M. T. (2003). Ethos on electronic mailing lists: Hyperthreading a virtual community for the price of a few e-tokens. *Readerly/Writerly Texts, 10*(1), 5–22.

Berlin, J. (1990). Writing instruction in school and college English 1890–1985. In J. Murphy (Ed.), *A short history of writing instruction: From ancient Greece to twentieth-century America.* Davis: Hermagoras.

Bruffee, K. A. (1986). Social construction, language, and the authority of knowledge: A bibliographic essay. *College English, 48*(8), 773–790.

Csikszentmihalyi, M. (1990). *Flow: The psychology of optimal experience.* New York. Harper.

Csikszentmihalyi, M. (1993). *The evolving self: A psychology for the third millennium.* New York: Harper Collins.

Cundall, M. K. (2007). Humor and the limits of incongruity. *Creativity Research Journal, 19*(2–3), 203–211.

DeJoy, N. C. (1994). James A. Berlin's social-epistemic rhetoric in a transformative frame: A conversation with Ira Shore. *Mediations, 18*(2), pp. 5–24.

Dormann, C., & Biddle, R. (2006). Humour in game-based learning. *Learning, Media and Technology 31*(4), 411–424.

Duncan, W. J., & Feisal, J. P. (1989). No laughing matter: Patterns of humor in the workplace. *Organizational Dynamics, 17*(4), 18–30.

Fetterman, D. M. (1989). *Ethnography step by step.* Newbury Park: SAGE.

George, A. L., & Bennett, A. (2005). *Case studies and theory development.* Boston: MIT Press.

Gerring, J., & McDermott, R. (2007). An experimental template for case study research. *American Journal of Political Science, 51*(3), 688–701.

Hertzler, J. O. (1970). *Laughter: A socio-scientific analysis.* New York: Exposition.

Holcomb, C. (1997). A class of clowns: Spontaneous joking in computer-assisted discussions. *Computers and Composition, 14,* 3–18.

Hubler, M. T., & Bell, D. C. (2003). Computer-mediated humor and ethos: Exploring threads of constitutive laughter in online communities. *Computers and Composition, 20*(3), 277–294.

Luck, L., Jackson, D., & Usher, K. (2006). Case study: A bridge across the paradigms. *Nursing Inquiry, 13*(2), 103–109.

Morkes J., Kernal, H. K., & Nass, C. (1999). Effects of humor in task-oriented human-computer interaction and computer-mediated communication: A direct test of SRCT theory. *Human-Computer Interaction, 14,* 395–435.

Mulkay, M. (1988). *On humor: Its nature and its place in modern society.* Cambridge: Basil Blackwell.

O'Quin, K., & Derks, P. (1994). Humor and creativity: A review of the empirical literature. In M. A. Runco (Ed.), *Creative Research Handbook* (Vol. 1, pp. 227–256). Creskill, NJ: Hampton.

Plester, B., & Sayers, J. (2007). 'Taking the piss': Functions of banter in the IT industry. *Humor, 20*(2), 157–187.

Robinson, D. T., & Smith-Lovin, L. (2001). Getting a laugh: Gender, status, and humor in task discussions. *Social Forces, 80,* 123–160.

Shen, C-C., & Chiou, J-S. (2009). The effect of community identification on attitude and intention toward csa blogging community. *Internet Research, 19*(4), 1066–2243.

Talamo, A., & Ligorio, B. (2001). Strategic identities in cyberspace. *CyberPsychology & Behavior, 4*(1), 109–121.

Williams, D., Caplan, S., & Xiong, L. (2007). Can you hear me now? The impact of voice in an online gaming community. *Human Communication Research, 33*, 427–449.

Wilson, C. P. (1979). *Jokes: Form, content, use and function.* London: Academic.

Yu, C-P., & Young, M-L. (2007). The virtual group identification process: A virtual educational community case. *CyberPsychology & Behavior, 11*(1), 87–90.

INDEX

Figure and Table pagination are in italics.

Singaporean vis à vis American/Israeli students, 267–268

Asia, 263

Canadian jokes about Newfoundlanders, 260

Chinese vis-à-vis Canadian university students
  Coping Humor Scale (CHS), 259–260
  Humor Styles Questionnaire (HSQ), 259–260

in classroom, 263–264

computer-mediated communication (CMC), 300–309

definition, 302

family humor communication 161–163
  examples and frequencies, *164–166*

German-American families in United States, 263

Humor Assessment (HA) scale, 82–88

humor in organization, 180–184

Humor Styles Questionnaire (HSQ)
  Chinese vis-à-vis Canadians, 259

Irish humor and Jewish humor, 261

in United States, 113

between regions of United States
  Humor Styles Questionnaire (HSQ), 260
  Multidimensional Sense of Humor Scale, 260

personality traits, 269–272
  New Zealanders vis-à-vis Americans, 270–272

receiver approaches to, 53–55

sexual communication satisfaction
  instrumentation, 126–128
  participants, 126
  procedure, 128
  results, 128–135

sources approaches to, 53–55

on teacher humor and learning, 220–221, 263–264

television advertising, 265–267
  See also Cross-cultural humor research

CAT, *See* Communication accommodation theory (CAT)

Cerebellum, 207

Cheerfulness, 210–211

Childhood, 64, 145–153
  antisocial humor, 149–150
  and applied humor, 150
  development of humor appreciation, 149
  gender differences, 146–147, 149–150
  humor message appreciation vs production, 147–148
  importance of study of humor communication in, 150–153
  incongruity theory of humor, 148–149, 216–217
  prosocial humor, 149–150
  smiling and laughter, 146–147, 205–206
  superiority theory of humor, 148–149, 216–217
  See also Infancy

Choleric humor, 191

Chopra, Dr. Deepak, 192

CHS, *See* Coping Humor Scale (CHS)

Cicero, 29
  theory of superiority, 283–284

Classroom humor, *see* Teacher humor

Clinton, Bill, 289

Clinton, Hillary, criticism of 282, 288–292
  aggressiveness, 290–291
  lack of perspective, 286
  unsexuality, 288–290

Closeness, 103

Clowns, 263

CMC, *see* Computer-mediated communication (CMC)

Cognitions, 103

in marketing schemes, 265–266

negative affects, 95, 111, 112

in organizational life, 176–177

paradoxes, 30

positive affects, 95, 111

to relay social information, 263

survival, 190–192

G

Gelastic seizures, 211

GELOPH, 270

Gelotophobia, 270–271

Gender differences

appreciation of humor, 267

aggressive humor, 113, 259

attitudes to sexual humor, 131–132, 260–261

blood pressure levels and humor, 210

in childhood, 146–147, 149–150

irony, 102

maintenance of identities, 176

postive humor use, 121

women managers, 179

General theory of verbal humor (GTVH), 39

Gesundheit Institute, 192

Goals of theory, 4–5

control goal, 5

description goal, 4

explanation goal, 4

prediction goal, 5

Goals-plans-action (GPA), 36, 41

consummatory approach, 41

inside-only perspective, 41

inside-out perspective, 41

levels approach, 41

outside-in perspective, 41

primary goal, 41

secondary goal, 41

Going Rogue, 286

Goldberg, Whoopi, 10

GPA, *see* Goals-plans-action (GPA)

Graham, Elizabeth, E., 3

Groups, 242–243

identities, 245–246

Gruner, Charles, 4

GTVH, *see* General theory of verbal humor (GTVH)

H

HA, *see* Humor Assessment Instrument (HA)

Hall, Jeffrey A., 119

Hartelius, E. Johanna, 281

HBQD, *see* Humorous Behavior Q-sort Deck (HBQD)

Health care professionals, humor use

constraints, 195–197

functions, 197

guidelines, 196–197

patient humor use, 197–198

practices, 192–193

therapeutic, 193–195, 211

Health education, and humor, 198–199

Health indicators, 191

Health messages, function of humor in, 198

Healthcare implications, 7, ch12, ch13

Healthworks, 198–199

Hefner, Hugh, 286

Hill, Patricia S., 255

HO, *see* Humor Orientation (HO) scale

Hobbes, 256

definition of humor, 256

I

Illness symptoms, 211

Immunity, 209–210

Incongruity theory, of humor, 11–12, 23, 39, 148–149, 152, 194, 216–217, 222

    jokes, 12, 244

Individual differences perspective, 6–7

Infancy

    mirth reactions, 144–145, 206

    role of maternal depression on social development of infant, 144

    smiles, 143, 206

    still-faced interaction, 144

    See also Childhood

"Inverted-U relationship", between arousal and pleasure, 10

Institutional Review Boards for the Protection of Human Subjects (IRBs), 152

Instructional Humor Processing Theory (IHPT), 56, 222

Integrative-assertion, 103–104

Intercultural communication, 242–249

    Communication accommodation theory (CAT), 246–248

    "creative flexibility", 243

    ethnic jokes, 249–251, 262–267

    examples, 243, 247–248, 249

    Expectancy violations theory (EVT), 248–249

    hazards of humor, 247

    location of, 244

    meaning, 243

    perspective, 243

    production, 243

    role of humor, 250

    success of humor attempts, 247

    See also Culture

Intercultural communications research

    and lack of studies on cross-cultural humor, 272–274

Interdiscourse communication, 243, 262

Interdiscourse humor, 262

Interlocutors, 246

Interpersonal Solidarity Scale, 127

Interpersonal solidarity

    case study findings, 126–135

        additional analyses, 131–133

        results, 128–131

    and sexual humor, 123–125

IRBs, *see* Institutional Review Boards for the Protection of Human Subjects (IRBs)

Irish humor, 261

Irony, 16, 99–100, 101, 102 194

    gender differences, 102

J

Jab lines, 244, 245

Jewish humor, 261

Joke competence, 38

Joke memory test, 59

Joke teller, relationship with butt of joke, 13, 96, 250, 284

Jokes and Their Relation to the Unconscious, 10

Jokes, 8–9, 244–245

    between Asian Indians and Asian Indian Americans, 249

    as conflict strategy, 160

    jab line, 244

    between nonnative speakers (NNSs) and native speakers (NSs), 247–248, 250–251

    "bucket", 182–184

    clarification humor, 26

    comprehensive theory, 15

    as expression of repressed sexual impulse, 11

    Hillary Clinton, 288–292

    incongruity theory, 12, 244

Patient humor use, 197–198

Perceived "funniness" ratings, 63

Personality traits, 269–272

Persuasion, humor in, 23–24

Persuasive power, of humor

    adaptive model, 266

    cognitive model, 266

Pet names, 121

Phlegmatic humor, 191

Pick's disease, 211

Planned humor, 43–44

Plato, 13

    theory of superiority, 283

Play frames, 244

Play, 40

Playboy, 286

Playful humor, 40, 42

Playfulness, 40

Poehler, Amy, 282

Polack, E. Phillips, 203

Political comedy, 282

    evasion of accountability, 293

    potential dangers of, 283–294

    power of, 282–294

Political humor, 283–294

Positive humor

    in couples, 121

    effect of, 96, 111

    and psychological health, 57, 61–62, 95–96, 134, 167–168, 194

Positive sexual humor

    case study findings, 126–135

    and interpersonal solidarity, 123–124

    and predicted outcome values, 125

    sexual communication satisfaction, 124–126

Post-graduate instructional communication, 232–234

"Potty humor", 8–9

Power, of humor, 282, 293–294

Pragmatic homonymy, concept of, 167

Predicted outcome value theory, 123–124

    case study findings, 126–135

    and expressive sexual humor, 125

    and negative sexual humor, 125

    and positive sexual humor, 125

Prediction goal of theory, 5

Private references, 121

Production and Appreciation Scale of Humor (PASH), 267

Production, of humor, 38–41

    categories of, 56

    in children, 147–148

    conversational laughter model, 38

    joke teller, 38

    stand-up comedy model, 38

    wit, the 38

    See also Humorous messages, production of

Provocation, 112, 114

Psychoanalytic theory, of humor, 10–11, 194

Psychological functions of humor, taxonomy of, 167

Psychological humor, and positive humor, 57, 61–62, 95–96, 134, 167–168, 194

Psychology of humor, 257

Psychometric intelligence, and humor ability, 59

Public speaking, 22

Punch lines, 10

Punk'd, 13

Punyanunt-Carter, Narissra Maria, 229

Purposive sampling, 162

Q

Quantum Healing: Exploring the Frontiers of Mind/ Body (1989), 192

Quintilian, theory of superiority, 283–284

R

Racist jokes, 217

Rancer, Andrew, S., 3

Reactive verbal aggression (RVA), 110
  negative affect, 112

Reader's Digest, 25

Reality-based humor, 264

Receiver approaches, to humor research, 53–55

Receiver characteristics, 114

Regan, Ronald (President), 24, 26, 29

Regression analysis for sexual humor use, 129, *130*

Relational benefits, 6

Relational satisfaction, 103–104

Relationships
  effect of aggressive humor on, 15
  humor in, 6, 22–23
  sexual humor in, 121–135

Relief, 9–10

Rennaisance, types of humor in, 191

Repressed feelings, and laughter, 10

Republic, 284

Resistance humor, 179

"Reward centres of the brain", 191

Rhett's syndrome, 212

Richmond, Virginia Peck, 73, 74–75

Ridicule, 112

Risky shift, 191

Robinson, Dr. Vera, 191

Rogers, Will, 26

Rosten, Leo, 242

Rowan and Martin, 15

Roy, 8

RVA, *See* Reactive verbal aggression (RVA)

S

Safety valve resistance, 179

Saliva (SIgA), assessment of, 209–210

"Sanctioned disrespect", 179

Sanguine humor, 191

Sarcasm, 99–100, 102, 112
  definition, 160, 293
  as a family communication standard (FCS), 160

Saturday Night Live, 282

Schema theory, 159

Schemata, 159

School Motivation Questionnaire, 270

Second-generation action assembly theory (AAT2), 43, 44

Security theory, 271

Segal, Dr. Bernie, 192

Seinfeld, 10

Self Esteem Inventory, 270

Self-defeating humor, 259

Self-deprecating humor, 11, 25
  for advertising slogans, 14
  by professional comedians, 14–15
  as superiority humor, 14
  by teachers, 218

"Self-derogatory linguistic image", 263

Self-disclosure, and sexual satisfaction, 127, 134

Self-disparaging humor styles, 62, 96, 217

Self-enhancing humor styles, 62, 95–96, 259

Self-focused attention, 112

Sensation Seeking Scale (SSS), 269

U

UHI, *see* Uses of Humor Index (UHI)
Unification function, 6, 22, 40–41, 44–45, 161
  cross-cultural, 262–263
  clarification, 25–27, 40–41, 95
  identification, 24–25, 40, 95
Universal humor, 264
Uses of Humor Index (UHI), 53, 55, 95
Using the Relationships as Cultures Perspective, 122

V

Verbal aggression, 6, 15, 112
  vis-à-vis assertiveness, 99
  forms of, 111
  vis-à-vis hostility, 102
  and physical violence, 102
  See also Aggressive humor
Verbal Aggressiveness Scale, 101
Verbal trigger events (VTEs), 110, 112
  adaptive humor, 113–114
  behavior criticism, 112
  character attacks, 112
  humor, 111
  innocuous statements, 111

maladaptive humor, 111–113
  reciprocal verbal aggression, 110, 112
Violence, physical
  and verbal aggression, 102
VTE, *See* Verbal trigger events (VTEs)

W

Wanzer, Melissa Bekelja, 51
WHAT, *see* Wit and Humor Appreciation Test (WHAT)
Wigley, Charles J. (III), 109
William's disorder, 212
Williams, Robin, 10
Wit and Humor Appreciation Test (WHAT), 57–58
Women in politics, 282–294
Word play, in online discourse, 307–308
Workplace, humor in
  See Organizational life, humor in
Wrench, Jason S., 73, 74–75, 229
Wuzzer, 123

Y

Yo Mama, 13